An Ethics of
Remembering

RELIGION AND POSTMODERNISM
A SERIES EDITED BY MARK C. TAYLOR

EDITH WYSCHOGROD

An Ethics of
Remembering

HISTORY, HETEROLOGY,
AND THE
NAMELESS OTHERS

THE UNIVERSITY OF CHICAGO PRESS
CHICAGO & LONDON

EDITH WYSCHOGROD is the J. Newton Rayzor Professor of Philosophy and Religious Thought at Rice University. Her other books include *Spirit in Ashes: Hegel, Heidegger, and Man-Made Mass Death* (1985) and *Saints and Postmodernism: Revisioning Moral Philosophy* (1990) also published by the University of Chicago Press. She has been a Guggenheim Fellow (1995–1996), a Woodrow Wilson Fellow (Fall 1988), and president of the American Academy of Religion (1992–1993).

The University of Chicago Press, Chicago 60637
The University of Chicago Press, Ltd., London
© 1998 by The University of Chicago
All rights reserved. Published 1998
Printed in the United States of America
07 06 05 04 03 02 01 00 99 98   1 2 3 4 5

ISBN: 0-226-92044-5 (cloth)
ISBN: 0-226-92045-3 (paper)

Library of Congress Cataloging-in-Publication Data

Wyschogrod, Edith.
  An ethics of remembering : history, heterology, and the nameless others / Edith Wyschogrod.
    p.   cm. — (Religion and postmodernism)
  Includes bibliographical references and index.
  ISBN 0-226-92044-5 (cloth) — ISBN 0-226-92045-3 (pbk.)
  1. Historiography—Moral and ethical aspects. 2. Difference (Psychology)—Moral and ethical aspects. I. Title. II. Series.
D13.W97   1998   97-41458
  901—dc21   CIP

⊗ The paper used in this publication meets the minimum requirements of the American National Standard for Information Sciences—Permanence of Paper for Printed Library Materials, ANSI Z39.48-1984.

CONTENTS

ILLUSTRATIONS

ACKNOWLEDGMENTS

To write about passionate involvement with the past, with the great silences of history, is to be in the debt of historians who have engaged in this painstaking process. As Hegel would say, they dared "to hold fast what is dead." I am especially grateful to those who have been of more immediate assistance—my family, colleagues, and friends whose criticisms and comments have been invaluable. Illuminating conversations with John D. Caputo, Robert Gibbs, Werner Kelber, Lucia Lermond, Peter Ochs, Susan Shapiro, and Mark C. Taylor have contributed to my thinking in a broad sense that would bear on the matters discussed here. I also should like to express my gratitude to the John Simon Guggenheim Memorial Foundation and to Rice University for the ways in which each has contributed to the support of this project. Thanks are due to the graduate students who helped with details of manuscript preparation, especially to Stephen L. Hood, Martin T. Kavka, and Eric E. Boynton. The work of the late Emmanuel Levinas and the conversations I was fortunate enough to have had with him have been of inestimable value in my struggle with the questions addressed in this work.

I am grateful also to the *Journal of the American Academy of Religion* for permission to reprint several pages from my "Fact, Fiction, *Ficciones:* Truth in the Study of Religion," vol. 62, no. 1 (Spring 1994).

PROLOGUE

What is it that must precede the conveying of history? Must there not be
the declaration of a double passion, an eros for the past and an ardor for the
others in whose name there is a felt urgency to speak? To convey that-
which-was in the light of this passion is to become a historian. Because the
past is irrecoverable and the others in whose stead the historian speaks are
dead, unknowable, she cannot hope that her passion will be reciprocated.
To be a historian then is to accept the destiny of the spurned lover—to
write, photograph, film, televise, archive, and simulate the past not merely
as its memory bank but as binding oneself by a promise to the dead to tell
the truth about the past. Nietzsche may have been right in proclaiming that
remembering the past is a sick passion; yet without the necrophilia of the
historian who gives herself over to overcoming the past's passing into oblivion, there would be only the finality of death.

   Can the historian ever bring back that which has gone by, ever tell the
truth about the past? The mundane view of truth as a matching of event or
pattern with what is said about it, a relation of homology between proposition and referent, has been undermined by powerful present-day criticisms
of both rationalist and empiricist theories of knowledge. Is the historian as
the lover who is spurned a faithless lover after all who seduces with a promise that cannot be fulfilled, yet knows all along that truth as the return of
the past in all of its *Leibhaftigkeit* is a chimera? Does she lie when she avers,
"I will tell the truth about the past, *je te jure?*"

   In making her promise of truth, the historian has perhaps blundered   *xi* into a category mistake. With the act of promising, she has moved from the discursive space of predication into the imperative, the non-space of ethics, thereby overstepping the limits of predication in the very act of promising. What does it mean to claim that the promise must be re-figured in the non-space of ethics when ethics is understood as the challenge to all that I am and have by virtue of the sheer existence of the other person? The history of ethics attests that, from the pre-Socratics to the present, philosophers have attempted to adjudicate the conflicting claims of self and other, to frame a concept of justice that would subsume them. But the appeal to a theoretical ground for determining the right and wrong of differing claims already reflects a weakening of what is exacted by the other who is anterior to theories of justice. The discursive space of authorization presupposed by theoretical accounts of justice is not a claim about what is intrinsically good, or an assessment of the good in terms of the consequences of actions, but simply the realization that there is another and that the other's existence obliges me to disown what is mine, to divest myself of myself and accept responsibility for the other. This obligation is impossible to fulfill, incommensurable with the theoretical analyses of justice which may supervene upon it and yet is their aporetic non-ground. The historian's responsibility is mandated by another who is absent, cannot speak for herself, one whose actual face the historian may never see, yet to whom "giving countenance" becomes a task. From the standpoint of history, to depict the dead or even the living other who is voiceless is to cordon off actual existence, to preempt in order to return it.

The historian is placed in a Catch-22. Obligated by her vow to restore the past in its actuality, she nevertheless recognizes the impossibility of doing so. Unlike the theologian who can speak apophatically, speak without speaking, the historian cannot resort to silence. How is she to breach the unsayability of what must be said? Must she not devise strategies to trick language into revealing its limits so that she can at once respect and defy them, artifices that are exhibited not in a straightforward manner but by resorting to other artifices? In what follows, the historian will be made to enter into conversation with Kant's and Hegel's accounts of history; she will force them to give up their secrets, expose the aporias in their philosophies, all the while showing how those philosophies have been formative for subsequent historiographic understanding. She will turn to ostension, deixis, and counterfactuality as strategies that will create the limits of historical discourse while calling it into question. Whether the resulting historical artifact is discursive or visual, she will compel it to take up into itself the conditions of its own errancy, not necessarily as recounting its historiographic claims one by one but rather as making visible the difference between the present of the text and the past that it brings to the fore.

The "present of the text" is not intended to refer to temporal coordinates but rather to contemporary social, cultural, economic, and political conditions as the ever-mobile de-centered standpoint where the historian who configures the past stations herself. The nadir point of recent history of which no historian can remain ignorant is the mass exterminations of peoples. No doubt, there are in this history affinities with wars and massacres of the past. But what sets recent events apart, the "present of the text," is the character of the mechanism of destruction: the bureaucratic and technological means used to assure the annihilation of the maximum number of persons in the least possible time, a process that I have described in detail elsewhere. No matter how far removed from her specific interest humanly contrived mass death may be, the historian is stationed "here" where the void exposed by mass extermination "is," a void that cannot be named but constitutes a unique moment, the entry of the nihil into time. I must breach the unnameability of this void by referring to it as the "cataclysm," a term that suggests its cosmological dimensions.

What is less clear is that the cataclysm exercises pressure to speak, not to name it, the unnameable, but rather to utter the promise from out of the cataclysm, to say "I," not as an ego but as one who promises to name the dead others. I call the historian who is driven by the eros for the dead and the urgency of ethics, and who speaks from out of the cataclysm that she cannot name, the "heterological historian." Her "truth" is deictic: "I, here, now vouch for what I say." She is aware of the aporias of *deixis* exposed by Hegel, Derrida, and others but allows it to remain in office, as it were, to guard her promise. In what follows, the heterological historian will appear as a character who slides in and out of narrative focus. Alternating disguises, she is a multiplicity of conceptual personae in something like Deleuze's sense of the term, a thinker through whom a particular thought-perspective is exhibited, someone frenzied who is in search of what precedes history; the passionate advocate of another; the Socratic gadfly who challenges received assumptions. On occasion, I speak in the first person, the I of the narrative voice bending back upon itself: I, the narrator, will doff the mask of the heterological historian and don yet another mask, that of the first person, in order to reveal and conceal the conditions of the errancy of my own discourse. The heterological historian is better able to speak for the other if alterity is disclosed in the feminine gender which will be used throughout.

Not only is the heterological historian caught up in the incommensurability of predicative and ethical language, but she is ensnared in a culture of images and information. The image is other than and a contestation of discourse. If the historian is to create a visual artifact, she must consider images not only in their sensory plenitude but in their capacity to signify aniconically and ethically. She may resort to the numerous technologies at her disposal in configuring the historical object. It is not, however, the image as manifested in the still photograph, in film, or as televised, all of which retain a residual notion of a stable referent, that challenges the historian. Rather it is the contention that the real, and with it history as we have known it heretofore, has come to an end. Jean Baudrillard claims that the age of images has been replaced by that of information, that the real has been supplanted by the hyperreal, a hallucinatory reproduction of the real. His critique may be viewed as parodic in intent, the invention of a covert moralist in the manner of such predecessors as Montaigne. Yet what is the historian to make of the breakdown of boundaries between actual death, the one reality that could not be transcended, and its volatilization as, for example, in the "visible interactive suicide" of Timothy Leary disseminated over the World Wide Web to become a media event?[1] Has Baudrillard not revealed the end of the actual as it has been conceived and its replacement by a hyperreality from which even death is not exempt? Or is there a way to both fissure and use the new culture of information? The heterological historian may ask whether images and information must be decoupled; images in fact may be the raison d'être for the shipping of information. Cannot images be de-commodified, become an-iconic, a concealing-revealing of alterity? In what follows, this line of inquiry will be explored in order to devise strategies for both using and escaping from images and from the volatilization of the real.

In considering the past, the heterological historian cannot ignore the sea change in the understanding of time that Husserl's analysis of internal time consciousness and Heidegger's account of the ecstases of time as lived by the Dasein have effected. Yet, in the culture of image and information, the irreverent tropes both of science fiction and of the more speculative reaches of modern physics, in which traveling backward in time is seen as a real possibility, express the historian's dream, the recovery of the past. The past to which the historian attends also can be usefully described by examining a binarism that has become a preoccupation of recent analytic philosophy. In a brief departure from the post-structuralist perspective of my narrative, I shall turn to the stretched and punctiform character of time, the former expressing the reality of pastness, presentness, and futurity, the latter acknowledging only that of succession, earlier and later. Each conception will be shown to have its utility for the historian. Stretched time enables her to speak about time's passing, about the recent and far-off pasts, and to lend emotional tone to thoughts about bygone, present, and future times. The historian's eros for a particular period of the past is an example of such affective coloration that attaches to time. The alternative view considers time as a sequence of now points that succeed one another and that help the historian to register the magnitude of historical change: before and after the fall of the Han dynasty, before and after the Russian Revolution. As Walter Benjamin has noticed, history is not merely a sequence of events that transpire in a continuous homogeneous time but rather a time of the now, a moment drawn from the past into the present because of some urgent claim it has upon us.

In retrieving the past, not only is the historian's task affected by her interpretations of temporality but also by how she views individual and collective memory. The critiques of representation already cited preclude a simplistic return to the claim that what occurred can be brought back in word and image, a view that has been governed by a double paradigm. First, past happenings were described as incised on a malleable surface, a seal on wax; second, words and images were seen as deposited in a storehouse from which they could be retrieved at will. Both tropes bypass the unbridgeable temporal gap that opens up between the "original" occurrence and its later mental "duplicate." In this context, I shall take account of Derrida's elaborate deconstruction of Hegel's depiction of memory in the latter's *Encyclopedia of the Philosophical Sciences*.

With the development of mnemotechnic prostheses from late antiquity to the Renaissance, the earliest known instance of an architectural model being the memory palace of Simonides, the scriptic and storehouse analogies lose something of their force. The techniques for remembering depend upon a system of associations between items to be recalled and features of some already familiar architectural monument. The independent appearance of a device that served a similar function in the Luba culture of Africa will be shown to provide a system not only of information retrieval but a conscious narratological focus for collective memory. It is to models such as these that the historian who wishes to track the genealogy of computer memory must look, as I hope to demonstrate.

I shall consider the way in which recent brain research ensconced in the culture of image and information largely departs from the traditional tropes governing the understanding of memory. The cognitive science advocate Daniel Dennett sees memory as a differentiation of brain states such that the determination of qualia is the result of differences of intensity of neuronal stimulation. Breaking with the view that time organizes the qualia, the sense of time is itself viewed as an example of an intensity shift in neuronal activity. Roger Penrose, Oxford University physicist, sees memory as accounted for by the gap between two types of neuronal activity, one governed by classical, the other by quantum physics. I shall consider the implications of these observations for the grasp of historical memory by allowing the questions of the heterological historian in regard to the political and cultural ramifications of these views to constitute a running commentary.

The heterological historian does not live and work in isolation but enters into the shaping of a community and returns to the community some aspect of its past. She refigures the self-sense of contemporary communities always already dis-figured (whether consciously or otherwise) by the cataclysm. Responding to the dangers of philosophies of community based upon the myth of autochthony as well as upon modern accounts of community in which social existence is founded on production, she ponders the impossible: a community that is deterritorialized and a/productive. Despite a certain awareness of these dangers, Jean-Paul Sartre's phenomenology of group formation depicts the emergence, consolidation, and decline of communities by falling back upon both the self-enclosure of the modern subject and the primacy of production.

The heterological historian who speaks from the cataclysm perceives that communities of production are communities of immanence organized around some specific work. As Jean-Luc Nancy and Maurice Blanchot insist, it is only with the de-nucleation of the self that a relation to exteriority becomes possible and a community that is not based on production, one that is "a community of those who have nothing in common," can come into being. Such a community is one of hospitality, of welcoming another. To be sure, it is impossible to bypass production so long as basic human needs persist. Yet the heterological historian may note that groups may arise where there is production that is "for nothing," a community of art, based on workless works that both preempt and resist image and information and that are marked by the cataclysm.

The task of the historian is to exhibit the past whereas the time scheme of community is that of the future. Its expression is hope, the gift that the members of the community bestow upon one another. The heterological historian may protest that the gift of hope makes a mockery of the cataclysm. Yet, if hope is to remain hope, it is not the promise of deferred happiness but hope for the present, a present that is always already marked by difference and that cannot come to be. The heterological historian is thus free to give over the gift of the past, one that has no return.

It is not my intention to write a history of historiography, to track lines of thought that might reach, for example, from Vico through Hegel to Croce, from Collingwood to Toynbee, but rather to elaborate upon the creation of the historical artifact after the cataclysm and in the new age of image and information. This task demands the mingling of numerous often irreverent voices: those of Western philosophy, itself marked by internal difference; of French post-structuralist thought; of analytic philosophies of time; of non-technical works that recount recent developments in brain research and the physics of time travel; of newpaper accounts of the murder and mayhem that marks our epoch; and of the heterological historian herself who is at the same time Plato's eristic youth and the crone Diotima, the one who both transgresses and polices boundaries. It is principally she who, before saying "Thus it was" or "It could not have been thus," is willing to pronounce the words "It *ought* not to have been thus."

ABBREVIATIONS

BT   Martin Heidegger, *Being and Time,* trans. John Macquarrie and Edward Robinson (New York: Harper and Row, 1962); *Sein und Zeit* (Tübingen: Niemeyer, 1943).

CDR Jean-Paul Sartre, *Critique of Dialectical Reason: Theory of Practical Ensembles,* pts. 1 and 2, trans. Alan Sheridan-Smith (Atlantic Highlands, NJ: Humanities Press, 1976); *Critique de la raison dialectique (précedé de question de méthode). Tome 1. Théorie des ensembles pratique* (Paris: Librairie Gallimard, 1960; rev. ed. 1985).

CJ   Immanuel Kant, *Critique of Judgment,* trans. J. H. Bernard (New York: Hafner Press, 1951); *Kritik der Urteilskraft,* in Kant's *Gesammelte Schriften IV* (Berlin: George Reiner, 1900).

CL   Roland Barthes, *Camera Lucida: Reflections on Photography,* trans. Richard Howard (New York: Hill and Wang, 1981).

DV   Andrzej Wajda, *Double Vision: My Life in Film* (New York: Henry Holt and Co., 1989).

FS   Jean Beaudrillard, "Fatal Strategies," in *Selected Writings,* trans. Mark Poster (Stanford: Stanford University Press, 1988); *Les Stratégies fatales* (Paris: Bernard Grasset, 1983), pp. 9–33, 259–73.

HCE Martin Heidegger, *Hegel's Concept of Experience,* trans. Kenley Royce Dove (New York: Harper and Row, 1970); "Hegel's Begriff der Erfahrung," in *Holzwege [Gesamtausgabe 5]* (Frankfurt: Vittorio Kostermann, 1980).

HPoS Martin Heidegger, *Hegel's Phenomenology of Spirit,* trans. Parvis Emad   *xix* and Kenneth Maly (Bloomington: Indiana University Press, 1988); *Hegel's Phanomenologie des Geistes [Gesamtausgabe 32]* (Frankfurt: Vittorio Klostermann, 1980).

IE Jean Baudrillard, *The Illusion of the End,* trans. Chris Turner (Stanford: Stanford University Press, 1994); *Illusion de la Fin* (Paris: Galilee, 1992).

Il Walter Benjamin, *Illuminations: Essays and Reflections,* trans. Harry Zohn (New York: Harcourt, Brace, Jovanovich, 1968); *Illuminationen: Ausgewählte Schriften* (Frankfurt: Suhrkamp Verlag, 1961).

OH Immanuel Kant, *On History,* trans. Lewis White Beck (New York: Liberal Arts Press, 1963); selections from Kant's *Gesammelte Schriften,* Konigliche Preussiche Akademie der Wissenschaften edition (Berlin, 1902–38).

Phen G. W. F. Hegel, *Phenomenology of Spirit,* trans. A. V. Miller (Oxford: Oxford University Press, 1977); *Phänomenologie des Geistes* (Hamburg: Felix Meiner, 1952).

PhM G. W. F. Hegel, *Philosophy of Mind being part three of the Encyclopedia of the Philosophical Sciences* (1830), trans. William Wallace together with Zusätze in Boumann's text (1845), trans. A. V. Miller (Oxford: Oxford University Press, 1971); *Enzyklopädie der philosophischen Wissenschaften im Grundrisse* (1830); *Dritter Teil: Philosophie des Geistes mit den mundlichen Zusätzen [Werke 10]* (Frankfurt: Suhrkamp Verlag, 1970).

PhN G. W. F. Hegel, *Philosophy of Nature, being part two of Encyclopedia of the Philosophical Sciences,* trans. Michael J. Petry (London: Allen and Unwin, 1970); *Encyklopädie der philosophischen Wissenschaften im Grundrisse* (1830); *Zweiter Teil: Die Naturphilosophie, mit den Mundlichen Zusätzen [Werke 9]* (Frankfurt: Suhrkamp Verlag, 1970).

RH G. W. F. Hegel, "Reason in History," in *Lectures on the Philosophy of World History,* trans. H. B. Nisbet (Cambridge: Cambridge University Press, 1975); *Vorlesungen über die philosophie der Geschichte* (Frankfurt: Suhrkamp Verlag, 1970).

RSW Jean Jacques Rousseau, *Reveries of a Solitary Walker,* trans. Peter France (London: Penguin Books, 1979); *Les Rêveries du promeneur solitaire,* Edition Bibliothèque de la Pléiade, 1959.

Sim Jean Baudrillard, *Simulations,* trans. Paul Foss, Paul Patton, and Philip Beitchman (New York: Semiotext[e], 1983).

SM Roger Penrose, *Shadows of the Mind: A Search for the Missing Science of Consciousness* (Oxford: Oxford University Press, 1994).

WOD Maurice Blanchot, *Writing of the Disaster,* trans. Ann Smock (Lincoln:

University of Nebraska Press, 1986); *L'Ecriture du Désastre* (Paris: Gallimard, 1980).

WP Friedrich Nietzsche, *The Will to Power,* trans. Walter Kaufmann (New York: Vintage, 1968); *Wille zur Macht* (Stuttgart: Alfred Kroner, 1956).

Z Friedrich Nietzsche, *Thus Spoke Zarathustra,* trans. R. J. Hollingdale (Harmondsworth: Penguin Books, 1961); also *Sprach Zarathustra in Kritische Gesamtausgabe* [Werke 6:4] (Berlin: Walter de Gruyter, 1991).

And when those immense structures go down, no one hears
. . . a flash and then it's gone
leaving behind a feeling that something happened there once
like wind tearing at the current,   ·
but no memory and no crying either. . . .
There was no one to tell us what it meant
when it meant what it did.

> John Ashberry
> "Flow Chart"

Re-signing History,
De-signing Ethics

It is a commonplace that history recounts events that have occurred in the past of some human community. This mundane view may provide a helpful starting point for inquiring into history's relation to time, language, and social existence. According to the everyday view, history is concerned with events once but no longer present, events that are somehow stored up, remembered, made conscious as that which is no more. Yet almost any manifestation of human activity may be singled out for historical scrutiny. It is no more surprising to find a history of naval architecture or of Chinese art than it is to find a depiction of the French Revolution.

Whatever her view of history, the historian is bound to ask, "What happened? How was it *then?*" When the answer is proffered as an account of what transpired in a stipulated time and place, it may be grasped as a transposition of codes, a decoding into narrative language of what has been encoded as a sequence of particulars.[1] On the other hand, the historian may respond with an explanation of long-term trends and adduce reasons, often shored up by statistical analyses, for how and why these trends persist or are modified. In either case, the process may be characterized as bringing into a system of signs, re-signing, that which was. There has been a vast expansion with respect to what is to count as the frame of reference in studying history so as to include visual and information technologies which do not leave discursive history unaffected. This sea change is of immense importance and will be considered in detail later. In this chapter I shall focus upon the question of historical writing.

The commonsense view of history presupposes that the historian aims to tell the truth about the past where truth is understood as a matching of event or pattern with what is said about it. Even if what is alleged about some specific detail happens to be false, the truth of a proposition is thought to depend upon its correspondence with an object or referent. Thus it is the criterion of truth rather than the truth or falsity of any single proposition that is thought to guarantee that the ultimate compilation of propositions, the whole, will be the sum of its true parts. So intimate is the relation of word to event that the term "history" refers, as Hegel observed, both to the *res gestae,* the historical object, and to the *historia rerum gestarum,* the verbal account of these events. Intrinsic also to the everyday view is the assumption that statements produced by the craft of historical writing are promises on the historian's part that her assertions are true in the sense that what is alleged to have happened did happen, that her claims are as accurate as proximity to the sources can make them. This meaning of veracity is embodied in Aristotle's famous distinction between historian and poet: "[The historian] describes the thing that has been, [the poet] a kind of thing that might be" (*Poetics,* 1451b).[2] This view of correspondence presupposes that the "original" and the narrated event are homologous, each layer transparent toward a more primordial one until the original event is disclosed. In accordance with Leopold von Ranke's often-cited claim, the historian conveys the thing that actually happened.

This description of recovering the past, of its re-signing, has been called into question by the critiques of post-structuralist and analytic philosophers alike on the grounds that the relation of language to both time and the referent have been misunderstood. Yet both post-structuralists and analysts who address these issues often fail to notice that their presumably new theories are often unrecognized repetitions of concepts previously explored in the thought of those whose concepts they believe they have transcended. I shall consider their positions and bring out the lineage of the iconoclastic arguments restated in their work.

I explore the claim that the promise to tell the truth about the past should continue to provide the warranty for the historian's assertions that re-signing, linguistic appropriation of that which was, need not disappear but is to be transformed. The question that presses not only upon the historian but, in other guises, upon the most urgent political, social, and cultural matters generally is whether the trenchant criticisms that recent philosophy has directed upon received views of truth effectively rule out the historian's promise. Can such claims avoid the paradox that, on the one hand, there is no straightforward way to match our propositions about events with events themselves, yet, on the other hand, the historian is justified in claiming she can tell the truth?

The promise to convey the truth about the past presupposes that the presentation of that which was is always already implicated in a pre-discursive ethics before it is a conveying of facts. But this space prior to historical description is one in which signs disappear, of de-signing. The historian when bound by a responsibility toward the dead for whom she claims to speak becomes what I call the "heterological historian." She assumes liability for the other, feels the pressure of an Ethics that is prior to historical judgment, an Ethics of ethics that is a de-signing prior to her construal of the historical object. Responsibility thus interpreted is Janus-faced: its moral authority is expressed in its disinterestedness, but its psychological force is experienced as a sense of inescapable urgency. The heterological historian is driven, on the one hand, by an impassioned necrophilia which would bring to life the dead others for whom she speaks. On the other hand, as "objective," she consciously or otherwise assumes responsibility for a dispassionate relation to events.

She does not yet raise the question of whether history is possible at all, an issue that will come to the fore in subsequent chapters concerned with the transformation of discourse into the circulation of information. In the present context she confines her attention to critiques of representation. She realizes that, if meaning cannot be attributed to the historian's promise, the solvent of criticism can only further destroy the already frayed affective and juridical bonds that hold contemporary societies together. Instead, criticism may regenerate the very cultural and social tensions spawned earlier by the epistemological fundamentalism that these critical analyses were designed to undermine.[3] Similarly, one by-now familiar tack, the slippage into a metaphysics of unamended difference and dissemination, can, in the context of a justifiable anti-colonialist discourse, backfire creating an intractable ethnocentricty and nationalism.[4]

THE HISTORIAN'S PROMISE

Before turning to the question of the promise, the one who pledges truthfulness must be identified. Who is the historian who promises? One of the ambiguities that attaches to the historian's role stems from a widening of the field of history in the culture of information and image so that persons with the variety of concerns already alluded to construct and disseminate interpretations of the past. The historian in the narrow sense has received academic training in the study of a period, theme, or concatenation of events within a geographical region, is the member of a profession and, as such, is usually recognized as belonging to a culture of experts. Because speaking about and for the past is a function taken on also by those outside the profession, the term can be more broadly applied. The historian in this wider sense is similarly bound by the promise that precedes discursive interpretations of the past in that she is committed truthfully to convey some aspect of it, often pictographically or through novel technological means. To provide the warranty for one's discourse is to enter into the terrain of ethics. Metahistorian Hayden White observes, "Every historical narrative has as its latent or manifest purpose the desire to moralize the events of which it treats."[5]

The historian's pledge means that she cannot absent herself from her work, even if the events of her life (as is usually the case) lie outside the historical matters at hand—the names, dates, currents of thought, and economic and social trends that she explicates. Textually invisible, the historian is nevertheless "there," the discursive void that constitutes the space of authorization for the coming together of the various rules and protocols that govern what can and cannot be said or exhibited in her work, for example, decisions about problematic lines between the public and the private, between the polite and the obscene. The promise that at first appears to suggest strictly epistemological questions—for example, what to count as the truth criterion for the historian and how that criterion is to be applied—can be seen to generate a quite different line of inquiry. Whose truth is being told, to whom, by whom, and to what end? Such queries not only bear upon the problem of historical knowledge but enter in searing ways into the affairs of everyday life.

Two personal anecdotes may help to make the point.

I had volunteered to guard a van on a New York City street for someone who was in the process of moving. Visibly stretched across the open back of the van was a new scuba diving suit, an oddity that attracted the attention of an old, homeless African-American man. After a brief conversation about scuba diving gear, I noticed that his left leg was swollen to twice its size. I pleaded with him to have it looked after at a nearby hospital and offered to accompany him, but he refused. I asked him whether I might help in some other way. "Just remember my name, Billie Joe. Don't forget Billie Joe," he said as he limped away.

Was the injunction to remember his name a means of informing me that he was one of the forgotten, that a transpersonal history was locked into the name Billie Joe, that he was a particular, as it were, that exhibited a universal meaning, that of destitution? Or was he pointing to himself proudly as the unique individual, a singularity, designated by this name? Was his history the inalienable property of a people and a culture upon which an outsider had no purchase? Yet if I, such an outsider, am prohibited from inquiring into the history of the other, is this constraint not tantamount to an endorsement of historical solipsism? If, per contra, I enter into the other's history, recount it, have I not created in his name a particular constellation of verbal or gestural instances having practical import, one that imposes a language of dominance and an alien historical identity? Would I come to remember this incident through the screen of later literary encounter, perhaps through the celebrated words of Toni Morrison's *Beloved,* who pleads in a moment of sexual desire, "I want you to call me my name."[6] Or, more insidious, was my offer and is the present telling of it not a gesture of narcissism, the self-congratulatory display of good intentions on the part of the relatively privileged?

The second episode occurred on a recent visit to Budapest. I noticed numerous posters on kiosks and store fronts throughout the city announcing an exhibit of Khmer dynasty art at a gallery in an out-of-the way quarter. Although somewhat dubious about the probability of a small gallery's negotiating a loan of objects so difficult to acquire, I was sufficently energized by the prospect of seeing them to undertake a visit. There were no artworks or artifacts on display. Instead, striking and detailed photographs of the ruins of Angkhor and other sites lined the gallery walls. In an anteroom were hung photographs of the piled-up skeletal remains attesting to the mass killings in Kampuchea under the Pol Pot regime. When I left the gallery, I noticed a bustling television studio in a building across the square with a Star of David conspicuously embedded in its facade. Upon inquiry, the studio's guard confirmed my suspicion that the building had been a synagogue and volunteered that, in 1944 when he was ten, what seemed to him a thousand Jews including a child who was his close friend were rounded up by the Hungarian Arrow Cross on the spot where we now stood, taken to the banks of the Danube nearby, shot, and their bodies dumped into the river.

Did the fortuitous contiguity of these two massacres mean that events concatenated within different cultural frameworks could be gathered into a common configuration in the absence of similar linguistic and cultural traditions? Does the comparison violate the tacitly understood right of each group to retain its singularity? Do resemblances of the sort that ordinarily seem to legitimize the breaching of vast differences, for example, the resemblance posited by Fernand Braudel between the situations of Ming China and France of the Valois with regard to the exposure of each to local wars, apply mutatis mutandis to differing instances of man-made mass death?[7] Or are events of mass death linked largely by their ability to provoke our outrage? Are political messages such as the proscription against racially or ideologically generated violence strengthened or weakened by such conjoining?

Such questions can be cordoned off in the form of a refusal to engage them, yet they continue to fissure everyday existence. Prior to the selection of a field of objects, prior to the orchestration of these objects into narrative, analytic, or specular form, the historian is assaulted by comparable questions. She may decide to ignore them on the grounds that historical objectivity requires detachment and precludes any *parti pris* in relation to past events or to distort and deny what she knows to have happened. Yet, when engaged in the task of describing that which was, irrespective of her metahistorical commitment to the standpoint of truth telling, she is under the threat of contestation in that the dead other both solicits rectitude, rightness of judgment, but also contests such judgment in that, by assuming the voice of the dead other, the historian appropriates that voice. To grasp the manner in which knowledge of the past is challenged by the other and to determine the way in which the relation to alterity serves as a precondition for historical discourse, it is important to reconstruct what is often meant by such knowledge. In that context, I shall consider the problem of historical knowledge in a preliminary way, sound it as a theme to which I shall frequently return.

HISTORICAL TRUTH AND THE END OF REPRESENTATION

On the commonsense view, it would seem that historical knowledge can be understood as a subset of some more general theory of knowledge usually conceived as representationalist, the view that "we can select among our beliefs and features of our world picture some that we can reasonably claim to represent the world . . . to the maximum degree independent of our perspective and its peculiarities."[8] Yet most current accounts, even those reflecting strong realist propensities, stress these features: the inseparability of thinking from its linguistic articulation, that what we hold to be true can be understood only against the web of all our beliefs, and, often, a constructivist view of the way in which the object of knowledge is constituted. Far from denying that narrativity penetrates the way we see events, Arthur C. Danto concedes the point but argues further that this process is akin to the way in which theories penetrate observations in science.[9] Even if the division between them often appears intractable, these features are common to both Anglo-American and continental philosophy, so that the words of the metahistorian Jacques Rancière apply across the philosophical continental divide: "Words, whatever the realists might say are more stubborn than facts."[10]

A phenomenological interpretation of cognition, as modified by the linguistic turn of structuralism, pictures knowing as the narrative explication of a series of occurrences such that that-which-is is manifested in linguistic signs. These signs acquire meaning by virtue of their differences from other signs and are unified into the synchronicity of a story. This amalgam is reflected in Emmanuel Levinas's account of knowledge:

> Linguistic signs which constitute a systematic unity, are able to identify a theme through the manifold ways of fabulation. Synopsis results from the unity of a theme which is identified in the narration. . . . Words then do not issue from an intention limited to the vain action of substituting signs for things and signs for signs. . . . The establishing and utilizing of verbal signs is borne by a narrating and thematizing intentionality.[11]

On this view, knowing is not an act of making transparent what is merely there, given, a content that is passively registered upon a receptive subject. Instead, knowing is both utterance and activity, an active proclaiming, declaring something as something.

In a quite different vein, Donald Davidson attacks representationalism by focusing upon the distinction between organizing system and that which awaits organization, between scheme and content. Sentences do not mirror a referent because "[n]othing . . . no thing makes sentences or theories true: Not experience, not surface irritations, not the world, can make a sentence true." As Richard Rorty declares, "The lines of evidential force . . . do not parallel the lines of referential direction" in that the former depends upon knowing the language in which the beliefs are expressed and the latter the rules used by speakers of the language.[12]

The structural/phenomenological view I have sketched treats thought-acts as the ascription of an identity and thus associates them with naming. The ascription of truth or falsity to propositions within a discursive system is contingent upon this primordial proclamation of meaning, of the acts of nomination which unite disparate discursive items. When he describes the name as designating links in a chain of communication, Saul Kripke's view of naming is, in that regard at least, in accord with the structural-phenomenological account. Kripke writes: "A baby is born; his parents call him by a certain name. They talk about him to their friends. Other people meet him. Through various sorts of talk the name is spread from link to link as if by a chain."[13] To know is to engage in a signifying and proclamatory act through which differentiated contexts or worlds are traversed and brought together through the permanence of the name.[14]

For Derrida, naming as a cognitive act exhibits, like cognitive acts generally, a proto-moral failure. The trouble with cognition is that it is in bad faith, disingenuous; it conceals the difference between itself and the items it links as well as the interim, however miniscule, that separates primary memory and anticipation from present perception. Thinking cannot go on atemporally: a before and after passes invisibly through discourse, a passing that philosophy in its classical and modern versions has tried to conceal. This covering over is what Derrida points out in his powerful, even if by now shopworn, expression *differance*,[15] a multivalent term that (among other things) refers to the interpreting of past and future as modes of the present and thereby hiding the diffractions of time. Like Freud's unconscious, these modes of "nonpresence" are constitutive of presence, cannot themselves be made present, and display themselves only as aftereffects (Derrida, *SP*, pp. 64 and 152).[16] To note the temporal diffraction or difference underlying thought-acts does not vitiate the need to confer an identity but brings to light "that a lack of foundation is basic and non-empirical and that the security of presence in the metaphorical form of ideality arises and is set forth again upon this irreducible void."[17]

The epistemic insecurity that attaches to the possibility of truth telling applies a fortiori to the relation with other persons. Knowing as a bringing together of what is multiple into a fragment of discourse, a unit of meaning, cannot be invoked to describe the manner in which other persons are encountered. This is not only because of the temporal diffraction that is concealed in acts of knowing generally but rather because the mode of apprehending the other is neither straightforwardly perceptual nor conceptual. To be sure, attributes of the other—tall, short, intelligent, stupid, greedy, generous—can be discursively rendered, but the manner in which the other as other is revealed cannot be predicative. The ascription of properties to the other interprets her as an object of thought, affect, or action so that her alterity is subordinated to a thought-act whose content she has become. Alterity no longer remains integral to her, an outcome that is inadmissible on logical grounds in that what defines otherness is its irreducible exteriority which, as such, defies cognitive encapsulation. Not only can the other not be manifested discursively but, it can be argued, she *ought* not to be so manifested. The effort to suppress alterity is an act of violence and thus inadmissable on ethical grounds. By the ethical relationship is meant one in which terms are united "neither by a synthesis of the understanding nor by a relationship between subject and object, and yet where the one weighs or concerns or is meaningful to the other."[18]

Historical narratives cannot avoid configuring the other in accordance with some model of cognitive apprehension however loosely construed. Yet when these epistemological vocabularies are applied to the other as other, they both fail phenomenologically and embody a category mistake. To be sure, the other can be envisioned as that which appears, as a phenomenon, or decoded as a token of which her society, culture, and economy, past and present, are types and thus as an object of categorial interpretation. Yet as other, she signifies prior to her corporeal appearing, prior to the meanings that can be conferred upon her behavior and to her anchorage in a psychosocial milieu. She is without a foothold in a terrain, deterritorialized, without psychic, physical, or cultural grounding,[19] a destitution that, in psychoanalytic terms, might be described as the absence of defense mechanisms without attributing ethical and ontological implications to the phrase.

The elusive manner of the other's self-manifestation can be depicted as enigmatic in the etymological sense, as that which is equivocal or obscure and that can only be conveyed in a non-discursive immediacy graphically characterized by the term "proximity."[20] The one who is proximate is encountered neither visually nor conceptually but as one who approaches; the approach in turn is defined as the manner in which the other is encountered. This relation of terms is non-viciously circular, suggesting rather that alterity and approach are reciprocally constituted. Because the terms "proximity" and "approach" imply spatiality, it could be inferred that they are explicable in terms of a Kantian synthesis of the understanding in which the other is constituted as a physical body, but nothing could be further removed from their signification in the present context. Proximity is rather a shift in orientation, a turning away from apprehension of the world and toward the reception of the other.[21] The non-spatiality of proximity is especially significant for the historian who does not encounter the other face-to-face but in the documents, artifacts, and visual and technological simulations that constitute the historical record. Whether living or dead, the other or others are bereft of the protective mechanisms provided by context "appearing" not as visible forms but as the contestation of form and thus as disfigured, as bodies that are subject to pain and death.

The other is a theme neither of historical analysis nor description but functions as an ethical placeholder in historical discourse, as a textually invisible demand placed upon the historian that she fulfill the promise of truthfulness, a promise that requires epistemic sophistication and historiographic inventiveness. Even the historian who deliberately substitutes that-which-was-not in place of what she believes to have occurred does so in fidelity to a principle or practice that is the placeholder for the pledge of veracity. Whether she will or no, the historian is covenanted to the dead and must, in making them speak, demonstrate without having to say so that she has fulfilled the promise. The claim of the other may be rejected, but nevertheless it is experienced as urgency, as pressure that cannot be evaded. Lyotard endorses this position in characteristically hyperbolic fashion when he affirms that "Satan would be God's best servant if it is true that at least he disobeys Him." Because disobedience confirms that responsibility for the other has been recognized, Lyotard concludes, "Satan is an ethical name."[22]

The relation to the other is an obsession not as a pathological idée fixe but rather as a passion for rectitude. To construct a narrative about the *res gestae* is not only to express that which appears but also to communicate that which cannot appear, the rectitude of the historian. To make that which cannot appear present itself is precisely the issue that Kant confronts in his analysis of the teleology of nature, in his aesthetic, and in his philosophy of history, problems I shall explore in Chapter 2.

I have argued that the Other can be neither the object of a thought, affect, or action, nor grasped in the manner of a content in that the other transcends the various modes in which content is apprehended. As other, she is an excess that necessitates a radical shift in the way time is experienced. In cognitive acts, the indicating and indicated terms are felt as inseparably co-present; thought-acts are non-different from their content. Cognition conceals the alterity that provides the warranty for its claims to truth because alterity belongs to another temporal "framework" than that of the cognitive act. That which is excessive, transcends incorporation into a thought, cannot be wedged into the time frame of presence for reasons other than those that affect cognition as Derrida has described it. In acts of knowing, there is a built-in lag time, a delay, a scission or fissure in the temporalization of cognition because the ecstases of time, anticipation, and primal memory preclude identifying our world relations as describable in terms of plenary presence. The relation to the other is an-achronistic all the way down in the sense that it does not merely come before a thought-act but is an absolute "before, a before for which there is no after. In non-phenomenological language, it is a relation in which one of the relata is more than, exceeds, the relation itself. In Emmanuel Levinas's words, "Consciousness is always late for the rendezvous with the neighbor."[23] The inescapability of the before accords a certain primacy to the time that has already passed by. The historian is particularly well-placed to offer powerful defiance of time's irreversibility. By rendering that which was in image and narrative, the historian engages in a rebellion against this irreversibility and places that-which-was before (ahead of) us. But how can the temporality of the before, of alterity, incise itself into the historical narrative?

THE NECESSITY OF NAMING

Earlier I described Billie Joe's request that I remember his name as an appeal that was not that of a generalized destitution, of a neutral alterity that obligates its addressee through the "transcendental structure" of ethics. Rather it was the importunity of an existing other who was *actually* destitute and not in this condition because *every* other is always already an an-iconic sign of indigence and vulnerability. How does naming enter into the question of destitution? Is naming not a conferring of an identity that links discrete discursive items and, as such, belongs to the order of knowledge rather than to that of ethics? On Lyotard's reading of Kripke, names situate the "where" and "when" of the subject under discussion in a system of spatial, temporal, and topical cross-references.[24] When the historical referent is a proper name it too is located in such a network of other names and relations, Lyotard contends. But proper names—Caesar, Marco Polo, and the like—should not be confused with objects of perception presented in "ostensive phrases," phrases that are related to a current origin such as the one who utters the phrase at a particular time and place. This is the deictic moment of perceptual acts. Lyotard is not endorsing a representational theory of knowledge but rather the claim that perceptual objects are exhibited by phrases of a type that differ from that of historical objects. Unlike the perceptual object, the historical object need not be related to an origin and is, as such, merely "quasi-deictic." Yet when in Hegel's phrase the *res gestae* of history are taken up into the *historia rerum gestarum*, when it becomes an object of historical inquiry, it enters into the discursive space of deictics so that the historian can say in Lyotard's words, "Look, there it is, the proof I was looking for."[25]

The historian can no longer appeal to the event, as if showing or indicating did not have its deictic aspect. To see this, consider that she is always already implicated in a history of metaphysics that receives its classical articulation in Aristotle's account of being *(prote ousia)*. For Aristotle, the specificity of indication, of the unity of the thing pointed to by the demonstrative pronouns this and that, and of signification, the sphere of meaning of the common noun, are distinguished. Benveniste and other modern linguists link the demonstratives (this, that, here, now) to the I that speaks in that both types of pronomial utterance are bound up with a unique and present instance of discourse. Thus he writes, "*This* [as] the object is simultaneous with . . . *here* and *now* [as] delimit[ing] the spatial and temporal instance is coextensive and contemporaneous with the present instant of discourse containing I."[26]

The historian is implicated in varying discursive types: description, an account of the historical object, but also attestation, expressed in its weak form as asserting only that it is she who has constructed the *historia rerum gestarum,* she who is its origin, and in its stronger form, the avowal that she stands up for, attests, the veracity of her account. The deictic feature of ostension, the first person attestation of that which is predicated, is now inscribed in the third-person narrative of historical writing.

Although Derrida nowhere alludes to the contrast between nomination and ostension as I have sketched it, the distinction remains an undertone in his account of the difference between the proper name as that which persists after death and the living bearer of the name: the post-mortem proper name is pure nomination, whereas ostensive phrases apply to the living bearer of the name who can speak in the first person.[27] The ambiguity of the proper name lies in its applicability at once to the historian, to the object of history, and to the reader or viewer so that all can be linked to the politics of the proper name. In developing this issue in the context of Nietzsche's writings, at once autobiographical and philosophical, Derrida asserts:

> A new problematic of the biographical in general . . . must mobilize other [than empirical psychological] resources, at the very least, a new analysis of the proper name and the signature. [What must be questioned] is the dynamis of that borderline between the work and the life . . . neither active nor passive, neither outside nor inside. . . . This divisible borderline traverses two "bodies," the corpus of works and the body, in accordance with laws we are just beginning to catch sight of.[28]

The signature borne by the written work is linked with the bearer of the name, the living individual such that between life and text there is a movement of reciprocal infiltration. Yet the proper name insofar as it exists apart from its bearer is the name of the dead or, floating freely, remains independent of the living bearer of the name.[29]

What has been said of the philosopher thus far is applicable ceteris paribus to the historian. Yet one should not be mistaken for the other. The deictic aspect of the philosopher's proper name is, to borrow Deleuze's apt phrase, a conceptual persona irreducible to psychosocial types, a pseudonym for the concepts he creates.[30] Even when the proper name in the strict sense is absent and the historical account is anonymous or a work of multiple authorship, the historian's pledge of truthfulness holds. Naming the historical object is a response to the other's mortality: to name is to make us forget the fact of death, to write over it. In *sensu strictu,* the name itself does not designate a property nor is it a condensed proposition to which truth or falsity can be attributed even if properties can be ascribed to the referent of the name and the truth or falsity of such ascriptions asserted.[31] Rather, the name is empty: its logical form suggests that its primary function is heterological, that of an ethical placeholder, an appeal to the historian to make manifest that which was. If, as Braudel has alleged, history can begin a minute ago, I am under obligation as the one who has spoken for Billie Joe to offer up predicates that "give him countenance."[32]

Names can be conferred to demean or even to consign to death. Those to whom a name has been refused or who have had names, generally common nouns, imposed upon them—"comfort women," the name applied to Chinese women forced into prostitution by the Japanese occupiers in World War II; Sarah and Jacob, names applied as generic terms to all Jewish women and men by the Nazis—have been encoded in a system of references which demands decoding. Like the virologist, the historian as cryptographer is at risk of contamination, either by virtue of a certain prior sympathy for the meaning constellation she is decoding or through the psychological power of the phrase regimen itself. This aspect of the historian's role opens unsettling questions. Returning to the personal experience described earlier, might the photographs of the Cambodian genocide that I saw exhibited in Budapest belong to the same phrase regimen as the account of the slaughter of Hungarian Jews on the banks of the Danube by virtue of something more than the accident of a spatial contiguity that united them in a single thought-act? Can the fact of mass annihilation inflicted upon those not inimical to one another create a single historical persona, a single proto-people as it were, upon whom a name could be conferred, a common not a proper noun in the absence of geographical, linguistic, cultural, and economic ties? Or would such a name attest not a web of beliefs but of silences and negations? Would such a persona fix the victims in a phrase regimen of perpetual victimhood or call attention to the way in which mass death cross-cuts cultural boundaries? And how does the name as an ethical placeholder situate those who are bound by cultural and geographic ties—the factions in Bosnia, Croatia, Krjina, and Slovenia—but are engaged in acts of reciprocal destruction? For the historian it is not a question of how likenesses are to be posited predicatively. Rather the problem exhibits the features of a Kierkegaardian dilemma: How does one compare incommensurables, Socrates and Jesus, Agamemnon and Abraham, without appealing to a hetero-logical order and thereby already begging the question?[33] The historian who feels herself obligated by the proper name does not call up the ghost of the bearer but rather continues the speech-acts of the dead.

THAT WHICH CANNOT BE NAMED: THE CATACLYSM

The cataclysm is the void exposed by the event of the mass annihilation of persons within ever more compressed time frames, a void that remains indescribable and yet constitutes a unique moment, the entry of the nihil into time. In saying this much, has the cataclysm not already been named, depicted? Do not refusals to name covertly circumscribe an entity in psychological or theological terms? From a psychological perspective, it has been claimed that horror numbs and blinds the historian and renders the void left by the event beyond the purview of historical narrative or analysis. Theologically the cataclysm is treated as the obverse of the sacred, a negative epiphany that can only be approached through the strategies of negative theology, a mode of negation that Derrida calls "apophasis . . . the voiceless voice." Yet even as the name God or some other theophanic appellation announces itself, it already proclaims what it hides as an object of desire.[34] Such readings of the void render it amenable to comprehension. Like the Lacanian unconscious, it would be structured like a language, so that the historian would have only to remove the screen of horror to recover the lost signifier and restore it to the chain of signifiers, thereby dispelling the apophasis of the void, its wordlessness and silence. The void is decoded into event sequences amenable to description and analysis.

But if this non-place is prior to historical descriptions, one in which signs disappear, then there is no-thing to distinguish it from the void of de-signing already invoked as the "locus" of Ethics. Is this non-place, as Hegel said of Schelling's concept of being, a night in which all cows are black? And is it not futile in the arena of history to depart altogether from intelligi-bility instead of merely seeking a more nuanced account of intelligibility?

Yet genealogical analysis can recover a philosophical legacy that imbricates the void and Ethics prior to the coupling of thinking and being. The Unlimited and cosmic justice are brought together in a single discursive formation in the fragment of the pre-Socratic philosopher, Anaximander:

> The Unlimited is the first-principle of things that are. It is that from which the coming-to-be of things and qualities takes place and it is that into which they return when they perish by moral necessity, giving satisfaction to one another and making reparation for their injustice according to the order of time.[35]

The *apeiron* and the void are undifferentiated, but the *apeiron* although *not yet* anything is an ontological storehouse, the womb of "things and qualities" in contradistinction to the void which has no offspring.

The text describes a moral balance sheet such that things make reparation for their injustice. Against Heidegger's claim that the Anaximander fragment points only to an overcoming of negativity in the coming-to-be or presencing of things, it must be argued that the *apeiron* is configured as an ethical topos against which wrongs are redressed through a process of reimbursement for the gift of being. Things and qualities act in conformity with a rule, the order of time, and thus know when and how to make restitution for their injustice. But unlike the cataclysm, the *apeiron* is timeless.

The persistence in contemporary physics of the trope of the boundless in its relation to time, things, and qualities is remarkable once the universe's primordiality conditions are stated in non-mathematical terms.[36] In a popular account of the original condition of the universe, Stephen Hawking posits the no-boundary condition, the idea that the universe is finite but has no boundary or edge, is smooth, orderly, and self-contained. From the standpoint of science (and thus from the physicist's perspective, the perspective not of the subjectivity of the scientist but that of the boundless itself) time has no direction. Because a minimum possible non-uniformity consistent with the uncertainty principle existed in the universe's original state, the universe was able to expand and will ultimately contract. As it expands, disorder or entropy increases accounting for time's seemingly forward movement. Both its expansion and disorder are the necessary conditions for our experience of time: we remember the past and not the future. Intelligent beings can exist only in the expanding phase which is one of disorder: we require time's directionality which, in turn, requires disorder. In our comprehension of the universe "[we have] established a small corner of order in an increasingly disordered universe."[37]

The cosmological process as described in the Anaximander fragment and by Hawking are conveyed in what is virtually a common set of metaphors. For there to be "things and properties" there must be disorder which issues (somehow) from the boundless. As soon as this occurs time, which in its own-being is non-directional, becomes directional. Things and qualities act in accordance with a rule of time generated by the complicity of the universe's disorder and expansion. A kind of back and forth exchange ensues: order and disorder alternate as it were. Order breaks down and restores itself in an ongoing process even if, in the long run, for modern physics disorder is likely to prevail. Can it not be said in the hyperbolic language of Anaximander "that [things and qualities] give satisfaction to one another and make reparation for their injustice according to the order of time?"

The discursive formation that links justice and the *apeiron* in Anaximander does not help us to think or to figure that which is "before" (in front of and prior to) the logos. The problem takes on special urgency in Plato's *Timaeus* where a way between the void and intelligibility must be negotiated. Derrida's analysis of the *Khora* of the *Timaeus* brings to the fore that which removes itself from all interpretation, yet which gives place to mythos and logos while exempt from the law of what it situates. Thus Derrida writes:

> *Khora* seems never to let itself be reached or touched, much less broached, and above all not exhausted by . . . tropological or interpretative translation. . . . *Khora* is not a subject. It is not the subject. Nor the support *(subjectile)*. . . . But if Timaeus names it as receptacle *(dekhomenon)* or place *(khora)*, these names do not designate an essence, the stable being of an eidos . . . nor of mimemes, that is, of images of the eidos. . . . [Khora] is not, does not belong to the two known or recognized genres of being.[38]

Like the *khora*, the *apeiron* is a progenetrix of forms; it does not supervene upon the destruction of beings but exists as a cosmological archive of forms and shapes. (It could be argued that the information culture is an effort to recreate such an archive by returning forms and shapes to their incipient state, recoding them as numbers in conformity with the Pythagorean principle that the world is made of numbers.)

What must be brought to the fore is the indeterminateness of Being that would ensue if one imagined not what is prior to beings but the disappearance of all beings. Emmanuel Levinas designates this impersonal anonymous residue, the Being that wells up when there is nothing, the *il y a*, the there is.[39] Just as mood is determinative for Heidegger's account of the Dasein's relation with its world, so too the *il y a* is disclosed through horror.

The *il y a* is not linked to a fear of death in that it is not an absolute nihil but sheer lambency, a pressure that weighs without there yet being a subject upon whom it impinges. Unlike the cataclysm, it is a proto-immortal being and thus not bound up with the moment. I shall defer the discussion of how the *il y a* and the non-place of ethics "mimic" one another in order to describe it in Chapter 2 in the context of Kant's analysis of the dynamical sublime. At present, it suffices to note that it is the emergence of the individual that effects a break with the *il y a*. Because tropes require some feature common to the items compared, there appear to be no resources for rendering emergence from the void. In effect there are metamorphoses without linkage—from the *apeiron* to justice, from the *khora* to the forms, from the *il y a* to the individual. Yet the question must be asked, What signals the emergence from the *il y a?* One can reply: the occurrence of an instance of discourse such that the deictic aspect of an indicative utterance manifests itself, that is to say, the I shows itself in an act of speech. Thus Agamben writes: "Pronouns and other indicators of the utterance, before they designate real objects, indicate precisely that *language takes place*. In this way, still prior to the world of meanings, they permit the reference *to the very event of language*."[40]

But the cataclysm is not the *apeiron*, the *khora*, or the *il y a*. How does the weight of the cataclysm manifest itself in the deictic utterance, not of any individual but in the I-saying of the historian? Such I-saying is not the assertion of a substantive self but rather of a promise to assume liability for the dead others by naming them. Derrida avers that in conferring a name "one does not offer a thing, one delivers nothing, and still something comes to be which comes down to giving that which one does not have, as Plotinus said of the Good."[41] The heterological historian goes about naming cautiously, is mindful of the slipperiness of names. "What can happen to a name given," Derrida warns, is "anonymity, metonymy, paleonymy, cryptonymy, pseudonymity."[42] Yet far from enjoining silence, the pressure of the cataclysm mandates discourse and image, the naming of that which has been reduced to the merely numerable. Neither the recency nor the remoteness of an event is germane to the responsibility imposed by the cataclysm. The psychological horror in the face of recent mass annihilations is likely to be far more profound than what is felt in encountering earlier events. Just as in Kierkegaard's view there is no difference from the standpoint of faith between the disciples who are Jesus's contemporaries and the disciples at second hand, from the standpoint of responsibility the cataclysm is determinative for historical discourse irrespective of the particular time that discourse describes. The cataclysm is bound-up-with/*is* the moment of the nihil. But the weight of the cataclysm is a force field from which the historian of any place or period, any social, political, economic, or cultural conformation cannot escape for it purely and simply demands that she speak out of that non-place.

HISTORICAL NARRATIVE

History, says Rancière, is concerned with a double absence, "that of the 'thing itself' that is no longer there—that is in the past; and that never was—because it never was such as it was told."[43] A claim is staked for linking historical truth to the power of naming an absence that is actually a reserve of presence waiting to be redeemed by the historical narrative. Earlier the everyday view of historical knowledge, the position that the "original," the remembered and the narrated events of the past are homologous, was shown to be parasitic upon a view of knowledge as representation, a naive epistemology that in the context of history took for granted a referent, the historical record embodied in chronicles and artifacts, as a quasi-presence. The historical object that exists only as a post hoc fabrication in the double sense of that which is merely made and that which is made up, a fiction, opens the problem of the loss of historical factuality and would seem to bely the historian's promise. Consider Arthur Danto's effort to offer a straightforward account of the historian's covenant:

> It . . . remains the ideal of history-as-science to eradicate discrepancies between historical reality and history-for-us. To the degree that it succeeds, we live no differently in history than we do outside history: we live in the light of historical truth.[44]

Roland Barthes's and Hayden White's accounts of the *historia rerum gestarum* exhibit a much more tenuous connection between event and narrative.

Roland Barthes proclaims the death of the referent, of facts external to language, as the object of historical study explaining that facts in and by themselves are meaningless. The historian constructs relations among signifiers so as to confer positive meaning upon otherwise meaningless series of facts. Like Nietzsche, Barthes asserts that for there to be facts there must first be meaning. The referent is at first extruded from the discourse so as to appear as if it were external to it and at the same time as the origin of the discourse; then the signified still lingering within the discourse is forced out and conflated with the referent so that the signifier appears to refer not to it but to the referent. It would seem that the illusion of the referent overpowers the signified and creates the sense of realistic discourse when in fact the real is merely a signified pretending to be a referent.[45] The signified gets confused with the referent and becomes the object of the historical narrative. Historical discourse cannot deliver the real but only the empty assertion "that it happened."[46]

White rightly rejects the myth of the given, the view that events are a field of lambent facts, merely "there," awaiting subsequent interpretation. What metahistorians have failed to take into account, he argues, is the metaphoricity of historical writing. The explanatory effect of historical narratives is achieved not by reproducing events, themselves already encoded in tropes, but through the development of metaphorically articulated correspondences between events and conventional story types. Thus, for White, historical narrative lies between the events described in the historical record and the icon or story type that will render them accessible. The narrative mediates between the events reported in it and conventional plot structures that cast unfamiliar events in a way that renders them meaningful.

White does not fail to note the conflict between what he calls "the desire for the imaginary" and "the imperative of the real."[47] Narrative is a sophisticated genre that confers signification upon a non-narrative and prior stratum of facts that is provided by annals, a chronologically ordered list of events and chronicles, incomplete stories that do not come to closure but simply end.[48] But narrative alone, White concedes, cannot account for "history proper"; the historian must "handle evidence, honor chronology." On the one hand, White argues for a constructivist view, the primacy of narrative, "form as content"; on the other hand, he argues for its anchorage in "history proper," the factoids of annals and chronicles. For White, history proper is akin to perception, thus "realistic."[49] Allowing for the difference between a narrative construal of historical objects and claims about the truth of our beliefs generally, White's non-foundational view of history as narrative roughly parallels Rorty's anti-representationalist contention that we can justify our truth claims only by appealing to a network of beliefs generally and to a commonly spoken language.[50] Rorty denies that we are tied to sense qualia except in the most trivial sense. But his assertion begs for explication. What is this ineliminable trivial sense? To suggest as Sellars does that raw feels and the sensations of infants are already knowledge in the sense that they are discriminative behavior as opposed to knowing construed as giving reasons, a view that Rorty appears to endorse, does not help. If "awareness is justified true belief—knowledge—[as] ability to respond to stimuli," then a two-tiered account of knowing persists, communally justified assertions on the one hand and response to stimuli on the other.[51] The persistence of this view is parasitic upon the ghost of the referent as an ineluctable presence that even the most radically coherentist and conventionalist accounts of knowledge retain. I hope to show that the referential aspect of historical knowledge must be reconfigured in terms that take account of the *res gestae* in terms of absence rather than presence, a claim that demands a prior analysis of past time that I shall undertake in Chapter 5.

Never abandoning his claim for the reality of events as contingent upon their narrative articulation, White insists that an event must be able to sustain at least two interpretations, "to be recorded otherwise . . . in an order of narrative, that makes [events] . . . questionable as to their authenticity and to being considered as tokens of reality."[52] White is not insensitive to the relativism that such a latitudinarian interpretation implies, even reaching a null point, as it were, where the referent is ruled out of existence. Does this position not provide an entering wedge for revisionist accounts of the Holocaust, for the believability of a Nazi version of Nazism's history, a crucial test case, on White's admission, for interpretive license? Are there not events that do not admit of alternative explanations? Positive historiography, White responds, constrains interpretation at the level of the event in that some even questionable interpretations leave the "reality" of the event intact, whereas "the revisionist interpretation de-realizes it [through redescription]."[53] Just as ostension was shown not to resolve the problem of naming, this assertion only takes the ambiguity a step further back. It may be concluded that White waffles between a strong theory of metaphor that is parasitic upon the inscrutability of reference and an anchorage in the putatively non-narrative texts of history as a domain of facts.

A quite different stress is placed upon the genre of annal and chronicle by Rancière, which casts a new light upon the placement of the historical referent, the result of a strategic difference in the discursive space of authorization, the placement of alterity in the narrative. To see this, it is important to understand that what guides Rancière's view of history is Walter Benjamin's conception of the historian's task as giving voice to the anonymous of history. For Rancière, this is best achieved by taking advantage of the power historical writing derives from its inner kinship with literature. A new genre emerges, a poetics of historical rationality that first appeared in the account of the French Revolution in the writings of nineteenth-century historian Jules Michelet.[54] The challenge to the contemporary historian is that, in the quest for large-scale trends, truth is often defined by the norms of the social sciences in which laws governing the permanencies and changes of social, economic, and political forces and the statistical determinations of trends has supplanted narrative. The difficulty with this model for Rancière is that the temporal articulation of events, the diachronicity of history, is subordinated to the atemporal generalizations of laws and trends. The historian is challenged to invent a discourse which folds its "scienticity" within the conventions of a literary discourse, "a poetics of knowledge [as] a study of the set of literary procedures by which a discourse escapes literature, gives itself the status of a science, and signifies this status."[55]

Continuing in this vein, he suggests that in "the age of democracy" in which phenomena can often best be registered in terms of statistical regularities, the new historian must commit herself to a triple contract: scientific, eliciting the latent order out of that which appears; narrative, conveying the process in the form of a story replete with character, episode, and event; political, that of communicating this history in an age of democracy. Rancière's view, if unamended, would make of Emile Zola's *Germinale,* for example, a consummate work of history.

The question of representing the historical object can be traced to the Platonic configuring of mimesis. According to Plato, mimesis is most deceptive when it fails to disclose itself. Thus tragedy, which purports to allow the protagonists to speak as if giving utterance to their own thoughts and affects without revealing the source of these utterances, is more deceptive than the poetic genres in which the poet discloses himself. Rancière contends that tragedy is criticized by Plato because it is closer to appearance and democracy, to bringing forward the *vox populi,* whereas the latter announces itself as mere appearance. Whether the Platonic text justifies this reading remains an open question, but the potential of the speech of the dead to speak for itself is, as it were, the desideratum for which Rancière is reaching. Thus, in describing the revolt of the Roman legions in Pannonia, Tacitus is shown to recreate the speech of an obscure provocateur, Percennius (*Annals,* Book I, chap. 16), without any interpolation of explanatory discourse. Only parts of the complex *Annals* are encoded as chronicle in the sense of an inconclusive narrative, but it is to one such segment that Rancière appeals. It is not Percennius but the Percennius created by Tacitus as a plausible type who offers the reasons for rebellion. The value of speech in the absence of explanatory or evaluative discourse is that it brings to the fore a voice that would otherwise be delegitimated.

> Percennius speaks in the same mode as the others . . . [He] speaks without speaking . . . expressing the value of the information without deciding on the

value of this information, without situating it on the scale of the present and the past, of the objective and the subjective. The indirect style . . . cancels the opposition between legitimate and illegitimate speakers.[56]

The importance of including Percennius's speech-acts is the disfigurement of the narrative voice. By paring away any internal evaluations of this discourse the speakers whose voices are heard in the chronicle are equalized. Thus, in contrast to White, mimetic speech is not the referent awaiting narrative articulation but that which the other did or could have spoken, an indexical sign of the absent other within historical discourse. On this view, inequality is registered as a deprivation of speech. To be sure, White has never denied that there is a politics of interpretation, that the narrative is situated in a nexus of concerns contemporary with those of the narrator and with our own, its intentional or unintentional addressees. But, for White, the ethical moment of a historical work is derived from a synthesis of plot, "an aesthetic perception" and argument, "a cognitive operation" so that the prescriptive emanates from the descriptive without further explanation.[57] He has not noticed that the ethical referent goes all the way down, that the alterity of the other grips the historian prior to her narration and not as an inference from it. This notion is reflected in Rancière's claim that "the disjunction cast on the speech of the other regulates itself through the rhetorical form of the disjunction of meaning and truth, through the suspension of reference."[58]

It may be concluded that depriving historical groups of speech is a juridical wrong but that it lies beyond the strategies of rectification within most Western juridical systems. The norms of those systems are generally traceable to the Aristotelian concepts of retributive and distributive justice, the assessment of proper punishment for wrongs committed and the apportionment of goods and honors in accordance with dessert by a duly constituted body of the polis. Normal juridical discourse presupposes the equality of the litigants, a society, despite certain unavoidable inequities, of peers. Such a society presupposes the background of a common juridical language that strongly resembles the way in which such a web of beliefs has been interpreted in Anglo-American analytic interpretations of the problem of knowledge by Quine, Davidson, and to an extent Rorty, and of social philosophy by Rawls, Nozick, and Walzer, to name a few. The assumption that not only current wrongs require adjudication but that the ethical dimension of historical writing can be construed in terms of jurisprudence has recently come to the fore in the recounting of twentieth-century genocides, perhaps most often with respect to the test case of Auschwitz. It is from this standpoint that answers are sought for such questions as: Who is authorized to speak for the victims? How is victimization to be ascribed? Does the conferring of voice mean that the victims of the Nanjing massacre or of Japanese medical experiments in China during World War II cease to be victims once inequities are regulated through the creation of speech-acts in the name of the victims?

Lyotard has redescribed the silence of the victims in terms of an inequality of power among speakers, a situation he names a *différend*. Like Derridean *différance*, the term is widely invoked but has not, for all that, lost its force. Lyotard avers:

> I would like to call a [differend] between two parties the case where the plaintiff is divested of the means to argue and becomes for that reason a victim. If the addressor, the addressee and the sense of the testimony are neutralized, everything takes place as if there were no damages. A case of differend between two parties takes place when the regulation of the conflict that opposes them is done in the language of one of the parties while the wrong suffered by the other is not signified in that idiom.[59]

The plaintiff, deprived of the opportunity to establish her victimization, is doubly victimized. By appealing to a regulative principle, Lyotard's view does not radically depart from the juridical presuppositions that bind together the multiple perspectives of Western moral and social philosophy.

HISTORY AS SCIENCE: *L'ESPRIT DE GÉOMÉTRIE ET L'ESPRIT DE FINESSE*

If historical writing is to concern itself with speech-acts (although not only with such acts) these utterances must be convincing. If so, should they not reflect the criteria that determine non-narrative truth in the social sciences which, in turn, based their notions of truth on the model of the hard sciences? For modernity, the aim of the scientific interpretation of the real was the formulation of hypotheses which, when supported by observation, would elicit the latent order of that which appears. What lent conviction to such interpretation was, first, the standard view of representation as correspondence of "word and object" said to hold true at the level of observation, and, second, the mathematization of concepts upon which the explanatory power of the hypothesis depended. Representation is enhanced when the discrete factoids, the unrelated elementary particles of knowledge, are given shape in the formal language of mathematics. In characteristically hyperbolic fashion, Rancière formulates the historian's dilemma from the post-

Enlightenment nineteenth century to the present: "Either narrative and its kindness toward chance heroes, or science dissipating their prestige."[60] Hayden White contends that, "as investigator, the historian is engaged in science; as narrator, in art."[61] The social implications of their relation resulted in the radical bifurcation of two cultures, as C. P. Snow had earlier described them, without the possibility of an internal discursive breaching of the one by the other.

There is an anticipation not merely of this disjunction, one which has become a commonplace of modernity, but also of the interpenetration of observation (the putative stuff of narration) already inscribed in Pascal's account of the difference between mathematical and intuitive mind, *l'esprit de géométrie* and *l'esprit de finesse*. Pascal depicts the mathematical mind as removed from ordinary experience such that its principles, once apprehended, are seen clearly and completely. Only through a failure of intellect does one reason wrongly from them. It is no surprise that at age nineteen Pascal invented a mechanical calculator. By contrast, the principles toward which the intuitive mind is directed are found in everyday use and require only "good eyesight." In Nietzsche-like fashion Pascal declares mathematicians, who reason well from definitions and axioms, "[are] otherwise . . . inaccurate and insufferable, for they are only right when the principles are quite clear," whereas intuitive minds are impatient with speculative and conceptual principles (*Pensées*, I, 2, p. 2).[62] The narrowness of the one and the comprehensiveness of the other challenge one another reciprocally in a play of difference.

More significant than the quarrel with an outdated positivist historicism is the contesting of historical writing as narrative by the *annaliste* historian Fernand Braudel, through the suppression of the difference between narrative and social science indirectly anticipated in Pascal's distinction between mathematical and intuitive mind. Unlike positivist historians, Braudel argues that history must be written from the standpoint of the present so that one can see where a past event is leading. He readily concedes that history is always already politically situated. This assumption distinguishes Braudel's position from a simplistic positivism that remains vulnerable to the charge of Hannah Arendt or Hayden White that scientism in history that purports to transcend politics encourages a decrease in political self-reflectiveness and is therefore hospitable to totalitarianism. He also remains faithful (if unintentionally) to Heidegger's view that history is not a quest for information but the imposing of a task, "that we question historically if we ask what is still happening even if it seems to be past. We ask what is still happening and whether we remain equal to this happening so that it can really develop."[63] But even if Braudel's scientism does not pretend to objectivity and acknowledges a present interest, it should be noted that the *annaliste* conception of history calls for the suppression of speech-acts or of naming as the "showing of countenance" of the other and tends toward a calculative proto-rationalism of the sort described by Pascal.

Braudel argues that the task of the historian is to depict trends and tendencies that extend over centuries and are related to relatively stable geographic features of a terrain and to long-standing mental frameworks. These tendencies then function as protoaxioms in that pure contingency is evaded and events derive from these long-range proclivities. The earth, nurturant and life-sustaining, allows for repetitive cycles as well as attitudes and behaviors. In his *History of the Mediterranean Basin in the Age of Phillip II,* Braudel does not focus upon changing political events, which are in his view "the flotsam and jetsam" of history, or even upon the *conjonctures,* longer cycles of recurrent trends, but rather upon the long event, the geophysically determined constancies that underpin the life of a region. The annaliste, as Rancière observes, is "a geologist of time" in appealing to "the spatialized time of the great permanencies."[64] The quest for a primordial geography conforms to a tradition that extends from state of nature theorists to Durkheim, one that attributes explanatory power, to that which is earliest and simplest.

For Braudel history should no longer be identified with the forward sweep of unique and unrepeatable events but, like the social sciences, with tendencies that recur and are supported by the evidence of regularities.[65] Such tendencies are uncovered through sophisticated statistical techniques. The new history would share its vocabulary and models with those of the social sciences, thereby both increasing its explanatory power and enhancing history's prestige among academic disciplines. Tailoring history to fit the model of the social sciences engenders a remarkable slowing down of historical change by setting limits to the conditions of observation. As Deleuze would say, "[T]he plane of reference of science is like a freeze frame."[66]

Sociological interpretation that conceals the diachronicity of the events it configures is, Braudel concedes, a far cry from history's "following the different rivers of time."[67] How can history both maintain its essential diachronicity and the slowing down of time into the rhythms of a region? If, as Braudel appears to believe, there is "a mathematical godlike time," a world time that is external to human time, "exogenous" and monochromatic, a Greenwich mean time of world history, dissemination can be both retained and returned to synchronicity. But the heterological historian may ask, "Can it?" If disseminated time can be recoded as world time, does it not vanish into world time just as individual speech-acts vanish into geohistory. The duplicity (in its etymological sense) of time that haunts Braudel's account is not first exhumed by Bergson and Heidegger but rather by Pascal in his portrayal of the reciprocal infiltration of *l'esprit de finesse* et *l'esprit de géométrie*. In an extraordinary aphorism that anticipates Nietzsche and illustrate's Braudel's problem, Pascal writes:

> Those who judge of a work by a rule are in regard to others as those who have a watch are in regard to others. One says, "It is two hours ago"; the other says "It is only three quarters of an hour." I look at my watch and say to the one, "You are weary," and to the other "Time gallops with you;" for it is only an hour and a half ago, and I laugh at those who tell me that time goes slowly with me, and that I judge by imagination. They do not know that I judge by my watch. (*Pensées,* I, 6, pp. 3–4)

The use of the watch metaphor by Pascal is meant to display how a practical person of sound judgment assesses time and should not be identified with the punctiformity of clock time as it is later defined by Bergson. To the contrary, one who judges by rule rather than practical sense best exemplifies calculative reason when applied to time.

FACTUALITY REVISITED: LIES, FICTION, *FICCIONES*

In an effort to draw the line between lying and error, Hayden White distinguishes a lie, the denial by an interpretation that an event considered by that interpretation is real, from an untruth, the drawing of false conclusions from an event whose reality is attestable at a basic level of inquiry.[68] The lie—the denial by historians that the Holocaust happened, rejecting the claim that Bosnian Muslims were massacred in Croatia or that the Hutu fleeing Rwanda were slain—would, for White, exhibit a moral failure, whereas untruth would merely manifest a lapse in the comprehension of the materials upon which the historian draws. Both modes of falsification presuppose that a referent extrinsic to the narrative could determine whether the failure is blameworthy, a lie, or an innocent mistake, an untruth.

But the heterological historian might ask, "Can the distinction thus drawn be sustained in light of the relation between the lie and fiction?" Before their difference can be determined, I am compelled to revisit the question of factuality alluded to in the discussion of representation and to exhume its genealogy in order to show how fact and fiction have mutually determined one another.

For the empirical philosophy of modernity, from the seventeenth century to the present, facts are what settle matters. The atomic constituents of our beliefs that no reasonable person could dispute, facts are what brook no disagreement. This view of facts works from the bottom up, as it were, from part to whole. Using the same ontological presuppositions, we could proceed from whole to part. On that view, facts are the sediment that remains after the whole that is to be studied is subjected to scrutiny. A researcher wants to learn why groupers, humphead wrasse, and other fish are disappearing from the coral reefs of the southwestern Pacific. By eliminating the co-present phenomena of climate change, underseas geological shifts and the like, and taking note of what is left, the poisoning of the reef ecosystem, the phenomenon to be accounted for, is explained. Facts can become facts by paring down a wider phenomenological field through the application of criteria of relevance to a portion of it.

Still missing from this account of fact and truth is a version of how the phenomenological field can be restricted with greater stringency through the application of finer-grained methods of control. By positing hypotheses that purport to explain natural phenomena and by regulating the conditions of observation, modern science tries to arrive at the truth about them. Observations conducted in this narrower framework may be limited either exclusively by the conditions of the hypothesis as in the observations of animal behavior, or by both hypothesis and the conditions set by the laboratory as in cell biology.

On this view, truth and fact are commutable terms. Thus both parts of the statement, "What is true is a fact and what is false is contrary to fact," can be construed as saying the same thing. The understanding of truth that is presupposed by the factuality blueprint I have drawn takes for granted, first, that our beliefs are so related to things and events that true beliefs can be distinguished from false ones; second, that strategies of justification linking the way things are to our statements about them will convert our statements into warranted beliefs; and finally, that inquiry should be undertaken from a standpoint of studied neutrality, be disinterested, reflect, in Leibniz's famous dictum, the view from nowhere.

If the notion of fact reflects the effort to say what is, fiction attempts to imagine what is not, to bring absence into presence, to construct a world that does not exist. If we reverse the binary oppositions fact/fiction, presence/absence, the liberation of the fictive may generate new possibilities for the study of history. We need not go all the way with George Steiner's view of fiction in order to endorse his remark that fiction "is a way to unsay the world, to image and speak it otherwise."[69] The binary oppositions themselves are the product of a long tradition so that the object of our study or our access routes to it cannot simply be signed away to fiction. Instead, we must remain attentive to the way in which the opposition fact/fiction is constructed as a co-dependence of the opposites upon one another, to the manner in which fictional narratives are formed, to the social forces they reflect, to the continuities and differences between the narratives communities tell about themselves and the meta-narratives others construct about them. Thus, for example, Todorov contrasts Aztec accounts of Cortes's conquest of Mexico with contemporary French accounts. Moctezuma laments: "From where did these calamities, this anguish, these torments come to us? Who are these people who are arriving? From where did they come? . . . Why did this not happen in our ancestor's time? . . . There is no other remedy my lords than to resign your hearts."[70] Montesquieu, on the other hand, suggests that the Aztecs and Incas could have been saved had they only been introduced to Western rationality:

> If a Descartes had come to Mexico one hundred years before Cortes; had the [the Mexicans] understood that all the effects of nature are a series of laws and communications of movements; had he made them recognize in the effects of nature the shock of bodies rather than the invisible powers of spirits: Cortes with a handful of men would never have destroyed the vast Mexican empire, and Pizarro that of Peru.[71]

The heterological historian would encounter little difficulty in observing the difference of power reflected in the two phrase regimens.

From the beginnings of Western philosophy, "the speaking otherwise" that would come to characterize fiction could not be dissociated from its opposite truth. In Greek thought, the co-implication of speaking what is and what is not is articulated not as fact and fiction but rather as myth and logos. Myth in the Greek sense is fictive but not yet fiction, precisely because the logos, and not fact, is its co-determinant.

In Plato's *Phaedrus* Socrates speaks of myth as proto-philosophy that can only be cashed out in terms of probability rather than certainty. Philosophy speaks clearly whereas myth stammers. Thus Socrates says:

> These allegories are very nice, but he is not to be envied who has to invent them . . . he must go and rehabilitate Hippocentaurs and chimeras dire . . . and if he is skeptical about them and would reduce them to rules of probability, this sort of crude philosophy will take up a great deal of time. (*Phaedrus* 229)

Worst of all, by depicting the crimes of the gods who cannot fall from virtue, myths lie (*Republic* 378). Yet in the *Republic,* Socrates devises the "audacious fiction" that citizens of the ideal state are earthborn, thus insuring absolute fidelity to the soil of the state from which they spring (*Republic* 414). It would seem that Socrates rejects myths that preserve ancient traditions about what he takes as the immoral exploits of the gods, whereas pedagogically useful myths are endorsed. This distinction produces a break in the idea of myth itself that provides an entering wedge for the discursive space of fiction. Traditional myths are presented as handed down, as acquiring their force from their antiquity, whereas constructed myths are constructed out of whole cloth or out of admittedly found elements malleable enough so they can accommodate didactic purposes.

The genre of the constructed myth is undecidable: as didactic it is "within the true," a proto-philosophical work; on its narrative side it is a conscious construction of the imagination that recounts events in largely non-dialogical prose that opens the space of fiction. More important as fiction, it is a lie, not blind error but intentional falsity.

In the turn from myth to fiction, the theme of the lie persists. Rousseau's account of fiction in *Reveries of a Solitary Walker* begins with a discussion of lying, an apology for his own questionable practices. Despite his horror of falsehood, he recalls only indifference toward his own fabrications. "By what strange inconsistency could I lie so cheerfully without compulsion or profit?" he asks himself.[72] To answer this question, he takes up the difference between withholding the truth and deliberate deception. While in the abstract truth is precious, he claims, astonishingly, that "in the particular or individual sense, truth is not always such a good thing; sometimes it is a bad thing and very often it is a matter of indifference" (*RSW,* p. 66). What determines whether statements contrary to fact are innocent or blameworthy is utility. That which has value is property whose value in turn is founded only on usefulness. Long before post-modern intellectual historians like Foucault identified discourse as a commodity, Rousseau deduces: "Truth without any possible usefulness can never be something we owe to one another; it follows therefore that anyone who conceals or disguises it is not telling a lie" (*RSW,* p. 66).

Rousseau also judges the guilt or innocence of a statement contrary to fact on the basis of whether it is injurious to another. One should be guided in this matter by the voice of conscience rather than by the light of reason, Rousseau concludes, and this is the point: "To lie to one's own advantage is an imposture, to lie to the advantage of others is a slander . . . to lie without advantage or disadvantage to oneself or others is not to lie; it is not falsehood but fiction" (*RSW,* p. 69).

It should be evident that we have departed from the terrain of Platonic myth and entered that of the modern subject, a space that is freed from the constraints of thought, where Rousseau and the Romantic subject are free "to roam and soar through the universe on wings of imagination, in ecstasies which surpass all other pleasures" (*RSW,* p. 107). In Chapter 2 I shall consider the way in which this space is reconfigured in the Kantian notion of the sublime and entered into Kant's conception of history. It suffices to notice in the present context that myth acquires its measure from the logos, the reason that is common to both cosmos and human intellect, whereas fiction says what is not and subjects itself to the standard posed by modernity, fact as utility.

If fiction is identified as a lie it could hardly be adopted as an instrument in the study of history. What then must narrative become if it is to provide a resource in this regard? Nietzsche's genealogical analysis of factuality provides not a resting place but a deconstructive moment contributing to the falling away of fact in the modernist sense. Fundamental to Nietzsche's position is the continuity of our concepts of truth with our acts of valuing. Moral judgments in a tradition that winds through Socrates, the biblical prophets, the Christianity of the Gospels, and medieval and modern philosophy involve the subjugation of the instincts through a renunciation of the senses. But moral judgments require truth for their support, so much so that truth and goodness become indistinguishable. "The true world attainable for the sage, the pious, the virtuous man; he lives in it, he is it," says Nietzsche.[73]

The vision that sustains morality segregates the true world attainable by reason from the apparent world: "The true world has been constructed out of contradiction to the actual world . . . an actual world that is merely a moral-optical illusion."[74] Nietzsche does not mean to substitute the apparent world for the real in that this would not alter the conceptual landscape one whit as Nietzsche recognizes: "The true world—we have abolished. What world has remained? The apparent one, Perhaps? But no! With the true world we have abolished the apparent one."[75]

The fact/fiction polarities I have been describing are much like Nietzsche's true and apparent worlds. Both take for granted the empirical strain that runs through modern thought, but demolishing the true world, Nietzsche argues, cannot leave factuality intact. The true world and the world of facts are inextricably related: they rise and fall together. If fiction is the negation of the real through a creation of a counterworld, then fiction when viewed against the background of factuality is a kind of lie. But against what concept of truth could a lie be measured if both the true world and the appearances are demolished. There are nonetheless lies in Nietzsche's world: "By lie, I mean wishing not to see something one does see; wishing not to see something as one sees it."[76] On this view, to lie is not to refuse to see things as they are but rather to refuse to see what one sees.

Could it not be argued, however, that the difference between historical and fictional narratives goes all the way down once we acknowledge that each is intended to belong to a different order of time. Thus Arthur C. Danto asserts: "The historian's statements are in history and belong to the same temporal order as the events that make them true. And this is not the case with fiction [even when the author is a contemporary of the characters s/he creates]."[77] But what appears to be a straightforward distinction is undermined when one considers the lie. Unlike error, the lie is an ambiguous form, belonging on the one hand to the historical time it purports to depict, on the other to the time stream of the illusion it hopes to create, that of fiction. Thus, for example, to which time stream does the narrative of the historian belong who, knowing his claim to be false and self-serving, writes that Stalin's slave labor camps reeducated counter-revolutionaries? And do all putative "fictions" belong to a time stream other than that of their "factual" counterparts? To which order of time does a fictional film about the life of Danton belong?

To be sure, as has often been noted, the breakdown of this distinction in Nietzsche's account of truth is a version of sophistic relativism. What is less obvious is the suggestiveness of Nietzsche's view for the study of history. First, truth is not disinterested, as White and Rancière who themselves were no doubt influenced by Nietzsche's concerns have demonstrated. Truth that, for Nietzsche (and *pace* White and Rancière), reflects the convictions and concerns of the historian, involves a reflexive paradox that only reinforces the claim: the statement that truth is not disinterested is itself not a disinterested statement.

Hermeneutical suspicion of this sort is linked to a deeper claim about truth: truth reflects interests in the shape of metaphors that come to seem canonical. The issue is addressed in what is by now a vintage Nietzscheanism:

> What then is truth? A mobile army of metaphors, metonyms and anthropomorphisms—in short, a sum of human relations, which have been enhanced, transposed, and embellished poetically and rhetorically, and which after long use seem canonical and obligatory.[78]

Narrative can no longer be dismissed as "only a story," a view parasitic upon the modernist's account of fiction because, as Nietzsche warns, any truth is enmeshed in a mobile army of metaphors.

By positing the narrative dimension of truth and value, Nietzsche has opened the way for transforming fiction into *ficciones,* a term coined by Argentinian fabulist and spinner of metaphysical conceits, Jorge Luis Borges. By *ficciones* I mean what fictions become when they take up into themselves the story of their own ontological errancy. Both fact and fiction are transformed when shards of the metaphysical history through which they have passed, in a return of the suppressed, percolate at the surface of the narrative. Such fictions may bring to the fore not the old metaphors for truth and certainty but, as Nietzsche and Derrida would later have it, their "worn-outness," metaphors that are like "coins which have lost their pictures and matter only as metal, no longer as coins."[79]

There is yet another issue bound up with the construction of historical narrative. Although narrative remains crucial for the study of history as White has shown, it remains on his reading a bodying forth of an ensemble of relations as a single whole, a whole that is still bound up with fact as its lexical opposite. Lyotard highlights the difficulty of the narrative genre understood as fact united in a story that has a climax and a conclusion when he writes:

> [The narrative] acts as if there were a last word. . . . The last word is always a good one *[un bon mot]* by virtue of its place. . . . The diachronic operator or the operator of successivity is not called back into question, even when it is modulated. It "swallows up" the event and the différends carried along by the event. Narratives drive the event back to the border.[80]

What has been missed in identifying narrative with fiction is the sea change in the conception of fiction in such writers as Borges, Beckett, Blanchot, and a host of lesser-known writers who not only dissolve narrative but take up the figures of narrative disclosure, what and how it reveals and conceals, into the narrative itself. Fictions have metamorphosed into *ficciones,* a sinuous literary form through which the alterity of the other can be made thematic without actually appearing. By bringing forth the silences of the other rather than by forcing silence into speech, by devising strategies of encounter that simultaneously attest and preserve that silence, silence itself becomes a speech-act. As Rancière remarks, "[I]t is the world of silent witnesses that the historian brings into *signifiance* without lies."[81]

The point is highlighted in Borges's tale, "The God's Script," in which an Aztec priest of the god Qahalom is confined in a vast prison with a jaguar he can glimpse over the wall that separates them. Upon the jaguar's skin is incised an eschatological formula that would prevent a final apocalypse, free the priest from the prison in which the Spaniards have incarcerated him, and make him more powerful than Moctezuma, but he maintains silence. What *ficciones* must the historian devise in her encounter with text and artifact? Perhaps like Borges's Aztec priest, the historian may focus not only upon the remains of the past but also upon what I have called the discursive space of authorization. She may say with Borges's priest: "I devoted long years to learning the order and configuration of the [jaguar's] spots. . . . More than once I cried out that it was impossible to decipher that text. Gradually the concrete enigma I labored at disturbed me less than the generic enigma of a sentence written by a God."[82]

It is one thing to be affected by alterity as signaling responsibility but another to see how alterity is reflected in the concrete work of the historian. Borges's tale, "Pierre Menard, Author of the Quixote," about the effort of a French symbolist writer, Pierre Menard, to recompose the Quixote—not to transcribe or copy it but to produce a few pages that would coincide word for word with the original—is suggestive of the historian's tasks. Trying to become Cervantes is both impossible and uninteresting. To recreate the past, "he would go on being Pierre Menard and reach the Quixote through the experiences of Pierre Menard."[83]

The pages Menard produces are identical with those of Cervantes, but the Menard work is a palimpsest through which the traces not only of Menard's many drafts but also of the intervening changes between the now of Menard's text and the then of Cervantes appear. Far from endorsing a fusion of horizons, of the historical situatedness both of Menard and of Cervantes, Borges depicts the effort at *Verstehen* on the part of the twentieth-century interpreter who must first master the minutiae of place and period, after which he strives but cannot attain. His effort does not lead to replication but rather brings into view the "lie" that fictions, even in their transmogrified form as *ficciones,* inevitably conceal: an unbreachable difference, that of the present of the text, the past it brings to light, and the conditions of its production. The challenge to the historian is to exhibit these conditions, not heavy-handedly as a laying out of hermeneutical principles or as the pretense of replicating the *cri de coeur* of the dead other but with the lightness already discerned by Pascal: "True eloquence makes light of eloquence" (*Pensées,* 1, p. 3).

FICCIONES AND HISTORY: FOUCAULT

It is no accident that Foucault begins *The Order of Things* by appealing to Borges's depiction of the classification of animals found in an old Chinese encyclopedia which juxtaposes items that cannot be thought of as belonging together in our own taxonomical system. The linking of what to the European are jarring anomalies precipitated Foucault's plunge into the description of discursive regularities that remain invisible but establish an order among things. It is not the oddity of the items linked by Borges's Chinese encyclopedia that struck Foucault but rather the transgressing of a boundary of what is and is not thinkable. "The monstrous quality that runs through Borges's enumeration consists . . . in the fact that the common ground on which such meetings are possible has been destroyed. . . . Where else could they be juxtaposed except in the non-place of language?"[84] Foucault's interest lies not in historical objects but rather in the epistemological practices that constitute them at a level he calls archeological. Defining this new mode of inquiry, he writes:

> Archeology, addressing itself to the general space of knowledge to its configurations, and to the modes of being that appear in it, defines systems of simultaneity, as well as the series of mutations necessary and sufficient to circumscribe the threshold of a new positivity.[85]

Disdainful of the historian's analysis of the "thus it was," indeed of ordinary ways of studying history, Foucault turns to an examination of the discontinuities or breaks in the history of consciousness. These ruptures are neither the result of specific events nor of the initiatives of individuals but rather the converse; events and behaviors are determined by the way the categories of representation force things to fall out at a given time and place. Rejecting Hegel's notion that there is an overarching spirit of the age, there are, for Foucault, only multiple language practices—biology, geology, numismatics, and the like, each with its own protocols and rules—that determine the objects of a science. On this view the knowing subject, the consciousness that knows and intends its objects as described by the conventions of Husserlian phenomenology that constituted the philosophical lingua franca of Foucault's academic environment, is dissolved into a system of discursive practices. Foucault's interest in depicting past historical phenomena is limited to their usefulness as examples of the discursive practices that constitute them. This does not preclude dazzling accounts of such varying particulars as the "Las Meninas" painted by Velazquez depicted in *The Order of Things,* the panopticon as an instrument of punitive surveillance in *Discipline and Punish,* or the sexual practices of men in Athens of the fifth century B.C.E. in *The History of Sexuality.* From the standpoint of preceding European historical writing from the nineteenth century to the present, Foucault's discussion of an artifact, institution, or practice often fastens upon details previously dismissed as marginal, as if the history of the West were being written from the standpoint of its detritus.

Yet Foucault's historiographic lens retains a constant focus. In *The Archeology of Knowledge,* he develops his notion of the episteme, "a discursive formation or ordered constellation of statements that point not to "'things,' 'facts' 'realities' or 'beings,' [but to] the law of possibility, rules of existence for the objects that are inscribed within it."[86] Statements do not represent the world but rather bring to light the conditions of emergence of the object of study. A statement's meaning is limited neither by its grammatical structure nor by what it refers to but by the pattern of significations it inhabits. Just as the affirmation, "The earth is round," does not mean the same thing before and after Copernicus, so too the assertion, "These are the facts," does not have an identical signification before and after the birth of modern science. In his earlier *The Order of Things,* Foucault deconstructs the episteme which sanctions the human sciences, sociology, psychology, ethnology, each with its own object of study or empiricity, by showing that the telos of the human sciences is not language but the one who, from within language, represents language.[87] Thus generic man rather than the discursive practices that constitute human beings of a given time or place is the subject of the human sciences, not human beings as they are which, in any case, cannot be known, but man, ungendered and without class, as fabricated by a discourse whose agendas are invisible to itself.

Foucault's focus upon the conditions of the production of a linguistic practice rather than upon the historical object it sanctions is not a covert reinstatement of the Platonic preference for the sort of poetic discourse in which the poet in speaking his name announces the origin of the poem. For Plato, the introduction of a narrative voice makes plain that the text openly proclaims itself as a semblance, an imitation, rather than passing itself off as the real. For Foucault, by contrast, disclosure of a cultural grid manifests the brokenness of speech-acts so that, for example, by describing the significations of madness at a given time, he brings the claims of the mad to the fore, their entrapment within the linguistic frameworks of a theology, penology, and later of medicine, all of which, by defining reason, has consigned the mad to silence.

Historical epochs as Foucault understands them are "an archipelago, a chain of epistemic islands, the deepest connections of which are unknown," as Hayden White graphically points out.[88] On Foucault's account, it is not possible to explain the shift from one episteme to another except to assert, "It happened." To entertain the view that such shifts can and ought to be explained would be characterized as a historically determined standpoint.

No more than post-Wittgensteinians need to find a master language game in order to bridge the multiplicity of language games does Foucault require a law that would explain the birth and death of a discursive paradigm. To invent a law would run counter to the notion of brute contingency that is one of the virtues of his description of epistemic shifts in the history of ideas.[89]

The outcome of Foucault's heady post-Nietzschean historicism can be perilous, as Foucault himself warns:

> At the end of such an enterprise one may not recover those unities that, out of methodological rigor, one initially held in suspense: one may be compelled to ignore influences and traditions, abandon definitively the question of origin, allow the commanding presence of authors to fade into the background; and thus everything that was thought to be proper to the study of the history of ideas may disappear from view.[90]

Like Pierre Menard of Borges's tale, Foucault in recreating an episteme does not re-present it but instead enters into it as Foucault, not because, like Menard, he wishes to reflect upon the temporal distance that separates him from the "original."[91] Rather he means to disseminate unities in order to redistribute the quanta of power hidden in discursive constellations that extend into the present.

Foucault's achievement is not without cost. By proposing a synchronic account of historical change in terms of discursive constellations, he loses the diachronicity of history. In seeking a way out of this self-imposed synchronicity, he introduces the discourse of desire, but desire made manifest in language is desire installed as the centerpiece of a new episteme and thus ceases to be what it is. To see this, consider first the relation of an archeological to an *annaliste* depiction of history. Like the annaliste, who foregoes the before and after of events in favor of enduring geophysical constants, Foucault recodes Braudel's *conjoncture,* the enduring cycle and the even more long-lasting geophysical constancies, the long event, into the language of statement and episteme. As Braudel himself has noted, "Mental frameworks too can form prisons of the long durée."[92] Yet positing discursive constancies does not preclude Foucault's effort to remain faithful to the Nietzschean diachronicity of "events, motions, becoming, [as] determinations of relations of forces"[93] (*WP* 552, p. 299). Whence then comes the impulse to suppress time's passing? Is this Foucault's concession to another Nietzschean aphorism: "A world in the state of becoming could not in a strict sense be comprehended or known" (*WP* 520, p. 281). Is Foucault driven to "create a world which is calculable, simplified, comprehensible" (*WP* 521, p. 282) in order to avoid being reduced to silence? Or is Foucault's conception of language propelled by still other concerns?

For Foucault, discourse has not only been pressed into the service of representation, but language has become capital, as it were, and capital requires redistribution. It is important to note that for Foucault discourse is not the slave of capital but rather one of its forms. Like money which replaces simple barter or exchange of goods in a Marxist framework, Foucault sees language in Western thought as valued for its transparency just as the abstractness of money is valued as an instrument of commensuration. But language conceals the fact of its commodification, its thing-like power, and, like money, its circulation in a field of exchange.

In a move as much Lacanian as it is Nietzschean, Foucault believes that desire provides an escape hatch from the constraints of the discursive formations of modernity. Yet desire itself cannot break free of the push-and-pull of epistemic constraints, as Foucault makes abundantly clear in his extensive writings on sexuality. Even if desire is envisioned as a transgression of limits, as exuberant life, once it is encoded as the subject of a discourse, as has often been remarked, it becomes tedious. For Nietzsche, desire is both vision and orgy, dream and intoxication in which there is "sexuality and voluptuousness" (WP 798–800, pp. 419–421). To follow Nietzsche one step further: "The sober, the weary, the exhausted, the dried up (e.g. scholars) can receive absolutely nothing" (WP 801, p. 422) from an art vivified by this orgiastic spirit. Desire described as commodified sexuality that awaits redistribution remains desire as commodity.

It is not difficult to fault Foucault both for inclusions and omissions in his selections of the voices he believes to have been suppressed by some discursive practice. Yet his achievement lies less in altering the fortunes of any particular constituency than in the invention of a genre, heterological history, one in which "the other is positioned between words and things."[94] The heterological historian must judge among competing silences, re-sign the history of the one who has been de-signed or silenced. Yet, with the breakdown of the epistemology of representation, what criteria is she to invoke in evaluating the claimants to truth while, at the same time, standing herself under the judging gaze of the dead other? "Who compels you to judge? And moreover—test yourself to see whether you could be just if you wanted to be!—As judge, you must stand higher than he who is to be judged; whereas all you are is subsequent to him," says Nietzsche.[95] The heterological historian who engages the issue of judgment as Nietzsche describes it, writes not under the sign, the semiological web, of Nietzsche but rather under the sign of Kant. It is to Kant that she must next turn.

∞

The historian who is driven by the urgency of a promise to the dead to tell the truth about them, a promise that is prior to her account of the facts, is the heterological historian. To be sure, she may be the member of a profession who seeks to dis-cover "what happened" and to re-cover these events by bringing them into discursive or visual clarity. Yet hers is a radically new persona. She is the agent of an irrepressible desire, a passion for the dead others who are voiceless and who exist both inside and outside the threads of an articulated narrative, hidden and awaiting exhumation.

But this persona must be undone by the paradoxes it generates. The heterological historian is one who commits herself to an impossible ideal of truth telling, to the notion that historical narratives replicate events, that discourse can at least approximate "what actually happened." Yet she cannot renege on the impossible promise that precedes the recounting of events "just as they were" and presupposes a constituency to whom the promise is given, the dead others who cannot speak for themselves. Inhabiting neither a region nor a territory—territorialization becomes an instrument of suppression of the other—the historian abides with the voiceless dead in the non-space of ethics, of the promise, yet empirical truth requires that the other be reinstated in a nexus of concrete events. When the historian speaks in the name of the other, she preempts the speech of the other, whereas if she remains silent the other is consigned to invisibility.

Nor can the historian recount the past in any straightforward sense, however eager she may be to replicate the vivacity and "thereness" of actual perception, to certify the deictic power of ostension in which an event is attested by an I who perceives and who is contemporaneous with the percept. Criticisms mounted by contemporary philosophy reveal the untenability of the claim that the past can be re-presented as if hypostatized in a perceptual "present." One reason for this failure lies in the misleading supposition that language can be cashed out by a referential nexus other than itself, an exteriority that it mirrors. Once the various versions of this epistemic claim collapse, the historian, compelled to name the dead other, cannot maintain that the denotations of the name are homologous with a referent. Instead, the name constitutes an appeal to a heterological order that must wend its way into the historical narrative.

If strict objectivity is impossible, how is the past to be brought into discursive articulation? If the referent is artificially pried loose from discourse, dubbed "the real" and then, in circular fashion, the real is called upon to justify the narrative, how can the historian escape the tyranny of narrative? And if she is committed to exhibiting historical wrongs, can past inequities be brought out by a standard juridical model which considers alternatives—"on the one hand, x, on the other, y?" Does not this paradigm presuppose the equality of the claimants when it is the inequality of power, the voicelessness of a claimant, that solicits the historian? The modeling of history upon the social sciences that appears to uncover much sought-after regularities presents still other limitations. By importing the static character of law into the fluid movement of events, change is hypostatized; events lose the diachronicity of time's passing.

Do these numerous double binds so thwart the writing of history that the historian's covenant to the dead others is vitiated? Or are they, in part at least, the result of certain binarisms generated in the history of Western thought: logos and myth, reality and appearance, fact and fiction. Both a narrative/constructivist and a factual/scientific account of the past are not new historiographic notions, for these alternatives were already presaged at the opening of the modern age by Pascal's disjunction of mathematical and intuitive mind.

It is Jean Jacques Rousseau who first frees the notion of fiction from its dyadic other, fact: liberated from fact, fiction cannot be a lie. To lie is to disguise a truth in the interest of utility or out of self-interest, but an untruth *not* motivated by self-interest is not a lie but fiction. In aptly discerning that truths reflect interests, Rousseau opens a chain of interpretation that wends its way forward through Nietzsche and Foucault. Is the historian then thrown back upon a fictional narrative that is a string of nonfalsifiable propositions, a tale spun out of whole cloth signifying nothing?

The contemporary fiction of Borges, *ficciones,* suggests an alternative. The premises, the metaphysical conceits of a narrative, are exhibited in the narrative itself, a disclosure that brings to the fore the discursive practices in which the narrative is embedded. As described by Foucault, these practices reflect constellations of power so that the historian who re-signs the history of those whose voices may have been stifled alters the balance of power. Rather than always compelling speech, on occasion, the silences of the other may be brought forward by the historian to become forceful acts of enunciation.

The dead other can be made to speak, but can there be metonymic substitutions for the cataclysm, the nihil exposed by the mass extermination of peoples that drives the discourse of the heterological historian? Tropes that suggest themselves range from the *apeiron,* the boundless of early Greek philosophy to the unbounded universe described by some physicists. But these cosmological figures treat the unbounded as an alternation of chaos and order, whereas the cataclysm remains the void from which nothing is generated except the excessiveness of that which cannot appear, the cataclysm itself.

But cannot the cataclysm become a sign, a gesture of abstraction comparable to that of modernist abstract art, or be conveyed by the fissured realism of postmodernity? To ask these questions is already to write under the sign of Kant. The historian who insists that the cataclysm "appear" is caught up in and prefigured by Kant's depiction of the sublime, of purposiveness without purpose and of formlessness that cannot be contained. Entrapment in the unrepresentable necessitates the historian's careful consideration of Kant's aesthetic and teleology of nature to which I shall now turn.

For I dipt into the future, far as human eye could see,
Saw the vision of the world, and all the wonders that would be,
Saw the heavens fill with commerce, argosies of magic sails,
Pilots of the purple twilight, dropping down with costly bales,
Heard the heavens fill with shouting, and there rained a ghastly dew
For the nation's airy navies grappling in the central blue,
Far along the world-wide whisper of the south wind rushing warm,
With the standards of the people plunging thro' the thunder storm;
Till the war drum throbb'd no longer, and the battle flags were furl'd
In the Parliament of man, the Federation of the world.

> Alfred Lord Tennyson
> *Locksley Hall*

"The rim bones of nothing" is just as truthful as "limitless space."

> Zora Neale Hurston

READING THE HETEROLOGICAL
HISTORIAN READING KANT

What does it mean to write history under the sign of Kant? It cannot mean to speak from within Kantian ethics with the voice of Kant—recall Borges's warning that one cannot write the *Don Quixote* today as if one were Cervantes—but rather to speak as oneself, the heterological historian from that contemporary place that is the cataclysm and to do so from within the space of ethics. It would be ludicrous to demand that the only subject of historical writing be mass annihilation, or that the moral claims of this annihilation be stated as a prolegomenon to every piece of such writing. Rather the cataclysm is the non-place from which the heterological historian writes. She is both "there" in the historical period she describes and "here" within the epoch of the cataclysm, driven by the demand of alterity. Like H. G. Wells's time traveler, "she covers herself with dust by rolling in a paradox."[1]

The issue of the historian's promise is embedded in Kant's philosophy in ways that both reinforce and traduce it. For Kant, philosophy is concerned with a priori knowledge derived from concepts, whereas historical knowledge is empirical. Kant's moral philosophy identifies right action with freedom, which likewise cannot be determined by empirical conditions; conversely, objects of experience, empiricities, can never generate morality. By displaying moral actions as they are undertaken in the world of nature, history, for Kant, is the theater that "represents" the unrepresentable moral law.

At the same time, the historian does not float above her own age, one of unprecedented mass annihilations within increasingly compressed temporal frameworks that brings to the fore the void or the unboundedness I have called the "cataclysm." Can this un-boundedness and the responsibility imposed by alterity be brought together so they belong to a common episteme? Or if the cataclysm is interpreted cosmologically, does it displace an ethical non-space? Does the de-signing of ethics in relation to the cataclysm lead to considering it as a regulative ideal (in Kant's sense) of absolute negation? These questions can be explored only in the context of their Kantian lineage.

Kantian philosophy may be described as the implementation of a blueprint, an "archi-tec-tonic." The etymology of the term is suggestive: "archi" derives from Greek *arkhein,* to begin; "tech" stems from a form of *teks,* one meaning of which is to fabricate, especially with an ax. Kant's system is an effort to build from a plan and to do so from the ground up, impossible without a prior tearing down. Kant as "archi-tect," master builder, may be contrasted with Hegel, the bricoleur who builds with found elements, the detritus of concepts Hegel's Absolute manages to save and without which there could be no system. For Kant, the conflict between the dogmatism of the rationalist and the skepticism of Hume would be overcome, the relation between the knowledge of nature and ethics explained. This Herculean task would in each of his critiques and other writings be assigned to judgment which would come to play the role of mediator linking a priori principles to their instantiations both in connection with the knowledge of nature and of the moral law. The term "judgment" is for Kant multivalent. Depending upon context, judgment refers to the connecting up of any one representation with others in the unity of a self-identical consciousness, the linking of one's proposed actions to the moral law or the designation of an object as beautiful.

Why should the heterological historian be concerned with the Kantian system when Kant lacks a full-blown philosophy of history? Kant's remarks on history are more than mere asides that display Enlightenment views on the political issues of his day. They are linked intrinsically to the major themes of his work, especially to the great divide in Kantian thought between morality and the world of nature, the former grounded in human freedom and the latter subject to necessary laws. It is just these two hetero-logical discourses that confront the historian. That which is demanded by ethics is inherently prior to experience but is instantiated in actual or possible actions. History, in turn, links the order of nature to morality in that history offers an arena for ethics to work itself out, a space for the enactment of Kant's dream of moral progress. As such, the actual affairs of history are projects of freedom providing an opportunity for humankind to create in the phenomenal world great works of self-betterment. Because morality is the task of free rational agents, nature cannot be the source but only the scene of moral action. Even Rousseau had seen that one's best natural impulses when "imported into society" and used unthinkingly become harmful (RSW, p. 95).

The historian's problem of de-signing ethics and re-signing history will provide direction for a new mapping of this familiar Kantian terrain. The heterological historian is interested neither in uncovering the fissures and tensions of the text in order to transcend its aporias nor, to the contrary, in showing that such an effort is futile. She is rather engaged in seeing how Kant's thought still affects the construction of history, what can and cannot be said before taking up the challenge thrown out by Kant.[2] With this end in view, a specific problem that arises in Kant's philosophy will be treated as pointing toward a question by the heterological historian, the historian's question stated, and each reply to that question taken up in detail from a standpoint that is both inside and outside Kant's system. The Kantian problem is expounded as if from the perspective of a disciple "at first hand." The reply to the historian's question does not bring the matter to closure but generates further thought-acts. Thus my text is a trialogue segmented into numbered thought-units, each unit alternating exposition, question, reply.

THE NIHIL AND ANALOGY

Kant I: The *Critique of Pure Reason* describes the world of nature as a lawfully organized system of phenomena about which we can attain precise knowledge. The subject is so constituted that it shapes sensations, the raw material of knowledge, so that knowledge is neither a purely passive replication of objects nor a construction of the mind. Space and time are the a priori forms of intuition that the mind imposes upon what is perceived, neither derivable from sensation nor presupposed by experience.

Not only are there a priori forms of intuition, but there are also a priori concepts, categories of the understanding as derived from the logical functions described by Aristotle, cause and effect being a principal category.

Knowledge of phenomena is conditioned by the form bestowed by the subject upon the material of sensible intuition, the work of the understanding which gives us knowledge of the empirical world. This view is summed up in the well-known apothegm: "Concepts without intuitions are empty, intuitions without concepts, blind." Imagination without the understanding would merely provide a world of images about which we could assert nothing. The manifold of sensations do not remain a buzzing blooming confusion but are combined into a this or a that, united by the concept of an object. Consciousness apprehends its own unity through the unity of what is given, a unity designated as the transcendental unity of apperception.

Knowledge about the world is not only the work of the understanding but also the result of the action of an unknowable core behind the phenomena, the thing-in-itself, of which the phenomena are the appearances. Although, strictly speaking, the category of casuality cannot be applied to the phantom things-in-themselves in that they are beyond experience, nevertheless it is necessary to think of them as somehow having efficacy.

What remains unexplained thus far is how the categories, which are rules of the understanding, can be linked to intuitions. The answer is that the faculty of judgment is responsible for applying the general rules provided by the understanding to particular cases. But this is not enough to support the connection of intuition to rules in that the difference in kind between concept and case requires further mediation. Thus one is compelled to introduce the schemata derived by interpreting a category in terms of time. Because time belongs to the world of sensible intuition, and although not itself a category, like categories is a priori, time can bridge the categorial and sensible worlds. The schemata are universal concepts which are the work of the imagination and which provide a rule for the making of images. Thus a schema is not itself an image but provides a rule for the creation of an image.

Having considered the faculties of understanding and judgment it now remains only to consider the third cognitive faculty as described in the first *Critique,* theoretical reason, the faculty that provides intellectual ideals presupposed in our thinking but unrealizable in experience. Unlike the categories which are constitutive of experience, the ideas of reason are regulative providing standards or norms which have practical utility. Ideas of reason fall into two types. God, freedom, and immortality belong to the first type. We cannot think these ideas by way of fault-free demonstrations, but this does not mean we cannot think them at all.[3] For example, even if God cannot be known as he is in himself, we can know God as he is in relation to us, by *analogy*. The distinction here is subtle. It is not here argued in the manner of Thomas Aquinas that we are in some sense like God but that we are related to God as clock to clockmaker. It is the relations that are analogous and not the relata.

Question I: Can mass annihilation be grasped as a regulative idea by way of the analoga or as as a historical object, an empiricity, by way of the schema? If analogically, by analogy with what regulative idea? That of an abyss? A nihil? If not, through what images that are not always already fissured by the nihil opened up by the analoga? Are regulative ideas and cognitive acts united in the event of mass annihilation in that that which is inherently unrealizable in experience is finally realized? Are the analoga and the schema now indistinguishable?

Reply I: If a regulative idea can be that which reason poses for itself as an intellectual standard or norm that is to guide practical reason, might there be a regulative idea of the nihil and, if so, what would it regulate? Does not human reason recoil, as Kant avers, from "the horror vacui . . . when an idea is encountered by means of which absolutely nothing can be thought?"[4] Kant called the apocalypse as a theological idea "moral terrorism" and denied its ultimacy. "Decline into wickedness cannot be incessant in the human race, for at a certain stage of disintegration, it would destroy itself" (*OH*, p. 139).

The question is one of whether the heterological historian can understand the cataclysm as a limited totality and thus as an object of representation, as a presentation governed by the schemata, fitting an example or a case to its rule without a rule to use for this purpose, or whether she is forced to conceive it as an absolute magnitude, an idea of reason. Common sense appears to dictate that mass annihilation belongs to the sphere of the calculable: so many persons killed in the Bosnian conflict, so many in Rwanda, Burundi, or the Sudan. The calculation of the number that might die is subject to the laws of probability: so many are likely to die if old Soviet nuclear arsenals are not protected against accidental or deliberate detonation. *L'esprit de géométrie* will suffice; the deaths of vast numbers is an additive phenomenon which the understanding can grasp. Is it possible that there is a numerical point at which the cataclysm begins? A hundred thousand dead? Six million? If thinking my death provides an entering wedge into the thought of non-being as Heidegger claims, what is added by thinking of mass destruction except magnitude? Does the mass destruction of persons, perhaps of all humankind, constitute a logical difference in the relation between death and the nihil because of the phenomenon's magnitude, the multiplicity of others?[5] From the standpoint of the understanding, the death of humankind could be seen as the elimination of one among numerous species.

If the cataclysm is beyond magnitude, events are singular. How are we to imagine the cataclysm as "expressing" a singularity? If mass death is to be bodied forth in images—not yet construed from the standpoint of ethics but merely as phenomenon—the present-day culture of the spectacle would provide innumerable graphic representations of these annihilations that would merely feed cognition as data of sensible intuition organized by the categories. A rule is needed that makes the presentation of the cataclysm as such possible. If the schemata are universal concepts which are the work of the imagination and that provide a rule for the making of images, then the heterological historian must first seek the rule by means of which she can justify the rule (a metarule, as it were) that commensurates the cataclysm with itself. But how could the schemata provide such a rule?

Are the schemata relevant to apprehending the cataclysm at all? The other's death is by virtue of the other's alterity always already more than what can be given in my representation, more than what the imagination could present. Her death is not merely different in kind from her phenomenal self-presentation in the sense that she is not object but person as existential philosophers claimed, but excessive, more than can be thought. If the other's death is not a phenomenon and is to be reinscribed in Kantian language, it can only be conceived as an idea of reason. Like God, freedom, and immortality, it cannot be represented but only thought analogically. But by analogy of what to what? Of my non-being to non-being *tout court*? Is non-being to be envisaged as being's other in terms of a binary opposition of being and non-being? Thus if, as Heidegger believes, "being is an access route to each singularity," then non-being is the denial of access. If we follow Heidegger, Emmanuel Levinas tells us, being is "a neuter which illuminates and commands thought, and renders intelligible" that which is the object of thought, so that without being there can be no thinking.[6] Nothing, nothing thinkable.

Is the cataclysm a re-presentation, a presentation, or an idea? The faculties are in a juridical relation with one another says Lyotard in his vivid troping of Kantian thought: "They keep making representations, remonstrances or grievances to each other through the confrontation of their respective objects. They thereby alternate relative to one another between the positions of addressor and addressee."[7] Kant's treatment of the French Revolution instantiates this difficulty, in that it confuses an object that can be presented in a cognitive phrase with what can be presented in an ethical phrase. But it is not "a confusion of schemata with exempla" that troubles the heterological historian. The ethical demand is already inscribed for Kant in his horror and revulsion at the Terror, emotions that cannot help infiltrating its cognitive "representations." For the cataclysm too, confusion is a necessary part of its "apprehension."

The historian who writes under the sign of Kant is challenged to find the rule according to which she creates the historical object and to provide the warranty for the rule. Is this not in effect what historians in the tradition of history and social science from Durkheim and Braudel through Foucault (for all their differences) have attempted to do? Does the historian who discloses a particular episteme not exhibit the deictic moment of discourse, the site of origin, the one who speaks the phrase, in the discourse itself? Is this not finding and disclosing a rule? Does the historian not speak deictically when she says, "Look, here it is hidden in the episteme, the proof I was looking for."

HETERONOMY'S RULE

Kant II: In both the *Critique of Practical Reason* and in *Foundations of the Metaphysics of Morals,* the notions of freedom and the moral law are developed. Human beings are shown to give a moral law to themselves, a law whose dictates, binding upon all rational beings, can neither be determined by empirical conditions nor issue from any source other than themselves. The moral law does not come from God nor is it the result of experience; it is rather the action of a will acting in accordance with its self-given laws. The subjective maxims which guide human actions must be subjected to the test of universalizability. For a merely private maxim to assume the form of a law it must be applicable to all: "Act only according to that maxim [subjective rule] by which you can at the same time will that it should become a universal law."[8] Actions in conformity with the law cannot be motivated by the desire for happiness: one can only hope to act so as to deserve happiness.

Yet this contention is unexplainably fissured by occasional counterthoughts. Consider the casual remark in the essay "The End of All Things," in which the morality of dessert, which is otherwise endorsed, invites challenge. Thus, in commenting about Christianity, one is forced to concede that in order to assure the adherence to duty one cannot appeal only to the notion of duty. There must also be "an indispensable complement" for the moral act to take place: "love as the free reception of the will of another person into one's own maxims" (*OH,* p. 82).

Question II: Is there a diffraction within universality such that a discursive space for alterity is opened, an as yet unthought phrase that precedes the categorical imperative and that "grounds" it? Is not the reception of another's will a concession to the indispensability of heteronomy? If that which is prior is neither law-like nor a feeling like the desire for happiness which cannot even motivate much less ground morality, then how are we to construe it? What does this heteronomous will demand of us?

Reply II: The question of whether there can be an Ethics that precedes the categorical imperative repeats the logical structure of the Augustinian query, "Can there be a time before time," and its answer, "Time prior to time is unthinkable." An Ethics prior to the ethics of imperatives cannot be thought. Yet there is an "indispensable complement" to imperatives, the will of the other. Kant can only think this opposition as one of duty and moral feeling and so names it "love." But is love in this context an intimate relation or rather the pressure of another's will that weighs upon my maxim? Kant does not say pressure upon my *will* but upon my *maxim.* The other's demand is a command in that it impacts upon my rule for proposed action and thus affects what I will do. More important, it is not the other's *maxim* that impacts upon my will, for I am not adopting his rule. Instead, it is the sheer pressure of alterity, of a will not my own, that impels me to form my maxims by responding to this alien will that obliges me.[9]

Kant leaves unthought the implications of this extraordinary intrusion of alterity that obligates me. The point of Kant's account of morality is precisely that moral action is contingent upon a perfectly free subject giving to itself a rule upon which the subject ought to act. But now Kant concedes that the autonomy of the sovereign subject is open to challenge. The implications of this challenge are drawn out in Levinas's description of the I as losing its self-coincidence, as called into question by the other. This calling into question cannot be a datum of consciousness, a point already sensed by Kant in his stress upon the impossibility of the other's will becoming either the object of my cognitive act or identical with my own will. Alterity can only weigh in as sheer demand, "a summons to answer, [not merely] as an obligation or a duty about which it would have to come to a decision; it is in its very position wholly a responsibility."[10] If I am my responsibility in the same sense in which I can say I am my body, I am nothing but this responsibility. I am at the disposal of the other, responsible for her, without as yet any content being demanded.

Yet heteronomic ethics poses two questions to the historian, one at the level of historical narrative, the other at the level of the historical object. With regard to the object, it may be asked how the demand of alterity helps the historian to adjudicate the conflicting claims of each dead other who insists: "Hear us, not them." If the claim of alterity lacks content, is non-linguistic, "says" what it says prior to language, it cannot be recoded in propositional form. Thus, if the work of the historian is to go forward, *sheer* alterity, an alterity that cannot be phrased either as description, question, or command, precedes and follows upon the narrating of the historical object emptily, as it were. Thus my earlier reference to the name "Billie Joe" had become the sign of a narrative that supervened upon the sheer urgency of a "presence" that broke into my complacency. Had "Billie Joe" not become in Rancière's terms "a social combatant," not as the symbol of a group but as a name designating speech-acts that affirm or challenge a certain relation between discourse and a state of affairs?[11]

What if the pressure of alterity emanates from sources who, despite their victimization, cannot be united into a narrative of fraternity, thus precluding such conjunctions as that of the Cambodian genocide and the Holocaust which could conceivably be brought together through the discernment of a common episteme? In the event of antagonistic alterities, the opposing claims of the belligerents contest any historical narrative and challenge the security of the historian with regard to the finality of her disclosures.

More primordially, Lyotard suggests that the constitution of a we as the subject of experience is challenged after Auschwitz because of a fundamental shift in the logic and grammar of this pronominal form. There can be no plural subject, no we, because what normally constitutes a community that can say we is a certain linkage of addressor and addressee. Because no common phrase universe unites the addressor whose fundamental command is "Die," and the addressee, there can be no law linking the command and the commanded.

For Kant, such a fissuring of the subject is unthinkable: what pure practical reason legislates must ultimately prevail in actuality, because nature is envisaged as generally amenable to rational human goals. Even if this were not the case, the purpose of the commanded action may be realized in the noumenal world, the world of which we can have no knowledge. The gap between the demand of alterity, that one place oneself at the disposal of others, and the empirical conditions for realization of this demand, which Kantian thought at once denies and points to, marks off a purely postmodern discursive space.

The demands of alterity create extraordinary difficulties in light of social, economic, and cultural forces that operate at a global level over which individuals have no control. The worldwide aggregate of information, images, and "material" commodities acquire the compelling character of what Kant might have called "forces of nature." If, as Heidegger has argued, all are trapped by such forces, how ought conflicts to be adjudicated? Prudential concerns having to do with global economy rather than the claims of alterity are invoked in the settlement of such disputes. Thus, for example, Germany has refused wartime compensation to the hundreds of thousands of Czech victims of Nazism until the Czech authorities apologize for the expulsion of the Sudeten Germans and do not renounce the possibility of restitution to them. What will determine the outcome is not the shadow of the cataclysm or a jurisprudence marked by alterity but rather the need of the Czech economy to enter the world market, and thus the necessity for acceptance by NATO and the European Union for which German support is required.[12]

Should an action that is almost certainly doomed to fail be performed so as to fulfill the demand of the other? Is not the symbolic significance of such failed acts open to multiple interpretations? And if so, are not actions that could be foreseen to miscarry when released into the discursive space of history likely to acquire unintended and opposed significations? Consider the deaths of the 1000 Israelite Zealots who under Eleazar ben Jair resisted the Romans at Masada after the Roman conquest of Judea in 66 C.E., an event that has been interpreted by some as futile and suicidal and by others as a model of heroic martyrdom. How is the historian to depict the designing of ethics with regard to the historical aftershocks of the eruptions of suicide/martyrdom that she must then re-sign in her narrative? Must the historian not turn from the "judgment of history" which, as a concept, is altogether different from the concept, "the historical narrative that stands under judgment?"

THE ENDS OF HISTORY

Kant III: The third *Critique* is written with the specific purpose of bridging the aporia between theoretical and practical reason, Describing the gap, Kant writes:

The understanding legislates a priori for nature as an object of sense—for a theoretical knowledge of it in a possible experience. Reason legislates a priori for freedom and its peculiar causality; as the supersensible in the subject for an unconditioned practical knowledge. (*CJ*, p. 32)[13]

A "great gulf" appears to separate what today is termed fact and value. "The sensible cannot determine the supersensible in the subject," but, Kant asks, what if the converse were true. What if the effects of the supersensible could be registered in the sensible? Is the concept of "a causality through freedom" an oxymoron or an intelligible notion? If we cease to think of causality not as a category but rather as a ground, the term becomes meaningful. Is there a ground both subjective and objective, embedded in nature and yet an idea of reason, a product of reflective judgment? Kant's answer: the purposiveness of nature can be understood in a twofold way, as having to exist in conformity with the concept of freedom and as a possibility presupposed in nature, specifically the nature of the subject as man (*CJ*, p. 32). Kant concludes that nature specifies its universal laws according to the principle of purposiveness prescribed to nature by means of the reflective judgment, which now mediates between the concepts of nature and freedom. What is more, there is pleasure in the apprehension of nature as having a purpose.

When judged subjectively prior to any concept, purposiveness is the subject of aesthetic judgments; when judged objectively as the harmony of a thing's concept with its form, it is the subject of teleological judgments (*CJ*, p. 29). In aesthetic judgments, we judge the object to be purposive, but we are unable to explain its purpose so that we experience a purposiveness without purpose as, for example, in apprehending the beauty of a tree. In the case of teleological judgment, we actually know what the purpose is. This distinction between types of judgment provides the ground for Kant's account of beauty. When the form of an object is merely reflected upon without reference to a concept and is judged as the ground of pleasure, it is called "beautiful," and the faculty of judging such an object is called "taste" (*CJ*, p. 28). Yet the feeling of pleasure engendered by the object is necessarily private. Is it possible to secure agreement about judgments of taste? Such judgments are valid for all, according to Kant, because there is a subjective yet common ground for them, a common sense [*sensus communis*] (fig. 1).

The advantage of turning to aesthetic judgment as grounding a philosophy of taste is perfectly clear in that there is now a court of appeal, the *sensus communis*, that is able to determine their validity. But what is the pragmatic

1. Suzanne Hélein Koss, *"Art and Nature: G-ddess Contemplating Field of Dandelions."* Courtesy of the photographer.

value of teleological judgments? Kant describes the representation of purposiveness in such judgments as follows:

> [Teleological judgment] refers the form of the object, not to the cognitive
> faculties of the subject in the apprehension of it, but to a definite cognition
> of the object under a given concept, has nothing to do with a feeling of
> pleasure in things, but with the understanding in its judgment upon them. *If
> the concept of an object is given, the business of the judgment in the use of the concept
> for cognition consists in presentation [exhibitio], i.e. in setting a corresponding intuition
> beside the concept.* (*CJ*, p. 29; emphasis mine)

This *Darstellung* or presentation may take place through imagination (as in
art) or by supplying the concept of purposiveness to "nature's product" (*CJ*,
p. 29) (see fig. 1).

Kant goes on to distinguish the beautiful from the sublime. Beauty
inheres in the form of the object and is discovered through quiet contemplation. The sublime, by contrast, is formless, exhibits no purpose, and is
apprehended in a state of excitation. Kant depicts this state as "a momentary
checking of the vital powers and a consequent stronger outflow of them"
(*CJ*, p. 83). Judgments of sublimity are universally valid, disinterested, necessary, and exhibit subjective purposiveness. The claim of universal validity
in the case of the sublime is particularly perplexing in that its object is formless and the state of the subject one of excitation. The universality of the
sublime is contingent upon the supersensible, upon moral feeling, Kant says.
Instead of generating a sense of pleasure, the sublime incites a feeling of
pain (fig. 2).

Kant distinguishes between the sublimity of magnitude, the mathemati-
cally sublime, and that of power, the dynamical sublime. Although Kant
speaks largely of objects of nature as sublime, he also adduces, astonishingly,
a concrete historical embodiment of sublimity: "War, if it is carried on with
order and with a sacred respect for the rights of citizens, has something
sublime in it" (*CJ*, p. 102; cf. *OH*, p. 19).

Kant examines the method of teleological judgment principally in his
account of the relation of such judgments to the natural sciences. But the
sciences, concerned with explaining natural phenomena, seem to require
determinate judgments. Teleology, which can provide a guiding thread for
the sciences, does not belong to the rules of science itself but "to critique
and to the critique of a special cognitive faculty, viz. judgment" (*CJ*, p. 266).
The student of archaic geological and living forms, who tries to imagine
the evolution of form as simply progressing from the simple to the more
complex, cannot do so. He must apply purposiveness to nature as a whole,

2. Kaspar David Friedrich, *Man Viewing Storm at Sea*. Hamburger Kunsthalle, Hamburg. Photograph by Elke Walford.

"the universal mother," or it would be impossible to think of the purposes of nature's products as demanded by science itself (*CJ*, p. 268). If there is a harmony between nature as a whole and its parts, then mechanical causality too can brought under the aegis of a grand plan governed by the purposiveness of nature.

Question III: Is the historian who depicts a given historical terrain compelled to account for why selected particulars are brought into just that terrain, under the aegis of the rules of just that empiricity? Is the "objective" historian obliged to inquire about the grand plan of that terrain, to think teleologically?

Reply III: It is a mistake to envisage teleology as *sheer* purpose. On this view, teleology would be an inner driving force that governs the course of events as in Heraclitus's philosophy, or governed by a will outside itself as in Calvin's theology in which not a sparrow falls but that God's will ordains it. Telos does not manifest itself in this fashion in the historical writings of modernity but rather as something like a guiding thread, a lead to be followed: for Ranke, nationality; for Michelet, democracy; for Toynbee, religion; for Burckhardt, art.

This mode of writing history is not foreign to Heidegger who tracks philosophy's history as a following of clues, the *Spuren* left by that history as a history of the meaning of Being, of the ontological difference rather than of events. It is a history that is the result of a single and decisive throw of the dice by early Greek thought and that unveils itself in conformity with this inner destiny to become one with its own history.[14] What has been noticed by commentators as disparate as Levinas and Deleuze is that destiny is not merely sheer or empty purpose but finds one of its existential expressions in a rootedness in earth that Levinas calls paganism and, for him, is at least compatible with, even if not identical to, the *Blut* und *Boden* ideology of Nazism. Deleuze identifies autochthony with territoriality, a proprietary relation to a given segment of earth. "[Heidegger] views the Greek as the Autochthon rather than as the free citizen (and as the themes of building and dwelling indicate, all of Heidegger's reflection on Being and beings brings earth and territory together)."[15] The movement of the destiny of Being is to reterritorialize the Greek spirit on European soil. It could be argued that Braudel's writing of history replicates the Heideggerian gesture of autochthony in that earth as a geophysical terrain is determinative for the history of events.

If history is tied to terrain and that terrain is inhabited by a people, is the idea of a terrain the necessary correlative of a people? How is the notion "a people" to be construed? Should the conception of peoples in their difference provide the telos of history? Says Deleuze: "A people can only be created in abominable sufferings." What brings them together is "their resistance to death, to servitude, to shame and to the present." He goes on to claim that the stranger may become autochthonous in the country of the other and the autochthon "a stranger to himself."[16] Does this blurring of the boundaries open the way for a history whose telos is, after all, that of a universal humanity as Kant envisaged it or, per contra, does it only provide an illusion of the transposability of identity in that whoever is currently perceived as indigenous remains privileged? Is autochthony necessarily bound up with bloodlines and these, in turn, with a privileged nobility that breaks into even the most hard and fast rules of economy? Thus, do not the emperor of Japan, the English peerage, or distant cousins of the Czar of Russia, claim privileges that are never wholly translatable into money but may transcend it?

What also remains invisible both in Heidegger's and Deleuze's account of peoples is the immense change likely to be effected in the construal of peoplehood through the recoding by contemporary genetics of human characteristics as information, DNA that encodes the traits of living beings. The transposition of information into a causal instrument that is decisive for physical, cognitive, and affective traits has already produced both positive and negative political fallout. But what has gone unperceived is that, if genetic engineering proceeds, the mystique of peoplehood may vanish into a vast new gene pool, perhaps creating a new humankind in a mannner undreamed of by Kant.

Yet the notion of peoplehood as presently imagined creates catastrophic collisions of ethnicities and conflicts between local cultures and at least putatively universal values. Is the heterological historian, in writing or visually depicting the history of an event, a trend, or practice, to honor the principle of difference or station herself in the discursive space of universality? Thus, for example, if the binding of women's feet in China or clitorectomy in Morocco are practices that the historian believes violate the rights of women generally, how is she to re-sign in history the de-signing of the "ethics of particularity?" If she argues that difference is to govern historical writing, does she not provide an entering wedge for the justification of practices she questions? Can the historian simply abandon the *teloi* of terrain and people that have played a role in the histories of African peoples or of the indigenous peoples of the Americas? New languages to deal with these particularities, translations as it were that bridge what may seem to be insuperable conceptual differences, are only now in the process of being forged.

If the historian is writing under the sign of Kant, the idea of telos can (oddly) be construed non-teleologically on analogy with Kant's account of the art object as purposive without purpose. History, says Deleuze, is the field for the realization of experimentation, for the creation of novelty. In a remark strongly reminiscent of John Dewey's pragmatic account of thinking, Deleuze asserts, "To think is to experiment."[17] History is not itself the experiment but provides the conditions that make it possible. Is the historian, who sees history as the field of that which can become but is constrained by the cataclysm, not writing under the sign of Kant?

THE AESTHETIC AND THE CATACLYSM

Kant IV: Kant's account of teleological judgment provides an entryway for understanding his view of the historian's task. The role of such judgments, it may be recalled, is to provide a *Darstellung* or presentation, "intuitions to set alongside the concept," that will display the concept's purposiveness. In relation to history, the concept for Kant is that of humankind and the field in which the purpose of humankind is enacted, the events of history.[18] But what can this purpose be? Because teleological judgments have supersensible and moral feeling as their ground, it follows that the idea that governs history must be a moral idea. For Kant, this idea is that of progress understood as a growth in goodness. The notion of moral progress in history functions in a manner comparable to the way in which God, freedom, and immortality as regulative ideas of reflective judgment guide the operations of practical reason. If the idea of moral progress is the work of the reflective judgment, it is *eo ipso* grounded in the supersensible. Thus the forces that propel history forward cannot be blind mechanical forces: history is a work of human freedom and, as such, not the outcome of a pre-conceived plan.

For Kant, human actions in history are the appearances of the human will, just as phenomena are "manifestations" of the things in themselves in the world of nature. The task of the historian is to determine the laws of these appearances. What may seem disorderly from an individual point of view is from the perspective of humankind "a steady and progressive though slow evolution of its original endowment" (*OH*, p. 11). Nature has provided humankind with all that is necessary to effect its transformation. In a fashion premonitory of Hegel, Kant argues that the chief means for bringing about a lawful society is through social antagonisms and their overcoming. Human development is only possible within a society whose fragmentation will ultimately be transcended through the establishment of a universal civic society, which will be characterized by the maximization of freedom under laws (*OH,* p. 16).[19]

Kant is not blind to the outlandishness of writing history that would be based upon his principles, a philosophical rather than an empirical history constructed in accordance with an idea of how things must fall out rather than with an attentiveness to how they in fact actually happened. Invoking

the division between fact and fiction, he writes: "But to originate an historical account from conjectures alone would seem to be not much better than
to draft a novel" (*OH*, p. 53). What could be the purpose of a philosophical
history? Kant alludes to the interest of future historians who, when documents disappear, will write history from the standpoint of their own concerns. The philosophical history Kant advocates is to serve as a goad to those
now alive to think about the future, about how they will be perceived by
history (*OH*, pp. 25–26).

   Yet on what grounds can we predict how what has occurred or is occurring will be interpreted in the future? Probabilities can be calculated, but
such calculation is unhelpful in the present-day lives of individuals. Instead,
says Kant, "an event that would serve as a sign [*signum, demonstrativum, prognostikon*]" must be sought that would signify atemporally and that would
occur within the framework of the history of states (*OH*, p. 143). Even if
the event should miscarry, the sign may serve to spark future repetitions. An
event that would serve as a sign is to be found not in what Hegel would
later call the acts of world historical individuals, not in the acts of the key
figures of the French Revolution (the decisive event of Kant's day as it
would later be of Hegel's), but rather in the disinterested sympathy of the
spectators. Thus Kant writes of the event that is a sign:

> [It] is the mode of thinking of the spectators which manifests . . . disinterested
> sympathy for the players on one side against those on the other, even at the
> risk that this partiality could become very dangerous for them if discov-
> ered. . . . This mode of thinking demonstrates . . . owing to its disinterest-
> edness, a moral character of humanity . . . which not only permits people to
> hope for progress . . . but is already itself progress. (*OH*, pp. 143–144)

**Question IV: Does not the quiet con-
templation of the spectator of the historical cataclysm in the age of mass
annihilation not suggest that the historical object is placed under the
aegis of aesthetic judgment? Is the
aesthetic gesture reinforced by condensing the cataclysm into a sign, a
mere movement of abstraction that
replicates the gesture of the abstract
artist rendering the cataclysm as an
abstract work of art? At the same
time, does not the depiction of the
cataclysm as an index of the moral
character of humanity not point to its
simultaneous refiguring as a *Darstellung* or presentation that will display a
hidden regulative idea? But in the
context of the cataclysm what could
such an idea be?**

Reply IV: To see the full import
of the Kantian sublime it must
be envisaged in the manner of
Nietzsche, as power. The imagination is magnetized toward the
transcendent, "which is like an
abyss in which it fears to lose itself," Kant says (*CJ*, p. 97). The
imagination is not unfettered
but is restrained by the rational
idea of the supersensible. Unlike
the beautiful, the sublime does
not reflect the harmonious play
of imagination and understanding but is rather a play of wild
antitheses, of reason and imagination later recoded by
Nietzsche through the lexicon
of Greek tragedy as the opposition of Dionysus and Appollo.
Prior to Nietzsche, Schiller had
already brooded over world history as the instantiation of this conflict:

> World history appears to me a sublime object. The world as an historical
> subject matter, is basically nothing but the conflict of natural forces among
> themselves and with man's freedom. . . . All the well-intentioned attempts of
> philosophy to reconcile what the moral world demands with what it actually
> performs are contradicted by experience . . . as [nature] impetuously tears off
> the reins by which the speculative spirit would gladly lead her.[20]

As Kant showed, imagination charged with creating images can never
apprehend the abyss because sheer magnitude cannot be encompassed in an
image; it can only be estimated by reason. As a faculty of images, imagination would have to devise a form for absolute magnitude as an absolute
totality by which is meant the unencompassable infinite. We are constrained
by "the objective impossibility of ever arriving at absolute totality by means of
the progress of the measurement of things in the sensible world in time and
space . . . as an impossibility of thinking the infinite as entirely given and not
as merely subjective [or as] an incapacity to grasp it, but objective" (*CJ*, p. 98).

This is why Kant offers in place of a description of the unrepresentable
cataclysms of history the sign of an event, the event as sign, an atemporal

abstraction that would signify rather than body forth the unrepresentable. But far from seeing this as a failure in the writing of history, it can be regarded as the first move of a new historical consciousness: the an-iconic depiction of the great cataclysms of modernity as signs.

The turn to signs is reflected in the artworks of modern abstractionist painters, sculptors, and architects. Some among them pare away the inessential to arrive at the essence of a phenomenon in the manner of Georges Braque, Picasso in his Cubist period, or Juan Gris. Others create abstractions *de novo* to stand for the unrepresentable in the manner of Piet Mondrian or Juan Miro. The former are painters of an essential figuration, the latter of a new hieroglyphics, a language of signs that reaches for an infinite that transcends representation.[21] In a striking move anticipatory of twentieth-century abstract art, Kant can be read as claiming that there is a work that is a sign of but not a figuring of the infinite: such a work is the sum of human actions in the theater of nation states that remain in conformity with the moral law. Is such a creation not an an-iconic work of art? In this context Kant writes: "Perhaps there is no sublimer passage in the Jewish law than the command 'Thou shall't not make to thyself any graven image, nor the likeness of anything which is in heaven or in the earth or under the earth'" (*CJ*, p. 115). Morality without iconicity is thus the measure of greatness.

Cannot Kant's dream of humanity's ever-increasing obedience to the moral law within history be recoded as a work that necessarily can never reach completion? Unlike the figural murals of Diego Rivera that attempt to depict a dream of progress, or Picasso's *Guernica* that strives for its obverse, the portraying of war that fissures hope, Kant's dream of humanity is better encoded in Christos's and Jean Claude's June 1995 wrapping of the Reichsteig in Berlin with a silvery fabric. As an event, the wrapping and unwrapping becomes a sign that signifies the mutiple modes of the veiling and unveiling of German parliamentarianism: the incineration of the Reichstag in 1933 by persons unknown; Hitler's reluctance to use the building during the Nazi period; very occasional meetings of the Bundestag in the Reichstag before German reunification, because such meetings were suspected by the East German government as covert efforts to restore Berlin as the capitol of West Germany. No photograph or film can capture the fluidity, the multiple sites from which the event was experienced. As Nietzsche recognized, artworks engender fear. Thus it is not surprising to find that in 1993 it was reported that "Helmut Kohl and party leader Schauble reject the wrapping. Schauble warns, experiment with the Reichstag should not be undertaken."[22] In its obedience to the moral law, humanity for Kant is like an artwork driven by an inner teleology that is paradoxically not aesthetic but moral. The moral perfection of humankind is both the means and the purpose of this work's creation. Nietzsche later describes such an auto-telic work as one that gives birth to itself.

The heterological historian who wishes to address the cataclysms of the twentieth century is abandoned to a de-signing of ethics that can be neither representation nor sign. At the same time, de-signing is also a recovery of the non-place of an alterity that is unrepresentable and that constrains the historian to uphold her pledge of truth telling. Neither cataclysm nor the other can be configured in her narrative because, as Levinas (in what is an amplification of a Kantian point) insists, the other is given as the infinite, as that which is always more. The infinite is the radically, the absolutely other, a being that cannot be contained in thought. Without being a cause, the infinity of the other has the "effect" of disempowering the self. The "logos" of alterity is a proscription against the violence of history.

What then is to be done by the historian who writes under the sign of Kant? She cannot bring forth the historical object through a movement of psychological empathy, of identification with the victim, for the historian is always already other than the victim. Even if she recounts her own history, there is a scission between narrator and the subject of narration. Instead, she must saturate herself in the political, social, and economic matters of which she writes without throwing off her situatedness. Does not the heterological historian then write as Borges suggests, not as pretending to be Cervantes but as Menard writing Cervantes?

Yet does not every such historical work undo itself? If the sign is a re-memoration, does it not threaten to perpetuate historical antagonisms by reevoking the cataclysm and, by remembering its dead others, invert an original binary opposition between victim and victimizer as justification for new violence? What is the historian to make of claims such as that of the Bosnian Serbs that their fighting Nazism in World War II justifies their annihilation of the present-day Croatians because Croatia abetted Nazism in that period? What is more, may the spectator's standing apart from violence, the sign of an event that creates a hope for the future, as Kant describes it, not reflect a sinister participation in violence? Consider:

> The Muslim men were herded by the thousands into trucks, delivered to killing sites near the Drina River, lined up four by four, and shot. One survivor, 17 year old Nezad Avdic recalled in an interview this week that as he lay wounded among the dead Muslims, a Serbian soldier surveyed the stony moonlit field piled with bodies and merrily declared: "That was a good hunt. There were a lot of rabbits here."[23]

Is the historian herself not a spectator who must often proclaim that the demands of alterity can be undecidable thereby consigning at least some victims to silence? Does the lapse of time between account and event not make this ever more likely? Is there with events, as with individuals, a dimming down (to use Heidegger's phrase) with age? Or must the historian, like Kierkegaard's disciple at second hand who claims that in matters of faith there is no difference between the later and the contemporary witness, station herself in an ethical non-space from which she will risk naming the historical object?

Kant's *Zweifaltigkeit* with regard to war is manifested in his admiration of war as an instance of the dynamical sublime on the one hand and the ideal of perpetual peace on the other. Hoping to root out the causes of future wars, Kant recommends eliminating standing armies, the prohibiting of acts that engender vengeance, the "employment of assassins, poisoners, breach of capitulation, incitement to treason in the opposing state" (*OH,* p. 89). If there is no residue of trust in the enemy, however miniscule such trust may be, no peace can be concluded. Perhaps in the hope of avoiding endless wars, Kant argues for the parity of states as lawfully constituted bodies who cannot engage in punitive wars. In an extraordinary anticipation of Hegel's master-slave dialectic, Kant asserts:

> Between states no punitive war is conceivable because between them there exists no relation of master and servant. It follows that a war of extermination, in which the destruction of both parties and of all justice can result would permit perpetual peace only in the vast burial ground of the human race. (Kant, *OH,* p. 90)

Question V: Can the presentation of the *res gestae* under the sign of the dynamical sublime provide the ground for re-signing history in the discursive space of a utopian politics grounded in alterity? Or, does the tempestuousness of the sublime and its apprehension through a feeling of enthusiasm lead to the aestheticization of politics as expressed in fascism? What would it mean to study history from the standpoint of the dynamical sublime?

Reply V: Kant actually begins the process of domesticating the Romantic notion of the sublime, in which the beautiful is linked with sense and action, by placing the feeling through which the sublime is apprehended under the aegis of reason and subordinating it to the moral faculties. His suspicion of reading history through the lens of an aesthesis of pure feeling is in conformity with an Enlightenment concern that historical writing not be brought under the thralldom of fiction. For historians like Ranke, writing objective history, history under the aegis of what I called earlier *l'esprit de géométrie*, would save history by returning it to the rectitude of fact. According to Kant, it is not the object of history such as war or revolution that is sublime but the reflective judgment itself which enables us to think it thus: "It is the state of mind produced by a certain representation with which the reflective judgment is occupied and not the object that is to be called sublime" (*CJ*, p. 89). If heterological historical works are *ficciones,* do these not, after all, constitute a literary genre oddly enough exempted from aesthetic judgments of taste as Kant defines it and ruled instead by an idea of the unattainable sublime? Do they not belong to the field marked out as the sublime but tamed through its inner relation to the supersensible rather than reflecting a wilder non-Kantian and romantic sublime? Have historical narratives as *ficciones* therefore lost their power to inspire what we envisage ourselves as becoming, as Nietzsche might put it? Would the writing of history not be better served by "a politics of interpretation" that would place the *res gestae* under the sign of the wild sublime? Is it the suppressing of or the reinstatment of the sublime that immunizes more effectively against Fascism as a mode of historical consciousness?

Two citations of Hayden White are worth placing side by side in considering this question:

1. The domestication of history effected by the suppression of the historical sublime may well be the sole basis for the claim to social responsibility in modern capitalist as well as communist societies. While this pride derives in part from the claim to see through the distortions and duplicities of fascist ideologies, it is possible that fascist politics is in part the price paid for the very domestication of historical consciousness that is supposed to stand against it.

2. In the politics of historical interpretation, [this perspective] is conventionally associated with the ideology of fascist regimes. Something like Schiller's notion of the historical sublime or Nietzsche's version of it is certainly present in . . . Heidegger and Gentile and in the intuitions of Hitler and Mussolini. But having granted as much, we must guard against a sentimentalism that would lead us to write off such a conception of history simply because it has been associated with fascist ideologies.[24]

Citation 1 rests on the premises that no reason can be found in the raw material of history for preferring one historical interpretation over another and that no such grounds can be adduced from the human and social sciences.[25] These sciences proceed as if the question of meaning were otiose and the self-evidence of fact could suffice to ground the historical sciences. Thus, it is better, White believes, to write history from the standpoint of the sublime in that such writing provides neither explanation nor description but inspiration as nineteenth-century Romantic historians understood.[26]

Does not the sublime in citations 1 and 2 replicate the role of writing as a *pharmakon,* a word signifying both remedy and poison in Plato's dialogue *Phaedrus* as Derrida describes it? For White, the sublime is the medicine that would cure the meaninglessness of objective history but could conceivably inject into both event and historical narrative the poison of Fascism. Are we to believe that the toxic nature of this *pharmakon* does not matter so long as the sublime can overcome the indifference of fact?

From the standpoint of standard logic, White's argument in citation 2 is impeccable: to appeal to the claimant, Hitler et al., rather than to the claim is to argue ad hominem, a common fallacy. Thus, odious as Hitler may be, the fact that it is he who utters the proposition "Vegetarianism is healthy" does not render the proposition false in that the facts about nutrition will verify or falsify it. But does not the ad hominem fallacy rest upon the notion that propositions are acontextual? Would the assertion "German culture has produced great writers" more easily gain approval if uttered by Thomas Mann or Günter Grass than if maintained by Hitler, if one knows in advance how the assertion of the greatness of German tradition entered into Nazi ideology?[27] Can the historian appeal to the event without appealing to the deictic aspect of utterance, as if the perspective of the speaker had no place in the narration? What is more, does not the implicit invoking of the ad hominem fallacy better suit the epistemology of the objective historian than that of the narrative historian who invokes the metaphoricity of historical narration?

White's unsettling willingness to gamble on the sublime that, on his own admission, helped to create the ethos of Fascism results in part from his entrapment in the binary oppositions of objective history/inspired history and of form/formlessness. If an uncontrolled aesthesis is to inspire history, it must make itself known as the absence of its opposites, objectivity and form, an absence expressed in the subjective idea of sheer might or magnitude. To ascribe empirical content to the sublime is to misread the unbridgable gap between objects and the formlessness of the sublime. The sublime cannot be an event—the creation of an artwork, for example—but rather an episteme (in the Foucauldian sense) not of statements but of powerful affects. In taming the sublime, Kant is trapped in a binarism that links sheer magnitude and force to cognition and the moral law. Is the writing of history under the sign of Kant doomed simply to repeat these dualities in a rebounding dialectic?

The Kantian sublime is recast in contemporary philosophy in Emmanuel Levinas's account of the *il y a,* the there is, the indeterminateness of Being that would ensue if all beings could be imagined to disappear, an anonymous residue, the Being that wells up when there is nothing.[28] In a double gesture, Levinas regenerates the binarism of Kant, then finds in the dynamism of the *il y a* not inspiration (as White argues is the case in relation to the sublime) but an entryway into the ethical. Like the dynamical sublime disclosed for Kant through negative affective states, the *il y a* is revealed through horror. The apprehension of one's individuality, what Levinas calls in the language of Husserlian phenomenology "the emergence of consciousness," effects a break with the *il y a.* Contrary to what might be imagined, the *il y a* is not linked to a fear of death in that it does not, like one's own non-being, open out into nothingness but rather into a timeless Being that can be said to mimic the formlessness and power of the sublime. In much the same way, for Kant the terrifying phenomena of nature, bold rocks, hurricanes, boundless ocean, are transcended, become sublime rather than merely fearsome, provided that the consciousness of the spectator rises above them as a consciousness that views them in security.

Before the binarism of Kant can be undone, it must be elaborated in the context of contemporary philosophy's linguistic turn. Just as the sublime is linked to the supersensible and the moral law, so too the *il y a* is explicated in its relation to what Levinas calls philosophy, a discursive formation within which the order of justice in society is given linguistic articulation and rational form. Between alterity and being, the placement of philosophy renders it a bulwark against the slippage of Being back into the *il y a.*[29] In this context, the *il y a* is the non-signifyingness that stalks language, nonsense that undermines coherence. Yet the Kantian duality form/formlessness appears to remain unaffected in the Levinasian version as the *il y a* and philosophy.

Yet it is within the inner circuitry of the *il y a* itself that Levinas undercuts the extreme peril of a purely inspirational sublime without returning to the Kantian binarisms, especially that of inspiration/cognition. Were the *il y a* marked off as a field from which Ethics was absent, the primacy of Ethics would give way to that of ontology in that the *il y a* as defined by Levinas is Being in the absence of beings, the absence of what Heidegger calls the ontological difference, the difference between Being and beings. Thus the *il y a* itself must advance Ethics even if in doing so it unmakes cognition. The ethical role of the *il y a* is to de-nucleate the self as the complex of mental acts. In characteristically rhapsodic language, Levinas declares: "The incessant murmur of the there is strikes with absurdity the active transcendental ego, beginning and presence. . . . Behind the anonymous rustling of the there is, subjectivity reaches [pure] passivity."[30] *The il y a:* untamed and taming, remedy and poison, it renders the self receptive to alterity.

∞

In re-signing history, the heterological historian is aware of the difficulties inherent in the claim that narration renders events just as they happened. Her narrative is so configured that its "truth" is contingent upon its subtle disclosure of the epistemic paradigms through which events are articulated and upon acts of naming that "give countenance" to the dead others, force their reticences to speak.

Such a work is necessarily incomplete because there is always more to recount. "That is *not* how it was then" demands not the conclusive refutation of an argument but rather an addition to the narrative. Such textual openness, however, reflects the expansive potential of historical narration and not the inherent unfigurability of the *res gestae*. That which can in no way be figured by the *historia rerum gestarum,* the cataclysm, a nihil whose sheer magnitude and unfigurable ethical force—a law prior to all law—resists emergence in word or image.

Beyond phenomenological description or law-like formulation yet with links to both, the cataclysm would seem to be refractory to Kantian interpretation. Thrust between the Scylla of the most empirical of phenomena—vast numbers of real people who suffer in actuality—and the Charybdis of the cataclysm's unthinkability as a self-same totality, can Kant's account of the knowledge of phenomena be rendered useful? In the world of phenomena, the understanding shapes sensible intuition while the link between them is forged by judgment. The categories or rules of the understanding are applied to intuitions, but, the heterological historian notices, this process is not yet enough to account for joining the categories to cases. The schemata, or universal concepts which are the work of the imagination, provides a rule for the creation of images, blurring, as it were, the boundary between the understanding and the sensible world. In her yearning for rendering the cataclysm in images, for some objective correlative of the cataclysm, might the schemata not allow the historian a middle passage such that the unfigurable might now be imaged?

In addition to intuition and understanding which together conspire to yield knowledge of phenomena, a third faculty, reason, posits regulative ideals unrealizable in experience and known to us through analogy. Might there not be a negative regulative ideal that would provide a guide for practical reason, an analogue for the cataclysm to which the historian could appeal? The existence of such an ideal cannot be proven but could be felt as pressure, as the moral weight of the dead others.

Yet if the moral weight of alterity is accounted for in the Kantian framework, the crucial question, "How can the supersensible be tracked in the sensible?" still remains unanswered. Kant's analysis of the beautiful and the sublime in *The Critique of Judgment* both prefigures and shapes this dilemma. The beautiful provides pleasure when apprehended, is grasped in quiet contemplation and judged disinterestedly in accordance with a common sense *[sensus communis]* so that judgments of taste can be universal and objective. An object judged to be beautiful is purposive, but we are unable to explain its purpose. By contrast, the sublime is formless, apprehended in a state of excitation, and induces pain. Its universality is contingent upon moral feeling. Two forms of the sublime, the mathematical sublime bound up with magnitude and the dynamical sublime which expresses power, are distinguished. Because the extent of the cataclysm is incalculable—it is commensurate only with itself—it cannot be judged as displaying mathematical sublimity but rather as expressing power. The heterological historian notices that, for Kant, a key historical manifestation of the dynamical sublime is war, a bursting forth of unrepresentable power. If war—for Kant, the French Revolution is the supreme exemplar—is indescribable, how are historians to transmit a sense of "what happened"? Through an event, says Kant, that serves as a sign, that which is seen not by participants but through the disinterested eyes of the spectators.

With the envisaging of war as a sign and thus tamed, what would it mean to transmit the *res gestae* under the form of the dynamical sublime? For Kant it is not the object that is sublime but the subjective judgment of the object. Subordinated to the moral faculties, the Kantian sublime differs from its Romantic counterparts, a sublime that provides inspiration and thereby overcomes the neutrality of fact. Like Plato's *pharmakon* in the dialogue *Phaedrus,* the inspirational sublime is both remedy and poison overcoming the spurious objectivity of fact by an appeal to inspiration but, at the same time, contributing a Romantic dimension to the ethos of Fascism.

If the heterological historian hoped that the sublime in its domesticated Kantian version could provide strategies for configuring the cataclysm, there is no indication of how sheer force should be linked to cognition and the moral law. The Kantian sublime must be thought otherwise than in terms of judgment and purpose, recast in post-Heideggerian terms. Reconsidered in this way, the sublime becomes the inchoate infra-cognitive *il y a* of Emmanuel Levinas's philosophy: being in the absence of beings. Shapeless and timeless, being replicates the formlessness and purposelessness of the sublime. Yet this dis-figuring of the sublime advances Ethics in that the *il y a* de-nucleates the self, "strikes with absurdity" the ego, beings and presence, undoes what Kantian ethics cannot abandon, the unity of a subject, a self-identical consciousness.

If the sublime provides an analogue for the imperative force of the cataclysm, we have seen that the schemata fail to facilitate the imaging of the unrepresentable cataclysm. But there is more. Linked to both concepts and sensible intuition, a schema, is a procedure or rule that stipulates the conditions under which a given category can be applied to experience, a rule constructed by the imagination. It is thus imagination *(Einbildungskraft)* that is charged with reining in the unruly images, policing them by seeing to it that they are lawfully produced while also trafficking in images.

The panic generated by the unleashing of images has haunted Western philosophy from its inception. In the contemporary culture of the spectacle, all restraints upon the production of images have been removed while the information culture has blurred the lines between image and concept. It is the coming into being of this world, one in which the historian is challenged to recast the *res gestae,* that I shall now explore.

It can be said that even though machines should hear never so well and speak never so wisely, they will still always do the one or the other for our advantage, not their own; that man will be the ruling spirit and the machine the servant; that as soon as a machine fails to discharge the service which man expects from it, it is doomed to extinction.

But the servant glides by imperceptible approaches into the master. . . . Man's very soul is due to the machines; it is a machine-made thing: he thinks as he thinks and feels as he feels due to the work that machines have wrought upon him.

It must always be remembered that man's body is what it is through having been moulded into its present shape by the chances and changes of many millions of years but that his organization never advanced with anything like the rapidity with which that of the machines is advancing.

Samuel Butler
Erewhon

THE HISTORICAL OBJECT AND THE MARK OF THE GRAPHEME: IMAGES, SIMULACRA, AND VIRTUAL REALITY

There has been a profound shift to a wider frame of reference in the study of history, so that historical work is now disseminated into an array of practices, a culture of images, from which the professional historian may be excluded: photographs, film and television dramas, museum exhibits, the preservation and replication of the material culture of the pre-industrial past in mock farms, villages, and theme parks. Computer archives and computer-simulated environments add to this panoply of visual simulations which reflect attempts to create a sense of the presence of the past.

These changes signal not a mere expansion of the means for acquiring and distributing historical information but a fundamental epistemic transformation and cultural upheaval. No longer can there be any hope of condensing meaning into any single historical event that would become a sign, as Kant had wished; instead, the sign dissolves into innumerable visual stimuli. Images themselves must now be read in a new way. Having no original they are not the replicas of anything. Language itself has become volatilized into the image; the voice has given way to the grapheme, the written mark.

From an everyday point of view, it might be argued that the grapheme is not pictographic in that the writing of Western languages is phonetic rather than hieroglyphic. Even within this commonsense framework, letters of the alphabet can be seen to function as sound images, seen before they are heard. But something much more far-reaching is intended. Derrida is convinced that everything heretofore designated as language must now be understood as writing.[1]

How is this seemingly counter-intuitive and global claim to be interpreted? The understanding of language as thought and activity, what heretofore has been denoted by the term "experience," should now be designated as writing. It is not merely pictographic and ideographic inscription that is to be thought of in this way but rather the very conditions of their possibility. Thus Derrida claims:

> We say writing for all that gives rise to an inscription in general, whether it is literal or not and even if what it distributes in space is alien to the order of the voice: cinematography, choreography . . . but also pictorial, musical sculptural "writing". . . . One might also speak of military or political writing in view of the techniques that govern these domains today. . . . It is also in this sense that the contemporary biologist speaks of writing and program in relation to the most elementary processes of information within the living cell [as well as] the entire field covered by the cybernetic program. If the theory of cybernetics is to oust all metaphysical concepts . . . which until recently served to separate the machine from man, it must conserve the notion of writing, trace, grammè, grapheme.[2]

The graphematic aspect of the culture of images first appears as spectacle in the event often seen as having initiated modernity's culture of the spectacle, the French Revolution. Today phenomena involving vast numbers of persons not only occur, but when they do they immediately become occular, events to be captured in still and moving images. How is the heterological historian to speak the language of her time so that she may be understood, speak graphematically, as it were, from within the cataclysm that cannot itself be pictured? How is she to counter the specular culture's claim to simulate anything whatsoever, thus even to picture the cataclysm? How is she to use images to demonstrate past actualities without manipulating affect through image?

In this chapter, I explore that aspect of the field of the sensible which is under the aegis of the visible, the graphematic character of the "real" as a relation to images. I analyze the image as the attempt to displace the being of the object with itself. I then turn to the images generated by still photography and the claims of photography to pin down that which is, a referent. Images do not float in isolation but are the object of a look, that of the camera's viewfinder that fixes or alters them. The gaze of the one whose look in effect has become that of the camera must be investigated in its effort to magnetize the image as referent.

The model of truth as correctness, as a matching of event to proposition, has been faulted earlier as deriving from a metaphysics that fundamentally misreads the presuppositions of propositional language. Yet representation is not jettisoned altogether in the culture of images. Those who rely upon early visual technologies, still photography and film, may think of the image as a truth icon, as that which registers what was there and that cannot be gainsaid. I shall explore the limited sense in which the credibility formerly attaching to representation remains alive in the culture of the spectacle as a breaching by images of the narrative construction of events. At the same time, discursive criticism will be shown to dis-figure specular pretensions to truth so that narrative and figure can no longer be segregated.[3] Rather, the claims of narrativity often collide with especial force when discourse and film both attempt to interpret what is allegedly the same event. By comparing the way in which aspects of the French Revolution have been depicted in the work of the celebrated nineteenth-century historian Jules Michelet with the film *Danton,* directed by Andrzej Wajda, the way in which narrative becomes ocular and image narratological, each unsaying the other, comes to the fore.

Finally, the specular culture deriving from the impetus to replicate that which appears conflicts with the unprecedented breaking away of images from an alleged original through the coding and recoding of images as information. Yet the fact that images can be stored and shipped as information suggests an identity in difference between the sensible and the codes that generate it. Photography, film, television, computer simulations—all have become actually or potentially atomic bits of information transposable into graphematic or acoustic images.

If the heterological historian's promise to tell the truth is to be meaningful, she must invent ways to disrupt specularity, not by ignoring or evading its cultural omnipresence but by creating a specific form of negation that is intrinsically related to it. Thus she may ask, "How am I to dis-figure this artifact, this photograph, this docudrama that has been con-figured by the age of images so as to re-figure it within the non-space of ethics?" "How am I to speak for the past from the non-place of much contemporary speech, cyberspace, such that the I-saying, the deictic character of ostension, remains?" The heterological historian will be seen as a disruptive presence who both adopts and disrupts the all-encompassing culture of images in which the distinction between the actual and the imag-inary is blurred.

RUNAWAY IMAGES

The "society of the spectacle," a term coined by Guy Debord, has been identified by him as the way in which modern conditions of production present themselves so that the spectacle is not merely or principally a collection of images but the manifestation of social relationships. The spectacle is not the product of technology but rather the concretization of a view of the world in material form, "capital become image."[4] On this view, capital is interpreted as the economic substructure described in Marxist analysis except that image rather than ideology is its superstructure. Yet if the being of images dissolves the "real" such that the distinction between materiality and ideality disappears and the real becomes what has come to be called the hyperreal, "a hallucinatory resemblance of the real with itself,"[5] can the difference between substructure and superstructure, as Debord sees them, persist? If nothing but images exist, there is neither the economy that determines them nor any vantage point other than the image itself from which to view images. Does not Debord's own position risk dissolving into a self-referential paradox to become nothing more than a flickering in the culture of images? What is more, Debord sees no possibility for the transformation of images into sources of either *jouissance* or critique. Not unaware of the nihilistic implications of this view and of his "avowed intention of doing harm to spectacular society,"[6] Debord not infrequently reverts to an ineluctable nostalgia for the "real" that preceded the spectacle. Thus, he claims that all that was once "directly lived" has become representation, thereby positing a new but unexplicated category of the "directly lived."

Debord's analysis can be seen as, in part, an outgrowth of Heidegger's position expounded in his essay "The Age of the World Picture," in which Heidegger contends that when being is interpreted as managed by technique, it gives itself as picture, as that which can be represented.[7] It is in this context that Heideggerian tropes for an authentic past, the fourfold, peasant culture, objects of human making, are contrasted with whatever is filtered through a *Weltanschauung,* the interpretation of the world as picture. Like Heidegger, Debord presupposes a lost original vitality that has become the object of a quest by the very forces that traduce it.[8] Contrasting the universal linear time of the spectacle with the greater vitality of ancient cyclical time, he reaches for a period when labor was somehow genuine, when consumable time was in conformity with the actual labor of those societies.[9] Moreover, by assuming a critical stance toward the culture of images, a vantage point exterior to it from which it can be scrutinized, Debord weakens the claim for the pandemic character of the spectacle. Just as the heterological historian stations herself within the catastrophe as an ineliminable condition from which she cannot stand aside, so too the culture of images itself creates conditions of observation that cannot be bypassed (see fig. 2). With the primacy of images, the notion of reality through which the image is seen also changes in a feedback loop such that reality can only be understood graphematically and the image, in turn, decoded as writing or seen language.

In the new age of images there are only images. Could it not be argued that the promiscuity of the image was already present in Plato's philosophy? From the Platonic standpoint, art objects, shadows, and the reflections of things are the wanton and wild images that escape regimentation by the logos. On the received view, the objects are less real than the realm of the ideas or forms: the more etiolated, the more real. Characterized by the properties of generality and non-materiality, they exist in a realm apart, remaining always the same yet infinitely replicating themselves in ontologically scaled-down models in the world of becoming. Mortals disciplined in the appropriate way can grasp or be grasped by the ideas or forms, the *archai* of which everyday objects are copies. Deleuze takes note of the standard view that the model is an original, the copy is derived from it, and that only then does the difference between them come to the fore. But in an astonishing inversion of the received view he claims:

> The true Platonic distinction lies elsewhere: it is of another nature, not between the original and the image but between two kinds of images [*idoles*] of which copies [*icones*] are only the first kind, the other being simulacra [*phantasmes*]. The model-copy distinction is there only in order to found and apply the copy-simulacra distinction, since the copies are selected, justified, and saved in the name of the identity of the model and owing to their internal resemblance to this model. The function of the model is not to oppose the world of images in its entirety but to select the good images from within and eliminate the bad images or simulacra.[10]

Plato chooses among the pretenders to truth doing away with the false copies in a process of selection which both precedes the form-copy distinction and makes it necessary. The simulacra mock resemblance, produce an illusion of it (the very essence of sophistry) so that the forms themselves are in danger of becoming indistinguishable from images.

That images are suspect is reflected in Aristotle's claim that the forms do not exist in isolation. They inhere in existing things and later in modernity's various versions of factuality that eliminate occult entities and proclaim truth to be the matching of referent with its description. So profound is the fear of the image's allure that neo-Platonism does not restore the realm of the forms but resorts instead to a doctrine of emanations. Yet far from being defunct, Platonism exhibits a remarkable sinuosity. Even if, as Deleuze remarks, "concepts are dated, signed and baptized, they have their own way of not dying while remaining subject to constraints of renewal, replacement and mutation."[11]

Platonism must undergo one further transformation if forms are to become images in a culture of images which have no originals of which they are copies. It is Hegel's obscure and baffling analysis of the inverted world that enables us to envisage how forms lose both their properties of abstractness and transcendence and become simulacra. For Hegel, things change into their opposites through inner dynamic laws of transformation. In discussing the laws of nature, Hegel contends that the supersensible world is a "tranquil kingdom of laws," a copy of the perceived world which, in accordance with Hegel's view of how things change, is converted into its opposite. Thus the supersensible world of laws returns to the perceived world but transforms that world and is transformed by it. The perceived world, in what seems to be a paradox, remains a world of particulars yet is also supersensible. There are no longer ideas or forms and their instantiations in Plato's sense but rather ideas of instances. Hegel's inverted world is Platonism stood on its head, a topsy-turvy world that instantiates a new form of intelligibility that we now call "simulacra" (*Phen* 157, pp. 96–97).

Still another variant of Platonism reappears in Walter Benjamin's account of the artwork in the age of mechanical reproduction. What has shifted in the early modern period is the status of the artwork itself; that which from Plato's standpoint is already a work of mimesis is now the "original," an *eidos* that is an artifact. The notion of participation that for Plato explains the relation of form to object cannot be carried over into the domain of the artwork. Unlike the eidos, the artwork is a physical object subject to decay and destruction, a frangibility that itself will be transcended in post-modernity by the proto-immortality of images provided by the information culture that succeeds mechanical reproduction without entirely eliminating it.

Walter Benjamin argues that copies traduce the quality of presence in the artwork in that copies lack what the original possesses: "all that is transmissable from its beginning," its history.[12] Reproduction jeopardizes the object's authority or, in Benjamin's much cited term, its aura, "prying [the artwork] loose from its shell" through the process of reproduction. The aura is drained from the authentic object which, in turn, leads to the leveling of objects turned into images in the specular culture that postdates Benjamin's analysis. His account also points to a deterritorialization of the artwork in that through its dissemination it loses its stationary quality, migrates, becomes nomadic—a position already anticipated in Rainer Maria Rilke's contrast of *Dinge,* objects handcrafted for simple mundane use that, unlike the products of technology, are replete with the meaning of the lives of their users. Heidegger's nostalgia for authentic objects in his analysis of the products of technique, a way of regarding the being of things from the standpoint of calculation, continues the work of mourning for the lost object, an imaginary other that as an absence cannot be captured in an image.[13] The attribution of aura has now been extended to include mundane objects whose ownership by celebrities from Elvis Presley to Jacqueline Kennedy Onassis can be established. Mechanical reproduction, Benjamin claims, freed the artwork from its residual embedding in cult and ritual, a relation that has been inverted with regard to the object owned by the famous and powerful. The ineluctable nostalgia for relics has resacralized the possessions of celebrities, the demi-gods of specular culture, so that aura has now been affixed to these mementos and is attested to both by the intense affect and the monetary values attached to them.

Is not too much being made of the contemporary cloning of artworks? Was not art for centuries reproducible by such techniques as founding, stamping, engraving, etching, woodcutting? The difference is that new technologies allow for the reproduction of works in great quantity, for alterations in size, for inclusion or excision of detail, and for bringing images into wide circulation. An "original" artwork for Benjamin is determined by spatio-temporal coordinates and a singular history that belong to it alone as validated by chemical and physical analyses as well as by historical records that establish its provenance. "The presence of the original is the prerequisite to the concept of authenticity" (*Il,* p. 220). The reproduction is not a conscious forgery and must be distinguished from it just as the lie must be distinguished from fiction. The reproduction is independent of the original whereas the forger manually copies it falsifying its aura.

To interpret Benjamin's view as a longing for originary presence is to miss the thrust of his analysis, the claim that releasing the artwork from its dependence on social and religious ritual frees it for new social roles. But the concept of aura remains suggestive in ways unthought of by Benjamin. What is destroyed by the culture of reproduction is a singularity, that which is transmissible from the beginning, the "original" artwork, that which exists uniquely as self-attesting (*Il*, p. 220). This self-attestation of the work can be seen as homologous with the presentation of the *res gestae* by the historian who vouches for it in an act of I-saying that authenticates it through the deixis of ostension: "Here it is, I promise you." The historian is not merely a medium of transmission but installs herself in events as an "eyewitness" of the events and carries forward the work of naming and speaking in the name of the dead others. She herself can be said to "give off" aura in a chain of transmission.

How when the ocular age of the grapheme overtakes the age of voice, of narrative and analysis, is the historian to re-figure her commitment to veracity? Can the historian as purveyor and consumer of reproductions, creator of photographs, films, and exhibits continue to speak from the cataclysm in the name of the historical object? Is aura superseded or does it migrate? And if it migrates, does it reappear in the political arena as the aestheticized politics of Fascism as Benjamin thought? Or are there self-authenticating possibilities, a language of deixis within the culture of reproduction itself?

THE HISTORIAN AND THE CAMERA: STILL PHOTOGRAPHY

The most significant form of reproduction in the early stages of the age of images is that of still photography. Whether seen as art or as document, photography is "note-taking on potentially everything in the world, from every possible angle."[14] Ostension or showing rather than signification or saying becomes the primary function of language, so much so that the "aura-l" has often been thought of as sound *image*.

Benjamin notices that aura as intrinsic to the art of portraiture is retained in early photographs of the human countenance. Yet photography does not come into its own until it loses its connection with painting and is used to establish evidence. With the work of Atget, "photographs become standard evidence for historical occurrences, and acquire a hidden political significance" (*Il*, p. 226). Even if the photographed scene is an artifact of camera angle and object arrangement, even if captions accompany and name the photographs's meaning, that which is captured is that which has to have been seen at some specified point in time and space from the camera's viewfinder. As Roland Barthes alleges, images recorded on glass plate or silver nitrate film "is a certificate of presence"; Barthes's claim that trick photography can lie about meaning but not about existence cannot be sustained today, but it can be argued that, in the absence of "trick shots," there is at least a promise of deixis, of being there where the viewfinder is.[15]

In Barthes's *Camera Lucida*, a *memento mori* for his mother, a work that surrenders to a certain bathos, the family photograph becomes the Proustian madeleine cake that opens the floodgate of memory. Yet Barthes is right to notice that its affective power derives from the fact that "photography mechanically records what cannot be repeated existentially," such that the photograph "is the absolute particular" (*CL*, p. 4). With photography had there not at last arrived a language of pure ostension so that the historian could say: "'Look,' 'See,' 'Here it is'; the photograph cannot escape this pure deictic language"? Would such a language not point to an identity without difference of showing and shown? In the immediate act of apprehension, Barthes proclaims, the photograph is never distinguished from its referent; we do not see the photograph but only the referent (*CL*, p. 5). The historian no longer names, describes, or analyzes: the object names itself.

Barthes's account reflects a turn to an extreme objectivism, to fact, apodictic and certifiable, established without method. If the photo is a pure emanation of the referent as Barthes declares (*CL*, p. 80), we have passed from Benjamin's Platonism, from the aura of the authentic artwork, to an Epicurean epistemology in which objects emit etiolated images and acts of perception are seen as the reception of these images.[16] On this view of the image, the task of the heterological historian as the collector of images is comparable to that of the chronicler who produces a list of sequential events but does not incorporate them into a narrative or an analysis.

Yet as we shall see, an image without discourse is not yet *deixis*, for attestation requires language if it is to name its object. Can language break into the culture of the spectacle from within the specular itself? For Barthes, a photograph is not merely a referent that merges with its neural configuration, a percept, but rather a cultural artifact that is subject to critique that emanates from a point *within* the picture itself. A photograph is first a political and cultural statement, its "studium." An affective response to it requires the reproduction of social norms, an "average effect" (*CL*, p. 26). Yet the real power of photographs is not lodged in reconciling viewer and image but rather in destabilizing the viewer through the picture's punctum, a detail in the photograph that functions as a partial object that wounds or punctures the viewer (*CL*, p. 45).[17] It is the punctum that forces the medium to self-destruct as signification and that may work catachrestically as an absurd expression that unsays the whole or metonymically as a string of images that extend it. Yet the historian does not know the significance of what she sees if she has only the unretouched photographic record; she knows only that, there where the camera stood, it was thus. Comprehension cannot be identified with apprehending the world as it looks but rather through the narrative orchestration of events.[18]

I have already pointed to some of the epistemic difficulties that inhere in narrative if construed as a matching of meaning with referent. But narrative articulations of events may also be acts of co-optation such that the deictic character of the photographic referent reinforces the version of the events as narrated and programs emotions in accordance with it. Consider the Yasukuni shrine near the Imperial Palace in Tokyo, a place where Japanese soldiers killed in warfare are venerated. The framework that gives meaning to the shrine is that of the Shinto religion's view of the sacrality of the dead ancestor. This context is used to glorify the kamakazi pilots and the soldiers who marched across Asia during World War II. Aesthetically compelling photographs of the dead in uniform and sometimes in heroic posture reinforce this narrative (fig. 3).[19]

A different rendering of the relation of the Japanese warriors of World War II to the Shinto cult of ancestor worship is to be found in the Japanese Garden of Peace adjacent to the Museum of the Pacific War in Fredricksburg, Texas, and located on the site of the old hotel that was the ancestral home of Fleet Admiral Chester W. Nimitz, commander in chief of naval operations in the Pacific Theater during World War II. The garden was completed in 1976 and constructed by a Japanese team.[20] A plaque commemorating Nimitz's pre-war friendship with Admiral Haihachiro Togo (1847–1934), a naval tactician much admired by Nimitz, reads: "The Garden of Peace is a gift to the people of the United States from the people of Japan with prayers for everlasting world peace through the goodwill of our two nations symbolized by the friendship and respect that existed between Admiral Togo and Admiral Nimitz." Strangely enough, plaques, many with photographic inserts of American seamen who lost their lives in the Pacific during World War II, line the nearby Memorial Wall. Thus divergent narrative lines emanate from the framework of the cult of ancestors. Photographs that resemble one another, each seeking its authentication from the same framework, validate alternative narratives (see fig. 4).[21]

Consider now the photograph of Aleksy II, Russian Orthodox patriarch who is celebrating mass at the Dachau concentration camp (fig. 5). It shows a movable altar whose entablature contains a painting of virgin and child, the backdrop for the patriarch and the priests in their robes of office. From this single photograph radically divergent narratives are easily envisioned. One might focus upon the chain of events leading to Dachau as deriving from traditional Christian narratives about Jews and conclude that, given the preponderance of Jewish victims incarcerated and killed in Dachau, the recitation of the mass is a desecration of the memory of the victims. Another interpretation might render the Russian Orthodox mass as a gesture of reconciliation with Germany on the part of the Russians who lost milliions of its citizens in World War II. Still another view (that of the article accompanying the photo), one neutralizing the critical thrust of the alternative narratives cited, holds that the presence of the prelate, "the first patriarch ever to set foot in Germany," is an acknowledgment of a growing influx of Russians in Berlin and elsewhere in Germany.[22]

When photographs are pressed into the service of differing narratives

3. Kaku Kurita, "Memorabilia of Japanese Soldier Who Died, World War II," *The New York Times,* July 30, 1995. Courtesy of the photographer.

4. Jeff Walker, "Plaques on the Memorial Wall." Admiral Nimitz Museum, Admiral Nimitz State Historical Park, Fredricksburg, Texas. Courtesy of the photographer.

deriving from a common more encompassing one, or when the same photograph gives rise to different accounts of an event-chain, is the ostensive power of the visual not rendered subservient to the linguistic signification of narrative? Is that signification, in turn, not predetermined by the discursive possibilities of the specular age and its system of distribution? Thus, for example, the purchase of the Bettman archive, a collection of millions of historical photographs, by Bill Gates shows that historical material will circulate in specular culture as a product. A news article reports, "Gates is building a huge library of digitally stored images that can someday be sampled and sold on computer disks or over computer networks" that will be marketed both to professionals and the general public.[23] Films and television docudramas may use such photographs as supportive of actual memories to prop up the verbal testimony of speakers.[24] In what then does the deictic force of photographs consist when they enter formulaic contexts that configure their meanings? Do they not become mere appendages to phrase regimens they do not shape?

5. Camay Sungu, "Aleksy II Celebrating Mass at Dachau." *The New York Times,* International, November 30, 1995. Courtesy Reuters, Archive Photos, New York.

What remains compelling in the photograph no matter how artfully posed and composed remains a certain extra-discursive verisimilitude to that which was seen. Thus Barthes writes:

> I call "photographic referent" not the optionally real thing to which an image or a sign refers but the necessarily real thing which has been placed before the lens. . . . Discourse combines signs which have referents . . . but these referents can be and most often are chimeras. Contrary to these imitations, in photography I can never deny that the thing has been there. . . . [Photography's essence] will therefore be "That-has-been." (*CL,* pp. 76–77)

Is there a way to understand the persuasiveness of the referent while taking into account its critical unsaying by the necessary intrusion of narrative discourse?

Events do not give themselves all at once in the simultaneity of a panorama before an Absolute Subject but are disclosed by the "not" that is imprinted, in Derrida's phrase, *sous rature,* in the graphematic surface of the photograph. To photograph is to freeze an occurrence such that one holds in front of oneself that-which-was and that carries with it the silent claim that if stationed *there* where the camera was it, the event-scene, could not have been apprehended as otherwise. The still photograph is the artifactual concretization of what is most crucial to Heidegger's Dasein as being *there.* Consider these texts of Heidegger:

> The entity which is essentially constituted by Being-in-the-world *is* itelf in every case its "there" *(Da).* According to the familiar signification of the word, the "there" points to a "here" and a "yonder." . . "Here" and "yonder" are possible only in a there—that is to say, only if there is an entity which has made a disclosure of spatiality as the Being of the "there." *(BT* 132, p. 171)

Giorgio Agamben cites this text in juxtaposition to another: "For me Dasein does not so much signify here I am, so much as, if I may express myself in impossible French, *être-le-là.* And *le-là* is precisely *Aletheia:* unveiling-disclosure."[25]

In the absence of "trick" photography, the material or graphematic trope for the *Da,* the there, is understood as a revealing and a concealing. In the photograph, what is revealed is the *Da* of that which was; what is concealed within this revelation is that which could have been yet was not. The photograph opens numerous metonymic chains but it also establishes the limiting conditions of what can be said of it. It may have been thus or thus, but it could not have been thus. Agamben writes that "thus" is neither substance nor quality. "Being that is irreparably thus is its thus. . . . Thus means not otherwise. . . . Not otherwise negates each predicate as a property."[26] The Japanese soldiers in their heroic postures, the Russian orthodox patriarch, the people in the snapshots appended to the plaques lining memorial walk were as pictured if one placed onself there where the camera eye had been.

Are the claims of ostension not undermined by profound changes in technology? Even in the early days of photography, dark room techniques including dodging, montage, and special effects created by the use of light and camera angles could radically alter the final work and thus already could have been said to affect photography's promise of self-attestation. Today, the production of images without light through infrared photography and holography are staples of the image culture. Technologies that penetrate the surface of bodies, X-ray, magnetic resonance imaging, and lazer-dependent techniques blur the boundaries between inner and outer. The world of moving images, of film and television and, more recently, computer simulations which are becoming ever more interactive, move even further away from the still photograph. Digital-effects experts now predict that synthetic human actors are likely to be available soon and "are busily advancing the day when the first synthespian . . . waits for a lingering close-up in an optical disk-drive rather than in a location trailer."[27] What becomes of the there of the Da-sein if its possibility of self-location is undermined by new technologies? Perhaps, as Gertrude Stein quipped, there is simply no there there. I shall consider this question when I take up the information culture and the issue of virtual reality. Suffice it to say that what is displaced by new technologies is localizability, the where of the there of Dasein's spatiality, but the there as a mobile and even multiply-located site of concealing-revealing does not disappear.

THE CO-OPTATION OF THE LOOK

To produce an image as a still photograph is to look through the viewfinder of a camera, see what the lens will transmit, and press a button that allows the image to be recorded on a light-sensitive silver halide treated surface. The film is developed through a chemical process that results in a photograph that, in turn, will be the object of a look. The photographic process mimes the ambiguity of the term "look": to look is the activity of gazing upon some object ("She looks at me"); in its passive sense, to look is a focusing upon the image that is the result of this activity and may denote an appearance rather than the thing itself ("This building looks old"). Not only is the look descriptive of what photography does, but it is also a common subject of photographs which depict persons or animals gazing at one another or outward at an unknown viewer.

In film and television the picture recording becomes kinetic so that the camera and the flux that it captures are mobilized diachronically in successive images. However, not only film and television but also still photography are diachronic media. Although the image in the still photograph does not change, it catches an *unrepeatable* instant in time, whereas film and television imitate the temporal succession of events themselves. Efforts to force film to arrest time's passing, such as in Andy Warhol's film *Sleep* in which endless footage of a man who is asleep and thus immobilized, only serves to disclose film's kinetic nature. The camera continues to roll, time passes and unsays the effort to stop it.

With the advent of Husserlian phenomenology, the act of looking has itself become the subject of philosophical inquiry. Husserl and his followers refused to regard perception as the passive recording of sense stimuli, as an interaction of neurons of eye and brain, but saw it as an intentional act. To claim that perceptual consciousness is intentional means not that consciousness is aware of its activity but rather that it becomes a source of directional lines of force aimed at the world which, in turn, fills or fails to fill the empty intention with content. Kant had already acknowledged mind's contribution to knowing acts but argued that time, space, and the categories structure our world relations in the manner of a grid that is placed over sensible intuitions without setting that grid in motion. Thus mind remained accommodating and receptive, cunningly contrived to accord with the world of phenomena even if such agreement could never be established beyond the shadow of a doubt.

Compared with the views of Kant and Husserl, it could be argued that Jean-Paul Sartre depicts intentionality as a preemptive strike against the world, radically shaping sensory input. For Sartre, the intentionality of the look is an active intervention in the world so that it does not yield a simple percept but becomes an act of violence. When directed at other persons, the look displaces the being of the other's consciousness so that she becomes identical with the materiality of her body. The look is also an act of theft, a stealing of the other's world such that the space around her flows toward the one who looks, deterritorializes the other. The other's space is made with mine, "an object has appeared which has stolen the world from me."[28] Looking has become an act shot through with cultural, political, and social meanings.

Michel Foucault describes the gaze as the expression of an episteme that has surveillance as its object. In the varying contexts of medicine, psychiatry, as well as the military and prison systems, surveillance, a putatively enlightened mode of social control, is actually shown to be a repressive exercise of power against the constituencies it purports to serve or improve. When optical instruments which expanded the field of observation of the physical world were developed at the beginning of the seventeenth century, architects designed institutional complexes so as to hierarchically organize a network of gazes that would enable authorities to survey the whole. The idea was to create the perfect eye, whose gaze nothing would elude, located at the center of a cordoned-off space laid out in accordance with the rules of institutional authority that could decode its signs.[29] The plan to increase visibility took hold in the military camp, urban housing, hospitals, asylums, prisons, and schools.[30]

Jeremy Bentham's panoptical design for a prison opens the inmates to total surveillance. Bentham's model, that of a tower and peripheral buildings, is laid out and illuminated to assure the visibility of inmates. Even in the absence of its exercise, the gaze that is there when no one happens to be looking confirms panoptical power. In what must appear as a rendering in physical terms of the Sartrian look, Foucault thinks of the Panopticon as a machine that dissociates seeing from being seen. At the periphery are those who are seen but do not see, at the center those who see but remain invisible. It required only a sufficiently advanced optics to develop hidden surveillance cameras that would find their way into airports, public buildings, and private residences, schools, offices, and stores, that replicate the panoptical gaze.

Recent post-structuralist criticism construes the subject-who-looks as a depersonalized complex of social and political forces that exercises power as specular: to watch is to control, to be watched is to be powerless. That the look creates its object is already anticipated in Sartre's trope of the keyhole peeper who spies upon another caught in his act of looking by an alien gaze that transfixes him as an embodiment of pure shame. The modes of specular control are protean: for Lacan it is the regulation of desire through the mirror image; for Deleuze, the parents in the Oedipal family romance that fix their gaze upon the child setting the limits for the child's adult sexuality; for Guy Debord, a social relationship mediated by omnipresent life-denying images; for Foucault, discursive practices that preform what is to be interpreted as knowledge.

The colonization of identity by a surveillant intelligence is captured in the visual tropes of Ridley Scott's 1982 film *Blade Runner.* Set in 2012 in a polyglot Los Angeles, the film shows the struggle of its tough hero who is hired to capture rebellious humanoids, replicants who do not know that they are replicants, only to discover that he is one of them. Originally manufactured by the Tyrell Corporation to colonize outer space, the replicant's memories and fantasies are implanted in them by their creator. Yet a humanity that breaks through the replicant's encoded identity is attested by love and pain from which they were presumed to be exempt.[31]

Film director Andrzej Wajda thinks of the look as expressing the director's intentions. When instructed to cast a "withering gaze," the actor must know precisely where the enemy is. "He speaks his lines, indicates his reactions—but that is not his real position. He is in fact standing in for the camera itself."[32] The camera eye is not exterior to the events and actions it registers but is the adversarial glance within the film itself.

HISTORY AS ARCHIVE OF THE MOVING IMAGE

What is new about images that move is not the fact *that* they do so. As astonishing as the mobility of the image remains, Plato's account of the shadows thrown by puppets on the wall of the darkened cave reminds us that images were long ago observed to move. What is new and of importance to the historian is that the film can replicate the passage of time in spatial images. What historical narrative accomplishes textually, the before and after of events as well as their simultaneity, all are now rendered visually. The acceleration and deceleration of motion that signify the speeding up and slowing down of time that so mesmerized early filmmakers, from G. W. Pabst and Buster Keaton to Chaplin, were often used to mimic what was perceived as the primary property of modernity: speed. The information culture will be seen to continue modernity's stress upon speed, but that which is moved, miniscule units of information, remains invisible until it is transcribed into phenomenologically accessible form.[33]

Even in the age of information, film remains the medium that bodies forth the modern subject, whose description is presaged in Husserl's phenomenological account of internal time-consciousnesss characterized by protentions, the anticipatory movement, and retentions, the holding-in consciousness of the immediately preceding moments that identify lived time. "The principal differences between memory and expectation are fulfilled by nexuses of intuitive reproductions. . . . We are concerned with such questions as 'Have I really perceived this?'. . . On the other hand, expectation finds its fulfillment in a perception. It pertains to the expected that it is about to be perceived."[34] For Husserl, consciousness intends its objects, foreshadows that which will come to fill or fail to fill an intention as content. Just as an intention is the telos of perceptual and cognitive acts, so too each frame constitutes the purpose of the preceding ones and, as purposive, holds on to them (*Il,* p. 226). There is a post hoc constitution of the past which is retained in the present as the telos of that present. This retention is intrinsic to Husserl's account of presence, as Derrida points out, in that the non-presence of the past is necessary for perceived presence to appear: "If we call perception the act in which all 'origination' lies, which constitutes originarily, then primary remembrance is perception. For only in primary remembrance do we see what is past; only in it is the past constituted, i.e. not in a representative but in a presentative way."[35] The moving images of film mime this primary remembrance in that what is projected on the screen is what is absent but has been captured as present by the camera eye.

Just as the camera fosters the sense of the presence of the past, so too the camera changes its place in the manner of the living, moving body which organizes the visual field. What is shown is guided by the camera's mobile perspective. The *Da* or being "there" of the camera is that of the audience whose perspective is where the camera is, stationary or moving as the case may be. Could it not be argued that the audience has been co-opted before any consideration of the content of a film, by the conferring upon it of a novel identity, that of the camera eye? The title of Christopher Isherwood's novel *I Am a Camera* purports to convey the objectivity of a technical instrument that cannot avoid telling the truth. But can the subject whose being is that of a camera escape the framing perspective of the camera eye?

In a pessimistic reading of media and information technologies, Baudrillard attributes to Benjamin the claim that these technologies involve the total co-optation of the viewer: "[In film] no contemplation is possible. The images fragment perception into successive sequences, into stimuli towards which there can be only instantaneous response, yes or no. . . . Film no longer allows you to question. It questions you and directly" (*Sim*, p. 119).

This interpretation fails to note that, far from excoriating the potential of film, Benjamin believes:

> For the entire spectrum of optical and . . . acoustical perception the film has brought about a . . . deepening of apperception. . . . [that] film . . . burst the prison-world of [banal everyday life] asunder by the dynamite of the tenth of a second, so that now in the midst of its far-flung ruins and debris, we calmly and adventurously go traveling. (*Il*, pp. 235–236)

Baudrillard sees the technologies of image making first and foremost as leading to a lie in the sense attributed to the lie by Rousseau as language that distorts what happened in order to harm another. Speaking of dissimulation and simulation, Baudrillard comments:

> To dissimulate is to feign not to have what one has. To simulate is to feign to have what one hasn't. One implies a presence, the other an absence. To simulate is not simply to feign. "Someone who feigns an illness can simply go to bed and make believe he is ill. Someone who simulates an illness produces in himself some of the symptoms" (Littré). Feigning . . . leaves the reality principle in tact . . . whereas simulation threatens the difference between . . . "real" and "imaginary." (*Sim*, p. 5)

Vital to the construction of film is the equipment that produces its images. Because the presence of equipment unseen by the viewer cannot fail to influence the words, gestures, and actions of those who are being filmed, the creation of so-called film and TV docudramas that claim to present authentic real-life situations, in fact, "lie." "There is no longer any medium in the literal sense: it is now intangible, diffuse, and diffracted in the real" (*Sim,* p. 54).

Benjamin is not unaware of the potential for the manipulation of images by a variety of social forces. He sees in new technologies, however, ways to facilitate what older art aspires to do but cannot. Thus Dadaism tried to create in painting and literature spatial and temporal diffractions that film renders more effectively (*Il,* p. 235). It could be argued that the new technologies of the information culture about which Benjamin could not have known lend support to Baudrillard's view that the medium enters into the "real." It is not, however, technological change that is the issue between them but rather a difference in the perception of the forces of modernity that in each case drives their accounts. For Benjamin, the fear is that of a generalized aestheticization of life that both causes and feeds upon Fascism whose ultimate expression is war, a view that perhaps reflects Benjamin's unstated allegiance to Marx's positive appropriation of technology as a means for suspending "the idiocy of rural life." In this regard, Benjamin's fear of artistic aesthesis is echoed in Levinas's worry about the power of art to disarticulate the order of discourse unless "safeguarded" by criticism.[36] Benjamin both valorizes and fears the power of the aura of the original artwork because, unrestricted, it may unleash a nostalgia for and a fetishization of a heroic past that inevitably leads to war. Baudrillard rejects the possibility of aura in the world of the hyperreal. In Herbert Muschamp's *New York Times* article on the movement to protect endangered monuments, such as the Temple of Anghkor in Cambodia or the Taj Mahal in Agra, he cites Baudrillard's warning against the "dance of the fossils . . . the transformation of something buried and living into something visible and dead."[37] Yet ancient monuments are linked to one another by the very global culture that the monuments call into question. Together they constitute a global artifactual narrative. Neither a replica nor a computer simulation, the idea of aura, of a material continuity with the past, is both vitiated and sustained.

What is more, unlike Baudrillard, Benjamin does not see the public as totally malleable but rather as "an examiner, even if an absent-minded one" (*Il,* p. 241). It is worth noting that filmmakers have often been surprised by audience appropriations of their work that are foreign to what they perceive as its patent intentions. Thus historian Eric Foner laments:

> You can never quite predict how an audience will react to a film. . . . A man who had made a documentary about Caryl Chessman [executed in 1960] had

made the film as a powerful statement against capital punishment. But a lot of people who saw the film said, "Great, they fried the guy at the end—and, boy, he really deserved it."[38]

The historian must not only be wary of unpredictable audience response but, as a producer or consumer of film and television docudramas or other visual simulations or as a putative non-historian creating avowedly fictional historical films, she must be attentive to the way in which visual artifacts construct otherness. In docudrama that renders events remote in time, the sites, artifacts, and documents relevant to the period as well as interviews with experts are relied upon whereas, in the case of recent history, photographs and filmed footage of the "actual" events is likely to be used. In the latter case, there are many matters concerning which there may be an illusion of great cultural distance between the events and personages of the *res gestae* and the historian herself. Yet the historian may share with her subjects the conditions imposed by modernity. The fact that homogeneity is dictated by global technologies, information and commodity distribution systems would seem to imply that alterity is contrived, that the subject of history as the marginal or exotic other is commodified, yet another collection of marketable images.[39] This specious alterity should alert us to understanding that alterity cannot be established in terms of a facile predication of cultural difference but must emanate from the non-place of ethics, an alterity interpreted as primordial vulnerability and destitution.

If there is an alterity that is prior to visible differences and if the trace of this difference is to enter into the historian's creation of the visual *historia rerum gestarum,* where is she to station herself? Perhaps between theory and practice or between several practices, as Homi Bhabha claims:

> "Between" is a very interesting place of enunciation, because it's also the place "in the midst of." It's not only between two polar positions, it is also a new place—formed when these two positions somehow ignite, incite and intitiate something. . . . One of the characteristics of this place "in between" is that there is always that moment of surprise, that moment of interrupting something. But from that moment of interruption emerges something new, something different, a displacement.[40]

The idea of the between is hardly new. For Hegel, mediation reconciles and overcomes the antitheses within the dialectical process and, as such, is between them. As that which sublates immediacy, it is the simple negation of immediacy, but it is also a negation that will in turn negate itself and enable the life of Spirit to move ahead. Mediation is Spirit's dynamism, its driving force, the means through which it becomes reflexive and overcomes earlier phases of its life. Kierkegaard destabilizes mediation by holding fast to the antitheses he favors as demanding existential choices: either the refusal to decide (the aesthetic) or decision (ethics), either ethics or obedience to God. The slash separating and uniting the either/or denotes the Kierke-gaardian between. The between as reactivated in Martin Buber's description of it, is the locus of an encounter between an I and a You in which individual identity is blurred in the heightened experience of the relation itself. Buber thinks of the between as the narrow ridge where an I and a You meet. Not a somewhere, the between is the arising of the event of relation itself.

In Homi Bhabha's account of cultural criticism, the between retains its meaning as a space of disclosure. It is the "there" in the guise of an un-bridgeable gap between the pronominal I, the time and place of enunciation, and the content of an utterance, the subject of a proposition. "The pact of interpretation is never simply an act of communication beween the I and the You designated in the statement."[41] For signification to occur these two places must pass through a "Third Space," which folds into itself both the general conditions of language and the performative conditions of the utter-ance which cannot be disclosed in the statement itself. The meaning of an utterance is rendered ambivalent in that neither pole of the relation is decisive.[42]

This challenge to certainty would render questionable any narrative of culture that purports to speak from the perspective of the subject of an originary past. Such questionability might be viewed as desirable when nar-ratives about the past express racial or ethnic superiority, for example, those of Serbian nationalism or of the Boers in South Africa. But how is the historian to protect herself against a cynicism generated by the ambiguity attributed to the historical object, so that she may proffer her version of events without apology? How is she to say, "Yes, I am not wrong, yes, there was a rape of Nanjing, yes, there were massacres in Cambodia, yes, hundred of thousands of Tutsi were slain in Rwanda, yes, the children of the Argen-tine *mujeres* of the fifth of May were murdered?" How is she to counter the rhetoric of a new politics, in the context of which it is possible, in October 1995, for an Austrian politician to be videotaped while addressing an audi-ence of veterans of the Nazi SS as friends and "upstanding citizens who still have character and who have remained true to their beliefs despite the great-est opposition?"[43] There can be no definitive resolution to the harrowing question of how the historian is to support her refusal to deny the horrors of history. Yet this assertion of inconclusiveness cannot provide an excuse for evasion: the visual historian may station herself "there" between the demands of alterity and those of its trans-position into visual imagery. This is not a space of certainty but one of ethical contestation such that the historian is bound to defend her stand.

The historian's situation in the culture of the moving image can best be clarified by considering the ontology of the image, that which the image reveals and conceals. The image refers to its object by way of resemblance, and requires thought to focus upon *it* rather than upon the object in contrast to the signs of discursive language which are transparent toward their objects.[44] The idea of resemblance does not reflect a return to an older representational view of the image; instead resemblance is a dynamic principle, an event of engendering.[45] There is a doubleness in the being of objects such that being escapes itself and releases the image. "We will say that the thing is itself and is its image. And that this relationship between the thing and its image is resemblance."[46] An image stops existence: it is not transparent toward something else. What is more, the image is not to be grasped as simply indicating an absent object. In a remark anticipating the virtualization of the real in the image, Levinas speaks of images as occupying the place of objects "as though the represented object died, were degraded, were disincarnated in its own reflection."[47]

The trope for the rupture with the world of discourse is not, however, the image but rather that which signifies beyond it, the face of another who cannot be invoked in speech-acts or by means of the attributes perceived in self-presentation:

> The Other manifests himself out of himself, and not on the basis of concepts. . . . The sensible presence . . . of skin with brow, nose, eyes, and mouth is not a sign making it possible to ascend towards the signified, nor is it a mask which dissimulates the signified. Here the sensible presence desensibilizes.[48]

This ethical disclosure of the human countenance is language whereas, by contrast, images are both infra-discursive and infra-ethical. Paradoxically the face is language and at the same time remains non-discursive. *The image is not (as might be thought) the obverse of ethics but, by holding beings and discourse in abeyance, bracketing them, opens a space of disclosure beyond iconicity that is homologous with the non-discursiveness of the face.*[49]

The relation of the image to the human face may be compared to the reciprocal contesting of the *il y a* and ethics described earlier. It may be recalled that the *il y a* is the non-signifyingness that haunts language, undermining its coherence, yet, in spite of itself, advancing ethics by denucleating the self as a complex of mental acts. Conversely the non-space of ethics from which the promise of affirming that-which-was issues, contests, and dis-figures that which is non-signifying.

How is it possible for the visual historian to station herself between the non-image of the face and the image that conveys the historical object so as to invoke the imperative of alterity? Must she not strive to present the image of an event as a countenance or rather allow the countenance to inscribe itself in the image? But the historian generally deals with large-scale phenomena whereas the face, if it is not to remain ineffable but is to act as an imperative, must be grasped through the trope of synechdoche, the part standing for the whole. Yet how can part and whole be discriminated in the non-space of ethics? Is it not possible to conceive of "having countenance" as expanding metonymically? Might it not be argued that, for example, the wounded body is a countenance or that nature has a face? Could it not also be argued that those who violate the imperative of another's face lose faciality? If the face is *always* proscriptive of violence and prescriptive of assistance to the other, then there is a democratization of faces that precludes exclusion. Both victim and victimizer have faces.

It is precisely in this context that a society of faces may be invoked. The face, or a multiplicity of faces—the visual images of the dead in the massacres of the twentieth century that attain force not only as singularities but by their collective power—are always and as such *reproaches* to egoity. The face of the one who refuses to respond, who turns back the reproach, tries to deflect it, discloses himself as an *image* of this reproach. Thus the face of the rapist may be doubly disclosive, of itself and of the reproach of the face of his victim. The historian who examines numerous photographs of the massacres by the Hutu of the Tutsi in Kibilira in 1990, later in the church in Nayarabuye and in the district of Butare, to name several of the most ferocious episodes, may see the faces of those ordering and carrying out the killings as reproached by the approximately 700,000 who died.[50] It has often been pointed out that in the age of atrocity the plethora of images of death, injury, and mutilation, a saturation point may be reached and the invocation of images rendered futile. But the visual historian's promise to present the *res gestae* is a promise to struggle against these odds.

The resources at the disposal of the visual historian to create the sense of the past are the technologies that body forth the image itself. Filmmaker David MacDougall points out that the commonplace strategies of taping and filming aging interviewees, background music, displaying old photographs or objects of the period without acknowledging either the way in which such evocations as well as the possible slippage of memory on the part of those interviewed may mislead viewers. But the historian as filmmaker is not without resources. She can, in films of memory, make absence manifest through the creation of signs that exhibit forgetting, distortion, and the time gap between event and memory. Thus the ironic use of objects and testimony may be introduced to provoke audience reflection. In this context the sign is not a proxy for the lost object but is rather its displacement.[51] MacDougall offers as an example of the filmic manifestation of absence, strategies used in Claude Lanzmann's 1985 film *Shoah:*

> Not only [does *Shoah*] ask us to query first-person testimony but to look at empty roads and fields where atrocities took place and search them for what happened there. We look in vain for the signified in the sign. In this constant reiteration of absence we are brought to the threshold of one kind of knowledge about history. In the failure of the sign we acknowledge a history beyond representation.[52]

Absence is one strategy in a larger repertoire of strategies that can be described as the *Ironisierung* of the denial of that which the camera eye would reveal were it there, there where the massacres occurred—for example, the denial that anything happened in these fields except the peaceful change of seasons. The empty fields are in fact a revealing/concealing of that which took place there. I shall call this visual troping "filmic catachresis."

Photomontage and cross-cutting may help to implement filmic catachresis by creating an effect of the simultaneity of events that occur at different places that unsay one another, or to the contrary, despite the difference of locale, say the same thing.[53] These techniques are familiar; they have been regularly used to illustrate class differences in Merchant and Ivory films such as *The Remains of the Day,* or in TV dramas such as *Upstairs, Downstairs,* without, however, creating a sense of intense dislocation in that the aestheticization of wealth unsays the critique of social class.

An extraordinary docudrama, *In the Name of the Emperor* (1995), an American film directed by Christine Choy and Nancy Tong about Japanese war atrocities in China immediately preceding and during World War II, avoids some of the difficulties to which MacDougall points through their employment of crosscutting and irony. Unknown to the Japanese occupiers, an American Episcopal missionary, Rev. John Magee, was able to conceal his movie camera to obtain footage of the victims who were burned, used for bayonet target practice, or gunned down. The handheld camera and poor film quality as well as voiceover reading from diaries kept by foreign observers and used as discursive elaboration enhances the poignancy of what is recorded. Close attention was paid to the mass rapes and often subsequent killing of Chinese women and to the later use of "comfort" women by

Japanese troops. Interviews are conducted with Japanese participants in the event who describe the brutal use of captive women in excrutiating detail. Italian and Japanese newsreel footage showing the triumphal Japanese entry into Nanjing are interspersed for catachrestic effect. Scholars and others who tried to bring the matter to public awareness in Japan and those who tried to minimize its horror are interviewed. At the 1946 Japanese war crime trials, Magee is shown testifying, but the trial which ended in seven convictions did not include the commander in Nanjing. What is more, the seven who were executed have since been given a place of honor in a national shrine honoring heroic ancestors.

Perhaps there has been no more caustic critique of memorialization cast in the form of regret and repentance than that of Baudrillard. It is not enough merely to note that from a psychological standpoint repentance may be the exception rather than the rule, as Richard Mollica, director of Harvard's program in refugee trauma, claims: "People who commit murder find it very easy to rationalize . . . and come to terms with it."[54] If the heterological historian is to justify her enterprise, Baudrillard's attack upon regret and repentance must be subjected to genealogical analysis and refutation.

According to Baudrillard, the real as we have known it has come to an end. With the replacement of the real by hyperreality, a duplication of the real through some medium of reproduction producing "a hallucinatory resemblance of the real with itself" (*Sim,* p. 142), the very possibility of history which presupposes linear time and geographical space also has come to an end (fig. 6). In this context, acts of memorialization can only reflect false consciousness exemplified in gestures of sanitization and revisionism. What of efforts not to sanitize but to speak in the name of the dead other? Baudrillard comments:

> Celebration and commemoration are merely the soft form of the necrophagous cannibalism, the homeopathic form of murder in easy stages. This is the work of the heirs whose ressentiment towards the deceased is boundless. . . . Publication of the tiniest of unpublished fragments—all this shows that we are entering an active age of ressentiment and repentance.[55]

He concludes that catastrophe itself is an illusion, that we are "liberated from any responsibility in that regard . . . the end of all anticipatory psychoses, all panic, all remorse" (*IE,* p. 121).

To be sure, the danger to which Baudrillard points is significant: the manufacture of images and synthetic memories. Baudrillard's alternative is to treat history as poetry, to envision it in terms of "a poetic reversibility of events" rather than as a linear retracing of them. For him, history like poetic language moves in tropes, loops, and swirls rather than in linear fashion. The logic of cause and effect is an artificial imposition upon that which merely happens. There is only a swarming of effects without causes. It is not only language but the *res gestae* of history, "the *Witze* of events," that are themselves ironic and perverse.

It is not difficult to detect in Baudrillard's view Nietzsche's claim that his age suffers from a hypertrophied sense of history that devitalizes and debases: "Excess of history has attacked life's plastic powers." This lifelessness is to be remedied by the *pharmakon* of the "unhistorical," the art and power of forgetting, and the "suprahistorical," that which bestows upon becoming some sense of the eternal. Disburdening humankind of history, Nietzsche contends, may produce a culture that is continuous with nature, "culture as

6. Suzanne Hélein Koss, *"Image of the Hyperreal."* Courtesy of the photographer.

a new and improved physis, without inner and outer, without dissimulation and convention, culture as a unanimity of life, thought, appearance and will." To rid oneself of history is to attain to a truthfulness that is in conformity with life itself.[56]

Does not this view of history reflect Nietzsche's *amor fati,* the Dionysian yes-saying "to the world as it is, without subtraction, exception, or selection" (*WP* 1041, p. 536), and does it not also necessitate the affirmation of the century's slaughters, its development of weapons of unprecedented destructive power? Once Nietzsche's aestheticized view of nature is taken for granted, this conclusion appears to be inevitable. What guides Nietzsche's vision is Nature in a state of nature, red in tooth and claw, such that, in the war of all against all, the forces of life appear as aestheticized manifestations of power. The lion's rending of the zebra is homologous with the victories of the Homeric hero. Disease lies beyond the horizon of a war-like nature, is non-natural, enters into it as a plot by nature, as it were, to destroy the beauty and elegance of its violence just as plebeian values are the result of connivance by the priestly castes in history. For Nietzsche the struggle against death is a battle against all of its tropes, sleep and disease (*WP* 231, p. 134). For Nietzsche, the standard of health remains "the efflorescence of the body," how much sickness it can overcome (*WP* 1013, p. 523). Yet Nietzsche's own view of perspectivism should have warned him that disease in the concrete biological sense is a mighty force of nature with respect to human beings, perhaps its highest power in that it recurs in ever new and more potent guises. *The heterological historian can reply to Nietzsche that the diseased body is the destitution of alterity written upon the face of nature, that de-signs its aesthetic surface.*

It can be argued against Baudrillard (as against Debord) that, if the hyperreal is pandemic, there can be no critical vantage point, for example, the "reality" of the poor, from which one can attack the culture of information. The ineluctable nostalgia for the referent or lost object cannot create its object in a world of the hyperreal. Yet Baudrillard does not rule out the possibility of eluding the information culture. Through poetization and irony, language becomes the means for escaping the penitential view of history. He proposes a gesture of reflexivity that circumvents any genuine mourning in a century that, he claims, does nothing but mourn. Would not Baudrillard's linguistic pyrotechnics, "anagrams, acrostics, spoonerisms, rhyme, strophe and catastrophe," not bend back upon themselves to mock the victims just as the culture of simulation does? Is there not a built-in cynicism in the amphiboly of tropic language such that it always already unsays what it says, so that it would replicate the gesture of simulation itself undoing simulation much as simulation has supplanted the real?

Consider the implementation of Baudrillard's recommendation that filmic (or theatrical) catachresis, in which the use of a once powerful political language now seen as defanged and harmless, may backfire by reintroducing what is intended as mockery. The *verbum ipsissimum* of the victimizers may be played as farce. Does such farce not debase the absence of speech-acts, the wordlessness of the victims? What is to be made, for example, of the Berliner Ensemble's production of *The Resistible Rise of Arturo Ui*, Berthold Brecht's allegory about the rise of the Third Reich, the last play directed by the brilliant and celebrated Heiner Müller in the Brecht Theater in Berlin? Each performance was preceded and followed by an actor's reading of Hitler's speeches from the theater's outdoor balcony and amplified to carry a considerable distance. Farce, according to the director. The image of Hitler, the little man with a moustache, is the persona created once and for all in Chaplin's film, *The Great Dictator,* he tells a group assembled to discuss the play.[57] During the play's run, the casual stroller (like myself) on the Friedrichstrasse, one of a number of as yet ungentrified streets on which the graffiti war between neo-Nazi and assorted other street gangs was conducted, could not help being struck by the ambience in which these words rang out. Could Hitler's speeches be viewed as farce? But can farce not regain the perlocutionary force of political speech and turn into instruction, speech-acts into directives for political action?[58]

THE FRENCH REVOLUTION IN NARRATIVE AND FILM

The French historian, Jules Michelet, brought to the reading of history the interpretive principles of Giambattista Vico's *New Science* and, from this perspective, conveyed the life of the Middle Ages and the Renaissance to his mid-nineteenth-century contemporaries. Yet it is not for these writings that he is principally remembered but rather for having delivered to the people of France—*le peuple* is in fact a coinage that he infused with meaning for a post-revolutionary generation—a vision of what he believed to be the most important event in history, the French Revolution.

In a remarkable series of inversions, Michelet's historical narrative, insofar as it succeeds in this endeavor, can be seen today to render the vast pageantry of Revolution in cinematic images premonitory of the moving images characteristic of film. By contrast, Andrzej Wajda's film, *Danton,* stakes itself on conveying events with something of the dispassionate reserve generally characteristic of the professional historical narrative. It is this slip-page within each genre that brings to the fore the graphematic transposabil-ity that is characteristic of the work of the historian in the culture of the spectacle: film re-signed as narrative and narrative de-signed as film. It is filmmaker Abel Gance who in 1927 saw the *graphein* in the image when he compared film to hieroglyphic writing and asserted that the eye had not yet adjusted to it.[59] It is this fluidity that requires exploration.

Michelet's voluminous study was intended to establish a certain identity, that of France, the Revolution, and the people who through it are brought to reflective awareness of themselves as a confraternity and a nation. "In the eyes of Europe, let it be known, France will have but one inexpiable name, which is her true name in eternity: the Revolution."[60] Simon Schama de-scribes the power of Michelet's account written after the Revolution's origi-nal fervor had been dissipated:

> It was the feat of the first generation of Romantic historians to celebrate the Revolution by lighting bonfires in their prose. Even as the elephant [a plaster cast symbolizing remembrance that stood on the Place de la Bastille] was slowly turning to dust and rubble, Jules Michelet's triumphal narrative made of the Revolution, a kind of spectacular performance, at once scripture, drama and invocation.[61]

Numerous meanings attach to the Revolution for Michelet: that of a heuristic principle that unites a multiplicity of events, that of an ideal or an eternal essence awaiting concrete embodiment in the France of 1789, and that of a re-naturalization of man. But none of these meanings suggest the cataclysmic power akin to a force of nature that Michelet attributes to the Revolution. Like Kant's account of the dynamical sublime as the formless in nature, which may be grasped in a state of excitation and which neverthe-less yields judgments that are universally valid and disinterested, so too the wild Revolution is the object of affirmative judgments that confirm the principles in whose name it was fought. Nature and the Revolution in their formlessness and might speak a common language. Thus, after one of his mountain walks, Michelet reflects: "What were then the subterranean revo-lutions of the earth . . . for that mass, disturbing mountains . . . to burst forth to the surface? What convulsions, what agony forced from the entrails of the globe that prodigious groan."[62]

Despite his indebtedness to Vico's claim that "memory is the same as imagination,"[63] and oblivious to his own hyperbolic style, Michelet insists that he is an analytic historian. Nettled by Taine's charge that his histories derive from imagination, Michelet writes: "I have made every effort to give history a serious and positive basis. . . . Yet everywhere people have written I was *a historian of a fortunate imagination.*"[64] Michelet's insistence on the inclusion of the historian in his narrative is not intended to show that history is a fiction based on subjective bias but rather that subjective purposivness belongs intrinsically to analytic history: "Of what is history made, if not of the self? What does history refer to, recount, if not the self [translation mine]?"[65] The centrality of the self is contingent upon Michelet's belief that knowledge emanates from the subject. Michelet discovers in Leibniz the dynamism common to nature and history and in Vico the universality that inheres in historical forces in the form of the self. Thus he says of Leibniz:

> [He] is sublime when, denuding being of every quality, reducing it to the simplest, the most abstract, the smallest, to the ultimate single individual or monad, he finds not the empty quiddity of the scholastics, but real living activity and reconstructs the whole world with atoms of will. The power of active life is such that it will envelop the world of nature and the world of history. (Translation mine)[66]

For both Leibniz and Vico, the subject is the source of knowledge. In a passage that could have been cited profitably by Heidegger as attesting modern philosophy's turn to the subject, Michelet proclaims: "Heroism of modern times: on what does it rest? The self. Descartes: *I think, therefore I am* (individually). Leibniz: *I cause, therefore I am* (individually). Vico: *I cause therefore I am* (as humanity), that is to say that not only my individuality but my generality is caused by me [translation mine, emphasis in original]."[67]

∞

Just as the camera invisibly infiltrates the images it records, Michelet installs himself inside his narrative as its specular intelligence and silent witness. Consider the comment of Andrzej Wajda, director of *Danton,* to whose work I shall turn shortly: "God blessed the film director with two eyes: one to watch the camera and one to take in everything going on around him" (*DV,* p. 76). Yet even if the self is imbricated in Michelet's history, that history is not autobiographical in any straightforward sense nor does the narrative voice replicate that of the realistic novel that Michelet derogated. An elaboration of how things fall out by sheer chance, the novel contrasts with history which recounts what affects collective interest and focuses upon "that difficult preparation that produces events."[68]

Who then is the self of the historian? For Michelet the historian is one who enters into a compact with the dead such that life is restored to them,

but, more important, the historian of the French Revolution offers reparation as one who has not been a contemporary of the dead. He brings the
living and the dead together in a single confraternity: "Thus is constituted
a family, a city shared by the living and the dead."[69] The self of the historian
is the composite of speech-acts that he creates, truer than the words of the
silent witnesses could ever have been had they been spoken, for they are
ignorant of the meaning of their deeds. The addressees of historical writing
are not only the present and future generations of readers but the dead
themselves who "must have an Oedipus . . . who will teach them what their
words, their acts, meant, which they did not understand."[70]

It may be recalled that Kant had already thought of the French Revolution in a somewhat similar manner, "as an event that would serve as a sign
[*signum, demonstrativum, prognostikon*]" (*OH,* p. 173)[71] that would signify
atemporally and that would occur within the framework of the history of
states to remind those who came later of its glories. Kant recognized that
the event unrolls in scene after scene for those who watch, that its very
purpose is bound up with its being observed. The sign that bodies forth
the Revolution's meaning is to be found in the silent spectators who place
themselves at risk by taking sides in disinterested sympathy—for Kant this
not an oxymoron—for one faction or another. What is read as a sign is not
the Bastille or the work of the guillotine in eliminating the monarchy but
rather the spirit of France in the first heady year of the Revolution, the
unity of the nation in which distinctions of wealth, gender, and class fade
away. For Michelet the living symbol of this spirit was the Festival of Unity,
on August 10, 1790, a mobile pageant orchestrated by the painter Jacques-
Louis David. Its most spectacular moment occurred when the symbols of
monarchy were being burned before the statue of Liberty—which had been
erected on the spot where once the bronze likeness of Louis XV had stood.
As the flames rose, 3000 white doves were released symbolizing "Christian
peace and republican freedom."[72] It is not difficult to read this event as the
prototype not only for happenings in France in 1968, but also (indirectly)
for such divergent occasions as the one that gave birth to the Woodstock
nation in 1968, the Million Man march in Washington, DC, in 1995, and
Jean-Claude and Christo's wrapping of the Reichstag in Berlin in 1995. To
exist as a historical spectacle in the postmodern age is to exist before a specular eye, that of the visual media.

Michelet's history trades upon cultural motifs that arise before the eye
in familiar guise. Like the cartoon that underlies a Raphael painting, themes
of New Testament narrative, crucifixion, resurrection, and apocalypse can
be discerned beneath events of the Revolution. "Christianity and the Revo-

lution are like salient and reentering angles, symmetrically opposed if not hostile," Michelet declares.[73] Thus the weary trek of Robespierre to the guillotine becomes an inversion of the crucifixion scene. Michelet describes what for him is the fickle and witless joy of the mob as they watched the condemned strapped to their carts on the way to the guillotine winding their way through Paris, which in its revolutionary fervor had become the new Jerusalem. Thus Michelet:

> Robespierre, had drunk with wormwood all that the world contains. At last he reached the gateway, the Place de la Revolution. He mounted the steps of the scaffold with a steady tread. . . . France will never be consoled for such a hope . . . he alone would have been strong enough to make the sword tremble before the law.[74]

It is Robespierre rather than the more moderate Danton who, for Michelet, lays claim to the soul of the Revolution, yet Michelet conveys the pathos of Danton's end in which he discerns the beginning of the end of the spectacle whose likeness would now live only through the historian. Later historians have found the fall of Danton and Camille Desmoulins extremely difficult to interpret and the indictment against them and the revolutionaries condemned with them unconvincing in contrast to Danton's compelling courtroom arguments. With the downfall of Danton and Desmoulin, Michelet sees the beginning of the end of the Revolution, the slide into the monarchist reaction. But it is the spectacle of the tribunal, the "last" act in a drama that cannot be brought to closure that remains one of the driving forces of his specular history. The highpoint of this drama turns on their testimony. Michelet writes:

> "Your name? your age? your address?—I am Danton; I am thirty-five years old. Tomorrow my address will be nothingness; my name will remain in the pantheon of history."
> "And I, Camille Desmoulins; thirty three years old, the age of the sans-culotte Jesus." (Translation mine)[75]

Danton's composure before his execution is legendary as is his final remark: "Don't forget to show my head to the people. It is well worth the trouble."[76]

The spectacle of Revolution that unfolds before Andrzej Wajda has expanded "far beyond the true name of France" (as Michelet would have it), exceeding even Michelet's wildest dreams. The nineteenth-century's miniature imitations of the Revolution are succeeded by the twentieth-century's IMAX versions of the Russian and Chinese Revolutions. For a Polish filmmmaker who worked after Jaruzelski's imposition of martial law in 1981, all of these events cannot but have circulated within the discursive space of the film. Must there not have been a reading back into Girondins and Montagnards, the world of Mensheviks and Bolsheviks, Mao's revolutionaries and Chiang Kai Shek's nationalists? Would it have been possible for the show trials in Moscow of the 1930s and the Slansky trials in Czechoslovakia in the 1950s not to have spilled over into Wajda's filming of the trial of Danton? Stanislawa Przybyszewska's 1931 drama that Wajda had already staged three times before took on new contours in the film of 1982.[77]

For Wajda as for Michelet, the specular character of the Revolution is condensed in the term *le peuple,* which is as much a rule of formation through which the events of the Revolution are interpreted as it is a subject of history. It is paradoxically Michelet, rather than Wajda, whose written history captures the purely specular character of the Revolution as panorama with its descriptions of crowds and festivals. Wajda, on the other hand, limits his use of crowd scenes, preferring to elicit them through condensations of word and image. Thus Wajda writes: "The very process of telling the story over and over forces me to eliminate unnecessary details. I emphasize what seems to me essential" (*DV,* p. 12). For him, *le peuple* has turned into a sign, which is evoked re-memoratively by both Robespierre and Danton to bring back the scenes of origin when their alliance was cemented, precisely because their actions reflected the will of *le peuple.* Thus Wajda's Robespierre remarks to Danton: *"Au fond nos convictions sont le même."*

What cannot be forgotten in filmic reconstruction is the de-signing of the dead others and their re-signing, not principally through narrative but through visual icons in the persons of the actors who substitute their own appearances, speech-acts, and gestures for those of the dead. Thus Wajda is inspired to make his film when, after seeing Gerard Depardieu play Danton on stage, he "realizes [he] had just seen Danton in the flesh" (*DV,* p. 32). If narrative cannot deliver its referent, how can the idols created by the culture of the spectacle produce credulity? Yet it is the simulacrum as image that persuades when recounted events fail to do so. Thus the dramatized scenes of the Nazi work camp in the Steven J. Spielberg film, *Schindler's List,* produces belief that may not attach to reports from contemporary eyewitnesses, in that the power of the image silences critique whereas the credibility of witnesses is challenged by a general cultural cynicism. When criticized for the historical inaccuracy of his films *JFK* and *Nixon,* filmmaker Oliver Stone does not plead artistic license but claims instead:

> The work of the historian involves great gulps of imagination and speculation, the resurrection of dialogues that frequently were never recorded. I am

not trying to denigrate the work of the historian but rather to say that the good historian must know how elusive this thing is referred to all too cavalierly by journalists as the truth, the truth, the truth.[78]

Yet it might be asked: At what point do the dramatized fictions intended to harness film in the interest of speaking for the dead become distortions rather than what I earlier referred to as *ficciones*? Can the technique of unsaying call attention within film itself to this danger?

In Wajda's *Danton,* a number of parodic repetitions at the film's beginning and end suggest the Revolution's move from moderation to extremism through a number of visual binarisms that unsay one another. At the outset, the people await the distribution of bread until at last a loaf is thrown into a basket held aloft by someone in the crowd. At the end of the film, the heads of the guillotined are similarly cradled in baskets of straw before the assembled crowd. Near the start of the film, a small nude boy standing in his bath tries unsuccessfully to recite the "Declaration of the Rights of Man" in order to ingratiate his family with Robespierre, who now resides in his home. Failing, the child is slapped by his sister. Near the end of the film, the boy's performance is nearly flawless as he recites the same Declaration to a Robespierre ill and stretched out on his bed. There are other less marked internal repetitions: a white veil is pulled over the face of the sick Robespierre, and a black curtain that veils the empty guillotine replicates this gesture.

There are also striking moments of anachronism in the interest of filmic catachresis. Those arresting Danton claim to be merely "following orders." After the conviction of the moderates, someone remarks to Robespierre who concedes he is unwell, "You're feeling ill just when you're entering history?"

Yet it is to painting as the art of image that Wajda appeals in the making of Danton, specifically to David's painting of the death of Marat, the same David who created the "happenings" of the Festival of Unity that so struck Michelet. In the famous painting, the dying Marat lies in his bathtub, the murderer's knife having dropped to the floor, in a posture that would lead one to interpret the painting's orientation as horizontal. Yet what strikes Wajda is that the principle of composition is vertical for reasons that he does not comprehend asserting merely that its verticality is both "arbitrary and indispensable" to the creation of the image (*DV,* p. 97) (fig. 7).

For Wajda the soul of film is image, or rather "that impalpable something between image and sound" (*DV,* p. 121). Recall that, in Levinas's philosophy, images occupy the place of objects as though the represented object died and were as disincarnated in its own reflection. For Wajda, a director who has brooded about the techniques of filmmaking, a key ques-

7. Jacques David, *Marat Assassinated*. Royal Museum of Fine Arts, Brussels.

tion remains the tension between a construal of the function of film as narrative and therefore discursive history and the manner in which the medium concretizes narrative. Thus Wajda asserts:

> Some directors learn their shooting scripts by heart. They are wrong. The shooting script is useful in indicating the general direction a film will take, but it should not be thought of as a four-lane highway. Otherwise you're leaving yourself no margin for the unexpected: those sudden possibilities that occur . . . because of . . . obstacles that arise on the spot that have to be dealt with. . . . There is no longer any map. (*DV,* p. 28)

There is no stable original script, no territory of which a map can be drawn.

Film time for Wajda can be described both diachronically and synchronically. Its diachronicity consists in the forward movement of its narrative, its synchronicity in the use of location for bringing together disparate narrative fragments. Although Wajda does not use flashbacks, he asserts that they do not interrupt diachronicity but rather constitute multiple diachronic narratives. Similarly, "All scenes filmed at the same location will be filmed together," Wajda writes (*DV,* p. 46). The production schedule for a film as he describes it resembles the diagramming of a structuralist analysis of a myth: each location functions as an archetype and all shots for that location are entered under that heading as mythemes. Space is similarly disseminated in that numerous takes assure that a scene is grasped not as a single shot but through its various fragments. In sum, "In place of the beautiful stately images of an earlier era, we have today a world that is fragmented and disintegrated, which in itself creates something dynamic and subjective," a situation made possible by technological innovations (*DV,* p. 72).

Although Wajda largely rejects television as a medium for his work—television camera movement and the possibility of erasure in video photography render creation too facile—he concedes that it has initiated a new form of specular culture. He describes an abandoned studio after the French left Algeria which seemed disconnected from events until someone activated the cameras and the demonstrators who entered the studio saw themselves on screen (*DV,* p. 30). If only, Wajda muses, television had existed at the time of the French Revolution—audiences in 1789 might have been able to see on screen the storming of the Bastille. . . . But there was no photographer present" (*DV,* p. 30).

IMAGES AND INFORMATION

It has been claimed that the age of images has come to an end, that the information revolution has reduced images to codes with the genetic code as the prototype of coding generally. The mode of rationality described in Pascal's account of *l'esprit de géométrie* and later probed in Heidegger's excoriation of the ontology of calculation that results in the production of things as standing reserve has conquered. According to Baudrillard, "We are witnessing the end of perspective and panoptic space (which remains a moral hypothesis bound up with every classical analysis of the 'objective' essence of power) and hence the very abolition of power" (*Sim,* p. 54). Instead, language is reduced to binary formulations "so that it can circulate not, any longer, in our memories, but in the luminous, electronic memory of the computers" (*Sim,* p. 2).

What is even more critical for Baudrillard is that the triumph of the information culture renders history inoperative. Because history requires real events, the transformation of the real into the hyperreal, the virtualization of reality, volatalizes the *res gestae* thereby terminating the very possibility of history. Yet history does not come to an end in that an ending still presupposes the linearity of historical time governed by the notion of an end time, an apocalypse and its fulfillment. Instead modernity's speeding up of all aspects of existence has "propelled us to 'escape velocity,' with the result that we have flown free of the referential sphere of the real and of history" (*IE,* p. 1). Baudrillard's cosmological trope ("humanity's 'big bang'") is based upon the view of modern physics that the universe is now expanding but that it will ultimately contract. It can be argued that, for Baudrillard, history collapses into the information culture (somehow) miming the physicist's model of a singularity, "a region of spacetime where spacetime curvature becomes so strong that the general relativistic laws break down and the laws of quantum gravity take over."[79] Although he does not actually refer to singularities, to interpret them in this way plausibly extends Baudrillard's "big bang" metaphor. What is normative for the historian, both time as experienced and chronometric time breaks down as a result of the "curvature," as it were, of the accelerating production of images such that images fly off without anchorage. Baudrillard argues further that marginalized cultures that have not entered history will have an opposite effect acting as dense bodies, inertial forces that may slow down this process.

In sum, Baudrillard's claims as they bear upon the work of the historian are these: the culture of images has been replaced by the information culture; temporal acceleration, the result of technological advance, has altered our relation to the referent so that the referent can no longer be linked to the real. Reality has become virtual; the voiceless, those who have no history, neutralize history as an inert absorptive mass, decelerating time.

Consider first the decoupling of image and information. To be sure, what makes the transmission of information possible is the conversion of a signal into numerical atomic constituents or bits, each bit having, for practical purposes, the numerical value of 1 or 0. Rather than encoding information analogically, in which case there is some resemblance between code and the phenomenon encoded, information has been digitized, breaking with any physically discernible relation between object and percept. "A bit, has no color, size or weight, and it can travel at the speed of light."[80] Digitization's advantage is that it achieves high levels of data compression thereby increasing the amount of data that can be transmitted. With the increased bandwidth or "number of bits that can be moved through a given circuit in a second" of fiber optic (glass or plastic) cable, the transmission of information is expected to expand even further.[81]

Consider next virtual reality (VR). As currently understood the virtual is not the replication of coded information but the reproduction of actual experience. It requires software programmed to create what is seen and to respond to new information as well as to instruments for transmission of this information as sensory input. Headphones adjusted to locate the direction of sound convey auditory stimuli. Visual simulation is achieved through the use of goggles whose lenses are adjusted to a computer display for each eye. Movements of the head are tracked by a sensor that adjusts what is seen in conformity with those movements so that the computer can synthesize the visual field. It has been theorized that bodysuits with sensors could replicate tactile sensations.[82] Experience becomes ever more sedentary as Paul Virilio observes: "From now on everything will happen without our even moving, without our even having to set out."[83] Although the virtualization of the real is parasitic upon the transposition of the visual into information, the illusion of reality is contingent upon replicating not only the body's visual and auditory capacities but also its tactile and kinesthetic experiences. The kinestheses, body movements, determine the horizon of perception and have not, as such, been regarded as constituting a sense. Tactility, in the tradition of early empiricism, has been viewed as the least distorted of the senses. Unlike sight, which alters size in inverse proportion to distance, the information provided by touch remains constant. What is more, there is a chiasmatic or crossover effect of touching and touched when, for example, one hand touches the other. The instruments thus far available in the virtualization of reality have succeeded in replicating visual and auditory experiences and some of those of the kinestheses by manipulating the visual field, but not those of tactility.

Virtualization as achieved through recent technological innovation does not yet reflect a paradigm shift in that it is fissured by the experienced presence of instrumentation that intrudes between simulation and subject. Instead, there is a more radical overcoming of the scission of the "there" than that experienced in television watching. The television viewer remains in a venue other than the one of the scene being observed and at the same time is there where the camera is. But VR is not simply a phenomenon of bilocation; instead the hyperreal is an elsewhere that shifts in conformity with one's actions which, in turn, are determined by the parameters of software programming and instrumentation. The effect of this technology is not to destroy bilocation but rather to virtualize the "actual" spatio-temporal locale of the viewer so that there is no stationary point of reference. Science fiction films such as *Blade Runner* and futuristic novels such as W. R. Gibson's *Neuromancer* envisage programming that would overcome this doubleness by becoming part of an individual's neurophysiological processes. Although such programming is highly unlikely, new technologies reflect an effort to simulate these simulations so that there would be no fissure between simulation and the real, no "there" other than the spatio-temporal coordinates of virtual reality. A world of pandemic simulation is anticipated in Descartes's account of the evil genius who deploys his power to create a world in which even the most solid truths give way to illusion.

What is missing in Baudrillard's assessment is the important sense in which "hard copy" as it were—the picture, the televised image, the computer simulation, the auditory image—are generally the *raison d'être* of the shipping of information. "Digitizing a signal is to take samples of it, which if closely spaced, can be used to play back a seemingly perfect replica."[84] What is more, the interface, the point of interaction between user and computer, relies increasingly upon images, upon iconic or graphical rather than character-based commands. George Lucas who created the computer technology for the film *Star Wars* sums up the purpose of simulation in the context of entertainment: "'The idea is not creating the perfect environment. It's creating the illusion of one.'"[85]

Genealogical analysis may help bring to the fore the provenance of digitization. The pre-Socratic philosophers of a physicalist bent distinguish what the world is made of as opposed to the way in which it appears, what it is in itself as opposed to the way it seems to the observer. Water, air, the four elements and atoms were proposed as the ultimate constituents of that which is. With Pythagoras, there is a radical paradigm shift: no longer is the world made up of one of its constituents targeted as an underlying substance that becomes a bearer of the qualities that appear to us, nor is it made of pulverized matter, atoms. Instead the link between what is and what is seen is broken. Pythagoras claims that the world is made of numbers, unchanging, immaterial, and eternal. The being of number becomes a speculative issue for subsequent Greek thought: Plato and Aristotle ponder the question of whether there can be a form for numbers or whether numbers are not already forms. With the radical transformation of mathematics from the arithmetic and geometry of the Greeks to algebra and calculus and later to more nuanced mathematical operations and with the mathematization of physical laws by modern science, it would appear that the Pythagorean view has been resurrected. In fact, the claims for mathematics by modern science remain more modest: mathematical expressions are descriptive of physical processes and not their underlying constituents.

Yet Baudrillard is right to notice a shift from the understanding of the relation of truth and being prior to the information culture and the sea change that follows in its wake. Belief presupposes a relation (however epistemically weak) between subject and object. Credibility has, in the contemporary world, supplanted belief and is a property of the object rather than that of the subject. For Baudrillard, belief is the willed adhesion to religious ideas, a holding fast to notions which were previously self-evident—God, immortality, resurrection. Because such faith consists of assertions that are unsupported by argument, they are vulnerable to philosophical critique (*IE,* p. 93). What is significant in this claim is not its manifesting of a breach between truth as self-evidence and belief as an assertion of the subject such that truth now resides in the subject, a point already elaborately developed by Heidegger. It is rather that, in the information culture, there has been a radical shift to the object. But the object, as we have seen, has been volatilized into the image which in turn is transposable into information. Credibility, the new epistemic claim of the information culture, is now applied to the relation between the image/object and the code.

What is more, with the information culture, "real" time is not the temporality of event sequences but of televised or computer-generated images. History has given way to news. On the one hand, history can no longer be articulated as straightforward narrative in conformity with time's arrow, its linear forward movement. On the other, the depiction of long-term trends, of the enduring geophysical terrain which provides a backdrop for recurrent tendencies envisaged by Braudel and the *annaliste* historians as the subject of history has given way to what they most feared, the flotsam and jetsam of events as the theme of historical inquiry. Now images of horror as reflected in news footage have become a specular chronicle and history an optics, history according to CNN.

Earlier I argued that the visual historian may station herself between the demands of alterity and those of the culture of visual imagery, a process that acquires added complexity when image is coded as information. Even if a particular technology does not demand such encoding, film, for example, the *potential* transposition of image into code is presupposed by the new episteme of the object. The culture of images reaches a height of abstraction in which everything can be translated into the binarism of the information code, 1 and 0. At the same time, *conceptual* abstractions and dominant cultural metaphors such as the idea of negation have reached an extreme point of realization in atomic, chemical, and biological weaponry. The idea of immortality has been "actualized" in the genetic code which can replicate itself and the life forms it generates indefinitely. Both extreme abstraction and total actualization reflect the telos of the information culture: the effort to reduce uncertainty to near zero. As we saw in Chapter 1, the critique of representation, as understood in both the analytic and continental philosophical traditions, gives rise to skepticism that allows at most for tentative and pragmatic epistemologies. The counter-movement reflected in the information culture arises not as a conscious response to the erosion of certitude but as the result of an entirely different set of social and economic forces that set in motion the need for data. Nevertheless, the new epistemology is best expressed in the definition of information as stated by Claude Shannon, the founder of information theory: "[I]nformation is the reduction of uncertainty,"[86] a view that cannot but be perceived as a throwback to modernity's quest for apodicticity. Such a reduction can be achieved, Shannon believes, by eliminating redundancy, an application it could be argued, of Ockham's razor: the elimination of unnecessary entities.

I suggested earlier that the heterological historian who works in the culture of images—this now includes the narrative historian—is stationed between the unstable image and the claims of an alterity that holds the image in check. The oscillation of the claims of alterity and image is the discursive space of the re-signing of history. But all this is not yet enough. Because the image is decontextualized, becomes a factoid, is shipped in code, still another demand is placed upon the historian, that of re-signing the image. She must give up strict temporal linearity in order to convey the coexistence of images through time and space in her discursive account or visual artifact by resorting to the flashback, the crosscutting to what is happening in a multiplicity of places. Yet simply excoriating the technologically generated image misses its potential for expanding experience as Benjamin had earlier noted in relation to the reproduction of artworks. To be sure, the historian cannot only remain subject to the hypnotic power of images but can use and escape them. She can arrest the flight of the deterritorialized panoply of images by fixing their milieu, by bringing to the fore the scission between a simulation produced by the culture of images and a territory. The historian's power remains deictic: she must be able to pursue the web of images to the point where she can stop them, where the etiolated image is halted by the density of a territory: "Stop. Here, here it is the church in Nayarabuye in which thousands of Tutsi were slain." The territory is also a graphematic surface, one replete with signs that will continue to be said and un-said but cannot be gain-said.

∞

The regimentation of images by concepts or by the stipulation of rules governing their production has given way in contemporary culture to an uncontrolled proliferation of images. This sea change is not the result of new technologies; rather technological developments have supervened upon a radical ontological shift. The real as materiality heretofore construed either as what is tangible or as its sign (in Marxist terms as commodity and money or its surrogates) is now envisaged as image, so that the distinction between reality and ideality dissolves. This complex of relationships is already pre-saged in Plato's account of the forms. On the received view, images are interpreted as copies of the ideal forms when, in fact, images precede the forms, and are either "good" or "bad" copies of objects, genuine images or simulacra. The ideal form or model is invoked post hoc in order to justify discarding the pretenders and thereby reclaiming the putatively real images.

The threat of the image can lead to an ineluctable nostalgia for the real. The desire to restore authenticity to the historian's retrieval of the event in word or image can be seen as resembling the effort to determine that a work of art is an "original," to recapture what has been called its aura. The histo-rian can try to station herself in the event she describes as if she were an eyewitness to it, just as a vetting of the historical chain of transmission of an artwork is thought to lead back to its origin and thus to establish its authen-ticity. Yet does not the dream of the recovery of the "aura" carry the danger of a reinscription of the sublime in its Fascist version?

Perhaps the promise of deixis can be fulfilled at least in recent times by way of the "true" shots of photography unaltered by technological means. Is not the photograph transparent toward its referent thereby providing the moment of pure deixis of the historian's dream? Yet the photographic image requires narrative orchestration if its meaning is to emerge and narratives differ in the claims they make about their referents. To be sure, but does the unretouched photograph not capture the there, the locale of the camera, and in so doing establish the limiting condition of historical narrative, for example, just *there* the ambiguous event occurred? Yet even in the absence of technological alteration the historian remains wary in that images, once isolable in the early days of photography are now inseparable from the plethora of images generated in a culture of media and information techno-logies and are distributed in formulaic ways.

Moreover, by constructing images, new technologies of simulation may preclude the relation of "being there" altogether. Such pure constructivism is already presaged in phenomenological accounts of "the gaze" and the "look" not as passive reception but as active interference in the world. By looking at the other, one reduces her alterity to that of an object. Contem-porary techniques of surveillance are socially prescribed extensions of the look: to watch is to dominate. The culture of images coerces the look of the viewer so that the world as constructed by images and as reflecting interests other than those of the beholder becomes *the* world.

The specular culture is largely not that of the static but of the moving image that replicates time's passing, the diachronicity of lived time. Film reproduces the modern subject's retention and anticipation of images in that each frame, in the interest of narrative coherence, clings to what immediately preceded it, makes it present. Thus film time acquires the authority attributed to perception. Not only does the film mime the logic of perceptual presence but it dissimulates in other ways. By hiding the technical instruments that engender its images the viewer is manipulated into believing what is seen. But, the heterological historian may inquire: "Is there not at work a culture of cynical reason, a distrust of the moving image precisely because it is a truism of present-day culture that images may be orchestrated as lies and does this knowledge not in some sense preclude naive credulity?"

What is more, the boundaries of genres have become fluid. If the film is defined as a sequence of moving images, the nineteenth-century French historian Michelet's portrayal of the French Revolution in fiery swiftly moving images of crowds, festivals, and executions is cinematic. By contrast, the more static images of Andrzej Wajda's depiction of the French Revolution in the film *Danton* is closer to traditional historical narrative. Michelet sees moving images as redressing the grievances of the dead others by putting words in their mouths, showing the dead what their words and acts actually meant, and trading on familiar religious imagery to heighten the readers' emotions.

The dilemma for the historian is not merely to acquire a more nuanced view of images, however, but to see whether it is possible to reclaim the image for ethics. Can the image, like the sublime, be so dis-figured that it might intrude into the non-space of ethics? For the heterological historian, the demand of alterity issues from the dead others, the multiple wounded and suffering bodies that form a society of bodies and, taken together, repudiate egoity. This past can never be recovered in face-to-face encounter but only as image. To be sure, the visual image disincarnates beings, becomes their reflection, but in so doing, the image opens a space beyond beings, unsays them (as the sublime transformed into the *il y a* was seen to unsay beings), and thus allows for the emergence of an ethical space of disclosure.

It has been argued that once the ontology of the image predominates, the real has come to an end and can have no moral claim upon us. Gestures of repentance designed to salvage the real are both futile and disingenuous and can only lead to fabricated memories. There is only that-which-happened, event upon event that can be poetized and ironized but not recreated. Yet the heterological historian can retort that ironization is recursive: by ironizing the culture of simulation, the culture that undoes history and memory, simulation is itself undone. The double gesture of irony returns simulation to the real, to a point where the flight of images can be arrested.

It has also been argued that the culture of images has been supplanted by the culture of information, that images along with ordinary language have become numbers. Yet if images become codes, codes are reconverted into images, pure abstractions into total visual realizations. To understand just how the *res gestae* came to be interpreted in this way, images of the past must first be seen as released from the individual cogito and later from the regimenting conditions of transcendental subjectivity to be replayed before a transpersonal subject, the Absolute of Hegelian philosophy, a process I shall now consider.

I found a weed
that had a
mirror in it
and that mirror
looked in at
a mirror in
me that
had a
weed in it.

W. Ammons
"Reflective"

WIRED IN THE ABSOLUTE:
HEGEL AND THE BEING OF APPEARANCE

History, the development of the Notion in time, necessitates the ascent and fall of peoples and civilizations. It is a spectacle of ephemera which arise, endure for an interval, decay, and give rise to new forms. It awaited only recent technological innovations to give concrete existence to Hegel's view of the backward glance of history as a parade of endless images. Hegel's history is an ocular display brought under rational control, with Spirit, the subject, creator, viewer, and object of this display. The *res gestae,* the stream of past events, has become a *historia rerum gestarum,* not as a discursive record but as a dazzling spectacle, premonitory of the culture of images. The rationality of Spirit so prized by Hegel cannot on his own terms transcend images in that they remain embedded in the Notion as its indispensable content. Nor can it persist as a panopticon, a fixed point at the end of history from which Spirit surveys all that belongs to it, for such a subject would merely replicate Spirit as the subject of feudalism that surveys all it owns. Instead, time continues to pass and Spirit opens out onto new perspectives. Thus the Notion has nothing to do with empty abstraction and everything with

114

the being-here of that which is not here, what we have come to call virtuality.

The boundary between being and seeming is blurred in the culture of images. In Karl Löwith's words:

> Hegel concludes the history of Spirit in old Europe. . . . in the sense of the *greatest fullness,* in which everything that has happened or has been thought up to now gets combined into unity; but he also completes this history in the sense of an eschatological end *[endgeschichtlichen Endes],* in which the history of spirit finally grasps itself. (Emphasis in original)[1]

Löwith's remark pinpoints two demons of Hegelianism, the unity of all preceding thought, the sublation of religion by the One-All of a self-reflective Absolute, and end time as presence.[2] The dissolution of this unity into spectacle and its reforming as a One-All must be explored as well as the implications of this dissolution for a view of time "after" (post/in the manner of) Hegel.

The drive to unity and the fissuring of this unity is replicated in the structure of Hegel's system as Heidegger shows. Reading-Heidegger-reading-Hegel brings to the fore the view that Hegel's philosophy is conceived as system from its inception. Hegel saw the *Phenomenology of Spirit,* the culmination of his work during the Jena years, as the first part of that system; its subtitle (later dropped) was the *System of Science: Part One, Science of the Experience of Consciousness.* Hegel next completed the *Logic* which became the first part of the *Encyclopedia* that would come to include the *Philosophy of Nature* and the *Philosophy of Spirit.* The *Phenomenology,* now seemingly demoted, is inserted as part of the latter work. On Heidegger's view, the *Encyclopedia* "presents the whole of [a] new system. It recognizes the *Phenomenology* . . . only as a segment of a segment of the third part."[3] Yet the *Phenomenology* remains for Heidegger the work that both drives and bifurcates the system. "[T]he *Phenomenology of Spirit* remains the work and the way that not only once but always prepares . . . the realm of expansion . . . for the encyclopedia-system. . . . [T]he *Phenomenology* is a foundational part for the system while being at the same time an affiliated component within the system" (*HPoS,* pp. 8–9).

The essential concern of Heidegger's Hegel is thus the key issue of the *Phenomenology,* the uniting of speculative theology (speculation about the being of the highest actuality) to ontology, a problem that receives its development before Hegel's Berlin period (1818–1831, the year of his death). Astonishingly, Heidegger passes over the work of these last thirteen years with an offhand remark: "Apart from his *Philosophy of Right* (1821) and a few book reviews, Hegel published nothing in his Berlin period that was of great significance for his philosophy" (*HPoS,* p. 5). Heidegger's refusal to attribute importance to Hegel's lectures on the philosophy of history is not likely to have been based either upon commonly cited worries about textual authenticity or the claim that they were merely "popular." Rather what seems to disturb Heidegger is that the concern with the Being of beings as the being of appearances dissolves into the appearances themselves, the concrete events of history. That Hegel thought otherwise is implied in his comment: "My lectures on the philosophy of history are giving me very much to do. . . . Yet it is a very interesting and pleasant occupation to have the peoples of the world pass in review before me."[4]

Because he is seen as espousing the view that events can be rationally deduced from the nature of Spirit, are pre-scribed in advance rather than de-scribed after they have occurred, contemporary historians have found little to admire in Hegelian historiography. It was, however, his intent to reconcile the working historian's view with that of philosophy whose aim it is to interpret contingent events from the standpoint of the rationality of the Notion and, in so doing, to resolve a fundamental aporia of his own thought. In a single breath, as it were, Hegel disclaims the a prioristic character of history's events—"our procedure must be pragmatic . . . events will always remain basic"[5]—while averring that "the sole aim of philosophy is to eliminate the contingent" (*RH,* p. 28). For Hegel the contradiction disappears once history is understood as intrinsic to the life of Spirit as a self-creating rational process, one that makes itself what it is: "a vast spectacle of events and actions in restless succession" (*RH,* p. 31). For Hegel, history is the work of reason expressed as an optics.

What does it mean to say "we must see with the eye of the concept" (*RH,* p. 30)? For Hegel such seeing means that not only are we to observe the events of history but that we must decode Spirit's program or, in his terms, fathom the cunning of reason. Hegel's well-known description of the types of historical writing may be viewed tropically as a depiction of the occular instruments whose progressive refinement provides an increasingly true, that is, rational, reflectively self-aware, picture of the historical object. The first type, original history, is a re-presentation of contemporary occurrences with no gap beween the consciousness displayed by the historical narrative and its object. Such histories generally take the form of annals written by those in power who reflect the spirit of the age in which they live, those who "see everything in its correct place" (*RH,* p. 15).

Reflective history, Hegel's second type, is panoptical, surveillant in that it provides an overview of a past object from the standpoint of the present.

Yet such histories often fall into anachronism, insipid moralizing or conceptually weak metahistorical analyses of history itself. The third type, the philosophical history of the world, is general without being abstract, the work of Spirit "eternally present to itself and for which there is no past" (*RH,* p. 24). Thus the projective and retrospective articulations of time are grasped synchronically by a timeless subject thereby situating history both inside and outside of time. For Hegel, the failure to grasp this typology is a sign of historical naiveté, a critical gesture replicated by contemporary specular thinkers, such as Debord and Baudrillard, who see a forgetting of the camera that is invisible to the viewer of film or television as creating a deceptive and spurious immediacy.

If historiographic typology provides the ocular instruments for viewing the *res gestae,* the ultimate purpose of this specularity is to grasp the intention of the process, the understanding of world history as the growth and development of human freedom. "[Spirit's] freedom does not consist in static being," Hegel says, "but in constant negation of all that threatens to destroy freedom" (*RH,* p. 48). Nor is Spirit free until it knows that it is free because freedom is just as much a matter of consciousness as of the absence of external coercion. True freedom is not, as Hegel will remark in his analysis of the French Revolution, freedom from all restraint—such freedom expresses itself as violence—but rather freedom from the arbitrariness of subjective will, from its particularity, so that the subjective will expresses the rationality of the universal will.

Because the historical process is governed by this inner *rational* necessity, the gap between the actual and the ideal is breached: "The actual world is as it ought to be" (*RH,* p. 66). This optimistic view is tempered by Hegel's well-known characterization of history as a slaughterbench, a process moved by the passions of individuals who embody the spirit of their times and who rise above conventional moral restraints to engage in war and other forms of bloodshed, thereby changing the course of history. Hegel appears oblivious to Rousseau's caveat:

> The man whose power sets him above humanity must himself be above all human weaknesses, or this excess of power will only sink him lower than his fellows, and lower than he would himself have been had he remained their equal. (*RSW,* p. 103)

The embodiment of Spirit's self-realization in history is the nation, and the scale upon which a nation's stage of development is measured is its progress in freedom by which Hegel means the pursuit of the rational ends intrinsic to the life of Spirit. It is in this context that Hegel puts forward his notorious evaluation of the nations of the world: those of the Orient know that One, the despot, is free, a freedom that "is mere arbitrariness, savagery and brutal passion" and thus mere license. The Greeks and Romans know that some but not all are free because they depended upon the institution of slavery to maintain their existence, thereby suppressing the freedom essential to human beings. It is only with Christianity and its realization in the Germanic nations, Hegel asserts, that freedom is truly realized (*RH*, p. 54).

Apart from the invidious hierarchy it establishes, it is obvious from this taxonomy that numerous peoples, sub-Saharan Africans, the peoples of the Pacific rim, the indigenous peoples of North, Central, and South America have been barred by Hegel from the theater of history. Far from ignoring them, Hegel both excludes and discusses them deducing their marginality from the double standpoint of natural existence which, for him, includes climate and geography on the one hand and subjective disposition on the other. With regard to climate, Hegel's meteorological determinism allots historical existence only to the peoples who reside in temperate zones, thereby exempting the inhabitants of tropical and arctic regions. Similarly, Hegel attributes causal efficacy to distance from and proximity to the sea as helping to determine the cultural characteristics of landlocked and maritime nations. Far from having vanished, this seemingly reductionist interpretation persists in the work of *annaliste* historians. Thus Fernand Braudel who resists idealist conceptions of history nevertheless remains Hegelian in ascribing importance to climate and terrain in determining the micropractices that make up the conditions of material life.[6]

More insidious is Hegel's account of the subjective dispositions, the *Volksgeister* of peoples barred from history, an exclusion more profound than that of previously historical peoples now consigned to the dustbin of history in that the latter have left marks upon Spirit. The term "primitive," a term whose lineage can be traced to the Greek construal of the barbarian and to the accounts of primal human nature in seventeenth-century state of nature theories (among other progenitors), embraces the traits Hegel attributes to those who are altogether excluded from history: social organization established through custom rather than law, simple technology, agrarian and herding economies.[7]

Although Hegel is sometimes critical of the treatment of colonized peoples by conquering Europeans, he nevertheless falls into a virulent biological as well as geographical determinism. It is inferior physique, he insists, that accounts for the surrender of the indigenous peoples of the Americas to European culture. Hegel reserves his most malignant criticism for sub-

Saharan Africa, characterizing its peoples as savage, lawless, and barbaric; accepting of slavery and tribal warfare; fetishistic; and fanatical (RH, pp. 173–190). For Africa, "history is out of the question," Hegel avers (RH, p. 176).

It is necessary to expose and analyze these comments which can only send shock waves through the contemporary reader. What ontological status is to be ascribed to those nations and peoples who are both Spirit and not-Spirit and whose appearing Hegel depicts in detail? Are they not from the standpoint of Hegelian ontology phantasms, images. simulacra who, as outside history, lack actuality? In this sense, does not the exclusion from the history of consciousness invert the real so that it becomes the hyperreal, a hyperreal that does not pass through the circuitry of consciousness but takes on the character it derives from its exteriority, that of an exotic or primitive object? In the contemporary culture of images, Hegel's legacy may be manifested as a staging of "the primitive," as a specular display, a commodity for anthropological investigation or tourist inspection.

That Hegel's account belongs to the chequered history of colonialism is patent. What is significant for Hegelian metaphysics in this history—in that very aspect of his thought that Heidegger dismisses as of little interest—is that precisely by extruding peoples and nations from the history of consciousness, something outside of the Absolute, a beyond of negation itself, an alterity that does not conform to the trajectory of Spirit's history puts the life of Spirit into question.

In what follows I shall, as in my discussion of Kant, focus first upon Hegel's interpretation of a specific issue; next, I shall question this interpretation from perspectives that lie both inside and outside the text; and finally I shall reply to the question.

THE SPECULAR ABSOLUTE: RELEASE FROM THE OBJECT

Hegel I: Nowhere is the specularity of Hegel's Absolute more perspicuously interpreted than in Heidegger's passage-by-passage gloss of the Introduction to Hegel's *Phenomenology of Spirit*. It is no accident that Heidegger gravitates toward the Introduction rather than the more frequently glossed Preface. The task of the Introduction is to alert us to Spirit's attempt to release or ab-solve itself from its thralldom to objects, to the detachment of knowledge from its relation to objects. It would seem then that knowledge would become hopelessly abstract. To the contrary, "this self-detachment of self-certainty from its relation to the object is its absolution," the only way in which the subject can see itself thereby transfiguring the naivete of its dependence on objects.[8] It is only through this movement that the Absolute arrives at its own truth. Thus Heidegger concludes: "The unity of *absolving* (detachment from the relation), *its completion* (the achievement of full detachment), and *absolution* (the freeing acquittal on the strength of full detachment) are what characterizes the absoluteness of the Absolute" (*HCE*, p. 39; emphasis in original).

The relation of "natural consciousness" to objects that is transcended in this movement of inversion is such that we see "what occurs behind the back of consciousness," the fact of appearing itself (*HCE*, p. 127). Natural consciousness is not linked exclusively to empiricism but, per contra, is inherent in all unreflexive knowing prior to its inversion (*HCE*, p. 62). Nor is it "the discard heap" of falsity and deception but rather a consciousness that is *unterwegs*, not-yet-true (*HCE*, p. 82). The itinerary of consciousness in its de-naturalization, in its production of new and truer objects, is named by Hegel experience *(Erfahrung)*. And experience is none other than "that which appears insofar as it appears" (*HCE*, p. 113).

Heidegger can be seen as importing Husserl's distinction between the natural attitude, the unquestioning apprehension of the world as real, and phenomenologically clarified knowledge, the turning to consciousness as itself an object of inquiry, into the account of natural consciousness and consciousness's turning in upon itself.[9] Although Hegel and Husserl differ radically with regard to their grasp of the character of the subject—for Hegel, Spirit is self-moving and suprapersonal, both subject and substance, whereas for Husserl the subject is an egology—for both "philosophy is the path of . . . presenting representation" (*HCE*, p. 58). If this is so, how far apart is Heidegger's description of Hegel's claim "[t]o appear by virtue of the radiance of that ray means: presence in the full brilliance of self-presenting representation" (*HCE*, p. 48) from Husserl's account of the reflexivity of knowledge:

> Only in cognition is [objectivity] truly given, evidently "seen." This evident seeing itself is truly cognition in the fullest sense. And the object is not a thing which is put into cognition as into a sack, as if cognition were a completely empty form. . . . But in givenness we see that the object is constituted in cognition.[10]

This view is corroborated by Kojève in his influential lectures on Hegel.[11] "The Hegelian method . . . is purely contemplative and descriptive, or better phenomenological in Husserl's sense of the term," he declares.[12] What is more, the ontic/ontological distinction as explicated in *Being and Time* is read back into Hegel's account of natural consciousness, for Heidegger, a consciousness which is always already implicated in an as yet unthought-out ontology (*HCE*, pp. 105–108).

Nowhere in Hegel's *Phenomenology* is the specularity uncovered by Heidegger's analysis of Hegel's Introduction more clearly revealed than in the depiction of the transition from revealed religion (itself the self-overcoming of the religions of nature and art) to philosophy. This stage in the life of Spirit is especially significant in that it is the final lap of Spirit's journey. The consciousness of revealed religion, still external to itself, appears to itself, becomes its own object, an in-itself for-itself, through the Notion. Hegel comments: "What in religion was *content* or a form for preserving an *other*, is here the *Self's* own act; the Notion requires the *content* to be the *Self's* own act (emphasis in original)."[13] Religion precedes science (*Wissenschaft*) in its self-manifestation, but only science brings it forth in its genuine appearing as self-knowledge. This sublation of revealed religion draws God into the dialectical process in which all contradictions are transcended, thereby achieving in its own way the death of God and the undermining of the finality of any concrete divine-human encounter. God is drawn into the vortex of philosophy, the last and final shape in which consciousness appears to itself as absolute appearance or appearance of the Absolute.

Yet if religion persists as the content of knowledge, the inseparability of that which is bodied forth in revelation and the reason that apprehends it are inseparable, and Christianity remains fissured by that which both is and is not sublated in Spirit's final phase. Derrida refers several times to this split in *Glas* and writes in a characteristic passage: "The Christian religion is already posited as absolute religion. Thus the cleavage stays in absolute religion; and it stays for all time and all the figures of Christianity."[14]

For Hegel of the *Phenomenology,* specularity permeates consciousness through and through. Not only are the shapes that pass by in the history of consciousness objects of sight but knowledge itself or science is specular. For Hegel, the binarism of appearance and reality later so crucial to Nietzsche's excoriation of representation melts into the distinction between the naive knowing of empty appearance and the knowing that is science, the apprehension of appearance as appearance. Unlike Nietzsche for whom the idea of appearance falls with the fall of reality, for Hegel the real is simply banished and "science in making its appearance is an appearance itself" (*HCE*, p. 48). By banishing the real and claiming that there is only appearance, the Hegelian inversion has virtualized reality. According to Heidegger, the Hegelian inversion of consciousness that allows phenomena to appear does not impose upon experience anything extrinsic to it. If presentation is intrinsic to experience and grounded in the inversion and, if the inversion as our contribution fulfills the relation of our nature to the Absolute, then we too are part of the appearing, part of "the parousia of the Absolute" (*HCE,* p. 130). Thus, on Hegelian grounds, we are forced to the startling conclusion that the being of appearance has swallowed up the divine and the human and has virtualized the real in an endless play of concept and image.

Question I: What strategies can the heterological historian invoke to circumvent the global character of virtualization, when virtualization is no longer the reproduction of experience but experience itself? Has not the specular absolute undermined even the information culture which depends upon the transposability of information and image to *reproduce* the real whereas absolute specularity as appearance allows for no gap between the virtual and what it reproduces?

Reply I: The Hegelian Absolute is an internally differentiated plenum, an ontological fullness in which negation is overcome. When appearance is absolutized it allows for nothing outside itself: there is simply no standpoint that transcends the One-All. The heterological historian appears to be doomed by the culture of the spectacle in that the fullness of presence that characterizes the Absolute precludes the void of the cataclysm as well as a standpoint that is extrinsic to the Absolute. An Absolute that could be transcended would simply signal its incompleteness and would be what Hegel calls the bad infinite, the repeated negation of the finite from which the Infinite cannot break free, a bug in the program that returns it repeatedly to its default setting. In short, if Hegelian phenomenology depicts the culture of the spectacle, is there any prospect for entering the discursive space of the cataclysm and for regaining the transcendence of a vantage point that is both inside and outside the specular Absolute?

Before this question can be addressed it is necessary to consider Hegel's distinction between the in-itself, what first appears as the object, and what that object is for-us, the being-for consciousness of the in-itself. Hegel (as cited by Heidegger) says: "A moment which is both *in-itself and for-us* is thereby introduced into the movement of consciousness, a moment which does not present itself for the consciousness engaged in the experience itself" (*HCE,* pp. 123–124). It is through this movement of awareness that a new shape of consciousness comes into being. There are, as it were, three subjects: that of the old object that is being sublated, the consciousness of the emergent object, and the for-us, for whom what emerges "exists at once as movement and becoming" (*HCE,* p. 124).

Who is this for-us, this specular "we" who looks on as the shapes of consciousness pass into one another? Is there in Heidegger's explication of the for-us an escape hatch for the heterological historian, one that does not posit either the subject's inwardization and a divine-human encounter in the manner of Kierkegaard, or that undermines the Absolute through a genealogical exhumation of its moral foundations in the manner of Nietzsche? When Heidegger asks in regard to Hegel, "Who is meant by 'we'? *[Wer sind die 'wir'],*" the response is, "We are those who in the inversion of natural consciousness, leave that consciousness to its own views but at the same time specifically keep the appearance of the phenomena in sight" (*HCE*, p. 126). This consciousness is not one before whose passive gaze the shapes of consciousness are unfurled but rather an active looking on, an inversion of consciousness that Hegel identifies as skepticism. While Hegel treats skepticism as dissolving a moment of knowledge into empty nothingness, Heidegger argues that in skepsis consciousness is able to grasp appearance itself. It is the reflexiveness of skepsis that is significant in that it enables us to look not at existents themselves but at the existents as appearances (*HCE*, p. 127). Skepticism is a metalevel strategy that considers the way in which representation works rather than being an expression of the represented.

What is crucial is that consciousness exists *as* the particular shape it takes on, whereas "skepsis takes hold of consciousness" (*HCE*, p. 66). Yet skepsis cannot be other than consciousness, but within consciousness it is that which transforms one shape into another, an inside that is outside and an outside that is inside. Heidegger calls to our attention that skepsis for Hegel is the power of seeing par excellence. "[It] renders the spirit for the first time competent to examine what truth is. For it brings about a state of despair about all of the so-called natural ideas, thoughts and opinions" (*HCE*, p. 55), ideas which obstruct Spirit's progress. Heidegger concludes that for Hegel "skepticism is the historicity of history," the process through which consciousness is transformed into absolute knowledge (*HCE*, p. 67).

It would seem that skepsis has the power to strike down commonsense beliefs in much the same world-negating way as the biblical text of *Koheleth (Ecclesiastes)* renders nugatory the value of the world by insisting that "all is vanity," a state Jean-Luc Marion calls caducity, that which is subject to fall.[15] But is skepticism overcome in the Hegelian system? Can skepticism ever be overcome? For Heidegger, the "we" that is the Hegelian subject "are those who skeptically pay specific heed to the Being of beings" (*HCE*, p. 149). Unlike other shapes in Spirit's history, skepsis cannot be transformed in that it is an undoing or unmaking. Thinking occurs between skepticism's negation of that which is posited and the undoing of skepticism itself.[16] But if that which puts everything into question is now *intrinsic* to the Absolute, the subject of skepticism *continues,* puts the One-All itself into question, renders it moot, caduce. Because the Absolute as pure appearance is internally differentiated and allows for the multiplicity of beings unified in the One-All along with the subject to be erased by skepticism, the appearances disappear. The result of this in-version is a re-version to existence without existents, anonymous being, an emptiness that apes nothingness, the *il y a*. This is the non-place that Blanchot's trope of anonymous murmuring that is not yet language and emanates from elsewhere renders compelling. In sum, skepsis has neutralized the appearances and, by rendering them null, has opened the space of the cataclysm from which the heterological historian works.

To understand the space exposed by skepsis, it is helpful to contrast natural catastrophe with the cataclysm, especially because they are often described in the same way. It is in fact Hegel who emphasized the distinction between events in nature as the negative of Spirit in contrast to the self-conscious events of history. Baudrillard, commenting on the ruins of Pompeii as the aftermath of a volcanic eruption discusses the psychological consequences of natural calamity: "This is the mental effect of catastrophe: stopping things before they come to an end, and holding them suspended in their apparition. . . . The last seismic movement is the pathetic repetition of the great original."[17] Despite his denial that monumentality and beauty determine the powerful impression made by these ruins, Baudrillard's descriptions of them speak otherwise. The depiction of Pompeii is written under the sign of Kant, of the majesty and awe of the dynamical sublime evoked by the traces of catastrophe. Were the volcano to erupt again, its power would dissipate, Baudrillard declares, and such an event would be parody.

Consider now Arthur Cohen's description of the cataclysmic annihilation of the Jews of Europe that he names the tremendum:

> The abyss consummated and torn out of the earth is now like the witness of
> a dead volcano, terrifying in its aspect but silent, monstrous in its gaping, raw
> in its entrails, visible reminder of fire and magma, but now quiet immovable
> presence. . . . We may climb to its rim to examine its forbidding ugliness . . .
> [and] preserve a scarifying moment when it was alive and active.[18]

The trope—volcanic ash, the earth as a maw that receives the dead— is virtually identical to that of Baudrillard yet it is unthinkable to envisage Auschwitz in the distant future as a ruin that could be aestheticized. As described by survivors, even the unintended effect of the superimposition of the beauty of a nature indifferent to history upon the world of the camps produces a profound and sadistic *Ironisierung*. The historian who positions herself "at the rim of the volcano" cannot treat cataclysm as natural catastrophe transformed by the patina of age but speaks or creates images from within the space of the cataclysm as the horizon of a historical thought that cannot, can never, be aestheticized. Lawrence L. Langer points out that the narrative conventions inherent in writing both aestheticize and moralize experience so that written memoirs of survivors differ markedly from oral testimony.[19]

If skepticism opens the way for cataclysmic speech and image making, it does not yet provide an account of how the historian can recover the *res gestae* such that she can station herself between the historical object and the demand of alterity. If, as I have argued, Hegel's Absolute is an Absolute of appearances, then the Hegelian inversion of the real has virtualized the reality of the appearances. In the world of virtuality, the *res gestae* and the *historia rerum gestarum* can no longer be marked off conceptually; all referentiality, whether conceived from the standpoint of realism or idealism, has disappeared, "characteristics" that taken together constitute the hallmark of the information culture.

Baudrillard's description of that culture can actually be construed as constituting a metaphenomenology of appearance that may provide an entering wedge for the grasp of alterity within virtuality. To be sure, Baudrillard denies the possibility of a subject that constitutes history and, a fortiori, of the historian as subject. The historian cannot evade the culture of appearances, but she may find that, by attending to the process of the de-ontologization of the real, an alterity is opened within virtuality itself. To see this, consider Baudrillard's de-historization of objects. From a commonsense standpoint, Baudrillard seems indifferent to the world's ills. Punctuated by incoherencies, his writing both mimics and mocks the "noise," the meaningless bits of code that infiltrate the new information systems that he describes. What is to be gleaned by the historian from his account, however, is that history has ceased to be real, and, if true, we cannot return to the point at which this change occurred because to do so would be to reinsert ourselves into the temporal structure that has dissolved. With this derealization, the *res gestae* of history which for Hegel have the being of appearances, disappear as history. "Perfect is the event . . . that assumes, and is able to stage its own mode of disappearance, thus acquiring the maximal energy of appearances," Baudrillard writes. A kind of historical entropy, the self-implosion of the energy of the appearances when history has lost its meaning, governs every event so that it "becomes a catastrophe, a pure event without consequences" (*FS,* p. 192).

This interpretation is dependent upon the notion that the real has become hyperreal, that appearance is not (as in Plato) a copy of the real but its duplication through a medium. "From medium to medium, the real is volatilized becoming an allegory of death [but also] reinforced through its own destruction" (*FS*, p. 145). The hyperreal is that which is always already reproduced in the wake of the death of the real. The object thus volatilized escapes systematization either in a system of exchange or in a nexus of utility, themselves notions that are parasitic upon a more primordial view of the object as sacred and expendable as expressed in cults of sacrifice (*FS*, pp. 119–124).[20] What is equally crucial is that in its escape the hyperreal object does not pass through the circuitry of the subject.

In the absence of the subject, we are left with a world of objects that possess a cunning of their own. Thus Baudrillard writes of the object:

> The metamorphoses, tactics and strategies of the object exceed the subject's understanding. The object is neither the subject's double nor his or her repression; neither the subject's fantasy nor hallucination; neither the subject's mirror nor reflection: but it has its own strategy. It withholds one of the rules of the game which is inaccessible to the subject, not because it is deeply mysterious, but because it is endlessly ironic. (*FS*, p. 198)

Baudrillard sees the *strategy* of the object, its cunning, as at one and the same time, its fate even if fate and strategy seem contradictory.

This triumph of the object that Baudrillard attributes to the globalization of communication may have quite another hidden genealogy, the clue to which can only be found in the cataclysm itself. I alluded earlier to Lawrence L. Langer's description of the gap between the rhetoric of the interviewers who try to elicit from concentration camp survivors evidence of both altruism and survival skills and that of the witnesses whose accounts speak otherwise. The survivor knows that she has been transformed; the cunning of her strategy is not that of planning but of fate. Thus the testimony of Eva K.:

> Interviewer: But you must be very strong and you must have had a will to have survived it. . . .
> Witness: I'm strong, *aber* [but] I never was doing anything really to live . . .
> Interviewer: To help yourself.
> Witness: My fate push me, you know, I not help myself.[21]

The pragmatic rules of everyday life of the autonomous rational subject do not apply in the concentration camp because there are no subjects in the

usual senses in which the term has been defined in Western thought. Chaim
E. testifies:

> We were not individuals, we were not human beings, we were just ro-
> bots. . . . It is hard to tell what a feeling that is. You think you are right, you
> know all the answers, and you try to find logic and things like that doesn't
> exist here at all. . . . So all the logic doesn't apply here.[22]

Chaim E. goes on to assert that even if the feeling of robotization can be
described, it cannot be evoked in its actuality in the hearer. Is this not what
Baudrillard means when he describes the Object as having "the passion of
indifference" as opposed to those of the subject which are "differential,
energetic, ethical and heroic."[23] This account appears to preclude widespread altruistic behavior in the camps; in actuality it highlights the complicity of strategy and fate and frees the victims of blame. This freeing is not
the result of litigation in Lyotard's sense of a differend, but prior to it by
virtue of the transformation that occurs in the cataclysm.

This fatalistic position enables Baudrillard to develop a phenomenology
of the object that inverts Hegel's plenum of objects. For Baudrillard, the
object is not that which is mastered, desired, or governed by the pleasure
principle but rather that which challenges. One can resist desire, but challenge is defined as "that to which one cannot avoid responding," a lure, the
entryway to an ecstasy that transcends meaning. Nothing could comport
less with the horror of the cataclysm than challenging the order of truth in
the interest of Nietzschean ecstasy or a synthetic eroticism of the hyperreal.
No-thing. Yet there is in this account of challenge a significant discursive
slippage which opens onto the Levinasian terrain of alterity. Because the
world is now interpreted from the standpoint of the object—in a virtual
world there are only objects—the other who is not a subject cannot be
another myself. "The other is not (as in love) the locus of your similarity,
nor the ideal type of what you are nor the hidden ideal of what you lack.
It is the locus of that which eludes you and whereby you elude yourself and
your own truth," Baudrillard declares.[24] The alterity thus described remains
within the order of the appearances which are now displaced "in order to
hit the empty and strategic heart of things."[25]

PLENUM AND VOID

Hegel II: In the specular consciousness of Hegel's Absolute in which
knowledge of the appearances is brought to fruition, everything transpires
as eternally present. But how are we to understand eternity and presence?

The conclusion of the *Phenomenology* states that "regarded from the side of their free existence, [the moments of Spirit] appear in the form of contingency [as] history," but regarded from the standpoint of philosophical comprehension they emerge in the shape of "the science of knowing in the sphere of appearance" (*Phen*, p. 493). Taken together they constitute Spirit's truth, thus leaving open the possibility that diachronicity persists even in the final phase of the life of the Absolute. At the end of *Philosophy of Mind*, Hegel claims, mystifyingly, "The eternal Idea *[Begriff]* in full fruition of its essence, eternally sets itself to work, engenders and enjoys itself as absolute mind."[26] This description can be read as suggesting the synchronicity of events in the permanently existing absolute Mind or, on the other hand, the eternal recurrence of these events under the aegis of mind. In either case, events no longer pass by; instead their chronological sequence, the before and after of their occurrence, appears as present in much the same way as the dates of a calendar indicate temporal succession, but diachronic time is apprehended on the calendar page in a single *Augenblick*.

In his *Philosophy of Nature*,[27] Hegel allows his philosophical imagination to linger on the issue of time without considering the subsequent etiolation it will undergo in Spirit's later development. As the idea in the form of otherness, Nature is pure externality. It is "before us as an enigma and a problem, the solution of which . . . attracts us in that spirit has a presentiment of itself in nature [and] repulses us in that nature is an alienation in which spirit does not find itself," Hegel declares (*PhN*, I: Intro, add., p. 194). But, he asks, does not God's self-sufficiency preclude his release into Nature, something inferior to himself, and he answers in *echt* Hegelian fashion: "The divine Idea is just this self-release, the expulsion of this other out of itself, and the acceptance of it again, in order to constitute subjectivity and spirit" *(PhN*, 1:247, add., p. 205).

Nature's self-expulsion occurs in linked stages of ascending complexity, the first of which is the science of mechanics, the philosophical inquiry into space, the positive, and time, the negative, dimensions of nature. Thus Hegel maintains: "The truth of space is time, so that space becomes time; our transition to time is not subjective, space itself makes the transition" (*PhN*, 1:257, add., p. 229). Heidegger stresses that this gesture is repeated in Hegel's analysis of time throughout the *Phenomenology* (*HPoS*, p. 144). At first, space is sheer undifferentiated externality in that there is nothing by virtue of which height, length, and breadth could be distinguished. The point is the first negation of space; through further negations the line and the plane are generated (*PhN*, 1:256, p. 226). What is crucial for Hegel is that the point in breaking away from undifferentiated space is not an in-itself: the externality of space in negating itself is also for-itself, a for-itself as time. Just as space cannot be differentiated without the negation that generates the point, so too the becoming of time dissolves into a similar punctiformity, the present as now (*PhN*, 1:257, 258, 259, pp.229–233).

Hegel's analysis of time putatively about mechanics has far-reaching but as yet hardly explored implications in that it provides the staging for two divergent accounts of time that have been determinative for present-day interpretations of time. On the one hand, it anticipates the sea change that occurs in the claim of modern physics that determining the simultaneity of events demands taking into account the observer's state of motion so that, Werner Heisenberg asserts, space and time can no longer be thought of as independent of one other.[28] On the other hand, Hegel's comments are premonitory of Heidegger's claim in *Being and Time* that "time needs to be explicated primordially as the horizon for the understanding of Being" (*BT* 18, p. 39).[29] To be sure, Heidegger insists that Hegel's account of the now is a description of the commonsense view of time (*BT* 431, p. 483). That Heidegger is staked on saying something other than Hegel and grows testy when perceived as repeating his predecessor is suggested by the following aside: "Philosophy is unfortunately not so easy that one simply picks up *Being and Time* and then subsequently moves around at random in the history of philosophy in order to flush out similaritites as proof that the matter has already been said a long time ago." Piqued at the criticism that he reads the history of philosophy arbitrarily, he goes on to say: "There is something peculiar in the lack of understanding of our contemporaries by virtue of which one can become famous all of a sudden, and indeed in a dubious sense. Fame is not only the ridiculous way in which we are honored nowadays" but also the way in which one is misunderstood (*HPoS*, pp. 146–147). Yet it is Hegel who posits the historicality of the subject (in spite of its differences from the Dasein) when he comments:

> [Past, present, and future] do not occur in nature . . . for they are only neces-
> sary in subjective representations, in *memory,* and in *fear* or *hope.* . . . There is
> no science of time corresponding to geometry, the science of space. . . . Time
> first becomes capable of such figurations when the understanding paralyzes it
> and reduces its negativity to a unit. (*PhN*, 1:259; Remark, p. 233)

Similarly, the formal structure of Hegel's claim that time is "the being which in that it *is, is not* and in that it is *not, is*" (*PhN*, 1:258, pp. 229–230; emphasis in original) prefigures that of Sartre's account of the *pour soi,* consciousness as that which is what it is not and is not what it is. Hegel of course denies that time as the for-itself of space in nature is genuinely subjective: as a "pure form of sensibility or intuition," time is still abstract negativity, not yet inwardized" (*PhN,* 1:257, p. 230). Yet Hegel's analysis provides the scaffolding for Sartre's grasp of the for-itself as an escape hatch for the in-itself. The in-itself ventures out of itself so that it can itself be confirmed.

In sum, time remains for Hegel the kinetic force of Spirit's metaphysical advance, the form of intuition through which Spirit achieves determination and develops as comprehending knowledge *(Begreifendes Wissen).* Spirit's fall into time precipitates the transformation of substance into subject, of nature into history. But time is also corruptive, that which Spirit must transcend. For Hegel, Spirit is doomed to appear as temporal so long as it falls short of grasping its notion, thereby annulling what Heidegger would come to see as the ecstases of time. The fallenness of Spirit is lived as temporalization, the long interval of time-bound human history that is surpassed in a final movement of inwardization in which difference is vanquished within the self-consciousness of the Absolute.

The metamorphosis of time into eternity that brings the manifold forms of Spirit's history into plenary presence is, from Hegel's standpoint, Spirit's finest hour, its entry into the eschaton under the aegis of Science. Hegel's account of Spirit's trajectory follows the contours of Protestant Christianity's world picture: prelapsarian bliss, the Fall, the advent of end time, and the final redemption of humankind, the gist of which is expressed in Karl Friedrich Goschel's remark, *"Denn der Geist erforschet alle Dinge, auch die Tie-fen der Gottheit"* ("Spirit searches all things including the depths of the Godhead").[30] In sum, the *Phenomenology* is Protestant Christianity *as* philosophy with respect to form and philosophy *as* Protestant Christianity with respect to content, an inversion of modernity's (especially Kant's) tendency to dissolve the formalism of the philosophy of religion into the concreteness of ethics.

Because it remains within the domain of picture thinking, Spirit in revealed religion falls short of fully reflexive self-consciousness, pictures but does not live in the annulled temporality of the eschaton. In Hegel's *Lectures on the Philosophy of Religion,* we are reminded that human beings are not pure thought, that mental life consists in percepts, feelings, and sensations to which the imagery of revealed religion appeals. "Religion must be something for all men," both those who have not transcended feeling and those who inhabit "the element of pure thought."[31] In the *Phenomenology* this affective phase is seen as picture thinking, an envisagement in images of the death of Jesus and his resurrection as the Christ and the continuing rememorialization of this event in the eucharist. When taken up in the memory of the Christian community, the death of the God-Man, at first merely natural, takes on its universal meaning.

The crucial point is that revealed religion which depicts the overcoming of time does not yet transcend time to manifest itself as an eternal present. Only philosophy can achieve this end. "[The community's] own reconciliation therefore enters its consciousness as something distant, as something in the distant future, just as the reconciliation which the other Self [the God-Man] achieved appears as something in the distant past" (*Phen* 787, p. 478).

Question II: Does not the inversion of the absolute, the transformation of a plenum of appearances into the void, not merely repeat the various transformations of time into the eternal present of the Hegelian absolute thereby subverting time's diachronicty? Have not events when read through the cataclysm, the inversion of the Hegelian Absolute, lost their meaning as history in that they no longer belong to the order of temporalization inhabited by the historical subject? Conversely, when history has lost its meaning does not every event sink into the cataclysm?

Reply II: In positing the abstractness of time in Nature, Hegel does not mean that time is an empty container or framework for things that come into being and pass away, things withdrawn from the stream of becoming. It is precisely at the point where Hegel rejects this view that his analysis becomes astonishingly contemporary. He writes:

> Time does not resemble a container in which everything is . . . borne away and swallowed up in the flow of a stream. Time is merely this abstraction of destroying. Things are in time because they are finite; they do not pass away because they are in time, but are themselves that which is temporal. It is therefore the process of actual things which constitutes time. The present makes a tremendous demand, yet as the individual present it is nothing, for even as I pronounce it, its all excluding pretentiousness dwindles, dissolves and falls into dust. (*PhN,* 1:257, add., p. 231)

What is more, he asserts in the *Phenomenology's* account of sense certainty that, should we try to pin down the now, we would find it to be a pure abstraction, a plurality of instants taken together, a universal (*Phen* 107, p. 64).

Hegel cannot of course follow these insights to any of their possible post-Nietzschean conclusions.[32] Insofar as Hegel projects contemporary approaches—the nihilistic potential of radical becoming and the need for its sublation on the one hand and on the other the merely formal character of present time as the now—he anticipates Zarathustra's lament that "all is empty, all is the same, all has been."[33] Yet Hegel promptly undermines this vision of temporal devastation by reverting to his view of time as eternal once it is reconfigured in the Notion (*PhN,* 3:257, add., p. 231), a subversion of time to which there is a ready-made Nietzschean response: "One must shatter the all, unlearn respect for the all" (*WP* 331, p. 181).[34] For Nietzsche, nihilism is overcome only by the belief in the being of becoming, a being identified as recurrence: "That *everything recurs* is the closest *approximation of a world of becoming to a world of being*" (*WP* 617, p. 330),[35] a recurrence that is not a movement of repetition, an endless miming of the same, but rather the return of difference.

When difference is understood as a cloning of the same, it is seen by later thinkers as mere determinateness established through negation. Thus Gilles Deleuze comments: "[For Hegel] difference is the ground, but only the ground for the demonstration of the identical. Hegel's circle is . . . only the infinite circulation of the identical by means of negativity."[36] Although the sublation of alterity and finitude in Hegel has, on occasion, been contested, their subreption in Hegel is taken for granted.[37]

It is this Hegelian negation of time in the Absolute that postmodernity will contest as the culmination of the metaphysics of presence. Derrida has most consistently brought this issue to the fore:

> Within the metaphysics of presence . . . we believe quite . . . literally, in absolute knowledge as the closure if not the end of history. And we believe that such a closure has taken place. The history of Being as presence, as self-presence in absolute knowledge, as consciousness of the self in the infinity of the parousia—this history is closed.[38]

What is meant by closure is far from clear. It can be construed as the end of metaphysics such that we can station ourselves in a beyond, an *au delà* of metaphysics. Or, in conformity with Heidegger's refusal to read the end as cessation, closure can be taken to mean not the end but rather the completion of metaphysics as having used up its possibilities. For Derrida, we remain both inside and outside of metaphysics so that pronouncements about closure are not apocalyptic proclamations of its end but rather metalevel analyses of the end.[39]

For the heterological historian, this portends the ineliminability both of the ontology of specularity and thus of presence and of the fissuring of presence. A deconstructive history depends upon thinking what is unthought in the Absolute and becomes possible only after the Hegelian movement of closure. But if closure is to be thought out of the resources of the Absolute such a thinking must always already be interior to the Absolute. Any truly contemporary philosophy of the One could now be thought only against the non-ground of a deconstructed All. It is worth noting that François Laruelle undertakes such an effort by envisaging the thinking of the One–All as eschewing totalization and as a non-philosophy.

> [Such a non-philosophy] is no longer tested as a totalizing pro-ject, a finite totality or a totalised finitude etc. but as a multiplicity of openings-without-closures, of transcendence without totalities, of ecstases-without-horizons, as well as non-decisional positings. (Translation is mine)[40]

Whereas Baudrillard's depiction of object-ity opens the way for an inversion of the appearances, Derrida's deconstruction of the logic of presence introduces the possibility of a differential history. Both inversions always already point to the Absolute's ownmost conceptual possibilities. For Derrida a differential history is "monumental, stratified, contradictory."[41] There is no concept, *differance,* that is productive of specific differences, but rather *differance* is "the nonfull, nonsimple origin, the structured and differing origin of differences."[42] It is by now a commonplace that *differance* has the double sense of an interval or spacing which allows phenomena to be distinguished and a temporal meaning as postponement, deferring, or delay. Such deferral does not mean the putting off of a present moment as the result of a decision, for decision starts from presence, but is rather constitutive of presence.

But how is the heterological historian who does not wish to fall into the naive referentiality of an older historicism to conceive of fact, narrative, and image in the light of this fissuring? Derrida's answer appears to be a reversion to a traditional view of reference as a court of last resort:

> Finally it goes without saying that in no case is it a question of discourse against truth or against science. . . . [Nor is there the intent] to return naively to a relativist or sceptical empiricism. . . . Paraphrasing Freud . . . we must recognize in truth 'the normal' prototype of the fetish. How can we do without it?[43]

If Derrida is right, what then is the point of deconstructing presence? A clue can be found in Derrida's early analysis of the primordial fissuring of the Living Present in Husserl's *Origin of Geometry.* It is precisely the duality that allows the phenomenon to appear and puts it into question. On the one hand, consciousness "must be restored to its own light" or "nothing would appear"; on the other, consciousness cannot "live enclosed in the innocent undividedness of the primordial Absolute, because the Absolute is present only in being deferred-delayed."[44] Such a synthesis is not a ground or foundation but maintains contradictory possibilities together.[45]

In what way would the narrative, film, computer simulation, or archive be marked by a difference from that of the avowedly objective historian? The deconstructive historian could not construct her artifact as a totality, first because inner heterogeneous forces annul the text's unity so that it is *essentially* incomplete; and second, because there is always some supplementary exterior condition to be added to what is a supposedly fully present origin that thereby threatens the unity of the object. Thus, in a description of the killings in Rwanda and Burundi, what might be read as tribal conflict between Tutsi and Hutu can be seen as reflecting the play of heterogeneous forces, for example, those of Belgian colonial influence. It could certainly be argued that it does not require deconstructive analysis to see this. The heterological historian attentive to deconstructive analysis, however, sees more: not only an event that *happens* to be more complex than originally thought but one that *inherently* requires the co-condition of the supplement, what appears to be merely added on but upon which a concept depends. When what supplements the event is negation or absence, paradoxically, this negation signals not a deficit but an excess of destruction that leaves its trace in the text. The cataclysm always already within and beyond historical narrative or visual presentation is the driving force of that presentation, is its supplement conveyed not as a futile moralizing but perhaps as a certain tone: the killing is unstoppable but must be stopped.

TERROR AND CATACLYSM

Hegel III: If history for Hegel is the cunning of reason working itself out through the history of peoples in the interest of freedom, the price for this freedom is the transformation of mere abstract negation into the concreteness of war and the slaughter of peoples. The cataclysmic event that transformed the thinking of Hegel and his generation was the French Revolution. Hegel's celebrated lines in the *Phenomenology* capture his early attitude toward "the unmediated pure negation" of the Jacobin terror:

> The sole work and deed of universal freedom is therefore *death,* a death too which has no inner signficance or filling, for what is negated is the empty point of the absolutely free self. It is the coldest and meanest of all deaths,

with no more signficance than cutting off the head of a cabbage, or swallowing a mouthful of water. (*Phen* 590, p. 360)

Yet philosopher Victor Cousin (1792–1867) describing his conversations with Hegel during the years from 1817 to 1831, declares that, despite Hegel's strong reservations about the Republic and his royalist leanings, "[Hegel] considered the French Revolution to be the greatest step taken by the human race since Christianity."[46]

To grasp the ambivalence of Hegel's attitude toward the French Revolution—his acknowledgment of its necessity and his fear of its aftermath—it is necessary to see it in relationship to the logic of modernity whose inevitable outcome Hegel believes it to be. In the *Phenomenology,* the conceptual itinerary of modernity is tracked from religious faith to the Enlightenment's attack on faith as supersitition, and thence through an inversion of Enlightenment reason as merely empty and abstract to its actualization in (for Hegel) history's most abyss-al moment of negation, the Jacobin terror. The religion of modernity is not that of Unhappy Consciousness but rather what Hegel calls a mere belief, a belief that flees from the world of actuality and inwardizes that world. At the same time, faith negates the vanity of modernity's world of culture from which, as religious consciousness, it had escaped. When this negation is exercised upon itself the result is that the new consciousness that is born sets itself to work on the picture thinking of faith, a consciousness that Hegel calls "insight." In what appears to be an explicit mimicking of Kant's statement that concepts without intuitions are empty and intuitions without concepts are blind, Hegel avers: "Pure insight has, therefore, no content of its own, because it is negative being-for self; to faith, on the other hand, there belongs a content but without insight" (*Phen* 529, p. 324). The consciousness of faith sees the real world as soulless and attempts to transcend it but can only do so as a projection into a beyond, a *future.* The only *present* reality is that which has emerged as the object of pure insight.

What leads directly to the Enlightenment and the French Revolution is that pure insight becomes a universal possession, a universality that is not merely abstract but is destined to become the demand for freedom by each and every citizen, freedom (as Hegel would later contend in his 1830 Berlin lectures on history) not for one or some but for all. With this democratization on the part of self-consciousness, every self becomes an I that is "self-identical and universal." Thus Hegel: "Spirit calls to *every* consciousness: be for yourselves what you all are in yourselves—reasonable" (*Phen* 537, p. 328). Now the entire force of the Notion as reason, as yet abstract and

contentless, is directed against faith which it sees as superstition and preju-
dice. Premonitory of Marx, reason sees the masses as victims of an insti-
tutionalized clergy who claim unique insight into truth and who, in complicity with political despotism, engage in a pincers movement against the
masses in order to pursue their own selfish interests. Reason hopes to
awaken the consciousness of the multitude without paying a price, but the
"unconscious idol" rebels. Citing Diderot, Hegel avers that "'one fine
morning it gives its comrades a shove with the elbow, and bang! crash! the
idol lies on the floor'" (*Phen* 545, p. 332).

In his lectures on the philosophy of history, Hegel offers a more concrete and piquant reading of these developments. The French understanding
of the truth of reason is expressed in a doctrine of specific rights grounded
in free will, the same principle that was given speculative elaboration in
Germany in Kant's philosophy as willing what is right for its own sake. What
for the Germans was tranquil theory became, for the French, a program for
action. Why this difference, Hegel asks? "[I]t might be said: the French are
hot-headed *[ils ont la tête près du bonnet]*; but this is a superficial solution."[47]
It is rather the rationality of Germany's Protestantism with its inner appeal
to conscience that provided the conditions for the peaceable development
of private right and the state's constitution. The German Enlightenment
was actualized in conformity with Protestant theology, whereas the French
Enlightenment remained hostile to a church that separates conscience from
the sacred. What is more, mired in a morass of luxury and extravagance
with neither court nor clergy, neither nobility nor parliament willing to
sacrifice its privileges, government could not police its own house.[48]

In the *Phenomenology*, which does not try to depict the *Volksgeister* of
actual history, the distinction between the German *Aufklärung* and the
French *éclaircissement* is less sharply drawn. Enlightenment reason generally
demeans faith's object, cheapening it by interpreting it as inaccessible save
in sensuous form, as a material object, a god of wood or stone. Moreover,
faith must justify itself by presenting historical evidence for its claims. But
for faith, its certainty, as Kierkegaard would later proclaim, rests on an unmediated relation to its object. Faith is excoriated for its renunciation of
pleasure and, more to the point, for relinquishing deeds in favor of contemplation. What, in fact, has the Enlightenment taught faith? Since everything
pictured by faith has been degraded into its materiality, absolute being is
ohne Eigenschaften (to borrow Musil's phrase), "a vacuum" of which no determinations can be predicated. Although the Enlightenment appears to dis-
parage the beauty and trust of faith, it calls attention to the doubleness of
faith: its life in this world and in a beyond. But the Enlightenment will

grieve over its loss of the world it has desacralized, one in which the *"être suprème"* of faith will be reduced "to the exhalation of a stale gas" (*Phen* 586, p. 358).

If the truth of the Enlightenment is the purity of its insight, its cold clear-headedness, it must turn its steely glance not only upon the subject but also upon the object which now becomes a pure thing. This split in the consciousness of the Enlightenment is expressed in the distinction between an Absolute that is pure thought without determination and matter devoid of qualities, a difference that is not ontological but rather determined by their starting points. It is only in the Cartesian cogito that the identity of subject and object is established. In one of Hegel's less persuasive transitions, thought and matter are caught up in a rotary movement that Hegel calls utility whose significance lies in its reestablishing the value of the object. "The Useful is the object insofar as self-consciousness penetrates it and has in it the certainty of the individual self, its enjoyment. . . . *[T]ruth* as well as presence and *actuality* are united. The two worlds are reconciled and heaven is transplanted to the earth below" (*Phen* 581, p. 355).

Consciousness discovers itself in utility, but utility is still a predicate of the object from which consciousness must withdraw in order to determine the truth of utility. Through this effort, a new form of consciousness is born, a self that gazes into itself and does so as absolute freedom. The world exists for Spirit to do with as it will because now the world and its will are non-different. This is for Hegel what is meant by a general will, a will that no power in the world can resist. As Kant had shown, the subject must fuse individual and universal will, a fusion that takes the form of a law. But individuality is still extant in law so that law remains exclusionary and lacks true universality. Hegel is now only a step away from revolutionary will. Fired up by the experience of his generation, in passionate prose worthy of Michelet, Hegel concludes: "Universal freedom can produce neither a positive work nor a deed; there is left for it only negative action; it is merely the fury of destruction" (*Phen* 589, p. 359).

Government under these circumstances is itself something divided, on the one hand executing the universal will, on the other an individual entity. As individual it can only be a faction, to be sure, the victorious faction, yet it remains what Rousseau (although not Hegel) refers to as a corporate will, something divisive that must be overthrown. The government has no defense to offer against what opposes it in that it lacks the universality it claims to possess and is *eo ipso* guilty. "Being suspected, therefore takes the place of being guilty; and the external reaction against this reality [lies in] the cold matter of fact annihilation of this existent self, from which nothing else can be taken away but its mere being" (*Phen* 591, p. 360). In the *Philosophy of History,* Hegel contends that virtue itself is defined in terms of support for the Revolution, but virtue can only be judged subjectively opening the way to a society in which suspicion is pandemic. "Suspicion attained a terrible power and brought to the scaffold the monarch . . . Robespierre set up the principle of Virtue as supreme. Virtue and terror are the order of the day. It exercises its power without legal formalities and the punishment it inflicts is equally simple—*Death.*"[49]

Question III: Does the inversion of enlightenment reason, its simultaneous expression and destruction in the Terror that supervenes upon the French revolution, also describe (in a movement of repetition) the relation of the logos of technique to the cataclysm? Does the connective "also" refer to a cataclysm that for Hegel was "already there" but did "not yet" exist in the Terror, or is the cataclysm without precedent?

Reply III: In a movement of striking repetition Heidegger's account of the essence of technology reproduces the essence of utility and its aftermath as conceived by Hegel. Does this analysis suffice to account for the cataclysm? What analysis could suffice in the context of that upon which analysis founders?

Consider first Heidegger's by-now familiar contention that technology is not to be construed instrumentally as it is in commonsense terms but rather as a way of revealing truth. Philological analysis shows that the Greek *techne* refers to the making of things and works of art as well as to a knowing *[episteme]* that implies expertise and understanding. Modernity has its own way of revealing truth, that of technology itself. It is generally alleged that knowing as interpreted by modern science provides the epistemic grounding for modern technology rather than the converse. However for Heidegger, without the prior mode of revealing belonging to modern technology, that of putting that-which-is to use, modern science could not have been given practical application. Technology sets upon and challenges nature driving toward a favorable input-output ratio in a never-ending process of production whose products are stockpiled as standing-reserve. This mode of gathering challenges human beings to reveal the real as standing-reserve, enframing *[Gestell]*, is not a consequence of human decision but a destiny *[Geschick]* that sends humans on a particular way of revealing, that of technology. To be sure, it is human beings who drive technology, but it is the essence of technology as a manner of revealing truth that drives them. The ills of the present age are attendant upon this transformation of the revealing of truth as enframing.[50]

It is in this context that Heidegger makes the claim that history too is determined out of this destining. Thus Heidegger:

> History is neither simply the object of written chronicle nor simply the fulfillment of human activity. That activity first becomes history as something destined. And it is only the destining into objectifying representation that makes the historical accessible as an object for historiography, i.e. for a science, and on this basis makes possible the current equating of the historical with that which is chronicled.[51]

For Heidegger it is not the cataclysm that determines the manner in which history is to be thought. Rather than providing an analysis of the being of technology in its primordiality, the efforts to describe contemporary reality "morphologically, psychologically in terms of decline and loss, in terms of fate, catastrophe, and destruction are merely technological behavior," Heidegger contends.[52] The contemporary historian is held captive not by the cataclysm but by the logos of technology that covers up the genuinely historical and allows history to appear only as that which is merely recorded. The nihil for Heidegger cannot be thought apart from Being.[53]

As early as the *Letter on Humanism,* Heidegger distinguishes Hegel's account of the "not" from his own position that "[n]ihilation unfolds essentially in Being itself." For Hegel, "the not appears as the negativity of negation in the essence of Being," whereas for Heidegger the nothing cannot give itself to thought without the prius of Being: "Because it thinks Being, thinking thinks the nothing."[54] If it is assumed that Heidegger repeats the conceptual gesture of Hegel in thinking the being of utility, is it possible to think after (post/in the manner of) Heidegger such that one thinks the "not" more primordially than Heidegger? What course would such thinking take?

For Heidegger, to think primordially is to question, and to question is to interrogate the nature of questioning. To question appears to have a double meaning, to ask about some subject, and to place this subject into question. In asking about some matter there is an anticipation of what is to be learned so that one must have some preliminary grasp of what is sought. Heidegger's concern, to query the meaning of being, presupposes some prior understanding of being, however dim. If there is something unsettlingly circular about this in that the meaning of what is interrogated is already presupposed, Heidegger reassures us that every inquiry into basic questions is guided by anticipating what is to be found in the manner of "taking a look beforehand." It is not a matter of pre-supposing something but rather of ex-posing the ground of the meaning of what is interrogated.

Yet to question questioning is not the same as to question the meaning of Being; in the former case the question is not simply the subject matter of an inquiry but also a placing *in* question of the question. Having something of the formal structure of skepticism, questioning undoes and reinstates itself. Primordial questioning points to the impossibility of the possibility of the question, and thereby circumvents thinking negation as unfolding in Being itself.

In *Writing the Disaster,* Maurice Blanchot tries to think negation as the destruction of traditional metaphysical interpretations of being, time, and history or, more primordially, as their original *Ur*-absence. At the same time he envisages the disaster as the actuality of the twentieth-century's cataclysmic events, which for him is concentrated in the Holocaust. Defining disaster, Blanchot writes, "I call disaster that which does not have the ultimate for its limit: it bears the ultimate away in the disaster."[55] Because the disaster is a sweeping away of all limit, there is neither self nor event to describe.

The weight of the disaster is felt not psychologically but epistemically as annulling the question of self so that both question and self disappear. It is no longer possible to contend either that historical catastrophe is merely an ontic event or that it is a blunder of Being. For Blanchot, "the disaster does not put me into question but annuls the question, makes it disappear—as if along with the question, I too disappeared in the disaster which never appears" (*WoD,* p. 28). Properly speaking, there is no experience of the disaster, not only because the I that undergoes experience has been carried away but because of the disaster's mode of self-temporalization. The disaster recurs in perpetuity not as something positive but as a "nonevent" that never did and never will happen in any straightforward sense. The time of the disaster is a time that always already was and a time that will be in the mode of not being it. Beyond facts and states of affairs, the disaster is always behind itself, "always takes place after having taken place," so that it lies outside experience (*WoD,* p. 28).

To speak of the Holocaust as a non-event appears to suggest its denial, a gross violation of the memory of the dead. Yet in this regard Blanchot's analysis should not be construed in a historical sense but rather as troping an intradivine disaster that intersects the historical one as a disruption of thought and language. Once these founder, the historical itself is no longer a sequence of logically comprehensible happenings but a theologically ambiguous non-event that resists description.

How does the historian who is to bring past events to the fore create visual or written artifacts about that-which-was, if the disaster impinges upon the cultural articulation of meaning as formulable in language and image thereby disabling them? How is the historian to move from ineffability to speech? Historical work reflects this struggle in what Blanchot describes as a double movement of giving and withholding, giving as the effort to bring otherness into speech and withholding as speech's effort to justify itself in a silent Saying anterior to speech. Such Saying is an unspoken covenant between speaker and hearer promising that her language will be marked by alterity. Unsayability becomes in-discreet: the Saying, the ineffable, escapes so that what cannot be said bursts into language. At the same time, the alterity of Saying is also held back by the Other who resists linguistic captivity.

What breaks into language in light of the disaster is not some content that eludes language but unsayability itself. How is such unsayability to make its way into the work of a historian who crafts a film or a narrative about the past? It has often been claimed that media bombardment by images of carnage desensitize the reader or viewer but, to the contrary, the sheer plethora of images may acquire cumulative power. What is gained in cumulative impact is lost, however, in the erasure of the distinctiveness of any particular event. The mountains of dead, the armies of refugees, the military presence that herds them together do not become visual cliches as has been argued but instead tend to fuse into a single event. Thus it is crucial for the visual historian to identify the historical object through accompanying narrative or easily deciphered internal evidence. "You are looking at Zagreb in 1945 and not at Banja Luka today." Yet the challenge to the visual historian is not only to specify that-which-was but to recover insofar as possible the singularity of the event. Such a recovery cannot be achieved merely through the inclusion of signs—a flag, a uniform, a famous landmark—that would pin down the time and place of the referent but rather by indicating the paradox of historical presentation: what cannot be shown or said must be shown or said.

Consider British photographer George Rodger's 1945 photograph of a child running along a road that abuts what appears to be a park strewn with corpses (fig. 8).[56] The site is concentration camp Bergen-Belsen, a fact we know only from the accompanying caption. The child is neatly dressed and seems well fed. He looks straight ahead seemingly oblivious to the dead. The child's glance refuses the negation of death, turns away from it yet cannot help reinstating it. The photographer as historian who captures and preserves such a moment becomes one with the internal narratological voice of the child. Subsequent historians may ask, "Why is the child not

8. George Rodger, "Ein jüdischer Junge läuft durch das Konzentrationlager Bergen-Belsen." *Life Magazine* © Time Inc.

emaciated?" "Why is he allowed to roam these grounds still strewn with corpses?" Or, they may link this photograph to other visual artifacts, perhaps provide a historical context for the liberation of the camps. Yet so long as the boy in his uncanny flight is permitted to break into the narrative of what is depicted, the child's face becomes the escape route for an unsayability that seeps into the visual image and contests any narrative articulation of what the camera captures, a world where death and life are virtually indistinguishable.

∞

Hegel's Absolute Subject sees in an *Augenblick* all that has happened, sees it both diachronically and in its unity as if the God of Protestant Christianity stood before a projector bringing the images he had filmed into plenary presence. Hegel affirms this history as progress, a history that is brought to closure in the self-consciousness of an Absolute Subject. How is the hetero-logical historian to understand the ontology of images which, for Hegel, are brought under control of the Notion? Is the formlessness of the cataclysm to be envisaged in terms of Hegelian negation, as the obverse of the Absolute Subject, or is the cataclysm beyond the dialectic of affirmation and nega-tion? And, if beyond, how is such exteriority to be interpreted?

It is no surprise that, when classifying types of history, Hegel expresses a preference for philosophical history that might today be characterized as doubly coded, because it includes both the observations of past events and a deciphering of the "cunning of reason" as exhibited in history. Spirit comes to discern that reason in history expresses itself in the growth of freedom, a freedom whose rationality is, for Hegel, realized in the nation-state, a view that continues to surprise contemporary readers. Written in terms of European supremacy and the exclusions of many non-Western peoples from the theater of history, Hegelian history becomes questionable when exposed to an alterity that it repudiates.

Can there not also be found in Hegel's system a *point d'appui* for under-standing the culture of images? It has often been noted that in the *Phenome-nology,* the Christian religion understood as picture thinking, the penulti-mate form of Spirit, persists as the content of philosophy, the final stage of Spirit's development. But form cannot be severed from content, so that images continue to infiltrate the Reason that has sublated them. What is more, philosophy knows not only the appearances of religion, its shapes and forms, but knows them *as* appearance. Reality as heretofore understood is banished. The ontology of appearance has virtualized the real so that absolute knowing itself cannot escape specularity.

Yet is there not in the trajectory of Spirit, a Moment that is unsur-passable, that unsays the Absolute subject, the "we" before whom the shapes of consciousness unfold? Heidegger notices that in the very constitution of this "we," natural consciousness in its immediacy is transcended, overturned in a movement that Hegel identifies as skepticism. For Hegel, skepticism is simply another moment to be overcome, but Heidegger shows that skepti-cism uncovers the appearances as appearances by nullifying the truth claims of common sense and reason. Like a virus that infiltrates information sys-tems, once inside the Absolute the power of skeptical undoing does not disappear. Instead, the internal differentiations of the Absolute are erased, and an emptiness like that of the Levinasian *il y a,* of being without existents, comes to the fore.

Once Hegel's Absolute has become a One-All of appearances in a post-Hegelian world, the distinction between the historical object and its description in word and image vanishes. If history is no longer "real" but has metamorphosized into the hyperreal, there is no place for the historian. What is more, along with historical consciousness the subject as such disappears, and in its absence we are left with a world of objects. Hegel's "cunning of reason" has been inverted into a "cunning of objects," a condition that can be described both as deliberate "strategy" and, paradoxically, as the operation of a certain "necessity" or "fate." It is in this barren sphere of the object that alterity would seem to disappear, yet, surprisingly, it remains. When the subject dissipates, the other cannot be another conceived as another myself, the recipient of an empathetic altruism, but only as an unfigurable singularity.

Does absolute knowledge as Hegel conceives it then signal the closure of history, such that a culture of objects becomes inevitable? Is this closure contingent upon the end of metaphysics? If so, is the historian to think that there is a vantage point outside or beyond metaphysics where she can station herself, or is she to believe that metaphysics has consumed its own possibilities and that her only alternative is to return to a naive referentiality? The heterological historian realizes that the historical artifact she has fabricated is inherently incomplete: there is always some condition that threatens her narrative, calls it into question. What differentiates her deconstructive account from that of the objective historian who subjects herself only to the principle of corrigibility is the heterologist's recognition that her narrative requires the supplement of the cataclysm. There is the danger, however, that both the power of the cataclysm as sheer force and the prodigality of images may convert the object of her narrative into a single fused event. Thus, if she is to keep her covenant with the dead others, she must remember the others' time, place, and corporeal specificity, the singularity of the event they inhabit.

But it is just this singularity that is unsaid in the eternal present of Hegel's Absolute. To be sure, time does not at first appear in Hegel's philosophy as presence. In his account of nature, time is described as the truth of space, the latter being mere undifferentiated externality. The dot or point is the first negation of space that, in breaking away from the in-itself of space, becomes a for-itself as time. The punctiformity of time does not vanish but is replicated at later stages of Spirit's history. In his descriptions of Spirit's trajectory, Hegel does not adopt the view that time is an empty container but asserts instead that it is the finitude of things that constitutes time. At the end of Spirit's journey, however, time's diachronicity is subordinated to the eternal present of the Absolute.

But is it an eternal present that poses a threat to time's diachronicity, or is it rather the speeding up of time in the age of images? And, if the claims of alterity do not disappear in specular culture despite time's acceleration, is the historian not obliged by her promise to the dead others to try to reclaim time's diachronicity? Does alterity itself not leave traces of a unique mode of temporalization that enters into the historian's discursive or visual artifact? These questions will be addressed in the following chapter.

TIME (OUR) Thunder against it. Deplore the fact that there is
nothing poetic about it. Call it a time of transition, of decadence.

Gustave Flaubert
Dictionary of Received Ideas

RE-MEMBERING THE PAST:
THE HISTORIAN AS TIME TRAVELER

It is a commonplace that what once existed but exists no longer belongs to
a past that is both irrecoverable and unchangeable. Past events cannot be
lived in the manner of firstness but merely relived in memory as the etiolated images, the replicas, of what they had been. Conventional wisdom
further suggests that one may wish to remember information previously
learned, or to reexperience bygone pleasures, or, on the contrary, to banish
from consciousness the recollected vicissitudes of disease, natural catastrophe, and historical calamity.

As custodian of the past, the historian must show why artifact and event,
trend and tendency, are worth present consideration. Yet to re-surrect or
re-member the past "just as it was" she must, *per impossibile,* be there *(Da),*
to somehow inhabit the past she wishes to recover. This desire to be present
to the past in its actuality is best expressed in the tropes of science fiction
and in the more speculative reaches of contemporary physics. The historian's
dream is to enter into the discursive practices which generate the material
146 and conceptual world she wishes to depict. Like H. G. Wells's time traveler,

she may inquire why, if gravity can be resisted in flight, cannot human beings hope "to stop or accelerate their drift along the Time Dimension and travel the other way."[1] Such speculation may be thought to trivialize the gravity of the cataclysm, but the historian cannot forget that in the culture of specularity and information, she must render the past in an idiom that is comprehensible within a framework in which reference is obliterated and images refer only to themselves. She must avail herself of present resources to deliver the message of the past, of an alterity that can never be spoken but lends urgency to her discourse: "It was not as it has been described previously by European travelers, but this, this is how life was in the late eighteenth century in the kingdom of the Dahomey."

The act of bringing back the past, of *Wiederholung,* reflects two distinctive views of time. According to the first, the past is envisaged *en bloc.* Each dimension of time is viewed as a freezing of some property of events as they pass by, their pastness, their presentness, and their futurity. Thus there are stretches of time that encompass temporally mobile individual events. This manner of speaking about time's passage enables us to think of the near and distant pasts, the immediate and far-off futures, as well as to give affective coloration to our relation to time's dimensions. We anticipate the future with hope or view the past with nostalgia. The alternative view considers time as a sequence of mensurable and disarticulated now points that succeed one another, that nest nowhere, but are simply marked off as earlier and later, before and after, time as the pure succession of individual occasions. The distinction between stretched and punctiform time goes all the way down. In the history of modern thought, from Kant and Hegel to recent analytic philosophy, there is no escaping time's doubleness, its stretched and punctiform character. Each view will be shown as opening another dimension of historical understanding depending upon whether, in any given context, the historian is in quest of cognitive yield, or whether she speaks from the discursive space of ethics. These differing descriptions of temporalization express a perspective in Nietzsche's sense of the term; each is an active context-producing account. Nietzsche contends that interpretations are not to be construed as relative to one another and, as such, susceptible to subjective judgment. Instead, an interpretation has the means from within itself both to illuminate phenomena as well as to undermine opposing views (*WP* 481, p. 267).[2] Alternative modes of seeing time insinuate themselves into the historian's work and re-mark the presentation of the historical object.

In conformity with Nietzsche, I shall support the claim that interpretations may both exhibit discursive power yet be reciprocally challenging. On the one hand, temporal continuity as phenomenologically experienced provides a useful framework for discursive or visual narration whose structure replicates that of experienced time. On the other, the before and after of time supplies the framework for the ethical dimension of the historian's work. The before and after may be short or long—"It was only a few weeks *before* the raj," or "The influence of the Buddhist king Asoka lasted long *after* his death"—but in either case the after reflects a radical alteration in social, political, economic, and cultural circumstances. William James succinctly sums up time's bifurcation when he claims that "on the theory of continuity, time, change, etc., would grow by finite buds or drops"[3] and also that experience is continuous. The "tiniest feeling comes with an earlier and later part and with a sense of their continuous procession," James writes.[4]

I shall argue further that accounts of the past are subject to a restriction beyond that of warring interpretations that challenge one another. What is said about the past can be checked by a negative determination. The historian may say that an event could have been W, X, or Y, but it could not have been Z. Eliminative propositions—"it could not have been Z"—will be exhibited as establishing constraints on what can be said or shown to have happened in the past, thereby placing limits upon what might seem to be the unchecked latitude of historical interpretation.

VOYAGES IN TIME

In arguing for a multiplicity of interpretations, Nietzsche does not rule out the possibility that their number might be infinite. With imagination thus unfettered, Nietzsche envisages the reversal of time providing an early blueprint for time travel. In a striking apothegm he writes: "It is a hopeless curiosity that wants to know what other kinds of intellects and perspectives there might be, . . . whether some beings might be able to experience time backward, or alternately forward and backward."[5] H. G. Wells's *Time Machine,* the locus classicus in mid-century science fiction for the depiction of time travel, defends its plausibility on the grounds that, properly understood, time and space are isomorphic. "Motion along any of the axes of space—length, breadth and thickness—is reversible whereas time moves in a single direction because our consciousness moves intermittently in one direction. . . . There is no difference between time and space except that our consciousness moves along it."[6] In a playful aside, the advantage of time travel for the historian is cited: "One might travel back and verify the accepted account of the Battle of Hastings."[7] For H. G. Wells time is only apparently different from space because time is bound up with consciousness.

Cultures of temporally distant ages described in the fiction of time travel differ considerably. This depends upon whether they are construed idyllically or derisively as such standard TV fare as the various *Star Trek* series, the film *Blade Runner,* or the novel *Neuromancer* demonstrate. Past or future ages are depicted either as arenas of progress or of decline but generally as the obverse of the creator's perception of the present. Such works describe imaginary societies that exhibit the positive or negative outcomes of current social, political, and cultural tendencies in inverted form. Thus Samuel Butler's novel *Erewhon* displays Butler's nineteenth-century suspicion of hypertrophied intelligence and of mechanical devices that imitate human intelligence, intellectual prostheses as simple as clocks and watches. H. G. Wells expresses the Nietzschean worry that a humanity ensconced in creature comforts has gone soft: "The too perfect security of the upper-worlders had led them to a slow movement of degeneration, to general dwindling in size, strength and intelligence."[8] The recent television series *X-Files* exhibits a sinister universe in which the communication of human to human and human to aliens from distant parts of the universe occurs telepathically unmediated by the outmoded technologies of radio waves or even fiber-optic cable. The envisaging of such communication is a reflection of a self-transcending science, a hyper-science that virtualizes the real as a free play of images that have become indifferent to physical law.

Two frequently cited cases have been constructed to highlight the logical incongruities thought to result from traveling back to the past. According to the first, if Louise travels backward in time, she may be able to alter past circumstances so that, for example, she could prevent her grandparents from marrying. In that case, she would never have been born, but of course Louise already exists. If, on the other hand, Louise was actually to become her grandparent's contemporary and was unable to effect any changes, what could account for her inability to act in the usual way?[9] The second quandary is depicted by philosopher Michael Dummett. A painter living in the present has up until now produced no works of any great merit. He is visited by a time traveler from the future who shows the painter reproductions of his works that future connoisseurs hold in high regard but that have not yet been produced. The painter now proceeds to copy the reproductions. Can it be said that the future reproductions are copies of paintings that are the result of the painter's creative effort, or that the paintings are copies of the reproductions?[10]

It has been argued that these inconsistencies arise only from the perspective of an obsolete classical worldview. They can be resolved by positing parallel universes in a manner consistent with the principles of quantum

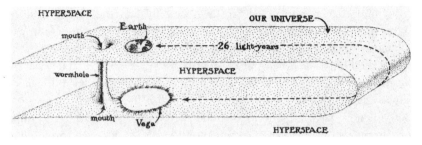

9. Diagram of a wormhole. Reproduced with the permission of W. W. Norton and Company, Inc. from Kip Thorne, *Black Holes and Time Warps: Einstein's Outrageous Legacy*, p. 485.

mechanics as they are applied in the many universes hypothesis proposed by Hugh Everett III. He holds that "if something physically can happen, it does—in some universe."[11] It should be noted that Nietzsche's contention that "all things that can happen have already happened" and "must also run once again forward" bears at least a family resemblance to this perspective.[12]

Thus, some physicists speculate that despite the verbal conundrums generated by travel to the past, there is nothing in the laws of physics to prevent it even if such travel is precluded by the present state of knowledge. Physicist Kip S. Thorne who holds this view envisions the process by means of which travel backward in time can come about. In what may be described as a fanciful narrative endemic to the age of the hyperreal, he declares that wormholes, a hypothetical warping of the topology of space (at least theoretically), can be converted into time machines. According to Thorne, wormholes consist of two entrance holes: "mouths" located at different points in space connected by a short tunnel such that entry at one end allows for exit at a distant location in the universe which is itself embedded in an imaginary flat space, hyperspace. The universe can be envisioned as lightly folded so that it resembles a pair of tongs with the wormhole providing a shortcut between the two prongs (fig. 9).[13] If a wormhole is to become a time machine, time must hook up differently inside the wormhole from the way in which time moves outside it in our universe. Inside the wormhole, the time flows at each mouth will be the same, whereas from outside the wormhole the two mouths will be seen as belonging to different reference frames. By crossing the wormhole in one direction, the traveler might go backward in time from the standpoint of our universe; by moving in the other direction she would go forward.[14] Within the wormhole the time traveler moves faster than the speed of light.

Thorne observes that Stephen Hawking rejects the possibility of time machines and advances what he calls the "chronology protection conjecture," the assumption that the laws of physics preclude the development of time machines because wormholes will be destroyed by electromagnetic vacuum fluctuations before they can actually become time machines. Thus Hawking is reported to have quipped that the world would remain safe for historians.[15] Hawking's well-intentioned comment aims at preserving the commonsense understanding of past, present, and future generally honored by the narrative historian. But visual historians are trapped by the temporal ambiguities of the hyperreal so that, for example, the viewer who has missed narrative cues may see what the historian claims is an "authentic" docudrama of the Assyrian, Roman, or Arthurian world, yet plausibly believe she is watching an "imaginary" depiction of the future.

Time travel, an artifact of the physicist's imagination, is not only compatible with but intrinsic to virtualization. According to Michael Heim, "[V]irtual worlds are not tied to physical reality, since any information that can be visualized can also be made into a virtual world that a participant can experience."[16] Not only can the viewer of the *Star Trek: Deep Space Nine* series "see" these worlds as spectacle, but the cybernaut who dons sense-altering equipment enters a new world with its own mode of temporalization, in effect a time machine of a limited sort.

The trope of time travel, now a staple of contemporary culture, destabilizes the *Da* of the Heideggerian Dasein upon which historical narrative has heretofore depended, in that the *Da* must now be both "here" and "elsewhere" in spacetime, "the four-dimensional 'fabric' that results when space and time are unified."[17] Yet this destabilization opens the way for historical imagination to envisage itself in two context-producing perspectives. On the one hand, within the wormhole, the historian traveling in time experiences past, present, and future as following upon one another, as they are manifested phenomenologically in everyday experience, because within the wormhole the mouths experience the same flow of time.[18] Yet when the historian in her imaginary journey emerges from the wormhole's second mouth, she cannot help being struck by the relativity of temporal frameworks and the dislocations it entails since the two mouths are in different reference frames, a relativity anticipated on a miniscule scale by the time differences experienced by travelers moving from one time zone to another. Because the historian, like the imaginary time traveler, inhabits two temporal frames of reference, that of the past and of her present-day existence, she may turn to the seemingly stable punctiform view of time, seeing events as earlier and later, to overcome her sense of temporal dislocation. In order to assess the possible cognitive yield and ethical implications for the historian of each standpoint, of time's flow and punctiform time, it may be useful to examine some philosophical treatments of these opposed perspectives.

TIME'S DUALITY: FROM HEGEL TO NIETZSCHE AND BACK

The historian who imagines herself as traveling in time cannot but be struck by time's doubleness, its character as both punctiform and stretched. On either reading, there is a passing of time: time cannot be immobilized. Plato, Plotinus, and most Christian neo-Platonists, to the contrary, envisage an immobilized time, a static and changeless present or eternity as contrasted with the change, coming into being and passing away of time.[19] In conformity with this Platonic tradition, Augustine sees time as the moving image of eternity. On Augustine's account, it is eternity without beginning or end that is stretched, whereas time itself is infinitely divisible, each instant giving way to the next. Thus in a disquisition on time addressed to God, Augustine declares:

> Your years are completely present to you all at once, because they are at a permanent standstill. They do not move on, forced to give way before the advance of others, because they never pass at all. Your years are one day; yet your day does not come daily but is always today, because your today does not give place to any tomorrow nor does it take the place of yesterday (*Confessions*, XI, 13, p. 263).[20]

Eternity is described as a holding on to presence such that its transience disappears, the ineluctable yearning for presence is fulfilled, and the allergy to time's passing is overcome.

For Augustine, time is unreal for much the same reason as its unreality will later be proclaimed by J. M. E. McTaggart, the British Hegelian. The now moves, shifts its position from future to present to past such that no moment of time can be stabilized and identified as time itself. The past and future cannot be time itself since the past no longer exists and the future has not yet come into being. If the present is time, it ceases to exist as it comes into being because it is always already giving way to past and future. On the other hand, if the present were to remain stable, it would cease to be time and would be eternity (*Confessions*, XI, 14, p. 264). On either hypothesis, time is unreal.

Because the instant itself is without dimension, time cannot, for Augustine, be punctiform. Like the infinitely divisible space of Zeno's paradox, time is always subject to further division. The present only appears to have length: "The only time that can be called present is an instant, if we can conceive of such, that cannot be divided into even the most minute fraction, and a point of time as small as this passes so rapidly from the future to the past that its duration is without length" (*Confessions*, XI, 15, p. 266). Whether the present is construed as a year, a day, a moment, or a nanosecond (had Augustine known of it), it defies conceptualization.

Time's passing when expressed in terms of sequence, earlier and later, before and after, is absent from Augustine's discussion of intramundane time but plays a crucial role in what might be termed the "metatemporal framework" or "God's eye view" of time. By asking "What was God doing before creation?" Augustine tries to think the meaning of "before time" in its most radical sense. How can there have been time before there was creation which gives birth to time? The expression "before creation" is an oxymoron. Before and after are bound up with the meaning of beginning, of the absolute novelty of creation, of a being that begins to be. The thought of before and after is, for Augustine, mind shattering: it is a mode of reckoning time that marks off the unthinkable before of "before creation" and after, the time that follows creation, an after that lacks a before. What is highlighted in the thought of Augustine and will come to the fore with Kierkegaard is the signficance of the Moment as the instantiating of an epochal shift, a fundamental difference between before and after. To be sure, in the ordinary course of affairs before and after are applied to the temporal relations of innocuous events that succeed one another, yet time's punctiformity expressed as before and after will be seen to become the perspective of the heterological historian by means of which she denotes momentous transformation. Suffice it to note, Augustine's analysis of before and after occurs in the context of a pivotal change that cannot be thought through to the end without issuing in paradox.

The significance of the before and after of punctiform time diminishes with the rendering of time as a structure of consciousness. For Kant, the *Zweifaltigkeit* of time is rendered as a property of the subject, a doubleness that is reflected in his grasp of time as a form of sensuous intuition and as the diachronicity of the chaotic flux of the sensa which the form of time subordinates to itself. There can be a past only because there is an a priori form that regiments the flux. Among modern philosophers it is Hegel and Nietzsche who, in Kant's shadow, develop time's doubleness in a way that is suggestive for the historian. Approaches to the understanding of time in Hegel and Nietzsche are legion. I shall consider both in the context of their attempts to think the bifurcation of time as punctiform and stretched, at once heirs of and rebels against the Augustinian tradition.

Nowhere has time as a series of points that precede and follow one another been explicated and criticized more carefully than by Hegel for whom the instants of time must pass over into stretched time. It is Nietzsche who, on the other hand, excoriates stretched time as sclerotic because presence is seen as lacking articulation, and who gathers up into the nonconcept of the eternal return the destruction of stretched time thus understood. Nietzsche's thought can be viewed as both preceding and following Hegel, preceding Hegel by thinking the flux that Hegel tries to rein in, and following him as affirming past and future in the eternal return. In an enigmatic formulation Maurice Blanchot elaborates this point:

> Nietzsche (if his name serves to name the law of the Eternal Return) and Hegel (if his name invites us to think presence as all and the all as presence) allow us to sketch a mythology. Nietzsche can only come after Hegel, but it is always before and after Hegel that he comes and comes again. Before: since even if it is thought as the absolute, presence has never gathered in itself the realized totality of knowledge . . . because it has not realized itself practically. . . . And . . . after supposes the completion [and] destruction of time as present such that the Eternal Return affirm[s] the future and the past as the only temporal authorities.[21]

Hegel's strongest criticism of time's punctiformity occurs in the context of his description of the certainty that common sense believes to be conferred by sense experience. What could be more conclusive than primal indication, the designating by an I or subject of a "this-here" or of a "this-very-moment," a now. But as soon as the I points to a now, the certainty of the now's existence vanishes; the immediacy that provides the warranty for its truth sinks into the past. If the now is to retain its truth, the I must, *per impossibile,* reenter the same point in time in order to become the I of that previous moment. Thus Hegel: "'Now' has already ceased to be in the act of pointing to it. The Now that is, is another now than the one pointed to . . . the Now is just this: to be no more just when it is" (*Phen* 106, p. 63). McTaggart will refine and embellish this Hegelian argument in the interest of proving time's unreality, an argument to which I shall recur and which continues to fuel intense debate in Anglo-American philosophy.

Hegel cannot bypass Kant's relegation of time to the subject by regarding time as an empty container withdrawn from the coming into being and the passing away of things. It is precisely when Hegel rejects the view that time is a receptacle for events that his analysis acquires a remarkably contemporary cast. In this light, consider again:

> Time does not resemble a container in which everything is . . . borne away and swallowed up in the flow of a stream. Time is merely this abstraction of

destroying. Things are in time because they are finite; they do not pass away because they are in time, but are themselves that which is temporal. It is therefore the process of actual things which constitutes time. The present makes a tremendous demand, yet as the individual present it is nothing, for even as I pronounce it, its all excluding pretentiousness dwindles, dissolves and falls into dust. (*PhN*, 1:257 add., p. 231)

In Spirit's continuous reinvention of itself, the view that time is a series of nows or an empty container is sublated. At the end of Spirit's history, when truth takes on the form of the philosophically comprehended organization of Spirit's shapes, time is taken up into the eternity of the Absolute, but Hegel refuses to see that the eternity of the Absolute is temporalized by that which it has devoured.

Nietzsche brings to the fore a feature of time's passing, the fact that discrete events repeat themselves, that is absent from Hegel's account. It is just this repetition that, Nietzsche contends, renders the world calculable (*WP* 624, p. 334). To grasp recurrence requires seeing moments of time that are homogeneous in some given respect. Whatever happens over and over again in the same way, "this regularity in succession" can be converted into a formula, a "foreshortening" of the sequence of instants (*WP* 629, pp. 335–330). It is mistaken to assume that such formulae somehow confer comprehension as though counting the beats in a musical composition would amount to understanding it (*WP* 624, p. 334). Because we experience regularity and see that things are unable to fall out other than in the way they do, we attribute lawfulness to sheer periodicity (*WP* 634, p. 337). But laws conceal only a difference of intensity in the energy pulses that succeed one another in the play of before and after.

Yet repetition is not, as calculative intelligence would have it, exact duplication, the recurrence of the identical. Were this the case, the present moment would remain frozen, unable to pass or to advance. The present must already in some way be past and future; otherwise it would remain statically present without being able to give way to the next moment. In Deleuze's version of Nietzsche, "it is the synthetic self-relation of present, past and future . . . that grounds the relation between this moment and other moments."[22]

Yet, for Nietzsche, the insight that things recur is not misguided. Instead, recurrence is to be understood otherwise: as an eternal return that is not mere repetition, an endless cloning of the same, but rather the return of difference. "Repetition appears as difference without a concept express[ing] a power peculiar to the existent," says Deleuze.[23] Such a post-structuralist reading of Nietzsche highlights an ontology in which "differences of differences reverberate to infinity. . . . [T]hings must be dispersed within difference, and their identity must be dissolved before they become subject to eternal return."[24] Thus interpreted, Nietzsche's principal concern is how to think the question of radical becoming so that being's actuality and thinkability do not simply disappear but are released from metaphysics, not as opposed to becoming but as remaining within its ambit.[25] Recurrence is Nietzsche's response to this ontological dilemma: "Recurring is the being of what becomes, 'That everything recurs is the closest approximation of a world of becoming to a world of being'" (*WP* 617, p. 330).[26]

The thought of the eternal recurrence as difference cannot be likened to the standard view that Nietzsche fails to achieve the perfection he strives for in that the debased recurs. Such is the reading given to the celebrated passage in *Zarathustra*, "'Everything goes, everything returns; the wheel of existence rolls forever . . . the wheel of existence remains true to itself for ever'" (*Z*, III, sec. 2, p. 234). But the eternal return is not to be thought of as a circular motion driven mechanistically by something outside itself; instead it is a process that is an-archic in the etymological sense. For does Zarathustra not say: "'Being begins in every instant; the ball There rolls around every Here. The middle is everywhere. The path of eternity is crooked'" (*Z*, III, sec. 2, p. 234).

To see the importance of this curve or bend, consider that on the cyclical view grounded in cosmology the final and initial states of a process must be identical, and the differences within each cycle must reproduce themselves endlessly. If the initial and final state of the process were to coincide, how would the process get started so that it could run through the differences within each cycle?[27] The cyclical view cannot account for intracyclical diversity. As Michel Haar writes, "The theory of the Eternal Return . . . consists precisely in according the most positive value, in attributing perfection, to the break in the circle. The break signifies here that the circle is a form without goal."[28] If the return is not a mechanical process, one that is teleogically driven and subject to laws outside itself, how is what is to return determined? What return is willed and willed as a creation: "It is the *thought* of Eternal Return that selects."[29]

This view should not be taken to mean that the eternal return precedes becoming as an empty thought-form but rather that it is founded on the thought of pure becoming as an ongoing affirmation of transience. Heidegger had already held that Nietzsche's eternal return is the "yes to time [as] the will to have transience abide." But for Heidegger's Nietzsche "what ceases to be returns as the selfsame in its coming,"[30] whereas, for Deleuze, if time is truly passing then there can be no identity, no selfsame: recurrence stamps itself, as it were, on this flux, "constitut[ing] being insofar as it affirms becoming. . . . Identity in the Eternal Return does not designate the nature of what recurs, but the fact of recurring difference."[31] Recurrence is thought and agency in the absence of a subject.

Like Nietzsche, Heidegger challenges the view of time as made up of measurable units as based upon calculative thinking rather than upon a more fundamental understanding of time. In his by-now familiar critique of hypostatized time, he shows that human existence is lived not as a series of discrete now points that pass by but rather as an ec-stasis, a reaching forward out of itself by the Dasein toward the Dasein's own non-being. Life is lived in anticipation of death, not as something not yet present—death will never be present to anyone—but rather as a not being able to be anywhere. Hegel had already noticed the importance of human mortality in deriving other expressions of non-being, for example, logical negation. But if, for Hegel, the negative is sublated in the life of the Absolute, for Heidegger non-being persists: human being is thrown, suspended over the abyss of its own non-existence, its life oriented by its own projected non-being. The critical point I want to note in this otherwise familiar scenario is that, because death is that *toward* which human existence moves in time, for Heidegger the most primordial mode of time is the future (*BT* 329, p. 377).

What then of the past? It cannot remain unaffected by a life that is futurally configured. The past too must be governed by this structure in that the I who existed before is the being who *even then* looked ahead, *even then* was always already thrown over the abyss of its own non-existence (*BT* 328, p. 376). For Heidegger, the future with its structure of anticipation and possibility prevailed in one's past thoughts and acts just as it does now and just as a more distant future will continue to provide the horizon for a nearer future (*BT* 385, p. 437). It is as if, for Heidegger, the content of the past is incidental to displaying the past's relation to the future: the past *für uns* is what is behind us, but the past *für sich* is, as it were, always already ahead of itself.

David Farrell Krell offers a nuanced account of the relation between Dasein's temporalization as past and future. Is it not odd, he asks, for Heidegger to tolerate the generally accepted terms for the present, *Gegenwart* and the future, *Zukunft,* while foregoing the expected correlative term for the past, *Vergangenheit,* choosing instead to coin *Gewesenheit,* the noun form of the past participle (*BT* 325–326, pp. 372–373)? Not if, Krell argues, Heidegger means to avoid turning the past into an "is," a static hypostatization of moving time. But the matter cannot be brought to closure with a substitution that is hardly innocuous. Dasein's futural existence depends on its having been: the future is a carrying back to a time to which one has always already come. Yet, as Krell concedes, Heidegger concludes in this very passage that Dasein's having been is contingent upon its being futural. Although Krell remains guarded about privileging the future and cites Heidegger's insistence upon the equiprimordiality of time's ec-stases (*BT* 329, p. 377; 350, p. 401), it is hard to disclaim the text that reads: "Having-been springs from the future in such a way that the future that has been *[die gewesene . . . Zukunft]* . . . (better, that is, having-been *[gewesende]*), releases the present from out of itself" (*BT*, p. 326).[32]

This point may be illustrated by the following example: I might inquire of a German-speaking stranger who accompanies an artist friend in a chance meeting at a gallery opening, *"Sicher sind sie auch Maler?"* If he responds with, *"Ja das war ich in die Vergangenheit,"* I take him to mean, "I was but now it is over and done with." The past is closed. Should he, however, reply as he might, with the single word, *"Gewesen,"* he is informing me, "I used to be a painter but am not now one, not one *any longer,"* thereby inserting through negation a covert reference to the today and the tomorrow in which he does not continue being a painter.[33] Even if he specifies a point at which he ceased to be a painter, the cesura only reinforces the "no longer" with its penumbra of past and future. "I stopped painting in 1994" only stipulates that he *surely* is a painter no longer. The love of Swann for Odette and of the narrator for Albertine in Proust's *Remembrance of Things Past* in some respects point to a *Gewesenheit* of this type. Like the "no longer" of the painter, the past of their amours is never finished and done with but constantly present as always already before them. The past is not first-order language to which second-order language can appeal: there is only "a resonance between two objects [that produce] an epiphany."[34]

Yet just as the projective movement of time governs the direction of Heidegger's thought, the significance of the past in both Bergson's and Husserl's accounts of time is subordinated either to the future or to the present. Despite the importance of Bergson's discovery of *durée,* lived time, the time of human experience over and against mensurable or clock time, the role of the past in configuring temporality is seen to be in the service of an ascending evolutionary process. Although no pre-ordained end governs evolution, life moves in the direction of creating future novelty. Husserl's depiction of the character of the present moment—of the retentions, what is preserved of past moments, and protentions, the forward-stretching anticipations that cling to the instant—has subordinated both past and future to the present.

But what is revealed in Nietzsche's account of recurrence and has been all but passed over in Heidegger's thought is the *primacy* of the past in determining the structure of time. In proposing the celebrated riddle to the dwarf, Zarathustra speaks of two paths, one that is ahead and the other that is behind us, paths that abut at the gateway he calls "Moment." The dwarf sees at once that the paths must somehow converge, that time is a circle, but the dwarf's merely superficial grasp of this point posits an identity without difference, a parity and symmetery that attest sheer replication. Thus Zarathustra remonstrates:

"From this gateway Moment, a long eternal lane runs *back:* an eternity lies behind us."

"Must not all things that *can* run *have* already run along this lane? Must not all things that *can* happen *have* already happened, been done, run past?"

". . . Must not this gateway too have been here—before." (*Z*, III, 2, p. 178)

What is most remarkable in this already remarkable interrogation of the dwarf is Zarathustra's final query: "'And are not all things bound fast together in such a way that this moment draws after it all future things? *Therefore* draws itself too'" (*Z*, III, 2, p. 179; emphasis in original). *That which was always already determines what will be, the future itself is nachträglich.* Does not the moment draw *after* it all future things?[35] Nietzsche's Zarathustra, like the time traveler who journeys to the future, sees not a straight line ahead but a curve such that the past is always already ahead of him. For Nietzsche, it is this curve that marks out time's stretch.

The idea of punctiformity is not absent from Nietzsche's thinking. To the contrary, the idea of before and after, of sheer succession, is crucial to his deconstruction of causality. The terms "cause" and "effect" are applied as if they were explanatory principles but fail to explain changes of state. "Two successive states, the one "cause," the other "effect": this is false. The first has nothing to effect, the second has been effected by nothing."[36] In fact, cause and effect can refer to nothing but the before and after of succession, a succesion that is itself determinable as the outcome of a struggle between different quanta of power.

McTAGGART'S PARADOX: TENSED AND TENSELESS TIME

The conundrums bound up with the bifurcation of time is elaborated in a by-now extended Anglo-American analytic philosophical literature whose complexity can only be suggested here. The problem almost always is considered independently of its historical or cultural embedding. This de-contextualization serves (perhaps unintentionally) as an act of reduction in Husserl's sense of the term, not (as for Husserl) a cordoning off of the existence of the world but rather of the culturally dense conceptual matrix, the discursive practices, from which such radical abstraction emerges. Yet if philosophical analysis is regarded as a mode of philosophical stylization akin to the abstractions of Mondrian, Miró, or the Cubists, or to the literary works of Beckett or Kafka, its formal elegance can be appreciated as well as its power to bring to the fore the logical and ontological implications of temporal passage.[37]

Time's passing has been construed in the analytic tradition in two ways, roughly comparable to what I have called "stretched" and "punctiform" time. On the view that temporal becoming consists in the passing of events from future to present to past, an event moves from the distant to the near future and thence to the present into an ever more remote past. Bertrand Russell, however, argued to the contrary that futurity cannot be a monadic property of events, that it is therefore meaningless to speak of an event as sloughing off this property. We need only say an event X occurs earlier or later than another event Y, a relation between events that remains true, come what may. On the first view, the status in existence of these events changes with respect to their temporal locations—present events exist but future events do not yet exist and past events no longer exist. Philosophers who believe that there is temporal becoming are called "tensers," a position captured in the sentence, "The French Revolution occurred long ago." Those who admit temporal descriptions of events only as earlier and later hold a tenseless theory of time and are called "detensers," a position captured in the sentence, "The French Revolution preceded the Russian Revolution."[38] As described by detensers, events that occur at different times have the same ontological status in that the truth or falsity of statements depicting them remains constant.[39]

The difficulties with the problem of time's passing received its most influential formulation in the work of J. M. E. McTaggart in the context of his celebrated argument for the unreality of time.[40] McTaggart, as an exponent of Hegel, develops this argument along the lines of Hegel's rebuttal of the claims of sense certainty discussed earlier. The two modes of ordering temporal series, one as reflecting temporal becoming—I shall call this mode "stretched" time—and the other, the static relations of before and after—I shall call this mode time's "punctiformity"—are referred to by McTaggart as the A and B series. Statements in the B series have permanent truth values: "It is true today and will remain so in the year 3000 that the French

Revolution occurred before the Russian," whereas "The French Revolution occurred long ago" changes its truth value depending upon the time of utterance. Although both temporal relations and temporal becoming are in accord with ordinary experience, McTaggart awards primacy to becoming to the A series. Because neither the events nor their relations change in the B series, if the B series is to remain a *temporal* series, says McTaggart, then its events must exemplify pastness, presentness, and futurity. Thus the B series is parasitic upon the A series. If this is conceded and if, in addition, it is agreed that a contradictory concept cannot be applied to reality, then it remains only to show that the A series involves such a contradiction, and McTaggart is home free. Just such a contradiction is demonstrated when it is conceded that events move from future to present to past because then each event *is* all three: future, present, and past. But an event cannot be all three in that these are irreconcilable properties. Tensers who want to save pastness, presentness, and futurity hope to elude McTaggart's conclusion by showing that tensed sentences are needed to describe tensed facts, whereas detensers believe that they can show that A determinations (pastness, presentness, and futurity) are otiose.[41]

The conceptual dilemmas that arise when reflecting upon the problem of time are of immense significance for the historian who works within the ambit of discursive practices that infiltrate her reconstruction of the past even when she does not notice their importance for her work. McTaggart's argument for the unreality of time hinges upon the notion of the moving Now, the Now that dissolves as it changes from future, to present, to past. But it is just this grasp of time's movement that informs narrative reconstructions of historical events. Thus it is of more than passing interest to the narrative historian to determine whether the A series can be saved without positing a moving Now and thereby avoiding the difficulties to which McTaggart and his followers have called attention. Although it by no means resolves the issue, the narrative historian who appeals to tense can argue that it is simply false to assert that, because time passes, an event must exhibit contradictory properties of pastness, presentness, and futurity, as McTaggart thought. Instead, if succession is rightly understood, it accords with phenomenological experience: an event E "is past, was present, and was (still earlier) future; E is future, will be present, and will still later be past; or E is present, was future, and will be past."[42] Yet there remains for the historian a corollary of the tensed theory of time that, on the face of it, constitutes an important objection. From the standpoint of the tensed theory, propositions change their truth value with the passage of time. Thus "John Major is Prime Minister of Great Britain," true in 1996, will no longer be true in the year 3000. But the narrative historian can reply that far from constituting a problem, time's passing supports the position that she holds from the start: historical narratives are *ficciones,* neither point-for-point mirroring of events nor sheer fabrication in the sense explained earlier. In sum, the conditions for ascribing truth and falsity to a proposition can now be seen as bound up with the movement of time that destabilizes the truth values ascribed to tensed propositions. Such propositions are not false in the usual sense as is the proposition "Hong Kong is a Spanish colony"; instead, epistemic fluidity is intrinsic to statements about matters of fact. Changing truth values are the way in which narratives reflect time's passage.

In the light of these considerations, it might be thought that interpreting events as earlier and later, the position defended by the detenser, could provide a feeling of solidity but that it had little to offer the historian. To be sure, the detenser avoids some difficulties associated with the tensed view of time in that the relation of before and after holds, come what may. The proposition "The Emancipation Proclamation precedes the Gettysburg Address" is as true in 1900 as it is in the year 2000. But the cognitive yield of such propositions for the narrative historian is small. If, as detensers claim, events exist temporally in relations of simultaneity, earlier than and later than, there is no ontological difference among the described events because there are no such properties as pastness, presentness, or futurity that can be ascribed to them. This ontological parity of events exhibited in the detenser's statements makes it difficult to account for the vivid feeling of emotional engagement one might feel when considering current matters: "Now, see them, the Armenians and the Azerbaijanis are engaged in a bloody conflict." This sense might be lacking in an aesthetically distanced response, for example, to the Roman historian Tacitus' account of the Roman occupation of Armenia, however powerfully rendered. Of what use is the detenser's account of events hanging in a timeless empyrean reminiscent of Plato's heaven of forms to the historian?[43]

It must not be forgotten that the detenser's view opens the discursive space for judgments of significance and that such judgments always already involve ethical determinations. By concluding that an event is of historical importance, the heterological historian judges that this event establishes a boundary between antecedent and subsequent political, economic, and cultural conditions. Whether such an event is of long or short duration, it effectively marks a sea change in the way subsequent affairs fall out. The historian would be remiss in failing to observe continuities, but she nevertheless marks off the historical terrain in terms of the radical alterations that occur after the event. The French, Russian, and Chinese Revolutions may be seen in this light.

It is useful to see the ontological underpinnings of the tenser/detenser debate in light of the differences between realists and anti-realists. Nowhere are these differences more subtly explicated than in Michael Dummett's by now classic 1969 essay, "The Reality of the Past."[44] According to Dummett, the realist assigns meanings to statements such that we know what has to be the case in order for a statement to be true. In the absence of these truth conditions the statement is false. The statement's truth value is independent of whether I know it to be true or false or whether I can acquire the means for ascertaining whether it is true or false. For the anti-realist, a statement is true or false independent of our knowledge or capacity for knowledge, but rather is so "in terms of the conditions which we recognize as establishing the truth or falsity of statements of that class."[45] One might say that for Dummett's realist, claims of truth or falsity are world linked, whereas for the anti-realist they are artifacts of language.

Truth conditions for the anti-realist may be expressed in statements that belong to some class other than the disputed class, that class of propositions whose truth or falsity is undetermined. If the truth of statements of the disputed class must be reduced to another class of statements, the anti-realist may be forced to a realist interpretation of statements of the second or re-ductive class, a concession that is clearly self-defeating for the anti-realist. Thus, for example, statements about someone's character may be reduced to statements about the neurophysiological correlates of that character trait which can only be explained in realist terms. But the anti-realist can avoid reductionism by arguing that "conditions that establish the truth or falsity of the statements of the disputed class are simply those we recognize as obtaining when they obtain without resorting to statements outside those of the disputed class."[46] In a down-to-earth situation, the realist would claim that to understand the statement "This cake is good" one would need the recipe used to make it, as opposed to the claim of the anti-realist who would merely say "Delicious! The proof of the pudding is in the eating." The anti-realist version of understanding a statement has the advantage of parsimony. The anti-realist, it would seem, applies the nominalist principle, *entia non sunt multiplacanda praeter necessitatem,* to explanations.

The anti-realist thinks we cannot grasp the sense of a statement apart from the way in which we have been taught to grasp the conditions of its justification. We therefore cannot imagine what it would mean to ascribe truth or falsity to statements *apart from* the criteria we have been primed to use in making such determinations. This claim can be viewed as a version of Nietzsche's assertion that "the strength of knowledge [depends] on the degree with which it has been incorporated, on its character as a condition of life."[47] It can be said concisely (if somewhat misleadingly) that for the anti-realist there is no exit from our discursive practices.

It is Dummett's contention that statements about the past are particularly well-suited to anti-realist interpretation. Consider now the position of the historian who subscribes to the realist view of truth. Recall that the realist insists upon knowing what has to be the case for a statement to be true. The realist historian will be obliged to argue for a truth-value link between statements uttered at different times: that which is the case that makes event A true will continue to make it true. Thus, by virtue of the truth-value or the what-has-to be the case link, she can assert that the proposition "In 1815, Texas was admitted as the twenty-eighth state of the Union" uttered in 1816 and the same statement uttered in 1996 are both true. The actual occurrence and the recounted event stand on the same ontological footing. The realist is for Dummett a detenser:

> [He] would like to stand outside the whole temporal process and describe the world from a point which has no temporal position at all . . . survey[ing] all temporal positions in a single glance: from this standpoint . . . the different points in time have a relation of temporal precedence between themselves, but no temporal relation to the standpoint of the description—i.e. they are not being considered as past, present or future.[48]

The anti-realist might agree about what happened to Texas in 1815 but would insist that she knows it by having learned the use of the past tense through conventions such as remembered instances of what was seen and done. Because there is no independent truth-value link that can be appealed to, it cannot be said that knowledge about the past is independent of our present or future knowledge of its truth value. This is of course the claim made by tensers and is, in addition, intrinsic to the time scheme of historical narrative. According to Dummett, "the anti-realist takes . . . seriously the fact that we are immersed in time. . . . [For him] the past exists only in the traces it has left upon the present, whereas for the realist, the past still exists as past, just as it was when it is present."[49]

Dummett distinguishes between two types of anti-realist: those who apply its tenets globally irrespective of context, and those who apply these tenets only to statements about the past. Nietzsche, Foucault, and Richard Rorty might be seen as belonging to the former class in that they believe that what we hold to be true across the board is the result of learned criteria.

The historiography of Hayden White as well as Dummett's own position approximates the latter in that both confine their anti-realism to statements about the past. The global anti-realist holds that there must be evidence now that there was evidence at the time of utterance that a statement was true, if we are to regard statements about the past as true. But the anti-realist only can say about the past that X was true so long as she ties it to some presently plausible past history of the world. If she is a historian, such an anti-realist might be imagined to say, "See, there is no one past history of the world in that every possible past history of the world stands on an equal footing. A statement about the opening of China to the West might be true in one possible history but false in another."

The moderate version of anti-realism would be particularly unsettling to the *heterological* historian in that no constraints upon the reconstruction of an event obtain apart from presently accepted linguistic conventions and *some* past possible history. For the historian of World War II, for example, this approach could vindicate the view advanced by Nolte and others in the context of the by-now notorious *Historikerstreit*—that the Nazi concentration camp system was a regrettable but understandable response to Soviet communism, that in fighting communism the Nazis merely imitated the Communist methods of reprisal against perceived internal enemies.[50] Such an approach takes for granted "a past history of the world," one in which the revisionist account of a segment of that history forms a part. It could be argued that for these revisionist historians the linguistic conventions determining truth and falsity are in conformity with certain memories of past occurrences. Yet what *now* determines truth and falsity for them may in fact be the self-serving "linguistic convention" that a statement is true when it assuages guilt, saves face, or encourages national pride. Such framework relativism has already been shown in Chapter 1 to create comparable problems for Hayden White who, in allowing for unconstrained interpretive freedom, conceded that Fascist interpretations of the Holocaust would have to be countenanced even if he would want the Holocaust to serve as a limiting case.

THE SPEECH AND SILENCE OF HETEROLOGY

How does the fissuring of time as it has been understood in this history figure in the inverted world of virtuality the historian now inhabits, a world in which objects have been volatilized into images and images into information that will be retranscribed into acoustic, visual, and even tactile simulacra? Consider again the past from the standpoint of the tenser, or the anti-realist about the past, or of the Dasein for whom time is lived ecstatically. By capturing temporal passage phenomenologically, each seeks to elude the aporetic result of viewing time as a series of disarticulated and successive droplets and, at the same time, to establish (against the Platonists, Augustine, and McTaggart) that stretched time is not unreal. I want to argue that, from the standpoint of time's continuity, the question is not one of the reality or unreality of the past but rather of its hyperreality. The past is always already hyperreal, volatilized, awaiting only the technological instantiation it has now received. A genealogical analysis may help to justify this claim.

Consider first the spatial world experienced as a nexus of material objects. Such objects invite circumnavigation, are made visible by gaining access to that which may be currently out of one's field of visibility. Thus, the world offers itself not only as spectacle but as resistance that can be physically overcome. The rock that is too heavy can be moved with a lever. Flight overcomes gravity. But it is otherwise with past time that, by contrast, occurs as a split, a scission, a fissure in the spatiality of the world as an organized assemblage. It is a commonplace of everyday phenomenology that what has passed by cannot be brought back materially: no, not, never. That which opens up through negation, the past, appears to offer itself to my grasp, but *the only way the past can return is as word or image.* "It was" is the unsurpassable negation that breaks into the materiality of the world and volatilizes it. The past is disclosed by the "not" that is imprinted, in Derrida's phrase, *sous rature* in what is actually imaged and told. The no, not, never is not merely a mode of time's disclosure, one of time's ec-stases, but *is* time as the break thrown open by the world between itself and itself in the mode of "it was before but cannot be again." *The only way in which that which was can return is through its volatilization in images.* Baudrillard is right to observe in his hypertrophied prose:

> The last bomb that no one speaks about, is the bomb that is not content to strew things in space but would strew them in time. The temporal bomb. Where it explodes, everything is suddenly blown into the past; and the greater the bomb's capacity the further into the past they go. . . . In an amnesic world like ours, everything living is projected into the past. . . . That is the real bomb, the bomb that immobilizes things in eerie retrogression.[51]

In a culture in which images are pandemic, does the negativity of time offer the possibility of a check on *which* particular images of the past the historian should choose to bind into a visual, acoustic, or discursive narrative? Does the "not yet" of the future in some way impinge upon the "no longer" of the past in such a way as to help the historian restrict interpretation? For defenders of stretched time, it is obvious that the future is dependent upon the past, but is there a place for the future in the past itself? A response to this question demands an inquiry into the relation of past and future, not by moving back toward the past from the future but rather by reversing direction from the "it was" to the "not yet."

What appears to distinguish the future from the past is the future's seemingly unique relation to possibility. As the present moves ahead, the multiple possibilities of the future drop away; the future is lived as an annihilation of possibilities. It is a commonplace that with advancing age people speak of the time they have left as a diminishing of their prospects. Yet does not a past event, like a present event, not exhibit a relation to *its* future, the possibilities it saw before it *then* when it was present, possibilities now annihilated. Recall that the historian who inhabits stretched time—the antirealist about the past, the tenser—might well entertain the view that her account of a past event is related to some past *possible* history of the world, a history in the making that at any possible point could have been or not have been. *To create a historical narrative she must grasp occurrences in the manner of holding-in-front-of-herself not only that which was but that which could have been.* It is this double disclosiveness of historical narrative, the inclusion of paths not taken, that places possibility within the conspectus of the past.

A proposition about the past, "I stayed home last summer," is not merely a statement of fact but suggests many rejected possibles: for example, my staying home may reflect a decision to avoid preparation for a camping trip I could have taken, or turning down an invitation for foreign travel I might have accepted, or numerous other rejected options. Historical narration is a constructive act whose grammatical structure, the indicative "it was," is, as it were, the limiting case of the counterfactual, "it could have been but was not," that circumscribes it. In sum, possibility's connection to the future is also intrinsic to its relation to the past: what the historian narrates is that which occurred surrounded by a penumbra of negated possibles each of which is expressed in the modal form: "X was possible but X did not occur."

The narrative historian's retrieval of the past requires the recovery of negated possibles. For example, in the period preceding and during World War II, Hitler could have honored his pact with Stalin and refrained from invading the Soviet Union; U.S. forces could have lost the battle of Iwo Jima; German General Von Paulus could have captured Stalingrad. If the past is to be retrieved, the not of that which can never be made present, the past's ungroundedness, its hyperreality, the field of images of that which could have but did not occur are intrinsic to that which is to be recovered.

The historian's re-construction of the past is delimited by a further more restrictive negation, that which could not have been even on the broadest possible interpretation. Thus, for example, I may think of Charlemagne as son of Pepin the Short, as King of the Franks, or as Emperor of the West, but I cannot think of him as Leo XIII, Pope of Rome.

To assert that which could not have been as that which was leaves open the possibility that such assertions are errors or intentional deceptions, in either case inviting revision of a historical narrative. But in the framework of the defenders of stretched time, is not deception intrinsic to language by virtue of the "original sin" of language, the impossiblity of a purely transparent language that would render discursive rectitude possible in the realist sense of the term? Caught by the imperative to tell the truth and the impossibility of telling it, the historian appears trapped. This Catch-22 situation would appear to release her from accountability for the historical artifact she has created.

But this is not the way things need to fall out. The historian is bound by the negative "grounding" of historical narrative: "it could never have been thus." The language of the defender of stretched time is necessarily faltering, a language always already fissured by negation. The historian therefore need not claim that she presents *absolute truth,* "It has to have been X, it could not have been otherwise." But she can claim a *kind of certainty,* grounded in a non-event, "It might have been X or Y, but I am sure it could not have been Z."

If the break with the truth-value link, the link between the possibility of truth telling and the historian's promise, remains unsettling, it would appear that the historian might be well-served by returning to some version of realism and assuming that a matching of referent and proposition is possible. Not so, if the historian wants to avoid becoming a creater of mere chronicles in Hegel's sense; not so, if the *historia rerum gestarum* is to be one of thick description rather than a recounting of a string of dated events. The historian who seeks complexity and phenomenological richness must give up the dream of absolute truth and settle for *ficciones,* not the absolute truth about what was but the certainty of that which could not have been.

Must it then be conceded that the punctiform view of time—"the finite buds or drops" (William James), the "manifestations of the wills to power" (Nietzsche)—that succeed one another are useless for the historian? Not at all. From a pragmatic point of view, the historian is able to define the upper limit of a moment and the coming into being of another moment. In the writing of history (unlike what may be the case in everyday life) she does so in terms of *significance:* an alteration of social, economic, political, and cultural forces. She may believe that the earlier event, trend, or condition is the cause of the later one but, prior to positing the cause-effect link she has, in actuality, rendered a judgment of value.

But how is the historian to determine significance? Before adducing reasons, before weighing evidence in deciding what is to be recounted, the historian attests or provides the warranty for her claim. "Yes, it is vital that we see what happened before and after Alexander's generals conquered the Bactrian kingdoms of northern India, why and for whom this was significant." "It is vital" is an axiological claim and not a description or an explanation. In asserting that an event is significant she speaks in the imperative voice about a matter of value and about a value that matters. Before elaborating upon this point, it is important to see how one moment goes over into the next.

For the historian, a past moment may be long or short, change may be sudden or slow, but, if the new moment is to be of interest, the change from before to after must be not only noticeable but non-trivial. To see this, consider the phrase "before and after Hitler," a phrase that can be contextualized so as to denote both inconsequential and significant change. The phrase may indicate the moment prior to and the moment subsequent to the birth of an infant to a couple in the town of Linz, in all likelihood the perspective of the townspeople at that time, but to the historian "before and after Hitler" is shorthand for massive transformations in the power constellations of Europe.

It is Kierkegaard who, in a theological context, draws attention to delimiting before and after as the result of a decisive event: what divides earlier from later is the Moment, the entry of eternity into time, that instant when the believer sees Jesus as the Christ, an instant that alters the character of the believer's life. Stretched time is of little consequence from the standpoint of faith, so much so that the Moment is no different for the disciple at second hand, the present-day believer, than it is for the contemporary disciple of Jesus. What counts, says Kierkegaard, is the Moment that renders "the before" a species of vanity ("caducity" as Jean-Luc Marion has called it) but that attaches significance to even trivial events in "the after."

To be sure, the historian does not speak of the significance of the before and after in theological terms, but like Kierkegaard's believer she is struck by that which is momentous. Change may be gradual or sudden, but the historian remains attentive to the point at which it is clear that a new state of affairs has come about. She may be involved in the mechanical task of data gathering but sees that her task will bring to the fore information that will bear upon a larger problem. Thus, examining tax records of landowners in South Carolina in the decade before the Civil War may shed light on the plantation economy and the role of slavery in sustaining it. The historian who proclaims, "See, these statistical records require your attention because they will help you discern how something momentous follows from understanding what they mean," has stationed herself in ethical terrain. She articulates the past from a perspective that Walter Benjamin describes as messianic, for her task is to redeem it. He writes:

> There is secret agreement between past generations and the present one. Our coming was expected on earth. Like every generation that preceded us, we have been endowed with a weak Messianic power to which the past has a claim. That claim cannot be settled cheaply (II, p. 254).[52]

Benjamin's impassioned statement bears a strong family resemblance to Arthur C. Danto's more austere account of the philosophy of history which he does not hesitate to characterize as "prophetic." In distinguishing the historian from the philosopher of history Danto writes: "Philosophers of history seek for the significance of events before the later events, in connection with which the future events acquire significance, have happened. The pattern they project into the future is a narrative structure."[53] Prior to making a determination of an event's significance and, a fortiori, prior to constructing her narrative, the historian assumes the standpoint of before and after that opens the space of ethical discourse. It is important to see that the historian who speaks from this perspective (that of the detenser) cannot, however, separate her claims about the event from the time of utterance or from the utterance itself. For the heterological historian, past, present, and future are always already indexical or token-reflexive expressions,[54] those that require knowing who utters an expression, when and where it has been uttered in order to determine the particular that is the subject of the reference. Proper names and the pronouns "I" and "you" do not refer to the properties of individuals but refer directly to the individuals they designate; similarly, "now" refers not to presentness but to the date of utterance. It is she who speaks now. Recall that Benveniste was shown (Chapter 1) to have argued that, from the standpoint of linguistics, demonstratives are linked to the I that speaks because the demonstratives "this," "here," "now," and the personal pronouns "I" and "you" both refer to a present instance of discourse. The "I" uttered by the historian refers directly and cannot be transposed into the descriptive phrase "the woman who writes about history." Nor does the historian explicitly say: "I, now, here, attest the significance of my claim." Instead, she is likely to maintain silence, a silence that affirms but does not refer to her as the bearer of discourse. Yet the unspoken indexical "I" inscribes itself in her narrative. Noting the ethical character of indexicals, Robert Nozick remarks: "Reflexive [self-aware] indexicality is the birthmark of ethics."[55]

When the historian makes a determination about an event's importance, she does so in indicative language for she cannot do otherwise. Prior to her utterance, however, she provides the warranty for its significance, attests that now, here, *je te jure,* language about the past that is about to take place must be heard.

∞

Time's diachronicity is threatened not only by its acceleration in a culture of images but by a series of powerful arguments that undermine the plausibility of positing time's flux. Not only can time be seen as a sliding from past to future but also as a series of dated events whose temporality can only be registered in terms of before and after, earlier and later. This perspective undermines the possibility of creating histories that are contingent upon the flow of time. Yet time's punctiformity, time construed in terms of before and after, opens the way for making determinations about the significance of events, for discerning historical turning points that allow the historian to say: "Now, after this has transpired, things are different from the way they were before."

In the culture of images which has further destabilized the movement of time, the notion of time travel has engaged both the literary and scientific imagination by providing tropes that enable the historian to reflect upon her sense of temporal bilocation. The time traveler stationed in the world she inhabits and, simultaneously, in a world of the past is the locus of their meeting. Moreover, the trope of time travel intersects with the volatilization of the real in the culture of images and intensifies the temporal destabilization confronting the historian.

Both the punctiform and stretched views of time have historically been challenged in the interest of establishing not the unreality of time's flow but rather the reality of an eternal present. Augustine questions time's actuality by indicating that time can be envisaged as a sequence of nows, each of which passes away. But the logic of considering time as passing or as a sequence of earlier and later events, of before and after, is itself undermined when Augustine tries to ponder the possibility of an after that has no before, namely, a before that preceded creation.

It is, unsurprisingly, Hegel, proponent of the eternal present of an Absolute Subject, who uncovers in one of Spirit's penultimate moments a powerful argument attacking time as a series of now points. What could be more certain, Hegel asks, than the immediacy of primal indication, of "this," "here," "now"? Yet as soon as the I points to a now, the now disappears into a past that can never be re-entered, vanishing the moment its existence is posited. McTaggart, a relatively recent admirer of Hegel, refines this argument. Positing the two views of time cited, the stretched and punctiform (earlier and later) views, respectively designated as the A and B series, he contends that the temporal relation of the B series is unchanging. But precisely because the relation of earlier and later is unalterable, it is no longer temporal. The stretched time of the A series too is undermined because the fluidity of temporal events allows for the positing of contradictory attributes—future, present, and past—to the same event.

Present-day proponents of the punctiform view known as "detensers" refuse to abandon what they see as the certainty that attaches to assertions of before and after, while advocates of stretched time, "tensers," see in the before and after view the loss of phenomenologically experienced temporal passage. When the historian envisages an event in terms of before and after, she sees it as marking off a sea change in historical circumstances. By contrast, historical narrative reflects the flow of time as past, present, and future. The differences between tensers and detensers are rendered far more complex when they are seen as bound up with the disputes between realists and anti-realists. While the ensuing debates resist easy summary, it can be said that, for the realist, claims of truth and falsity retain links to the world whereas for the anti-realist such claims are bound up with linguistic rules.

The detenser anti-realist view is anticipated in Nietzsche's claim that events repeat themselves, a periodicity that makes us think that events are governed by rationally comprehensible laws when, in fact, there is only a difference among pulses of energy that succeed one another. Yet this view is also undermined when Nietzsche's doctrine of the eternal return is interpreted as deconstructing sequentiality by alleging that the future is that-which-already-was, thereby rendering the future *nachträglich* and undoing the relation of earlier and later. In accordance with time's *Nachträglichkeit,* the historian holds the past she has contructed in front of her in a move back to the future.

It is Heidegger who offers a radical revisioning of temporal flux in his account of the ec-stases of time and of the Dasein's expectation of its own future non-being. Because the Dasein is always already ahead of itself, it can be argued that the future is the privileged modality of time for Heidegger. But, if so, the historian must note that that which was, the past, was in its own time futurally configured so that the future destabilizes a seemingly immobile past event. This undermining of diachronicity in the interest of a phenomenologically clarified view of time imposes a confusion of temporal modes that volatilizes the past.

Moreover, the past can be seen as threatening experienced materiality. If the world is viewed from the perspective of its character as solidity and resistance, it is apprehended as manipulable, as open to change. Yet the past is not part of the world's density in that it can never be brought back materially but only as word or image. "It was" *is* an unsurpassable negation that enters the world's materiality and, as such, whose material return is precluded.

If the historian is to configure the past in word and image, she must proceed by way of negation. We have seen that the past is always already infiltrated by futurity (as Heidegger's account implies) so that the past once was its future possibles, not those that can be realized but those that could have been realized. The historian must consider what could and could not have been *then,* recover and examine these negated possibles. The scope of her narrative is restricted by impossibility, that which could not under any circumstances have been. She can offer no absolute assurances of truth, but she can claim, as it were, a fallible certainty grounded in a non-event: it could not have been thus.

In her foray into the impossible, the historian must make the dead other re-member, speak through the literary and artifactual remains that constitute the historical record or, in their absence, through the burial places which encrypt the memories of the dead others. She may ask, ringing changes on Augustine's questions, "How am I to interpret remembering?" "Whom do I re-member when I re-member you, the dead others?" These questions will be considered in the following chapter.

I alone possess more memories than all human beings have had since the world became the world.

> Jorge Luis Borges
> "Funes the Memorious"

Beyond the expressible and the inexpressible . . . he floated on with the word, although the more he was enveloped by it, the more he penetrated into the flooding sound and was penetrated by it, the more unattainable, the greater, the graver and more elusive became the word . . . he could not hold fast to it. . . . incomprehensible and unutterable for him: it was the word beyond speech.

> Hermann Broch
> *The Death of Virgil*

SIX

RE-MEMBERING THE PAST

The work of the historian in retrieving the past is affected not only by her interpretation of temporality but by how she appropriates the "process" and "products" of remembering. From the commonsense point of view, events that have gone by are imprinted on a surface or stored in a repository in the form of words and images that can be accessed over and over again, re-membered. On this view, to re-member is to bring back, to re-present, what was previously encoded. The commonsense view conflates the major models of memory that have governed Western thought, that of inscription, incising upon a surface, and that of a storehouse into which one can reach to fetch up some particular of the past. According to the last of these views, what is brought back is either raw material to be worked up into a coherent narrative or detritus to be shunned and cast back into, as Augustine would put it, the great belly of memory. If remembering is a species of representation as the everyday view implies, the epistemic difficulty that pertains to representation as described earlier is reinsated: language about the past is second-order discourse without any first-order level to which definitive ap-

174

peal can be made. Even if, hypothetically, some original "scene" could be replicated, the gap that opens between first and later occasions creates an unsurpassable difference. It would be meaningless to speak of origins here because access to the past is constituted after the fact; firstness is conferred post hoc in the very act of remembering.

I shall take account of some criticisms of memory as representation, especially of Derrida's deconstruction and appropriation of the scriptic and storehouse models. The relation of mnemotechnic devices developed in late antiquity in the West and in the Luba culture of Africa in their relation to computer memory also will be examined. Next I shall turn to the way in which recent brain research brings to light the difference between first- and second-order discourse within remembering in the culture of spectacle and information. Memory is seen by Daniel Dennett not as a fissuring of present consciousness by past time but as the activation of differentiated brain states marked by differences of intensity of neuronal activity. As viewed by Roger Penrose, memory can be explained as a phenomenon of interfacing that occurs in the gap between neuronal activity that can be described in terms of classical physics and that which occurs at the quantum level. Thus difference is not absent from recent mnemonic models.

I shall argue further that computational models of memory developed by advanced mnemonic technologies can be seen as a stockpiling of memories that belong to no one. Such a decontextualization of that which is remembered radically affects the heterological historian's understanding of memory in its social, political, and cultural ramifications. Her queries and objections will constitute a running commentary throughout this chapter.

THE TABLET AND THE AVIARY

For those who believe that memory requires a body, what is most terrifying about death is that, in the absence of a body, there will be either no memory at all or no acquisition of new impressions from which new memories can be created. Aristotle and the Scholastics who followed him never deny that memory requires a body. Aquinas, to be sure, posits intellectual memory, the conceptual afterthought, as it were, of perceptual memory, the recollection that, when alive, one had a memory. In conformity with the view that after death there can be no new memories or even a reweaving of old ones—the imagination that would reweave memories also needs a body— it is clear that the dead cannot create new narratives. Souls that are cut off from the beatific vision that compensates the blessed for death, according to Dante, are stuck in a static past, the obverse of eternity.[1] The ambivalence of the affect that attaches to memory generally is highlighted in this context: living memory that allows for the production of novelty is a source of joy whereas memory brought to closure is a kind of death.

On the face of it, the matter would seem to be quite otherwise in the Platonic tradition. In perhaps the most familiar accounts of mnemonics in Western thought, Plato's *Meno* and *Phaedo,* what appear to be new cognitive acquisitions turn out to have been always already implanted in memory awaiting only the maieutic effort of Socrates, the master teacher, to bring them out. In *Meno,* the relation between the hypotenuse and the area of a triangle is interpreted as an a priori truth elicited, with proper prodding, from one previously ignorant of the axioms of geometry. For Plato, memories of sense impressions are of little consequence; the effort of remembering is to be directed toward the acquisition of rational truths. In *Phaedo* and *Republic,* the seeker after knowledge is led to the forms, to the good and the beautiful in their own-being and, above all, to what is true about truth. Haunted by the self-referentiality paradox that seems to attach to his view, Socrates argues in *Meno* that it is inevitable that some criteria for truth must precede the search for truth or one could not know what one is looking for. But when one works up to the disclosure of truth by appropriate questioning, one recognizes truth when it is found.

The two paradigms for the process of remembering that would come to dominate the way in which memory would be understood subsequently are explicated in Plato's *Theaetetus.* According to the first, memory is described as a kind of writing or imprint. It is imagined that there is implanted in the mind of each human being a wax tablet which is held before a thought or perception. The wax receives the impression "as from the seal of a ring" and retains it. If the imprint is effaced, the perception or thought is lost or forgotten; if incoming data is identified with an imprint with which it does not coincide, this mismatching counts as error (*Theaetetus* 191).[2] Plato distinguishes recollection, remembering in the absence of the object from recogniton what occurs in the presence of the object. According to the second paradigm, the mind is an aviary that warehouses birds while the birds themselves represent kinds of knowledge. One sort of knowledge is that which is learned in order to be stored for future use, knowledge that is "prior to possession," and the other knowledge is that possessed already and fetched up at will (*Theaetetus* 197–198).[3] I shall in due course elaborate upon the graphematic model as "script," and the storehouse view as "crypt," as these terms have entered into in the lexicography of deconstruction. At present it suffices to note that, despite the apparent discrepancy between mnemic materialism (in modern terms, the calling up of what has been experienced) and mnemic rationalism (the evoking of forms devoid of sensual imagery), both accounts are agreed upon several crucial points. First, both associate memory with the acquisition of knowledge and therefore attribute to memory an honorific sense. Second, even the most etiolated view of that which is remembered depends upon the body. Finally, both lean on the same tropes in the elaboration of mnemic conditions. Because knowledge, the desideratum of classical thought, hangs on a reevocation of the past, forgetting fissures knowledge, and becomes a source of fear in much the same way as degenerative diseases that insure memory's deterioration strike fear into the hearts of the aging today.

Aristotle's version of the scriptic model is especially instructive in that it quite consciously deconstructs itself. According to Aristotle, a sense perception is inscribed upon a corporeal surface such that a mind picture (Latin *simulacrum* or *imago*) is created. A percept terminates as an image in memory, as a form divested of its original matter stamped upon a malleable surface, the proverbial wax tablet.[4] These images (*phantasmata*) are then stored in memory.

> First Aporia: Aristotle notes that if we remember the object itself, we do not remember that which is absent. If we remember the image of the absent thing, how can we remember the absent thing that we are not currently perceiving? This difficulty is especially vexing in the case of feeling. "When one remembers, is it this impressed affection he remembers, or is it the objective thing from which this is derived? If the former, we remember nothing which is absent; if the latter, how is it possible that, although perceiving directly only the impression, we remember that absent thing we do not perceive."[5]

It is a version of this aporia that is meditated by Proust's narrator for whom the recollection of an affect produces the affect itself because the earlier affect is always already irretrievably absent.

The problem is doubly critical for the heterological historian who remembers on behalf of another: if she is to station herself in the non-space of ethics, she must re-member an affect that cannot be re-invoked but only (somehow) recreated. What is more (unless she is constructing a personal memoir), the affect she means to evoke is that of another. If this is so, on the one hand her remembering is at a degree of remotion from the original testimony, but, on the other, because of the character of re-membering itself, her post hoc reconstruction is no more remote than that of the one who experiences an event. From the perspective of historical narrative such an interpretation is not only grossly counter-intuitive but would appear to support a species of nihilism with respect to historical narrative.

It would seem that this interpretation of memory would fare no better from the standpoint of ethics than it does from the perspective of cognition. Yet the claim of the heterological historian is not merely "I remember the affect of the other," but "I am responsible for re-membering the affect of the other." Such re-membering provides an axiological force of gravity in the non-space of ethics, a *dédoublement* stemming from the double impossibility itself, the one inherent in the paradox of memory, the other in historical re-presentation. The historian is ob-lig-ated, tied in an etymological sense. "I myself, the historian, must feel the weight of this claim. I speak in a metalanguage but hear an object language which always escapes exact replication yet demands capture."

How is the historian to re-member affect? The psychoanalytically sophisticated historian may fear the charge of appealing to prurient curiosity in attempting to duplicate affect. Yet her narrative need not echo the emotions it depicts but may rely upon understatement. On the other hand, she may feel that the claims of alterity demand nothing less than a crying out, a shriek of protest, "whose justice, what rationality?"[6] The heterological historian understands that her discourse may be destroyed by an affect too powerful to control. Yet, as Derrida comments in speaking of the traumatism of an event, "When a discourse *holds* in some way, it is . . . because it has been opened up on the basis of some traumatizing event, by an upsetting question that does not let one rest . . . and because it nevertheless resists the destruction begun by this traumatism."[7]

Although affect infiltrates memory, it is time, for Aristotle, that is scriptic memory's most primordial feature. The scriptic model derives from time's fissuring of that which is. Aristotle reads this breach by interpreting memory as a function of that faculty charged with perceiving time, namely, the primary faculty of perception, the *sensus communis,* the unspecialized sense that unites and compares impressions of the five specialized senses. Individual memories may be bound up with determinate times or without any knowledge of when the original event occurred. But memory also requires images and, as such, belongs to the faculty of imagination, the faculty that forms the phantasmata and that belongs to higher animals as well as to humans, but in human beings is deliberative. Thus a penumbra of thought clings to imagination. "Imagination in the form of sense exists . . . in other animals but deliberative imagination only in those which can reason" (*De Anima* 434a).

Fear of the unfettered image, the image uncontrolled by thought, is

already evident in Aristotle. Imagination as the faculty of images that incite
to action in the absence of thought belongs to higher animals. Can it not
be activated in human beings? What is more, images other than those of
memory arise in dreams and hallucinations, wild images not regimented by
reason, the result of an arousal of affect. The *sensus communis* is inactive as a
result of the pressure of the blood on the heart, thought to be the inner
organ of perception, so that there is no longer an orderly process of retrieval.
The external senses continue their movement while one is asleep, and together with earlier unprocessed images they run rampant in dreams.

> Second Aporia: There is a leaching of images that either escape from the
> storehouse or are produced outside it, images whose proliferation threatens
> reason. No longer are impressions a fundament upon which reliable memo-
> ries can be built but an incursion upon the orderly process of cognition.
> Aristotle sees the difficulty: on the one hand dreams or hallucinations could
> be reliable indications (for Aristotle reliability would consist in their being of
> divine origin and having predictive power) or they could be the body's way
> of balancing the humors?[8]

In Freudian terms, one might ask whether a given dream is rich in bringing
repressed content to the surface, replete with symbols awaiting interpretation, or merely a random configuring of images, the detritus of the day.

The heterological historian is immersed in a culture of illusions and
phantasms, not one in which the images reflect reality but one in which
images bear no relation to the real, as Baudrillard would have it. There is,
he concludes, a frenetic need to *produce* the real and referential. With the
destruction of historical discourse, there is no longer a language in which
to frame prosecution and defense as a juridical discourse about the past. In
a manner reminiscent of Lyotard's description of the incommensurability of
phrase regimens, Baudrillard writes:

> Auschwitz and the final solution simply cannot be expiated. Punishment and
> crime have no common measure here, and the unrealistic character of the
> punishment ensures the unreality of the facts. What we are currently experi-
> encing is something else entirely . . . a transition from a historical stage to a
> mythical stage: the mythic—and media led reconstruction of these events.[9]

Because we have lost the ability to sustain memory, he renounces the possibility of factual proof.

In his criticism of memory, it would seem that Baudrillard is appallingly
insensitive to the horrors of the century. Yet, in his desire to shock, there is
something of the covert moralist who denies that proof is attainable yet

concedes that it remains vital.[10] Intent upon discovering the conditions that make denial possible, he finds them in the media's continual scrutiny of events. It is this ceaseless barrage of images that creates what earlier psychoanalytic interpretation called psychic numbing and that breeds doubt that these events ever existed.

Yet even if there is a moral purpose in Baudrillard's response to the loss of referentiality in the context of the cataclysm, his view is bound to evoke a *frisson* of horror. What is more, he does not hesitate to recommend "the [transposition of] language games on to social and historical phenomena . . . the heteroclite tropes which are the delight of a vulgar imagination,"[11] a Nietzschean playfulness as opposed to the sobriety of a search for the real.

The heterological historian need not allow her endorsement of Baudrillard's analysis of the letting loose of images and the effort by contemporary culture to gloss over the magnitude of the shift from the real to the hyperreal to preclude her concern with the historical object. Far from disappearing, the "real" intrudes into the specular in a way that cannot be overlooked. Thus she may observe in Baudrillard's Nietzsche-like vision of the present a neglect of that *cri de coeur* of the "other Nietzsche," whose gay science does not exempt existence from pain. Reading Nietzsche against himself, she may respond to Baudrillard's gloom not with playful troping but with Nietzsche's shrewd observation in the *Gay Science* that philosophies of pessimism, far from attesting to real suffering, merely substitute abstract ideas of suffering for experienced pain. Whether virtual or real, whether material in Aristotle's sense, or a visual expression of coded information, *bodily pain is the limiting condition of the hyperreal.* The heterological historian decodes pain, learns to recognize accounts that attempt to diminish or deny the pain of the other, such as the claim that the deaths in concentration camps were a consequence of war conditions widespread at the time, nothing more.[12]

Baudrillard propounds the view that the "anagram . . . the poetic non-linear convulsion of language" might be applied to history and that "beyond historical meaning, allows the pure materiality of time to show through." He concludes that by so doing "we enter beyond history, upon pure fiction."[13] The historian can respond that, in appealing to fiction, Baudrillard already concedes the necessity for narrative however loosely construed, and thus also for regimenting the chaos of images. And what could Baudrillard mean by the pure materiality of time? Surely not the hypostatization of pastness, presentness, and futurity. The materiality of time must mean the materiality of the events themselves in their successiveness, not unlike the time of Dummett's realist who pins down the meaning of the past as earlier and later without acquiescing in the directionality of time, of time's arrow, the giving way of past, present, and future to one another.

The fear of not remembering is bound up with the tradition of mnemotechnics, the creation of devices or contrivances, the chief of which would seem to be writing, the incising of marks to prod the memory to bring forth forgotten knowledge. Is not memory a retrieval of images stamped as if by a seal upon wax always already scriptic even prior to the invention of actual writing? Before returning to this point, it is important to consider a mnemotechnical model depicted in the *Ad Herennium,* a treatise by an unknown teacher of rhetoric compiled ca. 86–82 B.C., that incorporates scriptic elements but contains strikingly novel features. Erroneously believed to have been authored by Cicero, it acquired extraordinary prestige and became the most influential treatise about the classical art of memory in the Middle Ages and the Renaissance. The treatise describes a regimen for augmenting the deficiencies of natural memory by relying upon an association of places—a house, a space between columns, an arch and the like—and images. There is a rote invocation of the scriptic art in that the places are seen to be like the wax tablet and images like letters, but the rememorative process is one of association. The memory loci may be real or fictional but must be numerous and arranged in order so that "we can repeat orally what we have committed to loci, proceeding in either direction from any locus we please." Each fifth locus must be marked off by an image, a distinguishing mark. Frances Yates stresses that "the formation of the loci is of the greatest importance, for the same set of loci can be used again and again for remembering different material." The images which are to be associated with places might be of things, that is, subject matter, or of words, the language in which things are described. Images should be chosen that have strong affective resonances so that they will last for a long time.[14]

Here, in a perhaps unprecedented manner, computer memory is foreshadowed. With great ingenuity, an architectural model is furnished in terms of which the image may be translated into storable form and a translation rule supplied. To be sure, nothing as manageable as the digits 0 and 1 are provided into which information can be converted, yet in a functional sense memory has "gone digital" in ancient mnemonics: "[T]he same set of loci can be used again and again for remembering different material." The freedom to proceed from any locus one pleases suggests a primitive form of hypertext, the placing of the cursor on a word and eliciting all the contexts in which it appears.

The tale of a certain Simonides told by Cicero not only provides insights into the application of this technique but renders vivid the relation between dis-memberment and re-membering. To grasp the seductiveness of mnemotechnics, consider the tale of Simonides, not as it unfolds in Cicero's recounting of it but rather as it is conveyed by the Jesuit, Matteo Ricci, in 1596 to his audience of Chinese scholars whom he hopes so to impress with the power of his mnemotechnics that they would inquire into the theological matrix from which it derived.[15] Ricci hopes that with only slight modifications in architecture and imagery the principles of order and sequence would assure the utility of his mnemotechnic device to his Chinese audience.

> Long ago a Western poet, the noble Xi-mon-ide, was gathered with his relatives and friends for a drinking party at the palace, among a crowd of guests. When he left the hall for a moment . . . the great hall came tumbling down in a sudden mighty wind. [All the revelers were crushed beyond recognition]. Xi-mon-ide, however could remember the exact order in which his relatives and friends had been sitting, and as he recalled them one by one their bodies could be identified.[16]

For all intents and purposes, what Ricci has depicted might be described as a graphic interface, the locus of communication between the computer and the user, in this case a functional distinction within a single mind, that of the practitioner of the mnemonic art. What is remarkable, both in its Roman version and its later recontextualization for Chinese consumption, is the development and trust in a mnemotechnic that circumvents actual writing in cultures in which writing is highly developed.

In the mid-sixteenth century the now largely forgotten Giulio Camillo Delminio (generally referred to as "the divine Camillo"), using the same principles of mnemotechnics as the ancients, constructed a model theater he hoped would be pressed into the service of remembering, not incidental information but eternal truths as they were understood in the hermetic-kabbalistic writings of the time, especially those of Pico de Mirandola. Camillo replaces the fragile loci of the ancients by eternal places worthy of the eternal truths they would help to recall.[17] A recent exhibit of Luba art displayed art objects that are bound up with the complex cultural mnemotechnics of the Luba, a proto-Bantu people of today's southeastern Zaire, techniques reminiscent of the divine Camillo.[18] Numerous connotations attach to the Luba terms that might translate the word memory; these include a dispute to which one returns, speech, protest, demonstration, and intelligence. Memory in this context is a dynamic process that both retains and alters the past and whose content is expressed in highly developed narrative and visual art most frequently associated with royal history.[19] My purpose is not to enter into the intricacies of the Luba conception of history but rather to suggest a recurrent pattern in mnemonic systems in the absence of writing, in which relays between image and place (not unlike the connection between pixels and images) conveys what is to be remembered.

The principal mnemotechnic artifact of the Luba is the *lukasa*, a flat easily held wooden object which may be covered with beads and pins or sculpted so as to alternate incised motifs and figures in relief, all serving as polysemic reminders of royal history or sacred places. At the top and bottom of the board are representations of the head and feet of a woman—women alone are sufficiently powerful to contain the spirit of kings—and the board itself, the body of a tortoise depicting the terrain of the Luba (fig. 10). The complex mnemonics are in the charge of "men of memory" who belonged to an association responsible for guarding and transmitting sacred lore, the Mbudye who still wield considerable power today. Other memory devices—spears, staffs, bowstands, sculpted thrones—are used in individual and local contexts to reconstruct the past or to ameliorate present misfortune. The users of memory devices do not simply offer mechanical recitations of sacred history but press the past into the service of the present. Like the renaissance memory theater, the Luba mnemonic system depicts its historical truths in relation to place, except that place may be perceived not only cosmologically but also as the body of the king. V. Y. Mudimbe points out that myths of genesis are inscribed in the earth which reflects the body of the king.[20]

It is important for the heterological historian to notice not only the prestige that attaches to memory cross-culturally but also the embedding of what is remembered in ethical contexts that impact upon the dilemmas of the present. In its development by Cicero, mnemotechnics is wedded to rhetoric, not as a sophistical art of persuasion but rather as bound up with the Platonic conception of truth. The perfect orator is one whose powers of persuasion derive from the knowledge of truth and of the nature of the soul that remembers its past lives.[21] It is also important to note that, in the later Middle Ages, Albertus Magnus and Thomas Aquinas divorce architectural mnemonic from rhetoric, connecting it instead to prudence interpreted in standard Aristotelian terms as moral habit.[22] Memory in this context provides a link between intellect and action.[23]

The heterological historian may observe that, in the Aristotelian tradition, natural memory is preferable to artificial memory including the memory aids I have described. Natural memory is an endowment at birth so that objects are recalled spontaneously without training. But if what is remembered is an original imprint that can later be brought into plenary presence, Aristotle's worry about remembering the *image* of the absent thing as precluding a bringing back of the *thing* is reintroduced. And, if this is so, we are forced to conclude that natural memory itself depends upon an artifice, that of the image that replaces the "original." Artificial memory is a pleonasm in that memory is always already an artifice. Does "artificial" rememoration merely add another device to the process? What is brought to light through ancient mnemotechnics that is of interest to the historian is not the description, however intriguing, of a mechanism that will save the remembered content. Instead the contemporary historian can envisage what she is accustomed to regard as the prostheses of memory—chronicles, oral histories, photographs, films, videotapes, and computerized archives—as

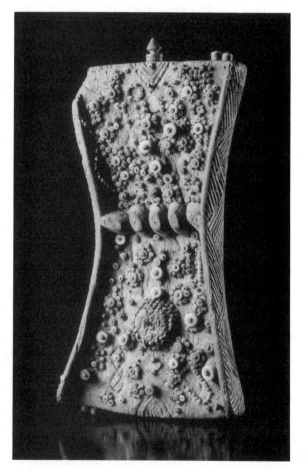

10. Dick Beaulieux, "Lukasa Memory Board of Mbudye." Courtesy Marc Leo Felix Collection, Brussels.

dependent upon the view that "natural" memory itself relies upon a supplement that is not exclusively scriptic. The "hardware" of this memory can be likened to the traditional view of mind itself in its capacity as a passive repository, but its "software" is an architectural iconic code that functions in proto-digital fashion.

What is more, when the mechanism of memory appears unable to escape its biological grounding, memory is delivered from its "animality," its neurophysiological base, through its embedding in the art of rhetoric in the age of Roman oratory and by moral habit in the Scholastic philosophy of the twelfth century. The re-membering of that which has been dismembered is always already set in a field of ethical concerns, those of persuasion and prudence.

"THAT THIS TOO TOO SOLID FLESH WOULD MELT"

Memory, according to Augustine, provides a dwelling place for the divine so that the effort to dispose of the vestiges of animality constitutes a driving force in his reflections on memory. In depicting his ascent toward the knowledge of God in the *Confessions,* Augustine shifts from the trope of memory as a great belly or cavernous storehouse to that of memory as a mighty power with which his very being is identified. "The power of the memory is great, O Lord. It is awe inspiring in its profound and incalculable complexity. Yet it is my mind: it is my self" (*Confessions,* X, 17).[24]

But, if memory retains vestiges of the flesh, must it not be regarded as a mere instrument toward some higher end? Is it not the Jacob's ladder by means of which Augustine will climb to the point where he can make contact with the divine life itself? "I shall go beyond even this force . . . which we call memory, longing to reach out to you by the only possible means and to cling to you in the only way in which it is possible to cling to you" (*Confessions,* X, 17). At the very juncture between the soul and God, Augustine has fallen back upon the most corporeal of senses, that of touch. What better metaphor for contact with the divine? As Aristotle had shown, in touch the entire body is the sensorium, and God must be felt with one's whole being. Yet, despite this effort to go beyond memory, in a remarkable turnabout Augustine will be unable to transcend it.

What puzzles Augustine is the means by which memory retains that which is not currently present to the mind, restores that which has been forgotten. It could be argued that it is not remembering but the enigma of forgetfulness that Augustine ponders and the resources that must be marshaled to overcome it. Thus he reflects upon the aporetic structure of forgetfulness. How might one recognize forgetfulness if it were to be found? Remembering the sound of the word does no more than convey what today might be called an empty signifier. Nor is it enough to know how to use the word; Augustine denies that the meaning is in the use. Instead he purports to lay hold of the thing itself.

> First Aporia: When remembering memory the faculty and its object are both present but, when remembering forgetfulness, memory and forgetfulness are present together. How can one remember the very object whose presence precludes remembering? "Who can understand the truth of the matter?" [*Confessions,* X, 16]. Does it help any to say forgetfulness is present merely as an image? If this is conceded, forgetfulness appears to be more than a mere privation of the being of memory but takes on a density of its own.

The analysis of forgetfulness is not without theological implications. In the absence of the knowledge of God, are we to assume God has been forgotten and can be remembered? In trying to recall a forgotten name, Augustine suggests, erroneous identification can be avoided by the process of elimination. If wrong names are ruled out and if every vestige of recollection is not obliterated, a fragment retained in memory may elicit the desired name. Similarly, in the absence of the knowledge of God, Augustine must discover a residue of something past that will enable him to find and cleave to God. Such is the experience of happiness. Everyone knows, if only dimly, what happiness is and longs for it, even if how one came by this knowledge—whether as an individual or through the prelapsarian state of Adam—remains unknown. Augustine disclaims those experiences of happiness that are bound up with the flesh, and by a process of elimination identifies happiness with the knowledge of truth which, on Augustine's Christian Platonic reading, is knowledge of God who is truth (*Confessions,* X, 20–24). Where is the dwelling place of truth, Augustine asks, if not in the memory? If God is in the memory must God not first have been outside it? But where can an incorporeal God have been? "We either approach you or depart from you, you are not confined in any place" (*Confessions,* X, 26).

> Second Aporia: If God is everywhere, God can never have been outside but always already both inside and outside of memory. How then can there be both an originary imprint and a later recollection of it?

The memory presents still further difficulties in that the the "resting place" God has chosen, "the sanctuary" he built for himself is the body, a fleshly abode in which memory resides. There is no escaping memory's animality in that a part of the memory, that which registers corporeal images, is "shared with the beasts." What is more, in depicting the conflict between experienced and remembered affect—I may experience joy but remember it in sorrow—Augustine is forced back upon a corporeal simile that, he concedes, "is ridiculous." Memory is compared to a cavernous stomach and remembered joy and sorrow are likened to the taste of plea- sant and repellent food that lie in the gut without being tasted (*Confessions*, X, 14).

> Third Aporia: The simile of the belly binds memory to the body yet func- tionally de-corporealizes memory. On the one hand the corporeal metaphor is needed to pin down what Augustine believes to be a mental distinction between experienced and remembered affects. Yet this corporeal metaphor has the effect of eviscerating memory in that remembered affect is seen as a mere "digesting without tasting," the very opposite of what in contemporary language is meant by a gut reaction.

In David Farrell Krell's apt phrase, "Augustine's ruminations would disem- bowel the mind, just as the power to remember joy joylessly would core the heart . . . [or] the power to think a tune without moving voice or lips would disgorge the voice from the throat."[25]

The heterological historian may note that the aporetic structure of memory described by Aristotle and later by Augustine anticipates *in nuce* contemporary critiques of re-presentation. The breach between impression and remembered image precludes any certainty with regard to their cor- respondence. Yet it is worth noting that if memory cannot be exact, that which is remembered is safeguarded by something like the heterological historian's rule of thumb, the admonition that *wrong* names must be ruled out. Thus Augustine circumscribes the field of truth by eliminating that which could not have been.

The historian also may observe that, despite Augustine's despair at the impossibility of grasping forgetfulness as an essence, there is a glimmer of light in the recognition that forgetting is an absence of objects which once may have been present. Augustine can then hope that some remnant of a particular absent object will show itself. Failing such an appearance, there is only oblivion. Might Augustine's account not be augmented by supplying what is missing in it, a theory of the sign such that in the absence of the object a sign appears which may lead back to the "original" impression? It is just here that Freud's theory of forgetting and re-memoration, especially in its early version, might be thought to supplement that of Augustinian forgetfulness. Augustine's notion of oblivion can be explained by Freud as the repression of childhood events, traumas too painful to be dredged up.

Such buried memories undergo a transformation and manifest themselves as symptoms. The keeper of the translation rules is not the sufferer but the other, the analyst who can convert a symptom as signifier into a signified. The concealment of the forgotten material, says Freud, is artful even if not deliberate. In Lacan's words:

> Freud's discovery was that of the domain of the incidence in the nature of man of his relations to the Symbolic order and the tracing of their sense right back to the most radical instances of the symbolization in being. To misconstrue this Symbolic order is to condemn the discovery to oblivion, and the experience to ruin.[26]

Without entering into an evaluation of psychohistory from the standpoint of its evidentiary power, suffice it to note that the heterological historian may be suspicious of an appeal to the author's unconscious intentions as explaining a text, or of regarding texts and visual artifacts as acts of sublimation. Having stationed herself in a non-space hollowed out by alterity, she does not coerce the discourse of the other claiming to bring it forth as truth. Distinguishing between the manifest discourse of the culture of appearances and the appeal to latent discourse in psychoanalysis, Baudrillard observes that latent discourse treats manifest discourse forcibly, making it say what it does not wish to say. The psychoanalytic interpretation of text, image, artifact, or living witness is, in this view, always already an act of violence that sublates the other's alterity. Can one not conclude that psychoanalysis may use the "truth" that it excavates from the unconscious to sanitize, for example, the actions of the torturer, thereby diminishing the sense of responsibility for his deeds? Can he not say, for example, that his childhood traumas determined his being drawn to the security units responsible for torture?

Baudrillard's alternative to coercion, seduction, defined as eschewing latent meaning, turning to appearances as the sites of play, risk, and diversion is, despite his denial, frivolous. How can the historian who speaks deictically from the non-place of the cataclysm enter into the enchantment of simulation? Yet, Baudrillard claims, if seduction is play and risk-taking, it is also its obverse, pure passivity. In a gesture that replicates the Levinasian repudiation of violence, Baudrillard may be read against himself when he writes:

> To seduce is to weaken. To seduce is to falter. We seduce with weakness, never with strong power and strong signs. . . . We seduce with our death, with our vulnerability and with the void that haunts us. The secret is to know how to make use of death, in the absence of a gaze, in the absence of a gesture, in the absence of knowledge, or in the absence of meaning.[27]

It is in this sense that the Augustinian pleading with God can be construed as a response to the Freudian latency hypothesis. Does Augustine not attempt to seduce God with his discourse of weakness? Thus he implores: "Terrified by my sins and the dead weight of my misery, I had turned my problems over in my mind and was half determined to seek refuge in the desert. But you forbade me to do this. . . . You know how weak I am and how inadequate is my knowledge: teach me and heal my frailty" (*Confessions*, X, 43).

What is the outcome for the historian who seduces with and is seduced by the vulnerability of the absent other? The historical object with which she is confronted becomes an appeal that breaks into "the blind and brilliant ambiance of the simulacra" (*Sim*, p. 150). The historian may resist the hyperreal world of images by refusing meaning and speech as is often the case when she is herself a witness of events, as in first-person oral and written histories by Holocaust survivors whose accounts are speech that refuses to speak, secrets that beg to be told yet resist narration. Films such as *Nanjing Massacre* and *Anne Frank Remembered* are also characterized by their reticences. Professional historians may want to contextualize these visual archives of memory, correct their inaccuracies ("it could not have been thus"). Yet, if the professional heterological historian has been in Baudrillard's sense "seduced" by vulnerability, she may feel compelled "to make use of death, in the absence of a gaze, in the absence of a gesture, in the absence of knowledge, or in the absence of meaning,"[28] to seduce her contemporaries with the other's defenselessness.

FROM "TRACE" TO SHINING TRACE

"I will not be here to tell it. Write it down so that you may not forget it and future generations may know of it," said the mothers and fathers of one's great grandparents. "Remember this, my great uncle died, died with prayer on his lips at the hands of the kulaks," said my father. "What then is the value of prayer?" he asked. Chain of filiation, inside and outside of a tradition transmitted but always already deconstructed. The medium of transmission, the viva vox of my father, the message, a skeptical fissuring of first and last things, of infinite divine understanding and mercy. Yet language itself shelters this broken understanding so that this mercy, this divine compassion, remained inscribed under erasure in my father's words. I attempt to decipher the trace, to decode it, to bring back the sense of his memories before the depredations of neurological degeneration had turned them into non-sense. I cast about in vain for the historical object, try to bring into plenary presence what came before and after the theological rift he experienced. Yet, as in Poe's celebrated "The Purloined Letter," in which the letter of the queen that everyone sought was hidden precisely because it was in full view, the historical object I was searching for did not lie outside the narrative itself. The trace of a lost theological origin, an inscription under erasure, the concealed patrimony, *is* the anecdote. But Derrida claims that "all the determinations of such a trace, all the names it is given—belong as such to the text of metaphysics that shelters the trace, and not to the trace itself. There is no trace itself, no proper trace."²⁹ Was what I was searching for not that which makes memory possible, a past which can never be lived in its originary presence? Did I not hope that the trace would replicate what still remained even in its brokenness, a belief in infinite justice and infinite mercy? Was I searching for an Ur-writing that could never be recovered so that I might then "write down" physically, materially, what I found and by tracing this trace "shine in the science of writing . . . like the sun?"³⁰

How was the trace I sought related to actual writing? Writing must be something more than a mere appendage, an instrument that would come to the aid of living memory, a prosthesis that would end in the atrophy of the faculty it was designed to supplement as Plato thought. Writing is a pharmakon, proclaims the Socrates who does not write, a *pharmakon* that is both remedy and poison. It is this doubleness of writing that Derrida will ponder by "tracing" in Socrates' gloss of an ancient Egyptian myth the derogation of writing and, by implication, the problem of secondariness generally, of mind/body, man/woman, reality/appearance, eternity/time.

An Egyptian myth of origins—do family myths not all bear a family resemblance?—of father and son and the rites/rights of patrimony. Socrates recounts the tale of the god Theuth who invented numbers, arithmetic, geometry, and preeminently letters, and who proudly presented these inventions to Thamus, king of Thebes who immediately removed power from the hands of Theuth declaring that it is not the creator but the user who must decide their value. Of writing, the king asserted, "It can only produce forgetfulness in the minds of those who learn to use it, because they will not practise their memory. Their trust in writing, produced by external characters which are not part of themselves will discourage the use of their own memory which is within them" (*Phaedrus* 274c–275b). It is Ammon-Re, the father of Theuth, the sun god, the living logos (of whom, one may assume, the Pharoah is an incarnation), who will be eclipsed by his son the inventer of writing, the unruly disrupter of the genealogical chain opposing the father, elbowing his way into the father's place. "He is thus the other of the father, and the subversive movement of replacement, simultaneously the father, his son and himself. Theuth does not allow himself to be assigned a fixed place in the play of differences." Plotter, trickster, and jokester, he is the Derridean wild card, putting play into play.[31]

Logo- and phono-centrism are now inextricably related, a pattern that, despite individual differences of interpretation, would appear and reappear in the history of Western metaphysics, Derrida claims. The origin of truth is ascribed to the logos; the history of truth cannot be told save as the de-meaning of writing as outside "full" speech. Had Aristotle not already concluded that mental experiences are universal and that voice as "producer of the first symbols, has a relation of essential and immediate proximity with the mind?"[32] Yet Saussure and the tradition of structuralist linguistics generally, heirs of the privileging of voice, are troubled by a perceived permeability of voice to writing. The written image of a sound is mistaken for the sound, Saussure laments. Do we then not speak as we write, Derrida asks? Does not representation mingle promiscuously with what it represents? What is critical is that "the point of origin is ungraspable," no longer a simple scheme of thought, spoken word, and written representation. The image has entered into the origin: "[T]he reflection, the image, splits what it doubles. The origin of the speculation becomes a difference."[33] Deconstructing this tradition is not a matter of simply inverting voice and writing, of showing that writing is not a nefarious device that destroys living memory, but rather that "the violence of writing does not befall an innocent language. There is an originary violence of writing because language is . . . first writing."[34]

If writing does not reflect speech, is not the image of speech, then it must be considered as outside speech. Yet we have seen that it is lodged within speech, splitting it, in that speech is already writing. Yet Derrida recognizes that it is somehow counter-intuitive to deny the derivativeness of writing. For this reason, it must be shown that an original natural language never existed in the first place but rather that language is impossible without an arche-writing, a writing of which there can be no science and which can never be brought into plenary presence. This arche-writing rendering possible the spoken word and the written mark or *graphie* is in contact with ordinary writing that speech is always seeking to displace.

This breaching of speech cannot be thought without recourse to the trace, "the arche-phenomenon of memory," without which signification would not occur. Identifying the trace with arche-writing, Derrida sees the trace as spacing, the opening of exteriority, of an inside to an outside, and as temporalization, "the non-presence of the other inscribed within the sense of the present."[35] Yet is not a writing as an outside that is inside already suggested in several crucial contexts in the history of Western thought? Good writing, for Plato, is truth written in the soul, as distinguished from bad writing, writing as the representation of speech (*Phaedrus* 278a). Absent from Derrida's account is the biblical reference to a second covenant with Israel in which the Torah will be incised in their hearts: "I will put my law within them and I will write it on their hearts" (*Jeremiah* 31:32). In a move reminiscent of rabbinic hermeneutics, Augustine speaks of Moses' reception of the word of God which, through the very act of writing, is seen as an effraction of the one Truth, a writing that invites undecidability. "I declare resolutely and with all my heart that if I were called upon to write a book which was to be vested with the highest authority [such as that of Moses] I should prefer so to write it in such a way . . . [so as not to] impose a single true meaning so explicitly as to exclude all others" (*Confessions,* XII, 31, p. 308).

The heterological historian may ponder whether the chain of filiation in the myth of Theuth described by Derrida can lead from daughter to father in a *dédoublement* of the difference between father and son? Lacking patrimony, can the daughter, like Theuth, the son, be treasonous? Is hers too "the orphan's distress . . . that not only needs to be helped by a presence but also needs that help to be transported to [her]. . . . Yet in lamenting the orphan one also accuses [her]—and writing—of pretending to distance [herself] from the father with an air of complacency and self-sufficiency."[36] Was Augustine's early life of sin directed against his mother, Monica, not an inversion of the rebellion against the father? Would he not in a second inversion re-member this Christianity that was not a patrimony but a legacy of the mother, one that he would appropriate as his own?

FLICKERING MEMORIES: IMAGES AND SIGNS

What is the heterological historian to make of Derrida's claim that all dualisms and monisms, whether idealist or materialist, dialectical or those of common sense are "the unique theme of a metaphysics whose entire history was compelled to strive toward the reduction of the trace,"[37] She could reply that in the culture of information and spectacle the "movement of signification" opened by the trace never occurs because there is a plethora of mobile instantly transmittable images that have been cut off from an ontotheological matrix and for which the historian has no grammar. Even in what appears to be a straightforwardly phonocentric exercise in mnemonics, taping the testimony of witnesses, the historian records and hears a voice that is an acoustic image replicating another such image through the intervention of a complex technology. Spoken language, auditory signifiers in the sense attributed to them in structural linguistics, demand a linear notion of time. But in the culture of images, linearity has given way to circularity; time has been commodified in a system of irrational circular exchange. Having become speed, time finds its parodic extreme in slave labor, concentration and death camps in which human labor is forced to mimic the speed of the machine.

The question to be pondered by the heterological historian is whether the non-space of the archi-trace until now seen as crucial for envisaging memory and mnemonics is so bound up with language that the transformed culture of information and specularity cannot be conceptualized in relation to it. Are writing and speech, the binarisms of the metaphysical tradition whose conditions of possibility have been opened up by a consideration of archi-trace, and *differance,* to be supplemented—ringing all the Derridean changes on this term—by another binarism, that of code and simulacra, the former anticipated by Pythagoras and Leibniz, the latter in the flickering shadows on the walls of Plato's cave? In concrete terms, does a contemporary historian, for example, of imperial Rome, who re-members the campaigns of Germanicus in the discursive language of narrative history, not become a time traveler immersed in the past who, however unwittingly, *sees* the encounters of the legions of Rome and the Germanic tribes anachronistically as TV news footage? Must this not affect her narrative not necessarily by rendering it more lively—Tacitus and Gibbon wrote as vividly as one could wish—but as reflecting this specularity. The linear progression of such a discursive text may give way to the alternation of the flashback and present-day news footage, "objective" description may cede its place to the specularity of closeup and panning. Such writing is always already intertextual in its appeal to antecedent histories and multimedial in its imagery. What would such a history look like? Marion Hobson describes it as "having no tidy seriality . . . an interminable network, branching out in listening posts to somewhere else."[38]

Consider the complex mnemonics of the 1995 film, *Anne Frank Remembered,* directed by Jon Blair. Through intricate intertextual relays, Anne Frank's diary, a work that has become a key text of Holocaust memory, opens out into an interplay of texts, stories of other lives derived through interviews with Anne's surviving friends and those who knew the Frank family, with Miep Gies, the gentile woman who provided food for the Franks and the others who joined them in hiding. The life that is always already in transit, always already in danger of incineration, is presaged in the film's opening scenes of moving train wheels, a burning forest. Deterritorialization and nomadism suggested by moving trains do not liberate in the age of the cataclysm but become parodic inversions, the wandering of the refugee. It is precisely because the images of train wheels and fire are commonplace that they can stage the temporal reference points, the beginning that has no beginning, and the end, the fire that is inextinguishable. Shots of family artifacts suggesting the spurious normalcy of a life soon to come to an end are interspersed with those of public events. Memories of a rebellious Anne, her quiet sister, demanding mother, and easy-going father become daguerrotypes of life before the disaster.

The content of the Anne Frank diary has become virtually a cultural given in an age of mass death. After the deportation of Jews begins, Otto Frank prepares a hiding place for his family to which they repair on July 6, 1942, a secret place that will not remain secret. Anne turns to literature, writes and rewrites her diary, not only because life has become impossible but in the interest of a mnemonics that will carry forward her proper name which would come to signify the lives of the others who died. The artifacts of the hiding place become traces of a past that will not pass. The sequel to the story of the secret hiding place is equally familiar. The family is betrayed; Anne with her mother and sister are sent to Westerborck, a Dutch transit camp from which she is transported to Auschwitz. There is no "tidy seriality" in the film, only the narratives of the other others whose lives intertwine with Anne's and whose stories are now being heard, perhaps for the first time. Among them is Hannali Gosler, Anne's friend, who ends up in another sector of the same concentration camp, a friendship now marked by the barbed wire that separates them. Across this wire, Hannali throws a Red Cross food package to Anne. After it is stolen, she throws another that Anne catches, a gift that could have no return. Hannali Gosler tells the tale as though she herself had done nothing special. Mrs. Emden, friend of Anne's sister, recalls bodily humiliation, nudity intended to mock and shame the camp's inmates.

Before the hiding place is raided, it is Miep Gies, the gentile woman, who keeps the secret of the hiding place and every day supplies the little group with food and news from the outside. It is she who pleads with the arresting officer—"Lieutenant Silberbauer, are we not both Austrian by birth?"—to allow her help to continue after the family's arrest. She is advised at the peril of her husband's life to remain invisible, to keep away from the untouchables of Europe. But she perseveres, will not heed the survival rule of Berthold Brecht's *Mother Courage* to lay low, all to no avail. It is Miep Gies who remains the custodian of memory for she has managed to secure and save Anne's diary. Another gentile Dutch woman, a resistance fighter incarcerated with Anne, remembers Anne's last days, conveys them to her father. Re-membering that time and place—face to camera, no leading interviewer's questions—she invokes silence and breaks it: "I remember the smell of burning flesh, of disinfectant and smoke."

Should the professional historian not be wary of films such as these because they arouse strong affect and thus diminish historical distance?[39] It has been pointed out that historians invoke discursive narrative to criticize visual history as if discourse could recover the past in its own-being. But the rhetoric of objectivity no less than the techniques of visual media is a style and not an instrument for recovery of "the facts." The visual no less than the narrative historian is not without constraints. Committed to a factuality and to accumulated historical knowledge whose apodicticity cannot be guaranteed, she can view such knowledge as opening on to a past construed as a field of unrealized and realized possibilities. What must be excluded, that which under no conditions can be said, establishes the limiting condition of her narrative. At the same time, the historian's artifact is not an affectless chronicle of events related seriatim but evinces a passion for the dead others whose past she is committed to re-membering.

LA CAGE AUX FOLLES: FROM TABLET TO AVIARY AND BACK

The path between scriptic and specular memory is circuitous and requires careful analysis. It may be recalled that in *Thaetetus* scriptic memory is envisioned as imprinting a seal upon a wax tablet. When the imprint is erased, the percept or thought is lost, forgotten. In the paradigm of the aviary, the caged birds represent both knowledge that can be called up at will and knowledge that has been acquired with an eye to future use. The aviary is a kind of bank for excess wealth that can be drawn upon in an economy that hoards its capital and invests it when the opportunity arises. What the scriptic model cannot explain is memory as a reservoir; what the aviary model lacks is an account of precisely what is stored and how it is retained. Can forgetting be explained as the death of the birds, in which case the content of memory is irretrievable and the cage becomes a crypt? Or is it possible that there is no forgetting at all, only a vast ever-expanding chamber of memories? Is there any breaching of this disjunction?

Although the resolution of these dilemmas is not Hegel's intent, the effort to transform images into the pure immateriality of signs can be envisaged as a drawing together of these tropes. In invoking the mediation of signs and language in the *Philosophy of Mind,* Hegel turns to an immaterial semiology unhampered by "nature and physical modes" (*PhM* 440,

p. 179).⁴⁰ In light of the virtual semiological frenzy of contemporary philosophies of language, the importance of signs had until Hegel's day been played down in Western thought. Thus Hegel writes: "In logic and psychology, signs and language are usually foisted in somewhere as an appendix, without any trouble being taken to display their necessity and systematic place in the economy of intelligence" (*PhM* 458, p. 213). Only after the mind has freed itself from any content extrinsic to itself, has transcended its immediacy as soul (man as natural being), and as consciousness ("the reflected or correlational grade of mind") (*PhM* 413, p. 153), can it turn attention to its own features as subject so that now mental vision, ideation, remembering, and desire become the themes of a psychology (*PhM* 440, p. 179). At this stage, the truth of mind is still abstract. Only with the suppression of difference, when the "formal identity of subjectivity and objectivity has developed into an actual difference and made itself into an identity of itself and its difference" will mind's truth be established (*PhM* 440, *Zuzatz* note, pp. 180–181).

Hegel dissociates his analysis from the developmental unfolding of cognition in the individual as it is described, for example, in Condillac's empirical psychology. Instead, Hegel treats mental faculties as mind's creative self-activity, its strategy for getting hold of itself and freeing itself from what is merely contingent and outside it. Hegel leads up to memory by analyzing both cognition in its function as intuition in which intelligence identifies with what is outside itself, and representation in its role as mind recollecting or inwardizing intuition. It is representation that critically mediates between intuition and mind as thought. As Derrida points out in a gloss of Hegel's semiology:

> By means of *Erinnerung* the content of sensible intuition becomes an image, freeing itself from immediacy and singularity in order to permit the passage to conceptuality. The image thus interiorized in memory is no longer there . . . but preserved in an unconscious dwelling, conserved without consciousness. Intelligence keeps images in reserve submerged at the bottom of a very dark shelter, like the water in a nightlike or unconscious pit, or like a precious vein at the bottom of a mine.⁴¹

Plato's aviary has become a pit of images without consciousness, uncontrolled by reason, a *cage aux folles*.

Mind as intelligence frees the image from the space and time of externality and resituates it in a spatiotemporal framework of its own. It can then be "stored up out of consciousness" but, as such, remains merely potential like the germ or seed of things. Actual remembrance occurs when the image is referred to an intuition that triggers recollection and makes the image a possession of intelligence. "This synthesis of the internal image with recollected existence is representation proper" (*PhM* 454, p. 205). The work of reproductive imagination merely hauls up but does not connect the images with one another. Once retrieved, imagination concatenates the images in a chain of associations and, by linking some property common to them, for example, the redness in roses, engenders general ideas, but, because this process received its impetus from what was external, it remains merely passive.[42]

With the creation of signs, mind as productive imagination transcends the confines of this passivity by giving objective existence to what was still simple "auto-intuition." Mind "aims at making itself be and be a fact, [becomes] self-uttering, intuition producing: the imagination which creates signs" (*PhM* 457, p. 211). It is at this point that the hidden Hegelian philosophemes of time, difference, marginality, the supplement, come to the fore. As Derrida describes mind's trajectory, "the night pit, silent as death, [leads to] a pyramid brought back from the Egyptian desert which will soon be raised . . . over the Hegelian text"[43] Derrida's Nietzsche-like observation that this path is circular points to the undecidability of the locus and status of the sign: pit or pyramid, tablet or aviary.

Hegel asserts that sign and language heretofore marginalized, "treated as an appendix," are indispensable for grasping the work of reason. With the emergence of productive intelligence, "the right place for the sign is to be found." The connotation belonging to the intuition is "deleted" and intelligence's own connotation conferred upon the sign. Crucial to the present context is Hegel's linking of semiology and memory. Distinguishing his account from the commonsense view of memory as recollection, he proclaims, "Memory . . . has always to do with signs only" (*PhM* 458, p. 213). Intelligence may still authenticate itself by an appeal to images, in which case what it creates are symbols, expressed tropically as allegory in which the symbol resembles the symbolized. Liberated from images and resemblance, the general idea produces the sign. The connection between general idea and sensuous material is arbitrary: the sign is not only a cognitive advance but an advance in human freedom. The appropriate reservoir for the sign is not the pit but the pyramid, a structure erected aboveground that conceals the labyrinthine burial chambers below. Thus Hegel writes: "The sign is some immediate intuition, representing a totally different import from what naturally belongs to it; it is the pyramid into which a foreign soul has been conveyed, and where it is conserved" (*PhM* 458, p. 213).

Hegel passes from a consideration of the sign to language as a concatenation of names. Intelligence unites meaning to the name; retentive memory becomes a holding bin for names. The name has become "the thing in the ideational realm" (*PhM* 461, p. 219), an imageless representation which is thought itself: "We *think* in names." With the introduction of names, Hegel converts memory into a mental book, a "within-book *[inwendiges]*" that has replaced a "without-book *[auswendiges]*" (*PhM* 462, p. 220). To be sure, memory can be merely mechanical, but if it is to be more than this, if it is to become thought, in accordance with a familiar Hegelian scheme, objectivity and subjectivity must be united, in this case by the representing intellect. What persists, however, when intelligence becomes thought is memory's re-cognitive character, the re-possession of what is already one's own.

Having created a passageway between pit and pyramid, between image and sign, it would appear that Hegel has succeeded in intercalating these tropes such that the image, the content of the pit, when inwardized becomes the sign, the hieroglyphs of the pyramid. But can the heterological historian trust this mediation? May she not ask, "Is Hegel's account of memory not merely a reworking in the framework of dialectics of Aristotle's effort to transcend images?" To be sure, the materiality of the image, its construal as something spatial, is conquered by Hegel in the same way that space as a point is overcome in the *Philosophy of Nature,* by its transformation into punctiform time. Thus Hegel says, "[T]he truer phase of the intuition used as a sign is time" (*PhM* 459, p. 213). It is as spoken that the sign first enters the "ideational realm and as that which is voiced or uttered, its existence vanishes" (*PhM* 459, pp. 213–214), thus attesting to its internal temporal diffraction.

When the heterological historian undertakes to remember under the sign of Hegel, she cannot ignore the evanescence of the voiced sign: time is the condition of the possibility of signs. In a succinct if arcane formulation, Derrida describes the relation of time to signification. Speaking of the *Da,* the "there" of time, he maintains:

> With the stroke *[du coup]* of time, its incompleteness, its inner default, the semantic void that holds it in motion [is marked]. Time is always of this vacancy with which *Sa* [an acronym for *savoir absolu* and the French third person possessive pronoun] affects itself. Because it affects itself with this, *Sa* empties itself with a view to determining itself, *it gives itself time.* It imposes on itself a gap *[écart]* in signing itself. The *Da* of *Sa* is nothing other than the movement of signification.[44]

How is the historian to find the trace of time in the sign? Like Dummett's realist, Derrida depicts singular events as dated particulars, but in conformity with Hegel each such date is a wound that is itself time's passing.[45] If the heterological historian is stationed in the non-space of ethics, she must tolerate the wounding by time without allowing herself to be overcome by it for she works in the discursive space opened up by wounding and re-covery.

She is confronted also by another aporia of Hegelian discourse, a danger intrinsic to historical writing, the effacing of the victim's name. The threat is less one of deliberate exclusion—does the good historian not select care-fully so as to leave out no details of significance?—than the danger that, in the very act of re-memoration, the name will be separated from its bearer, become an empty signifier. Is this equivocality not reflected in the accounts of victims of man-made mass death whose personae may be preempted by a variety of interests? Yet the historian recognizes that no historical account can remain disinterested.[46] She must rely upon a discerning ear, one that hears difference, that hears with the ear of the dead other. She must name, narrate discursively or visually, not despite but because of the inherent poly-semy of names. The heterological historian is commanded to rescue the name from its historization in a narrative of events that could not have been. As an act of responsibility that she cannot renounce, the historian must "hear as she speaks, as acutely as possible."[47] What remains as yet unthought in Derrida's analysis is that, in the age of the hyperreal and of specularity, hearing is always already infiltrated by images: the acoustic and the visual are permeable to one another.

If Hegel considers semiology an advance in the development of mem-ory, the historian must be warned that he is contemptuous of those ancient mnemonic devices that depend upon images and would, in all likelihood, have included in his condemnation the *lukasa* of the Luba had he known of it. The reasons for his rejection of mnemotechnics are of interest to the contemporary heterological historian who is involved in the use of their contemporary counterparts. Hegel alleges that ancient mnemonics are in-efficient: first because the meaning of the ideas to be remembered and the images with which they are correlated are unrelated; second because such connections must be made quickly and can only be "shallow, silly and ut-terly accidental," soon to be forgotten (*PhM* 462, p. 220). It is not too far-fetched to find in Hegel's condemnation a presaging of the criticism of badly designed, inefficient software: computers should "filter, sort, prioritize, and manage multimedia on our behalf."[48]

From Hegel's remarks, it is clear that not only does he (like Aristotle) fear that a reversion to images would return the mind to the tenebrous materiality of uncontrollable images, but that mind would lose that toward which, for Hegel, it had been heading, the freedom intrinsic to thought. Hegel could not have envisaged the freedom of the Mbudye "men of memory," their creation of sinuous narratives that link past to present. Instead, he saw mnemotechnics as the process by which rote memory replicates previously imprinted content without alteration. Nor could he have foreseen the semes and pictograms of vast information systems into which the pit of images would be transformed. Yet the Hegelian fear of the unfreedom of the image is not foreign to that of the contemporary historian who is surrounded by the simulations of the hyperreal, in Baudrillard's language, "the cool universe of digitality [that] has absorbed the world of metaphor and metonymy" that she attributes to the past" (*Sim,* p. 152).

THE MIND IS A BONE: SKULL, BRAINS, AND MEMORY

To the idealism of Hegel, no doctrine could be further from the truth than that one is one's body and that mind can be understood in terms of biological processes. To such a view, Hegel tartly replies, the high is reduced to the low; it is mere picture thinking such as occurs in nature when the organ of generation is also that of micturation: "[To] remain at this level of picture-thinking behaves as urination" (*Phen* 346, p. 210). Hegel rejects as "idle chatter," as mere opinion, the nineteenth-century "science" of the physiognomic reading of inner states. Any interpretation of such states would require introspective reporting when, in fact, inner states are ineffable. To the physiognomic view, Hegel opposes what today might be called behaviorism on the grounds that acts are publicly verifiable: "The deed is something simply determined . . . it is murder, theft, or a good action or a brave deed and what it is can be *said* of it" (*Phen* 322, p. 194). He is equally critical of the putative science of phrenology, reading the bumps and hollows of the skull as indicative of character. It is the brain that mediates between this outward manifestation, the skull, and the essence of Spirit, and must be seen as partaking of both although Hegel is chary of positing a direct causal relation between brain states and skull protruberances. What is crucial for Hegel is the thing-ification of Spirit: *"[T]he actuality and existence of man is his skull bone"* (fig. 11) (*Phen,* p. 200).

Because surgical trepanation existed in nineteenth-century medical practice, the skull could be viewed as an intermediary between outward behavior and the brain beneath it. But once the importance of brain activity is recognized, the skull is seen as relatively unimportant. If the brain can be interpreted as a thing, Hegel's arguments can be recontextualized and applied *mutatis mutandis* to the claim that states of consciousness can be inter-

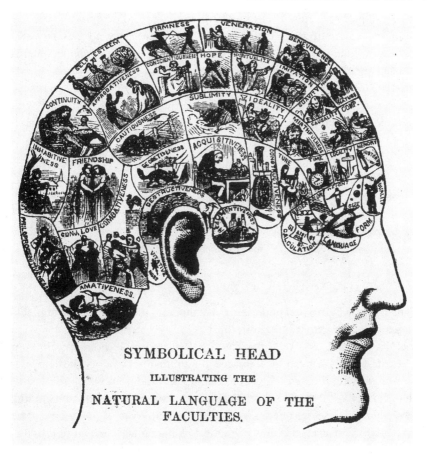

SYMBOLICAL HEAD

ILLUSTRATING THE

NATURAL LANGUAGE OF THE
FACULTIES.

11. Diagram of phrenology's view of the faculties. Reproduced from Samuel B. Wells, *How to read Character: a new illustrated handbook of Phrenology and Physiognomy for students and examiners with a descriptive chart,* New York, Fowler and Wells Co., 1884.

preted as brain states and, as such, premonitory of more complex contemporary deliberations. If Hegel's arguments were to be recast in terms of brain rather than skull, he would hold, first, that mental acts and the brain are heterogenous; thoughts, looks, and gestures cannot be read from the examination of the brain, an inert organ. Second, it has been claimed that even if the organ does not feel, feelings might be localized and thus ascertainable by investigating brain states. Hegel would reply that feelings are too vague and indeterminate to support any meaningful correlation between affect and organ (*Phen* 333–334, pp. 200–202). Third, if categories for positing correlations between states of mind and brain are laid down, they must be homogeneous with those used to understand brain states and thus necessarily abstract and impoverished. In what could be taken as presaging contemporary questions about felt qualia, it is worth comparing John Searle's question, "How is it possible for physical objective quantitatively describable neuron firings to cause qualitative, private subjective experiences?"[49] with Hegel's reservations about the identity of mental properties with physical states. Hegel writes:

> On the one side, then we have a multitude of inert areas of the skull, on the other a multitude of mental properties, whose number and character will depend on the state of psychology. The more paltry the conception of Spirit, the easier becomes the task from this side; for partly the mental properties become fewer, and partly they become more detached, rigid, and ossified, and therefore more akin to the characteristics of the bone (*Phen* 335, p. 202).

MATTER MATTERS: BRAIN STATES AND MENTAL ACTS

The two paradigms that undergird contemporary materialist views of memory are not altogether foreign to the account of correlating brain states and mental acts that Hegel rejects. The first, a materialistic monism posited in the interest of what can be envisaged as a unified field theory of the real, is consistent with the ontology of modern physics and from which consciousness is not excluded. By naturalizing consciousness it purports to demystify and liberate conscious phenomena such as remembering from an oppressive metaphysical matrix. But now matter is no longer phenomenologically construed as that which offers resistance to impact but is rather coded information. The second is a materialism grounded in social philosophy that tries to show how the products of a materially construed mind can be commodified.

According to the more radical versions of the first, conscious phenomena are nothing more than the effects of the brain's activities just as material objects are nothing more than the nuclear particles that go to make them up. Much of the effort to render this position plausible consists in decoding the language of sensations, thoughts, and memories and encoding it into brain process language. Because there are numerous difficulties in positing a straightforward identity of brain state and mental state, some radical materialists argue it is better to examine the conditions that justify ascribing mental states to people but insist that the conditions of ascription themselves be observable material conditions. Thus, what is observable is not likely to be simple behavior, for example, withdrawing one's hand from the fire, screaming and so on as justifying the imputing of the term "burning sensation." Rather to clinch matters it is thought better to examine complex neurophysiological data to justify the ascription of pain.

Radical materialists reject the Cartesian view that there is some switching station where mind and body communicate and a single consciousness masterminds the process. Instead, it is argued that mind is nothing more than a multiplicity of information-processing bits, that consciousness is not a special faculty but a qualitative enhancement of the bits that are already there.[50]

Daniel Dennett, a leading exponent of this position, contends that what is there are memes, complex ideas that form themselves into easily remembered units, ideas such as wheel, wearing clothes, a sonata, chess, or calculus. "Borne by language . . . 'images' and other data structures, [memes] take up residence in an individual brain . . . thereby turning it into a mind."[51] Evolutionary utility explains the endurance of some memes rather than others.

It could be objected that higher mental processes like remembering are not like the "ouch" of a burning sensation that can be reduced to neurological mechanisms. Dennett argues to the contrary that the increased complexity of a mental process requires no special explanation. "There is no single definitive 'stream of consciousness,' because there is no central Headquarters . . . where it all comes together. . . . Instead of such a single stream there are multiple channels in which specialist circuits try . . . to do various things, creating Multiple Drafts as they go. Most . . are short lived . . . but some get promoted to further functional roles [accounting for higher order mental processes]."[52] But what explains the experience of consciousness? Dennett is persuaded that consciousness can be explained in terms of "memory-loading" and "broadcasting," the invoking of previous learning as it bears upon current problems. That these features seem to be the effect of an occult consciouness is, he argues, a magical trick or illusion created by nature.[53]

In the case of memory there is a special relationship to time: the content is inseparable from its pastness. What physical descriptions could cover the before and after, the sequentiality of experience? For the radical materialist the question dissolves. All that there is are changes in movement and location in various parts of the brain, changes that do not converge anywhere. At some point, Dennett contends that "the corner is turned from the timing of representations to the representation of timing."[54]

In fact, the heterological historian may notice that Dennett's account of time is flawed in that he can be shown to assume one of the central claims he is challenging, the claim that experience presupposes temporal comprehension. If all there is is change in movement and location in various parts of the brain, and the "corner is somehow turned" from sequentiality to the representation of time as Dennett alleges, movement and location suggest that time is something actual like material objects that existed earlier but are understood later. But if time is not like material objects, as Dennett acknowledges, the predication of sequentiality which enables the corner "somehow" to be turned trades on some sort of ongoing awareness of time all along. The breach between the realist view about the past as before and after and the anti-realist view that time's passing is primordial (as described by Michael Dummett in Chapter 5) has, in the context of neurophysiology, been suppressed and given a developmental thrust: sequence turns into a representation of past, present, and future.

What stands fast in Dennett's account is, first, his assertion that there is no "central headquarters" where everything comes together in consciousness and, second, that multiple channels produce multiple drafts of what is remembered. The past does not manifest itself all at once as spectacle before a subject, but is imprinted, in Derrida's phrase, *sous rature,* in that which is actually imaged and told. For the historian, something of the scriptic character of language, of the economy of signs, must remain. What is ineliminable and right in Dennett's modeling of memory is just this scriptic character, a point he explicitly acknowledges: "The Multiple Drafts model makes 'writing it down' in memory criterial for consciousness; that is *what it is* for the 'given' to be 'taken'—to be taken one way rather than another."[55]

But if memory is scriptic, the heterological historian can reinscribe memory in another interpretive framework, that of writing and text. Dennett concedes the Derridean point that "there are no origins, there is only production, we produce ourselves in language.'"[56] and refers to this position as semiotic materialism.[57] There is no reason why from a metonymic perspective the subject position of the historical narrator cannot be seen as dispersed in an infinite web of memes. The materialist reading of consciousness does not escape the issues of interpretation raised by the linguisticality of mind; in the absence of this built-in textual or scriptic character, its account of consciousness would exclude all but a description of electromagnetic impulses.[58] The necessity for signs is summarized in inimitable fashion by William James:

> If we knew thoroughly the nervous system of William Shakespeare, and as thoroughly his environing conditions, we should be able to show why . . . his hand came to trace . . . those crabbed little black marks which we for shortness sake call the manuscript of *Hamlet.* We should understand the rationale of every erasure and alteration therein. . . . The words and sentences

would be taken, not as signs of anything beyond themselves, but as little out-wards facts pure and simple.[59]

DIFFERANCE IS IN THE NEURONS

Despite his penchant for a certain Platonism with regard to mathematics, Roger Penrose's account of mind may be characterized as materialist, but in contrast to Dennett and to the premises of much current neurophysiolgical research he holds that consciousness cannot be grasped computationally. On the received view, nerve impulses are understood as on-and-off switches in the electronic circuitry of a computer. While macrolevel brain processes can be understood digitally, microlevel brain activity cannot be grasped without recourse to "the mysterious superpositions of alternatives that are character-istic of quantum action," that allow "occurring" and "non-occurring" at the same time.[60] What is needed is a new understanding of "the area that is intermediate between the small scale level where quantum laws hold sway, and the everyday level of classical physics" (*SM*, p. 15).

On the standard view, nerve signals travel from a neuron's center along an axon, a long fibre that splits into separate strands at various places, each terminating at a synapse, or cleft, where the signal is transferred to the den-drite or branched structure of another neuron (*SM*, p. 353). But, Penrose points out, that is only part of the story. He notes that complex actions of one-celled animals who lack a nervous system are controlled by its cytoskel-eton whose parts include long fiber-like microtubules. Remarkably, each of our own neurons has its own cytoskeleton whose microtubules emit chemi-cal neurotransmitters that govern synaptic transmission, ordering the varia-tions in synaptic strengths and the locations of synaptic connections. The activity of these microtubules can no longer be accounted for in terms of classical physics but are best explained in quantum mechanical terms (*SM*, p. 366). He goes on to say that we ought to envisage "genuine quantum oscillations of some kind taking place *within* the tubes, with some kind of delicate coupling between the quantum internal and classical external as-pects of each tube" (*SM*, p. 375). Quantum organization within the micro-tubules is "tapped off" to influence changes in the synaptic connections. Penrose concludes:

> Consciousness would be some manifestation of this quantum-entangled in-ternal cytoskeletal state and of its involvement in the interplay between quan-tum and classical levels of activity. The computer-like classically intercon-nected system of neurons would be continually influenced by this cytoskeletal activity . . . The neuron level of description is . . . is a mere shadow of the

deeper level of cytoskeletal action—and it is at this deeper level where we must seek the physical basis of mind. (*SM*, p. 376)

What is crucial for Penrose is that quantum effects do not disappear but operate at a larger scale or macrolevel of activity. "Subtle quantum effects, such as non-locality, quantum parallelism (several superposed actions being carried out simultaneously) or effects of counterfactuality . . . [should have] significance when the classical level of brain activity is reached" (*SM*, p. 351). It is just this instability that enables us to perform non-computational feats enabling us to claim that our minds have features that cannot be simulated on a computer. This can be seen as constituting an advantage, one already prefigured in William James's account of the actions of what he calls "the higher nerve centers." Speaking of the advantage of vagueness, James writes:

> We may construct a nervous system that reacts infallibly and certainly, but it will then be capable of reacting to very few changes in the environment. . . . We may, on the other hand, construct a nervous system potentially adapted to respond to an infinite variety of minute features in the situation; but its fallibility will then be as great as its elaboration. . . . In short a high brain may do many things. . . . but its hair-trigger organization makes of it a happy-go-lucky, hit-or-miss affair. It is as likely to do the crazy as the sane thing at any given moment. A low brain does few things, and in doing them perfectly forfeits all other use.[61]

John Searle's objection to Penrose's non-computability account of consciousness hangs on the claim that Penrose wrongly conflates the manner in which we solve mathematical problems with the way in which we model conscious processes. Searle argues that even if it is true, as Penrose maintains, that mathematical results cannot always be accounted for by theorem-producing algorithms, it does not follow that we are unable to simulate the cognitive processes we use. "The aim is not to get an algorithm people are trying to follow, but rather one which accurately describes what is going on inside them."[62] Searle's objection can be construed as an appeal to the metalanguage/object-language distinction saying something like: "See, we can have a language *about* what happens in us, *about* our object language namely non-algorithmic mathematical thought, but our metalanguage need not mirror our object language." It could, however, be replied that, if we are to produce a metalanguage that *simulates* (like an architectectural drawing) what goes on inside us in non-computational thinking, we must be able to reproduce what is non-computable or arcane in the thought object itself, and this is precisely what we cannot do. We may be able to provide a phenomenological description of sorts—this is in fact what Penrose has achieved—as theories about art and poetry typically do. But we cannot claim to have produced a simulation. Thus the instability described by Penrose goes all the way down.

For the heterological historian, such questions cannot be consigned to the arcana of cognitive science in that the shifting metaphors through which memory is explored are intrinsic to the contemporary accounts of memory with which she must contend. She must notice that Penrose's account of brain activity builds temporal undecidability into the deepest level of neuronal activity. Thus Penrose:

> Indeed it would be unwise to make too strong an identification between the phenomenon of conscious awareness, with its seeming "flowing" of time and the physicist's use of a real number parameter to denote what would be referred to as a "time coordinate." . . . Can we be specific about the relation between conscious experience and the [real number] parameter that physicists use as the "time" in their physical descriptions? Can there really be any experimental way to test "when" a subjective experience "actually" takes place in relation to this physical parameter? Does it even mean anything in an objective sense to say that a conscious event takes place at any particular time?
> (*SM*, p. 385)

The heterological historian may observe that the unexplained difference between the quantum level and that accessible to classical physics disturbs the standard picture of neural activity so that replicated at the level of brain processes is a Derridean self-dividing difference, one that haunts the history of metaphysics, the difference that underlies being-present but is covered over in classical accounts of representation. Unlike the smooth transitions that characterize the movement from one brain state to another in Dennett's mind model, such that quantitative changes in excitation produce observable changes in experience, in Penrose's account difference goes all the way down in the very fissuring of the neurotransmitter substance. Signals relayed from one neuron to another cross "tiny gaps" or "synaptic clefts" which depend upon the differential strengths of the neurotransmitters and determine the success or failure of the neural communication (*SM*, p. 348). Could it not be said in Derrida's terms that this synaptic crossing "gives itself time . . . imposes on itself a gap [*écart*] in signing itself," is at the neurological level "nothing other than the movement of signification."[63]

What is equally striking are the explanations to which Penrose appeals in interpreting the manner in which our notions of actuality have been unsettled by the interface between classical physics and quantum mechanics.

The heterological historian perceives that it is through an appeal to counter-factuality that some understanding of this relation may be gleaned. How, Penrose asks, does the counterfactual possibility of an occurrence, something that does not actually happen, influence what does happen? How do counterfactual conditions produce real effects? He speculates that when the neural computer is poised to undertake an action but refrains from performing it, the sheer fact that it might have performed the computation produces an effect that is different from what would be the case if it were unable to perform it. "In this way, the classical 'wiring' of the neural computer at any one moment could have an influence on the cytoskeletal state, even though the the neuron firings that would activate that particular 'wired up' computer might not actually take place" (*SM*, p. 376).

Although analogies with everyday thought might be pursued, Penrose refrains from doing so. It is, however, worth considering such applications in the context of historical narration. The heterological historian has already been introduced to statements of the form, "Without Mohammed, Charlemagne would have been inconceivable," the claim of Henri Pirenne. She may apply counterfactuality to a narrative by essaying variations of a formal or psychological type as Borges suggests, to what can be described as the metonymic dimension of history, a free speculative variation in the form: "it could have been w, x, or y." (Charlemagne could have but did not refrain from waging war in the Pyrenees, Islam might have but did not obtain a foothold in Italy.) Second, as Borges remarks, the historian "sacrifice[s] these variations to the 'original' text and reason[s] out this annihilation in an irrefutable manner."[64] The historian is then relying upon a negative counterfactual statement, what I call "the moment of historical elenchus": "Here I stand. It could not have been thus." The first is history's metonymic, the second its deictic moment, each indispensable. Because metonymy operates in accordance with the Derridean logic of the supplement, the moment of difference, narrative ambiguity, addition, improvisation, and the subliminal, if historical narrative were deprived of its deictic moment of attestation, the historian, unrestricted by the laws of discourse, would enter a realm of runaway fantasy. She would become deaf to the command of the dead to show that "it could not have been thus."

OWNERLESS MEMORIES: ARTIFICAL LIFE
AND BIOLOGICAL COMPUTERS

There is still another model of memory that must be understood within the paramaters of a computational ontology, such that memory becomes ownerless, the memory of no one, as information appears in unprecedented new conformations that extend to the encoding of life. With the discovery of the genetic code by James Watson and Francis Crick in 1952, as Lewis Thomas describes it in *The Lives of a Cell,* living human beings are "shared, rented, occupied," the nuclei of our cells carriers of DNA inherited from ancestral cells. "Our genomes," he goes on to say, "are catalogues of instructions from all kinds of sources in nature, filed for all kinds of contingencies." The current laboratory interspecies exchange of DNA through gene splicing is anticipated in the process of evolution itself. Viruses, for example, "transplant grafts of DNA, passing around heredity as though at a great party."[65]

Until recently, it was uncontested that life and the blueprint for an organism's reproduction and functioning as well as its history which *are* its DNA were indissolubly associated. Life was seen as marked off by non-life through the possession of a genetic code. Genetic engineering which alters the forms of so-called wet life forms still proceeds on this premise.[66] It is now argued, however, that the theory of life must be broadened so as to embrace non-living, non-organic beings; a science of artificial life that will create living systems is in the process of development. The heterological historian may be reminded of the antecedents of artificial life, Faust's homunculus or the *golem,* the artificial man created by the seventeenth-century rabbi, the Miral of Prague or Mary Shelley's Frankenstein. It was the celebrated Hungarian mathematican John von Neumann who first suggested in 1956 that computers and human beings are merely different classes of automata,[67] thereby assuming that natural evolution could somehow be replicated digitally. Would it, however, be possible to reproduce a system of freely evolving creatures as this process occurred in nature, to create cellular automata that would be connected to the physical world?

Artificial-life enthusiasts continue to pursue this aim. As though bestowing actuality upon Nietzsche's description of differential forces, Tommaso Toffoli in the mid-1970s claimed that "behavior arises as an emergent property of a number of variable forces. . . . CA's [cellular automata] do not merely reflect reality—they are reality."[68] In a further Nietzsche-like proclamation, Toffoli contends that biological automata would become a model for physics rather than the converse. What is more, time in this paradigm is not unidirectional but calculationally reversible: we should be able to tell what happened in a previous instant. He managed to construct a complex proof showing this to be possible.[69]

The great dilemma in computer modeling remained whether computers could produce unprogrammed responses. Simulating the complex flocking movements of blackbirds, Craig Reynolds developed a program that appeared to generate novel activity. Just as for Dennett there was no homunculus in the mind, for Reynolds no master bird directed flocking activity. Instead, flocking is decentralized, each bird following its own rules. "The group behavior then emerged from that collective action."[70] Individuals modified their actions in accordance with their neighbor's activities and encounters with obstacles, responses that were unprogrammed. It remained only to develop and implement the birds' rules for computer simulation.

Perhaps what needs to be replicated is the ability "to spit in the face of entropy," Christopher Gale Langton remarks. He characterizes the emergence and persistence of life as the result of just the right amount of complexity:

> On a precipice to its left was a barren region where enough information could move, to its right was a swirling maelstrom where information moved so wildly that chaos ruled. . . . Life took advantage of that proximity to draw its information processing abilities, but it dared not stray too far from the frozen areas that allowed it to keep some information stable.[71]

That a computational machine can mimic life is not impossible to imagine, but it would appear totally counter-intuitive to reverse the process by envisaging turning a vat of DNA into a computational mechanism that would solve mathematical problems. Dr. Leonard Adelman of the University of Southern California, who is said to have opened the field of biological computation, demonstrated that, if DNA molecules were synthesized in a particular sequence, a problem could be solved by letting the molecules remain in a test tube to produce a new molecule that is the problem's answer. Thus:

> Conventional computers represent information in terms of 0's and 1's physically expressed in terms of the flow of electrons through logical circuits. DNA computers represent information in terms of the chemical units of DNA. . . . In an ordinary computer a program instructs electrons to travel on particular paths; with a DNA computer, calculation requires synthesizing particular sequences of DNA and letting them react in a test tube.[72]

DNA computers would be infinitely faster, more energy efficient, and occupy far less space than conventional computers.

What is the heterological historian to make of technical issues that may appear at best as frivolous speculation and at worst a science fiction nightmare in a genocidal age? She would be right to be wary of putative technological advances that blur the boundaries between life and machine, of the possibility, however remote, of a Hal-like computer that could not be de-programmed. Have not the relatively simple computational possibilities of bank computers and digitized phone-answering systems not already dehu-manized daily life? Yet, as a historian, she may notice that what is common to both a-life research and biological computation systems is a desperate quest for memory, a frenetic search for what enables us to store in word image or archive that which might otherwise be lost or replaced by a de-based word or image. So powerful is the quest for memory that Dr. Adel-man remarks, "To some a computer is a physical device in the real world . . . [but] a computer is something that we externally impose on an object. There might be a lot of computers out there."[73] What magnetizes the search is the capaciousness of DNA memory beyond that of all of today's computer memories combined. Another researcher explains that "to retrieve data it would only be necessary to search for a small part of it—a key word for example—by adding a DNA strand so that its sequence sticks to the key word wherever it appears on the DNA."[74]

For the heterological historian, these conceptual forays are not merely recondite problems in the complex field of information storage and produc-tion. They are part of an economy that is both specular and speculative. According to Lyotard, information is knowledge and knowledge is capital: if brains or their electronic memory surrogates are knowledge-producing technologies, they too must be construed as commodities. For Lyotard, the last phase of the historical process eventuates in the stockpiling of informa-tion and an ever-increasing reliance on technologies of data processing. Un-like Dennett for whom the multiple channels of computer models provide analogies for brain activities, what is crucial for Lyotard is the potential of these technologies to *supplant* brain processes. In controlling memorizing, the new technologies eliminate time-bound difference by compressing temporally separate events into a single time, a detemporalization that need not depend on brain conditions.[75] In short, by creating autonomous systems unconstrained by phenomenologically experienced corporeality, the con-temporary economy creates memory borne by hardware, memory without a body. Thus Lyotard:

> Among the material complexes we know, the human brain is the most capa-ble of producing complexity . . . as the production of the new technologies proves. . . . And yet its own survival requires that it be fed by a body, which . . . can survive only in the conditions of life on earth. . . . One of the essential objectives of research today is to overcome the obstacle that the body places in the way of [these] technologies, [namely,] the new extended memory.[76]

In the past, Lyotard contends, "ethnocultures" conserved information by gathering up dispersed local memories into historical narrative, so that narrative itself became a technical apparatus for converting the emotional charge of events into meaning and information. But far from considering the new technologies a sign of progress, Lyotard decries "the barbarism, illiteracy and impoverishment of language [and] . . . remodelling of opinion" he believes they have created. The electronic global information network, Lyotard claims, will dispose of the memories of culturally borne narratives so "that in the last analysis it [global memory] is nobody's memory"[77] just as Dennett's memes are, in the end, nobody's memes but simply information that takes up residence in a mind, Lyotard's materialism, unlike that of Dennett, is shot through with pessimism. The Hegelian subject is regenerated in materialist guise as a repressive "cosmic memory . . . of which Leibniz could have said . . . it is on the way to producing a monad much more complete than humanity itself was ever able to be."[78]

Lyotard's account of the storehouse model may be considered as an ever-expanding memory bank that stores information to be retrieved in the interest of attaining a purchase upon time by neutralizing events, stopping the flow of time, gathering and conserving what is extended in time as a single temporally flattened stock of information. Thus Lyotard: "What is already known [the content of the storehouse] cannot . . . be experienced as an event. Consequently if one wants to control a process, the best way of so doing is to subordinate the present to what is (still) called the 'future' since in these conditions the 'future' will be completely predetermined."[79]

Lyotard's description can be viewed as providing a postmodern context for envisaging what Emmanuel Levinas calls totality—that socio-political whole dominated by war and violence in which individuals, unknown to themselves, are reduced to being the bearers of forces that command them and from which they derive their meaning.[80] There is a functional convergence between the repressive character of the totality and Baudrillard's pessimistic reading of the social control exercised by the culture of simulation with its volatilization of meaning, a meaning that is sought but irrecoverable. Lyotard's view brings to the fore what enables the totality to continue in postmodernity, the constructed *memory* of totality, one in which historical narratives are encoded in structures that preempt their diversity. Highlighted in Lyotard's description is a cosmic memory that produces its own metanarratives suppressing, in Dennett's terms, multiple drafts, the multitrack interpretations of sensory input.

Narratives generated by the totality attempt to acquire the sort of consensus sought by science.[81] Thus, they do not gain their truth from what I described before as history's mode of negation: the constraint imposed upon historical narrative by the condition "it could have been w, x, or y but it could not have been z." Instead, the meta-narratives that can be identified with the concept of totality become necessary narratives written in the mode of "it could *only* have been thus."

But it is precisely the stationing of the heterological historian just at that point where she neither ignores nor is overwhelmed by the cataclysm, is neither inured to alterity nor so wounded by it that she cannot speak, that enables her to evade totalization. Can she not from the non-space of ethics transform a vat of DNA with its unheard of stockpiling potential into a memory palace, a lukasa board upon whose retained events she may draw in her depiction of the past? Like biological life as described by the a-life researcher Christopher Langton, the heterological historian is situated "on [that] precipice between a barren region where information could move, and a swirling maelstrom where information moved so wildly that chaos ruled."[82]

∞

The culture of information and image has transformed the historian's expectation of continuity with a past whose events could be interpreted as having political, social, cultural, and economic significance. The movement of events remembered as belonging to a people has given way to a plethora of images and of "raw" information that can be ascribed to no one. Memory has been brought to closure not by death, an event that Aristotle and Aquinas saw as precluding both perception and imagination and thus as ruling out genuine memory, but rather by a vast excess of factoids, meaningless constellations of picture and discourse. As a result, there is currently a need to *create* the real and the referential. Yet pain and suffering do not disappear but remain the limiting condition of this otherwise volatilized hyperreality.

Memory in the history of Western thought has been construed through metaphors of imprinting and storing, through images of a wax tablet or seal upon which percepts and thoughts are impressed, or as a warehouse in which knowledge is either stored for future use or is already "there" awaiting recollection. But explanations of memory have aroused mistrust not because they have been undermined by the phenomenon of forgetfulness but rather because of an inherent instability in the mechanisms of memory. Plato's simultaneous reliance on and suspicion of the scriptic model is brought out in Derrida's deconstructive reading of the dialogue *Phaedrus* in which Socrates demonstrates that writing is the supplement of speech, of the living logos and, as such, remains secondary to it. But Derrida shows that originary presence cannot be what it purports to be, self-identical, unless it can be repeated and repetition is dependent upon rememoration, an imprint or writing: "no repetition without the graphics of supplementarity."

For Aristotle, the memories of both individual things and concepts provides the materials from which knowledge is constructed, memories that are images or simulacra. But images cannot be fully regimented by the mind's topoi, its principles of ordering. The runaway images of dreams and hallucinations threaten mental stability, a condition presaging intramentally the disorderly dissemination of images in contemporary specular culture. Aristotle is troubled too by the question of what it is we remember when we recall a feeling, the affect itself or its image, a problem that is compounded for the heterological historian who promises to remember the wounds and outrages of another.

For Augustine, memory is a mighty power, the dwelling place of truth and the means through which knowledge of God must be sought. But, if God is to be remembered, must he not first have been known? And, if once known, how can God have been forgotten? It is not by direct remembering but only by remembering past happiness that there is hope for finding God. Yet no image of *true* happiness can be dredged from memory because images remain sensible, so that, like the logos of the *Phaedrus,* Augustine's memory requires a supplement, that of the sign.

Because an account of semiological memory is not developed in Augustine, we may have recourse to a modern view: Freud's description of repressed mental content and its transformation into the symptom, the sign of an original trauma, so that the way is now open for recovering buried memory. Yet the heterological historian cannot fail to notice that it is the psychoanalyst who frames the rules of discourse and forces the unconscious of the other to speak. There is, however, an alternative to the coercion, the pressure exerted by a semiology of the unconscious. Instead of relying upon the strength of signs, passivity or weakness invites or seduces the other to give up her secrets just as Augustine's weakness and pleading may be seen as a seduction of the divine. Does the heterological historian too not seduce with and for the weakness of the other?

Yet, Hegel might object, unless images are transformed into signs, memory becomes either a chamber of metastasizing simulacra reminiscent of the mind of Borges's Funes the Memorious or a reservoir of dead images, a crypt. Elaborating upon these alternatives, Hegel sees memory as starting with the inwardization of images, of sensible intuitions conserved unconsciously in a mind that has become a dark pit. Even when freed from its externality, the image remains merely passive until inward intuitions are transformed into signs. Memory is cleansed as it were from the taint of images only when it is semiologically reborn. Unlike images, signs cannot be thrust into a pit but must be conserved above ground, on the face of a pyramid that conceals the crypt below. Hegel's tropes help to describe the discursive space between the unstable sign and the runaway image from which the historian issues her narrative.

Still another ancient model of memory is that of associating items to be remembered with the architectural elements of a building that can be called upon repeatedly to help remember new images. Thus memory is transformed into a mnemotechnic, into an information retrieval system reminiscent of the digital computer. In like manner, the Luba people of Africa use complex memory devices, especially the lukasa, a board whose elaborate decorations are polysemic reminders of past history. But far from being a mechanical system for the recovery of information, the *lukasa* preserves memories linked to present events, to the living history of a people. The visual historian might wish to explore techniques interspersing present interests and past events so as to expose the errant seriality of historical narrative, to stand inside and outside each of these perspectives.

Hegel objects to ancient mnemotechnics on the ground that there is an associative but no conceptual link between physical image and the object to be recalled. A remarkably similar criticism is leveled by Hegel against the claims of the nineteenth-century so-called science of phrenology that inner mental states are associated with specific regions of the skull. If brain states are substituted for skull configurations and Hegel's argument recast in contemporary terms, Hegel could be seen to contend that states of consciousness and brain activity are heterogeneous so that the one can provide no knowledge about the other. Moreover, if feelings are reduced to brain states, the interpretation of brain states is far too abstract to provide meaningful correlations with the indeterminacy of feeling.

Contemporary materialist accounts of memory as a conscious process attempt to free interpretations of mind from a discredited metaphysics, especially from the Cartesian view that there is an inner homunculus that masterminds the interaction of mind and body within a single consciousness. Materialism itself is no longer phenomenologically construed as in Hegel's day but is understood in terms of the occult entities of the physical sciences or as coded information. Now, the language of thoughts, emotions, and sensations are translated into that of brain activities. Hegel's anti-materialism did not, however, preclude his turning to behavior as a far better correlate of inner states than the skull's ridges and hollows. Many contemporary accounts find straightforward behaviorism simplistic but adopt a version of behaviorism in which what is observed are not actions but brain activities.

They demand to know what conditions justify the ascription of mental states, but these ascriptions must be cashed out by observable material conditions provided by neurophysiological data.

For Daniel Dennett, the brain is an aggregate of information processing bits while consciousness is a qualitative intensification of the bits already there. Language is central to this process in that what is stored are conceptual simples, memes, ideas that form themselves into units ranging from wheels to chess. The sense of time's passing can be explained as a change from a succession of representations to the representation of succession. The heterological historian may sense something question begging about this account in that the felt succession of representations already presupposes a prior sense of time. Even if Dennett is right to exclude a "central headquarters" in consciousness, right to see remembering as a scriptic process, the historian may ask whether by encoding time's passing in the language of brain states Dennett has failed to notice that temporalization is primordial, that it goes all the way down.

Roger Penrose's version of materialism presupposes a two-tiered account of brain processes: at the macrolevel the laws of classical physics obtain while at another more subterranean stratum the laws of quantum physics hold. But the events at each level interact in a "delicate coupling" that affects the way thought occurs. It is the instability of the quantum level that enables us to perform non-computational tasks and allows for a salutary vagueness in our thought processes. The heterological historian observes that temporal undecidability, the result of an incommensurability between the physicist's use of a "real number parameter" and the subjective experience of time, is intrinsic to neuronal activity. Thus she sees repeated in brain activity a Derridean self-dividing difference. Moreover, she discerns that, for Penrose, counterfactuality is not only a conceptual artifact of Western logic but is built into neural activity: an action that might have been performed produces neural effects other than those resulting from being unable to perform an action. Does not a roughly comparable difference between the counterfactual and the impossible describe the discursive space in which the historian configures her narrative? Does not the ambiguity of "it could have been" allow for sinuosity in a narrative that is also constrained by the negative "it could not have been?"

Although the heterological historian is challenged by materialistic views of mind, each brain-mind is a singularity, its memes owned, that is, possessive pronouns, my and mine, hers and his, can be ascribed to them. What is more, the brain is seen as living so that life is still marked off from non-life. But new technologies have opened the possibility of creating sophisticated cellular automata that would replicate the activities of neural systems, even those that are unprogrammed. Conversely, what appears to be purely biological material, DNA molecules, can be used to represent information and thus create a biological computational system that would speed up calculative processes. Although she is unlikely to master the physical theories thought to render such visions "actual," the historian cannot fail to observe that these technological innovations reflect a frantic quest for the expansion of memory. The memories themselves have become ownerless, commodified in a global culture of information. No longer are memories carried forward as the shared experience of peoples but instead circulate as timeless information in a global system of information.

How can the decontextualized memories of specular culture, memories now compressed into a single undifferentiated time, enter into the formation of communal consciousness? Are communities as previously understood possible without chronologically articulated social memories? Does the insistence upon the retrieval of what has gone by as the rightful possession of particular communities only increase the violence already present in specular culture? In the light of these worries, can the heterological historian help to maintain the impossible dream of non-violent communities? These matters will be considered in the following chapter.

One of them asked us from where did we come? I replied that we were coming from my town, then he said where? I told him that it was very far away to this town and he asked again were the people in that town alives or deads? I replied that the whole of us in that town had never died. When he heard that from me he told us to go back to that town where there were only alives living, he said that it was forbidden for alives to come to the Dead's town.

Amos Tutuola
The Palm Wine Drinkard

THE GIFT OF COMMUNITY

Is it possible to shape a community of shared experience in the wake of the cataclysm? What role does the heterological historian play in refiguring social existence always already disfigured by the cataclysm? Her part can only come to light as she reacts and responds to conflicting conceptions of communal life and situates herself in dynamic relationship to them. Classical discourses consider community in terms of autochthony so that, as Plato seems to hold, communal bonds are strongest when engendered by emergence from a common soil. By contrast, modern accounts of community are often grounded in relations of production and exchange. Each of these social entities, both the autochthonous and the productive communities, can be considered communities of immanence. The heterological historian asks whether communities can be formed in relation to an incommensurable outside, an outside that is neither a topos of transcendence nor of ecstasy. Can the cataclysm be understood as such an unsurpassable exteriority, an outside that cannot be poetized and that fissures communities of imma-

nence?

Jean-Paul Sartre will be seen to follow the pattern set by modernity. Describing what he calls totalization, the dynamic open-ended social process that characterizes human life lived historically, Sartre develops a phenomenology of community that is contingent upon the formation of a common consciousness by its members. Inspired by what he saw as the unfolding of communal self-awareness in the French Revolution, Sartre sees a collective, a mere series of persons unaware of the telos that unites them, that becomes the group in fusion through the discovery of a common purpose. Later the group may ossify when its originary passion cools. But in the final analysis each of these communities may be defined in terms of production.

It can be argued against Sartre that communities of production governed by the logic of modernity as revealed in the self-enclosure of the subject are barred from relation with an outside, that the object of production is caught up in a nexus of economic exchange. The historian who speaks from the cataclysm cannot help noticing that communities of production are communities of immanence, windowless monads whose driving force is that of an objective task that is begun but not completed and whose end is realized with the death of its members in the interest of some community yet to come.

Only with the de-nucleation of the self and a relation to exteriority can heterological community come into being. The link with exteriority inaugurates a community other than that of production, the community of hospitality. Yet production as such is ineliminable if only because basic human needs must be satisfied. Is there not, however, a pre-originary form of production that is gratuitous, workless, one that resists ensnarement by the culture of images? Could communities formed in this way not be compared to an artwork whose value is not determined by labor, a non-work fissured by the cataclysm?

Community also embodies a mode of self-temporalization, that of the future, which is manifested as hope, the gift that those who have no-thing in common give to one another. But what must hope be if it is not to constitute a mockery of the cataclysm, a pious sentiment? A fundamental rethinking of hope that precludes a reasonable expectation of happiness, in the manner either of eudaemonistic ethics or of philosophies of political utopianism, is required. If hope is a gift, the gift too must be reenvisaged in terms of a relation between its gratuitousness, on the one hand, and its inevitable involvement in the sphere of economy, on the other. What is more, a gift does not depend upon its pre-conditions but is purely contingent. In Derrida's words:

There must be event—and therefore appeal to event and narrative of event—
for there to be gift, and there must be gift or *phenomenon of gift* for there to
be narrative and history. The gift like the event as event . . . must let itself be
structured by the aleatory; it must appear chancey.[1]

The description of the coming-into-being of community that follows
is not to be construed as the positing of a transcendental condition or structural requisite that makes community possible but as an account of that
aspect of community that constitutes a reserve or excess in the being of
community, an outside that is also always inside. Because they are subject
to change, communities do not float timelessly above the conditions of existence but *live* these contingent conditions. The heterological historian will
be shown to intervene as critic and contributor to these social processes.

UNSAYING RATIONAL COMMUNITY:
AUTOCHTHONY AND DESIRE

"No one knows where Moses was buried, but we know where he lived and
we still know all about his life. Nowadays everything is the other way
around. We know only where the burial places are. Where we live is unfixed and unknown. We roam about, we change we shift. Only the burial
place is known."[2] What is the heterological historian to make of the extraordinary change in sensibility, the de-formation implicit in this description? A
superficial reading might situate this shift within the binarism of settled existence and exile. To be sure, the exilic life of the refugee is endemic to the
world marred by the cataclysm. Flight from zones of mass killings and severe
economic hardship has become a commonplace. Far less obvious is the fact
that the myth of autochthony, the myth that depicts human beings as born
from the earth, has nevertheless not disappeared. On the one hand, the idea
of autochthony has spawned proprietary claims that still result in fierce local
wars; on the other hand, the idea of place persists, but locales have become
sites of mourning, not of life but of death. Burial places are the fragments
of vast memory palaces, reminders less of the events awaiting historical remembering, than of the historian's responsibility to remember. What accounts for this displacement of autochthony not by the nomadism of exile
but by death? How may community be envisaged "out of" (in the double
sense of "from within" and "beyond") the cataclysm?

The myth of autochthony as it manifests itself in Western philosophy
begins innocuously enough as an insertion into Plato's account of the ideal
state, one in which the bonds that unite individuals are envisaged in terms

of interests that must be rationally adjudicated. Fundamental to this perspective is the assumption that common categories can be applied to the individual and to the state, that relations within the soul may be likened to those of classes within the state. Thus psyche and polis differ only in size and not in kind insofar as the rational governance of affect and action remains the aim of both. Where the description of soul predominates as in *Republic,* intrapsychic relations are construed in epistemic terms: knowledge of the eternal unchanging forms provides the warranty for the right ordering of soul and state. The justice of the just individual and the just state are one (*Republic,* IV, 435). Where the state as it actually exists is foregrounded as in Plato's *Laws,* it is the laws of the polis that incarnate the truths of reason. But, if the laws are *embodiments* of justice, the penumbra of corporeality that clings to them opens the possibility of slippage. "Do you imagine that there ever was a legislator so foolish as not to know that many things are necessarily omitted which someone coming after him is to correct, if the constitution and the order of the government is not to deteriorate?" the Athenian Stranger asks (*Laws,* VI, 769). It is in part the difference between the epistemic certitude of *Republic* and the fallible practical wisdom of the *Laws* that has led interpreters to see the former as the creation of youth and the latter as the product of the reflective wisdom of age, a move from rational certitude to a reckoning with contingency. To the Athenian Stranger who commends the rule of law, Cleinias remarks, "Truly you see with the keen vision of age" (*Laws,* IV, 715).

I rehearse these well-known differences to introduce the myth without which the implementation of Plato's plan for an ideal state as envisioned in *Republic* would founder, the myth of the autochthon. Imagine, says Plato, a state that imposes a period for procreation during which an elite will couple. Those born of these couplings would not know who their parents were but would be told that they are earth sprung, that the state is both mother and father. "They are to be told their youth was a dream; during all that time they were being formed and fed by the womb of the earth. . . . When they were completed, the earth, their mother, sent them up" (*Republic,* III, 414). Would they not be inclined to regard the state with a filial affection that would assure fealty to their brothers and sisters and compliance with the laws of the state? Plato appears to be seeking a basis in nature for the state that is more natural, as it were, than nature itself, one in which no counterwill to the state could arise: earth, a manifestation of nature, must become the womb that nurtures the citizens.

Although Aristotle's *Politics* is grounded in the concepts of his metaphysics and ethics, his method purports to be largely inductive. The Platonic philosophemes—the superiority of the soul to the body, of reason to pas-sion, the identification of a thing's essence with its telos—persist but are articulated in a different register. For Aristotle, the state is a subset of com-munity, its highest and most comprehensive form. But unlike Plato, Aris-totle sees the family as a *sine qua non* for the development of economic and political life. If Aristotle does not depreciate the family, it is because it is better understood, truer to experience than the fantasy of earthsprung prog-eny. Yet even if the myth of autochthony is absent in its full-blown form, Aristotle presupposes the strong ties linking all those born as Hellenes and goes so far as to maintain that, theoretically, Hellenes need pose no threat to one another. There is no mistaking Aristotle's view of the benefits of autochthony once the idea is watered down and rendered plausible. The Greek race alone, he avers, at once spirited and intelligent, combines free-dom with good government and, "if it could be formed into a single state, could govern the world" (*Politics,* VII, 1328a).³

∞

The heterological historian could scarcely hope for the reinstatment of the myth of autochthony either in its strong or attenuated versions. How could she endorse an appeal to what would be reincarnated, despite important differences, in the social Darwinist principle of *Blut und Boden* in nineteenth-century racial doctrines? Although Aristotle moderates the force of the autochthony myth, it is taken for granted that earth and ethos can assure the preeminence of a people, a superiority he attributes to Hellenes, that entitles them to rule. But if rational community is always already rid-dled by the aporetic structure of autochthony whose binding force is not reason but affect, there is another mode of fissuring the rule of reason, that of a nearly invisible alterity whose traces may be discerned in the eros of Plato's *Symposium* and in the depiction of friendship introduced almost par-enthetically in Books VIII and IX of Aristotle's *Nichomachean Ethics.* The great speech on the excessiveness of desire disrupts the work of the logos, a disquisition launched in sobriety by Socrates at a banquet at which drunken-ness, madness, and folly enter from outside to undermine the work of the logos. We shall see that desire as interference and exteriority is retained in the discourses on community of Bataille, Jean-Luc Nancy, Levinas, and Blanchot to break with received accounts of community based on utility and production.

Socrates shows that, although the objects of love may differ, love loves what it lacks: "He who desires something is in want of something, and he who desires nothing is in want of nothing" (*Symposium* 199). One does not desire what one has or is. As lack, love cannot be identified with the object of its desires. Love is the affective register in which that which is not expresses itself. To praise love is to slip into a category mistake such that one praises love as if it were one of its own objects. Encomia about love are meaningless. As Christian neo-Platonism would come to recognize, the true language of love is apophatic. Yet, as Socrates learns from the crone-wisdom of Diotima, love is a power, not quite a god—the gods lack nothing—nor a mortal, but a great spirit. Love is outside the binarisms, beautiful and ugly, wisdom and ignorance; thus it is not ugly and ignorant because it is non-beautiful and non-wise.

Crucial for the recent French re-figuring of this myth is Diotima's depiction of love as creating communion and communication with the gods. The task of love is to "interpret . . . between gods and men conveying and taking across to the gods, the prayers and sacrifices of men, and to men the commands and replies of the gods; he is the mediator who spans the chasm which divides them, and therefore in him all is bound together" (*Symposium* 202). In a genealogical allegory, Diotima reports that when Aphrodite was born, a feast was held at which Plenty (Poros), the son of Metis or Discretion, grew drunk and fell asleep outside the house in the garden of Zeus. Poverty (Penia) who was hanging about the door noticed Plenty's inebriated state. "So Poverty considering her own straitened circumstances, plotted to have a child by him . . . lay down at his side and conceived Love" (*Symposium* 203). But Diotima points out the defects of love:

> He is always poor; and anything but tender and fair, as the many imagine him; and he is rough and squalid, has no shoes, nor a house to dwell in; on the bare earth exposed he lies under the open heaven, in the streets or in the doors of houses, taking his rest. Like his father too, he is always plotting against the fair and the good; . . . he is terrible as an enchanter. (*Symposium* 203)

The heterological historian attentive to textual stratigraphy may notice that there is a layering of the narrative's chain of transmission, a banquet within the banquet, and that this layering opens the narrative to that which is outside that configures the inside. The first story of the banquet is told by Apollodorus who had it from Aristodemus who was there, and who transmits the Socratic discourse, itself a remembered story told by Diotima. In her tale, a banquet is described that is re-described at yet another such occasion. The dialogue is constructed as a system of memory relays with no originating first-person account, even that of Aristodemus, the eye witness, who only repeats discourses always already remembered. In the disquisition about love, discourse is discourse of another, repeated, described, hearsay about that which is outside the present moment of narration. It is the discourse of Poverty, one that can never be rendered as a fully present logos, that provides an entering wedge for the way community is seen in Levinas and Blanchot.

In some brief remarks about the *Symposium,* Nancy portrays love as subordinated to philosophy, as pressed into the service of thought. "For all its generosity, the *Symposium* also exercises a mastery over love."[4] He does not fail to notice love's frailty and vulnerability, yet it does not continue to fissure thought in an ever-recurrent lack that is intrinsically incapable of fulfillment. For even if love is double and contradictory as it is in the long tradition of the discourse of love from Plato to Freud, for Nancy it resolves or surpasses its contradictions. What is instantiated in the *Symposium* is a perpetual reconquest of love by thought. Yet the wounding by and of love, its built-in anguish that cannot be surmounted and that infiltrates Diotima's account, is missed in Nancy's interpretation precisely because the desiring aspect of love is overlooked. Far from segregating love from desire, the affect directed at an object that one may or may not possess from a yearning aimed at what one does not possess, Diotima's discourse converts love into desire. In speaking of loving what one does not have rather than what one has, what is really meant is expressed more naturally by locutions of desire: one does not desire what one has but what one does not have. If love is indeed lack as Diotima claims, it is what we generally name desire. This is not merely an arcane dialectical point but one that will be seen as crucial to understanding the relation of community to the desire for an alterity that remains irreducible and unobtainable.

At first glance, Aristotle's account of friendship hardly seems to disrupt the description in the *Politics* of the well-ordered state as the exemplary rational community. More often than not, Aristotle makes friendship appear as self- rather than other-regarding. Friendship may indeed be based on utility or on the sheer pleasure in the society of others, but its real aim is facilitating the good life of the individual as citizen. In pinning down the reasons for behavior that is other-regarding, Aristotle in the *Nichomachean Ethics* often recurs to that which is good in one's relation to oneself: wanting to be who one is, being in harmony with oneself, concentration of soul and consistency in choosing pleasures and pains (1166, a1–b30). These qualities that enable one to do what is best for oneself should be wished for and fostered in the friend who is a version of oneself.

Yet it is noteworthy that the Greek word for friendship means the attraction between two human beings and that friendship for Aristotle is a community of love. It is here that Aristotle introduces the notion that it is better to give love than to receive it. "People delight [in being loved] for its own sake [not as a means] and friendship is desirable in itself. But it seems to lie in loving rather than in being loved" (1159a, 8–35). Breaking with the eudaemonistic thrust of the *Nichomachean Ethics,* that is, the notion that human beings ought to aim at their own happiness, he argues that one wishes the other well for the other's sake and not for one's own. The argument is not a consequentialist one, that is, I should desire the other's happiness because his happiness is likely to guarantee mine, but rather deontological, that is, I do good for the other for its own sake and not for any benefit that may accrue. In a favorite example, in support of the feasibility of preferring loving over being loved, Aristotle speaks of a mother's satisfaction in the prospering of her child even when he has been handed over to another (1166a, 5–9).

The heterological historian may reflect upon the double aporia created by autochthony and by other-regarding love, each of which threatens the classical view of the state as governed by rational rule. Reason alone is not enough to insure the state's well-being but requires a supplement. Strong affect based upon consanguinity is generated by the earthsprung for one another, an exclusive love that begets a community of immanence, one closed to exteriority. Only those born of the same earth are bound by the ties of love, ties that bind only within this limited totality. Such love cannot be construed as lack for, if it were, it would be powerless to achieve communal loyalty; the love of the earthsprung for one another must be repletion, but in that case it ceases to be (on Plato's definition) love.

On the other hand, the reverse autochthony of the burial place is engendered in destitution, pure lack, and can produce no object. History written under the sign of autochthony must be heroic history, a tending and preserving of the past, an incessant remythologization of the divine origin, of how it was in *illo tempore.* The reverse autochthony of burial places cannot generate such a recalling, an anamnesis of a divine origin: we know where the burial places are, but "where we live is unfixed and unknown." To speak from the burial place is to inhabit a terrain that is not a terrain, an exteriority that is the non-place of ethics, the "space" of authorization of historical narrative.

HUMANITY'S ESSENCE IS PRODUCTION

On the classical view, the state is a rationally ordered community whose end is the well-being of its citizens. Power belongs to the good who are also wise, that is, rational, in the sense of acting in accordance with the logos as well as being temperate. Three forms of community have been seen to fissure the classical ideal of rational social existence while claiming to advance its interest: the myth of autochthony, that gives rise to a polis grounded in natural existence; the encomia for love, that attest to the intimate community of the banquet; and the discourse of fraternal amity, that eventuates in a community of friends.

Just as for Plato the rational community is to avoid its opposite, for Augustine the community of the good, the heavenly city, must be cordoned off, separated from the earthly city. In a movement of inversion, however, it is not reason that unites the inhabitants of the heavenly city but love from which desire has now been prescinded. Thus Augustine proclaims that the earthly city is beset by "litigations, wars and quarrels" although there may be some good in it insofar as the just prevail and peace is promoted, but it is only the heavenly city that promises never-ending peace.[5] "Isaac, the child of the promse typif[ies] the children of grace, the citizens of the free city who dwell together in everlasting peace, in which self-love and self-will have no place, but a ministering love that rejoices in the common joy of all," Augustine proclaims.[6]

What is striking in the modern overturning of the classical and Christian views and comes to the fore with especial force in Marx is the introduction of production as the foundation of community. Jean-Luc Nancy maintains that, despite the Marxist hope for a community without class divisions and "technopolitical" domination, it is precisely the contention that human beings are the producers of their own essence as production that caused the Marxist ideal of community to founder. Recent conceptions of community have been linked to the embodiment of still another essence, that of being human. It then becomes the task of society to produce this essence in the shape of community. For Nancy, essence circulates as economic, political, and technological production within a locked totality, an "immanentism" without exit that is "the general horizon of our time."[7]

Although Jean-Paul Sartre knew the early writings of both Levinas and Blanchot that presaged Nancy's critque of communities of production when he wrote his massive work of social philosophy, *The Critique of Dialectical Reason,* he took no account of them.[8] Conversely, Sartre's depiction of social existence as founded on production, admired and struggled against by Levinas and Blanchot, is nevertheless not the subject of extended analysis in their more recent accounts of social existence, nor is it a focal point of Nancy's 1986 inquiry into the nature of community. Yet Sartre's version of community as an attempted synthesis of conflicting tendencies in social thought—the lament for a Marxism he saw as destroyed by Stalinism and a plea for a

12. Suzanne Hélein Koss, "Communities of Production: Growth in the Desert."
Courtesy of the photographer.

Nietzschean intensity of experience—powerfully infiltrates later discussion.[9]
Arguing that the mode of production is basic to the determination of social
structure, Sartre is convinced that social fragmentation and alienated atom-
ized individualism are the consequences both of Stalinist communism and
the capitalism immediately following World War II, before the society and
culture had been transformed into spectacle and information (fig. 12).

A crucial aspect of Sartre's account of community in the *Critique* is his
description of totalization, the open-ended process of human life as it is
lived historically. Distinguishing between totality and totalization, Sartre describes totality as functioning heuristically. It is, on the one hand, a being
distinct from the mere sum of its parts; on the other, its self-relation is
determined by a relation of its parts among themselves, each of which embodies the totality in a kind of macrocosmic-microcosmic parallelism.
"They lie heavy on our destiny because of the contradiction which opposes
praxis," Sartre asserts (*CDR,* pp. 45–46). Totalization is a dynamic open-
ended activity into which conscious participation enters as one of its moments. Dialectic is defined by Sartre in terms of praxis, a totalizing activity
whose rules are produced by the process itself. As something produced, the
totality has the status of a thing, a residue that is the result of past action
whose inertia may resist praxis with a counterforce of its own. This reifica-

tion of praxis is what Sartre calls the "pratico-inert." Crucial for Sartre is the notion that knowledge is intrinsic to the activity of totalizing such that "critical investigation is the very life of the investigator" (*CDR*, p. 51), a conviction reminiscent of the notion of existential commitment intrinsic to his earlier work. That which is totalized embodies knowledge acts, so much so that the Sartrian critique, bending back on itself, is not exterior to the totalizing process. There is nothing outside dialectical reason so that Sartrian dialectic, unlike that of Hegel, offers no panoptical vantage point from which the totality can be surveyed. Nor is totalization as an idea or formal principle separable from historical context.

A critique of dialectical reason only could have arisen in a post-Hegelian, post-Stalinist world, one of alienation that has become internalized and chronic: "[The individual's] free activity in its freedom, will take upon itself everything which crushes him—exhausting work, exploitation, oppression, and rising prices . . . His liberty is the means chosen by the Thing and by the Other to crush him and to transform him into a worked Thing" (*CDR*, p. 325). A kind of atomization of the individual is evinced in the simplest everyday social encounters such as that in Sartre's celebrated (if jejune) example of people queueing for a bus on the Place St. Germain. "Through the medium of the city, there are given the millions of people who are the city, and whose completely invisible presence makes of everyone both a polyvalent isolation . . . and an integrated member of the city. . . . the mode of life occasions isolated behavior in everyone" (*CDR*, p. 257). The mood of Sartre's analysis is not one of bleak pessimism but rather of hope, a fixing upon the process of totalization as an entering wedge into the creation of community. Only now, in the post-Stalinist period, he declares, can we have critique in its etymological sense as that which can "set limits to the scope of totalizing activities in order to restore to them their validity" (*CDR*, p. 50).

The heterological historian caught up in the culture of image and information will recognize in Sartre's reinscription of Marx's analysis of capital an anticipation of Baudrillard's account of the hyperreal. For both, the subject has become a captive of the object, "a freedom captured by the order of the thing" in Sartrean terms. Thus, in effect, the subject as a spontaneity is dissolved, even if Sartre, in conformity with his earlier existential analysis of consciousness, fails to acknowledge this shift. Are we not now dominated by the order of things, and does not the object, as Baudrillard thought, possess a cunning of its own? Has there not in Sartre been a partial volatilization of the object in contrast to the standard Marxist view in which the object, even if alienated, still belongs to a nexus of exchange and utility?

Yet Sartre's materialism remains tied to a phenomenological interpretation of matter as that which is inert, which offers resistance and counter-resistance and can be altered by human activity. It is because Sartre holds this view of matter that he does not entirely abandon the notion of freedom and envisions his historical situation as providing an opportunity for social transformations. But the heterological historian does not inhabit the hodological spaces from which Sartre's examples are drawn. To be sure, there are still bus queues as Sartre describes them, but they are embedded in new matrices within a world of etiolated materiality. Such a transformation volatilizes space into time. Paul Virilio explains this change: "In our banal and daily life we are switching from the extensive time of history to the intensive time of momentariness without history—with the aid of contemporary technologies."[10]

Sartre is unable to evade the question of who is to undertake the task of social critique. Because there is no exteriority, no perspective outside the totality for him it must, at least theoretically, be those inside it whom he identifies as anyone at all *(n'importe qui)*. He reasons that if the totality is expressed in its parts, and the individual is a segment of the totality, then the life of the individual is a singularization of this totality. And if each and every individual is such a singularization then everyone, Sartre claims, is anyone at all. "If the historical totalization is able to exist, then any human life is the direct and indirect expression of the whole and of all lives to precisely the extent that it is opposed to everything and everyone" (*CDR*, p. 50). If critique is the task of an investigator who will link the whole and its parts, he will make the leap between his own life and history. Caught up in the totalizing process, like all the others, he too is an "anyone at all." This anyone remains a consciousness, an epistemological *point d'appui* that is at once consciousness certain of itself and consciousness of the object.

The heterological historian may see from Sartre's analysis that once she enters the discursive space of historical recounting she, like the historical investigator he describes, becomes "anyone at all." As a historian traveling in time, she cannot elude what the earlier Sartre had called situation, the conditions of her own time and place. But now situation itself has been volatilized in a world of images and hyperreal objects that have a cunning of their own so that social existence has moved beyond the conditions depicted by Sartre. May the historian not escape to the non-space of deixis, the "locus" of authorization of her discourse, the exteriority of the cataclysm and of alterity? Can she not station herself "there" where the hyperreal is fissured as the place from which her narrative is to issue? But if she tries to evade her historical condition by conferring a panoptical privilege upon ethics, would she not then transform ethics itself into the locus of all that has thus far been subjected to a critique by ethics: representation, the transparency of language, the truth of presence? Such evasion would convert the non-place of ethics into a *Da,* a site of interpretation and appropriation. Ethics cannot be a safety zone, an escape route from the entrapments of contemporary life—all are caught up in that life—but a demand placed upon the historian by the dead to re-member them in the always already pre-figured discursive space in which she finds herself. Thus she cannot in the culture of images and information avoid with Luddite simplicity its technologies nor the languages they have generated.

It should be recognized that, for Sartre, totalization does not preclude negative phenomena: absence, need, lack, nothingness, that formed so prominent a part of his early work; they remain crucial to his social philosophy. But the indigence of the *tout autre* opens out into production rather than into ethics. "Everything is to be explained through *need [besoin]*" as "the link of *univocal immanence* with surrounding materiality insofar as the organism tries to sustain itself" (*CDR,* p. 80), he argues. For Sartre the foundation of the possibility of history is construed as a community's self-reflexive relation to its materiality (*CDR,* p. 125). In its most primal form, need is the indigence of the organism, hunger, and its relief. Thus there is a "natural" grounding for that which is most fundamental to social existence, economic scarcity. Yet he claims that even if scarcity is to be found everywhere, it is a necessary but not yet a sufficient condition for history which, in his view, does not arise in all societies. In a long disquisition on what he calls non-historical societies, he expounds a mixed discourse which accepts the stereotyping of non-literate societies as governed by atemporal archetypes characteristic of the ethnology of his day. At the same time he decries the role of colonialism in foisting a historical identity upon the colonized (*CDR,* 125–126).

Because scarcity itself is not a static condition but a dynamic relation between human beings and environment, the latter already replete with social meaning, need and scarcity are not the same. Human labor is the praxis that aims to satisfy needs in a material field of scarcity. It is just this persistence of scarcity as a result of historical conditions that carries with it the sense that the other is a threat and thus that violence is possible. War is not only destruction, it is also labor, "a labor of man upon man" (*CDR,* p. 136).

The discerning historian will note that if labor transforms social existence and Sartre identifies war with labor, he cannot easily renounce violence. Nor can he envision the inception of the state in terms of a social contract theory in which power is transferred to the sovereign in the interest of putting an end to a war of all against all. She may observe too that Sartre is in fact not especially interested in the discovery of an absolute origin of the state but rather in the transformation of one form of economic and political life into another. Violence is likely to continue so long as naturally or socially created scarcity persists.

In examining social existence, Sartre views the interpenetration of individual and environment as orchestrated either receptively and passively as a collective or dynamically and actively as a group. The collective unifies individuals as a series, one that does not fundamentally change the praxis of those so organized. To recur to the bus stop example, all those who are waiting for the bus are, as it were, standard interchangeable parts. Yet each individual is alone, a monadic existent waiting to board the bus (*CDR,* p. 257). Alterity does not exist at this level: no Other is different from any other Other (*CDR,* p. 261). If there are too many persons, there may not be room for all, a potential dispute that can be settled by accepting seriality as a principle of adjudication, in this case, who came first. There is no appeal to something distinctive in individuals that sets them apart from one another. As yet no common consciousness exists, but merely a negative unity, an alterity that remains impotent. It is common praxis, in this case a habitual and pragmatic one, that characterizes what remains a mere collectivity of individuals. But for Sartre, "Neither common need, nor common *praxis,* nor common objectives can define a community unless it makes itself into a community by feeling individual need as common need, and by projecting itself . . . towards objectives that it produces in common" (*CDR,* p. 350). For one to speak of a group there must be scarcity, the perception of an individual need as a common need and a driving passion against the inert.

It is in the context of the French Revolution's upheavals that Sartre discovers the process of the emergence of community through the formation of a common consciousness. A mere series may become a group in fusion, one having a common purpose that nevertheless remains confined to a specific time and space. The entire city of Paris becomes such a group when the people of Paris, expecting arms, find only rags and, thus deceived, work in concert to capture a cache of arms stored in the Bastille. The structure of the group in fusion depends upon a mediated reciprocity, that of relation with the third such that the binarism of self and other is broken. This complex relation is well-summarized by Joseph Catalano:

Sartre notes that relations within a group are ternary and not . . . binary. Each person approaching the group is not an individual other joining the group as a common other. Rather each person is related to every other through the group itself.[11]

Crucial for Sartre is the overcoming of reciprocal alienation and object-ification that appears otherwise to be built into social existence so that, when I see the other, I see my own lived objectivity. If the group is to maintain its existence, it must organize its practices even if to do so portends ossification. This hardening of identity occurs as the result of its effort to prevent fragmentation once its objectives are achieved, and the intense affect that generated the original fusion cools. The group comes to see itself as mirrored in its previous praxes and now dedicates itself to preserving its past being. The white heat of collective response and common purpose dissipates; what remains is the institution which may come to serve the very ends that the group had been formed to combat.

The heterological historian cannot fail to observe that alterity in Sartre remains subordinated to consciousness, individual and collective. Nancy declares that Sartre does nothing more than "coat the classical individual subject with . . . a sociological paste: they never *inclined* it outside itself, over that edge which opens up its being in common."[12] The historian may note that alterity is constituted only to be sublated in the interest of an action that begins with the self in a movement of empathy interpreted as common interest, one's own lived objectivity. For Sartre it is not the other but oneself that one sees: "The third party is my objectivity interiorised. I do not see it in him as Other but as *mine*" (*CDR*, p. 377).

EXTERIORITY AND COMMUNITY

An etymological analysis of community points to its derivation from *kom* which can be traced to the Greek *koinos,* shared, and Germanic *ga,* together, with, and from the root *mei,* signifying to hold in common. But *mei* in its various forms also means to change, go, move as in mutate; to hold in common, as in communicate; gift, as in munificent; and to change one's place of living as in migrate. The significations of community may themselves be shifting, an errancy that will be seen to reclaim all of these meanings in spite of the privilege often granted to community as a group sharing proprietary interests. The notion of propriety itself refers to the proper, that which is one's own, what belongs to the individual. These considerations suggest that the fervor generated by a common enterprise may not, as Sartre thought, eventuate in community but rather that production as the grounding for community only reinforces the logic of modernity. On the one hand, this logic is reflected in the self-enclosure of the detached individual, the subject closed to relation. On the other, work is production, and the object produced—image, information, or artifact—is caught up in a network of circulation and exchange which transpires both inside and outside the subject. Yet after exploring its derivative forms, it may be possible to refigure production so that it need no longer be construed as work.

The heterological historian has been warned that re-presentations of the past can themselves become commodities, not only to be reified in institutions as Sartre believed, but subject to refiguration to feed the hunger for images that can be manipulated in the interest of powerful affects that these images both serve and generate. As Pierre Vidal-Naquet remarks in relation to revisionist accounts of the Holocaust: "In our spectacle oriented-society, it is an attempt at extermination on paper that pursues in another register the actual work of extermination. One revives the dead in order the better to strike the living."[13] A community is coerced into producing itself in the shape of an argument, a discursive artifact to defend that which should need no defense: "We find ourselves forced to prove what happened. We . . . find ourselves obliged to be demonstrative, eloquent, to use rhetorical weapons, to enter into the world of what the Greeks called *Peitho,* persuasion, which they had made a goddess who is not our own."[14]

Communities based upon production can be envisaged in several ways, additively as the sum of discrete individuals each of whom is seen as a bundle of potentialities awaiting activation in the interest of the same project, or, on the other hand, as a unified body incarnating a single will. The first community is calculative, interested in the circulation of goods and their symbolic equivalents, money and credit; the second, one of affective intensity, in its extreme form a merging of the social body which can only be consummated in the death of all. The latter communities are exemplified in Fascist groups or suicidal conventicles. Among these are the community in Guayana in which mass suicide was mandated by the Reverend Jim Jones, or that of Waco in which a mass will-to-death operated in complicity with adversarial outside forces so that its leader, David Koresh, was able to create a mood of imminent apocalypse. The calculative community, by contrast, is invested in living within the self-enclosed circuitry of the culture of information and spectacle.

Thus far the heterological historian finds herself still within the sphere of the Sartrean dialectic of seriality and group in fusion. But in subtle meditations upon the shifting positions of George Bataille, both Nancy and Blanchot reflect upon a commonality created by a shared task and by group fusion. Such communities are not communities at all but solidary monads—in the latter case that of a single social body, in the former that of atomic constituents acting mechanically and in concert in response to the magnetic force of an objective task. Communities of fusion realize their end only in death; in the community of shared tasks, the deaths of individuals are subordinated to the interest of a remote future community, one whose goals, extrapolated from the present, is to become ever more productive. Bataille had already mounted a fierce if by now familiar attack upon utility: "Indeed, present day political and technical thought which is reaching a kind of hypertrophy, has gotten us ludicrous results in the very sphere of useful ends . . . SERVILE MAN averts his eyes from that which is not useful, which *serves* no purpose."[15] His point is that productivity vitiates the very principle of utility it purports to serve. The pseudo-immortality of regenerated images and artifacts, on the one hand, and, on the other, war and mass extermination have become ends in themselves and the products of the productive process. Characteristic of both is an immanentism that suppresses the relation with an outside, an alterity that would resist pre-emption.

Yet, the historian might inquire, if its members have nothing in common, no work or discourse to which appeal could be made, would a community not disintegrate? How would it maintain itself without recourse to shared projects that express its power? And is the willingness to die for a community not the ultimate expression of the social bond between self and others? It is not the conatus toward death that troubles Nancy in the work of Bataille but the mystification of death. This transforms the willingness to die out of simple and understandable opposition to that which is intolerable to an arcane more-than-mortal bond between subjects. In fact, Nancy does not contest that community occurs in and through death because death alone evades transformation into a product other than itself, one of sheer negation. It is not possible, he contends, "*to make a work* other than a work of death," a work that is workless and that is ultimately "inscribed and acknowledged as community."[16] Production is not to cease, but rather the gratuity and worklessness of the artwork becomes the pre-originary condition of community.

That death itself could become a television event or that dying could be disseminated from a Web site suggests that death can remain a workless work even in specular culture. Thus Timothy Leary, the advocate of psychedelic experience to the generation of the 1960s, attempted recently to orchestrate his death in cyberspace, to transform his dying into a "visible interactive suicide." The result, however, was not a workless work but rather the denial of death which had become hyperreal in its volatilization as image and information.

It is not death as my ownmost possibility, as Heidegger describes it, that reveals community but rather the deaths of others: what comes to an end is the I of all the others, a multiplicity of I's that do not coalesce into the commonality of a we. To exist as a community excludes the possibility of its member's forging a subject. But the de-nucleation of the subject is a self-negation that takes the self to be nothing. For Bataille, sovereignty becomes nothing and in its destitution is exposed to what is outside itself, an excess, which does not yield to appropriation but remains always other. Bataille writes: "'I am NOTHING': this parody of affirmation is the last word of sovereign subjectivity, freed from the dominion it wanted—or had—to give itself over to things."[17] To be in community is to be in relation with "an incommensurable outside" that interrupts self-consciousness. But as Nancy comments, for Bataille, "[C]ommunity is the ecstatic consciousness of the night of immanence, insofar as such a consciousness is interruption of self-consciousness."[18] The outside is a topos of ecstasy that Bataille means to restrain by invoking the otherness of community; ecstasy and community in a reciprocal movement of derealization, he believes, can avoid the danger of fusion.

The heterological historian may wish to affirm Bataille's uncovering of the relation of community to an outside but she may be suspicious of the pursuit of ecstasy, a quest that Levinas would identify with the sacrality of the *il y a* and thus remain unconstrained by the responsibility of one for the other. Does not ecstasy reintroduce the questionable forces that drive the community of fusion or of lovers in quest of a *jouissance* that Blanchot depicts? The community of the erotic pair as engaged in orgies of death and sacrifice has become a cultural icon in the Bonnie and Clyde motif of such American films as Oliver Stone's *Natural Born Killers*. Here killing becomes a gratuitous work and liberates a *jouissance* that appears to be self-justifying. Must exteriority then not be rethought otherwise than ecstatically, otherwise than as a ceaseless re-figuration of the inebriated community of Plato's *Symposium?* The Platonic banquet unites the celebrants through the ecstasy of chemically induced madness constrained by the sobriety of Socratic reason that, in turn, must itself have recourse to a myth of the divine origin of ecstatic love to account for the gestation of reason itself. What is most challenging for the heterological historian who sees the danger of an ecstasy derived from exteriority is the possible identification of exteriority with the non-ground of the cataclysm. Does exteriority reinstate this ecstasy of the banquet and of the celebrated Hegelian description of history as the bacchanalian revel at which no member is sober as the romance of the abyss?

Exteriority in its ethical sense cannot be envisioned exclusively in terms of the cataclysmic but rather in its doubleness both as cataclysm, the non-space of mass extermination and as an exteriority that is the prelinguistic Saying that precedes language as a concrete act of communication with another. Although it transcends description, the cataclysm may be envisioned cosmologically; therein lies its power to compel. Just as it is impossible to evade a force of nature, the cataclysm cannot be bypassed. Yet once imagined as a natural force, it carries the danger of a mythologization which would poetize a history written from out of the cataclysm, so that the resulting historical artifact may reflect a will to power that becomes totalitarian. It is here that Saying constrains mythologization, a speaking to someone which conveys nothing, communicates no information but is simply a reflexive act, signification signifying itself. It is both a response to another and the vouching or providing a warranty for that which is articulated in language as constituting such a response.[19]

The Other to whom I speak may be, as Levinas believes, proximate, the neighbor, or distant, at a height, as one's teacher in an asymmetrical relation with oneself. In either view, community *is* the assumption of responsibility, *is* living in the manner of one for another. Obligation to another is not distributed piecemeal but is assumed to the fullest extent by each member of the community. In a less extreme form and framed in another philosophical idiom, something like this consideration may lie behind Robert Nozick's argument against what he calls the bucket theory of responsibility. According to that theory, a fixed quantity of responsibility exists for each wrongful act committed, and this quantity can be determined by the amount of punishment that would accrue for a wrongful act. Someone persuaded by another to engage in such an act should not receive a lesser punishment than someone who decides independently to commit such an act. If this is so, the entire quantity of punishment will have been exhausted, leaving nothing over for the one who persuades him. But Nozick contends, per contra, "responsibility is not a bucket in which less remains when some is apportioned out; there is not a fixed amount of punishment or responsibility which one uses up so that none is left over for the other."[20] It would seem there is always an excess, a more of responsibility that can be tapped.

If Bataille's account of community allows us to think, the break with the subject, exteriority, and unworking, the bearing of obligation upon community in light of the interrelationship between the cataclysm, and a pre-originary Saying cannot be extrapolated from his thought. The cataclysm is the de-ontologization of space so that no geodetic metaphor suffices to delimit it; it deterritorializes and renders questionable the relation of ethnicity and earth. Yet it is impossible to eliminate altogether hodological space in actual social, political, and cultural groups in that space persists in the localizations of virtuality; in fact, such an expunging would only accelerate the subversion of local communities by the culture of images. Instead, the cataclysm inaugurates a questioning of the relation of inside and outside that inhibits the theft of historical identity and difference, of exploitative social relations. At the same time the cataclysm does not subordinate the aleatory conditions of existence to a transcendental scheme. It is here that Saying may function as a contesting of appropriation and a recognition of alterity, a contesting that inaugurates the necessity for justice. Even if the relation between the pre-originary conditions of community and justice in the concrete remain obscure, for Bataille "without justice the communitarian enterprise can only be a farce."[21]

How can actual justice be brought about in the light of its pre-originary conditions? Justice begins when the third person enters into my relation with a single Other, not as breaking into an intimate communion of two but as always already there in the countenance of the single Other: the Other is an an-iconic indication of all the others. As Sartre understood, the other must be "anyone at all," the not-I rather than a someone, a person with special characteristics. It is with the entry of the "anyone at all" as a third party that justice is awakened. The other is at once unique and irreplaceable but not yet set apart by individuating attributes. The possibility of rectitude is created by all the others, thus demolishing the monopolistic claims of any one other. Yet this very condition explains the relation of alterity to justice in that one is forced to parcel oneself out so as to meet the claims of the others, to commensurate self and other who, *per hypothesi,* cannot be encompassed within any common measure. In actual social existence, these multiple claims must be adjudicated so that rules that may be applied to cases are required.

At the interface between this pre-originary justice and actual social existence is born the possibility for injustice. In administering justice, the difficulty of applying abstract rules to concrete cases arises. As Lyotard argues, the inequity between plaintiff and defendant in a judicial process may occur when the rules governing the decision-making process are inscribed in the language of the stronger. The plaintiff may become a victim of a judicial language inimical or, at best, foreign to him so that "everything takes place as if there were no damages." It is only with the alteration of the rule or a change in the balance of power that rectification becomes possible. It should be noted that there are "pre-originary" incommensurabilities that cannot be dissolved. The heterological historian is positioned between two phrase regimens, descriptive and moral. Should she remain exclusively under the aegis of moral discourse to become the plaintiff, as it were, she loses contact with the descriptive density and diachronicity of the historical object; if she speaks "factually" she loses sight of her responsibility to the other to convey what happened. It is this discursive space of an irresolvable differend that she inhabits and that poses an ever recurrent challenge to the creation of the *historia rerum gestarum.*

It could be argued that an advantage of a community, whose pre-originary condition is exteriority as the commanding presence of the Other, lies in the power of exteriority to break into the culture of information and spectacle. Yet it also could be concluded that the stringent regulation of a life governed by the claims of alterity would be austere and joyless, that even a modicum of happiness demands not only the weight of obligation but also certain rights. To be sure, joy is always already fissured by natural catastrophe, personal misfortune, and historical calamity, and inestimably so in the epoch of the cataclysm. Yet most lives are touched by moments of joy such as those derived from contact with nature, artworks, and from sociality itself. Under the constraints described, are not the pleasures that remain likely to be pallid and watered down the civilized pleasures excoriated by Nietzsche?

The underlying assumption of this critique is that joy demands freedom and that, in the context of social existence, such freedom is expressed in terms of rights. In Levinas, Blanchot, and Bataille, the discourse of rights is framed otherwise than in recent Anglo-American discussion. The language of rights is absent insofar as responsibility is the pre-originary condition of community. Yet even if not made explicit, rights are implicitly construed as spheres of freedom in a nexus of reciprocally constraining rights, a situation analogous to that intended by analytic philosopher Robert Nozick's remark, "Rights have hooks." Nozick explains:

> The right to engage in a certain relationship is not a right to engage in it with anyone, or even with anyone who wants to or would choose to, but rather it is to do it with anyone who has the right to engage in it. Rights to engage in relationships or transactions have hooks on them, which must attach to the corresponding hook of another's rights that come out to meet theirs. . . . The right is a right to a relationship with someone else who *also* has the right to be the other party in such a relationship.[22]

For Levinas and Blanchot, the sphere of freedom would appear to be re-strained if not crushed on the one hand by the domination of the culture of the spectacle and information, on the other by an irrecusable responsibility. Because for thinkers of community who follow this route community is fundamentally grounded neither in rational rules nor in proprietary inter-ests, responsibility is divorced from rights.

It is not, however, the case that responsibility precludes freedom but rather that freedom requires justification prior to its exercise, not by argu-ment and counterargument but rather by alterity itself. Levinas writes:

> Freedom must justify itself; reduced to itself it is accomplished not in sover-eignty but in arbitrariness. . . . Freedom is not justified by freedom. . . . To account for being or to be in truth is not to comprehend nor to take hold of . . . , but rather to encounter the other . . . in justice.[23]

Being on behalf of others does not demolish the subject; instead the I is generated in a single apprehension of self and other. Born in prior responsi-bility, the I is a necessary if illusory construct if any action including that on behalf of the other is to be undertaken. The introduction of freedom at this level takes into account different desires among individuals, desires which are at the same time constrained by the responsibility to others.[24]

Yet joylessness is far from a necessary affective outcome of the commu-nity whose non-ground is exteriority. To respond to the other who is "out-side" is a movement of extraversion. The root of the word respond is the Greek *sponde,* libation or offering, an engagement of oneself in a ritual act. By extension, to *respond* to the other is to welcome, to extend hospitality, to promise to receive the other, to mitigate his sorrow, to join his grief or, if possible, to engender his joy. What is more, responsibility is intemperate rather than prudential. In the subordination of self to other, there is an immoderate abandon, a transcending of rule-bound transactions. The rela-tion with exteriority is errant, nomadic, "an absolute adventure in a primal imprudence," not as the production of ecstasy but rather as the encounter with an unknown.[25]

If the subject is a place of intersection and communication, the interface where information is received and activated, does the being with others of such a subject not reintroduce the community of production? What then is to result from this freedom other than the fulfillment of basic needs or subjugation to the production of information and consumer goods, or to fiscal instruments that are no longer tied to products but circulate as wealth? What remains outside the production process is the disclosure of that which resists disclosure, the artwork. But is not the art work infra-cognitive and dangerously non-ethical? Is the poet as described by Heidegger not subject to a seizure by language and had not Andre Breton and the surrealists proclaimed that art was a spontaneous dreamwork? If, per contra, the artwork is thought to subserve ethics, is that not an endorsement of a straightforwardly didactic view of art? But art need not re-present "just" and "proper" actions, nor is it "barbaric" to write poetry after Auschwitz as Adorno had declared.[26] The art work as a gratuitous "production," one that is for and of no-thing depicts the formless in form, much as the apophatic disclosures within discursive theology point to an unsayable transcendence. The "work" of a disseminated subject that is not an othering of self but an unsaying may circulate within the culture of images, command a price, but it cannot be entirely commodified in that it undoes or un-writes the very predicative and iterative schema that propagate it. Without requiring any particular style or medium, the artwork, perhaps counter to the artists' intentions, functions as a kind of *analogia entis,* an analogue of an ethics that is itself beyond form. The work's errant word or image "gives sign" in a non-purposive relation with another. Once released, such signs seep into the enclosed world of immanence, "go from Self to Other . . . give sign to undo the structure of language."[27]

THE GIFT OF THE FUTURE

Community has been shown to be bodied forth in its preoriginary structure as hospitality and in the fashioning of the workless work of art. But these pre-conditions are not without risk. A community of hospitality whose language is that of welcome to the other can, in its de-formation, issue in violence that is paradoxically bound up with the renunciation of violence. To be sure, welcoming the other entails the abandonment of hostility toward that other; but the acceptance of a proscription against violence, even one without which there would be no community, is to accede to the incursion of an alterity that inhibits and forbids. Language is not only communication but always already inter-diction, the no-saying of a speech that prohibits, even if such prohibition is on behalf of the other. The community whose non-ground is hospitality is one of peace, but it must remain attentive to the potential violence of an alterity whose very existence is proscriptive and, as such, coercive. Law is the transformation of this attentiveness, this vigilance, into specific injunctions intended as safeguards against an excess of violence. Yet it is virtually a truism that law itself may engender violence. Thus the community of hospitality must remain one of watchfulness so that welcome and response remain in excess of violence.

No less than social existence as hospitality, the community that unfolds as the forming of that which cannot be given form, the art "work," is also at risk. The potential for the commodification of the artwork need not be belabored. More insidious is the indistinguishability of the artwork from the world it may be criticizing. Thus, for example, arrangements of objects generally found in other contexts become artworks only when site specific. Consider Cindy Sherman's installation of multiple grand pianos, each topped by a reproduction of a free-standing bust by Brancusi. Placed in a warehouse, these objects would simply be a collection of musical instruments together with multiple reproductions of a work by a celebrated modern sculptor. Only in a museum or gallery can the same arrangement serve its culture critical function. Similarly, Nam June Paik's installations of old television sets become artworks only in a setting that annnounces that what is displayed is intended as art rather than as a random grouping of objects.

If hospitality and the artwork are the non-ground of communal existence, how does the heterological historian's creation of the historical artifact figure in the development of community? Consider first the time scheme of community. Two modes of ordering temporal series, one as reflecting temporal becoming, stretched time, and the other the static relations of before and after, time's punctiformity, have already been described. The former enables one to think of time as a succession of discrete occasions, the latter to envisage expanses of time and to affix emotions to the dimensions of time, hope, nostalgia, and the like. The community of hospitality is a relation with exteriority and, as such, eludes presence. Similarly, the community of pre-originary production, that of the artwork, does not represent a given form but rather dis-figures presence. Yet an ineluctable yearning or hope for presence remains. Is there not, however, an inner contradiction in the phrase "hope for presence" in that hope is bound up with that which is not yet, with the future rather than the present?

THE GIFT OF HOPE

Can it be said that community is the gift of that which is not yet, of the future, that those who have no-thing in common give to one another?[28] What is it that would be given, by whom and for whom? Consider first the nature of the gift that community gives to itself, time that is not yet but is to come, the future. If the future is a *gift* in the usual sense, it cannot be a future of despair that is given but rather one of hope. Yet the heterological historian attuned to the cataclysm might ask, "What could be the object of such a hope?" Surely not the recreation of an imagined past nor utopian philosophies of the future nor the psychedelic visions of popular culture. Nor can hope be the hope of oblivion, an anodyne for the pain of history, the "slaughter bench," as Hegel aptly calls it. Such a forgetting would destroy community whose non-ground is alterity, the appeal of the dead others to force the culture of images to speak their names.

In his startling analysis of hope, Blanchot declares, "Hope is to be reinvented. . . . [It] is true hope insofar as it aspires to give us [now] the future of a promise, [that is,] what is. What is presence."[29] Hope then is the hope for presence. Although the historian may already be persuaded of the impossibility of getting hold of the present, this impossibility continually vitiates itself. Derrida writes: "How could the desire for presence let itself be destroyed? It is desire itself. But what gives it . . . breath and necessity— what there is and what remains to be thought—is that which in the presence of the present does not present itself."[30] It is this inextinguishable longing for the present and the impossibility of laying hold of it that constitutes hope. Hope relates to a future that is always yet to come but may never arrive. To remain hope, hope must desire the possible, yet it wants what escapes the domain of possibility, the plenitude of a presence that cannot be appropriated. Like the dialectic of love in Plato's *Symposium,* hope desires a fullness that would demolish it. On the other hand, if hope ceases to be related to that which is as what is possible and only to that which could not be, the impossible, hope would be identical with despair. If linked to the possible as probability, then hope is for that which is likely to happen and degenerates into a calculation of the odds. If hope is for the improbable, it must be recognized that the improbable is not the opposite of the probable but belongs to another dimension. It lies outside the realm of proof and not merely as that which at the moment defies proof or is only minimally probable. The improbable is, Blanchot affirms, "a meeting point between possibility and impossibility."[31] The expression, "hope against hope," captures this sense, the first hope being an indication of what is possible, the second of an improbability. Hope as that which never coincides with what-is is powerless and cannot be violent. This is perhaps why the messianism of biblical prophecy links hope to establishing a kingdom of peace.

Yet hope as the interface of possibility and improbability, as that which is not only improbable but also possible, can become programmatic and, as such, is hope that enters into history. Historical possibility is not only the absence of impediment to realization of an event, but rather, as Blanchot points out, possibility is excess, "to be plus the power to be." The heterological historian sees that world relations are relations of power and that discourse is an expression of such relations. If discourse as information and image are manifestations of force, violence inheres in language. Yet language is not open violence, but to the contrary, so long as discourse continues, open violence has not yet occurred. Language, says Bataille, "is secret violence disarming open violence [and thus becomes] the hope and guarantee of a world freed from violence."[32] Thus language, hope, and the future are imbricated in community as conditioning its existence. Yet they are not to be viewed as transcendental structures or pre-existing forms protected from contingency. The conditions that in-form community are also those that de-form it: alterity, the artwork, and hope are incursions into existence.

The historian as one who re-members the past is not immune to setting this violence into motion if she is to make us see, "It could not have been thus." Vidal-Naquet remarks that "for the historian to purge as [well as] he can the work of all that is fabricated, legendary or mythical is the very least to be expected and obviously constitutes a never-ending task."[33] The heterological historian, having examined the past, may abhor its violence yet is compelled to make the dead other speak as the gift she bestows upon actual communities. She must remain perennially wary of the historical lie by affirming that it could never have been thus. She is also aware that the historical lie is forcing language to declare as actual a mythologized past and is thus structurally homologous with torture which makes the victim speak the language of the regime she opposes. The historian who wishes to uncover the camouflages of the past, its lies, and to restore the name of the other is aware that language may incite violence, that she risks fixing an identity that may create a target for violence. The professional historian, the journalist, the filmmaker or keeper of archives has the responsiblity to coerce the dead other into speech yet to uncover in language the antidote to violence.

How and in what sense then is the *historia rerum gestarum* a gift? The commonsense meaning of gift-giving takes for granted that someone gives something to another. But this definition is question begging in that it presumes we know what giving is. Derrida claims that the very conditions that produce the gift render it impossible.[34] If we nevertheless trust our pre-comprehension of the term as indicating a donor, object, and recipient, the gift is self-nullifying in that the recipient is always already enmeshed in a system of exchange. Should the recipient return the gift, she has converted the gift into a loan; if the recipient fails to return the gift, she is placed under obligation: "I owe X a counter-gift or at least thanks," or its opposite, "X was in my debt; he has now repaid it so I owe him nothing." Thus a gift may turn into what it is not as the German word *Gift* (poison) suggests. Once it is recognized that a gift has been given, there is no emerging from the *cul de sac* I have described. Only by forgetting, not recognizing the gift as gift, can there be gift. Has Derrida converted the gift into the *Ursprung* of a Nietzschean ressentiment thus precluding magnanimity?[35]

Consider first that what the community gives itself is time. But what could this mean since time is not a possession that one can give or take, make over to oneself as a legacy? One can only consider a metonymic exchange within time but not one in which time is the object given. Exchange is itself circular, the object always returning in one form or another to its starting point, a circularity commensurable with the configuring of time in the history of metaphysics. Is there any escaping this circle? Does time's circularity preclude the possibility of gift-giving as taking place within the ambit of time? "A gift would be possible, there could be a gift only at the instant an effraction in the circle will have taken place, at the instant all circulation will have been interrupted and on condition of this instant. . . . This instant of effraction must no longer be part of time."[36]

The heterological historian who has committed herself to giving the gift of inscription, to inscribing events into a system of traces, has abandoned the desire for return. Her writing may be the project of a subject, an ego that writes, but as gift *it takes place*. Not personal generosity, but a "forgetful excess," a dissemination that precludes return, describes the giving of the gift. Derrida is persuaded "that only a problematic of the trace and thus of dissemination, can allow the question of the gift and forgiveness to arise . . . signalling towards something altogether other than the traditional opposition between a (living) speech and a (dead) writing."[37] Does this doom the heterological historian as giver of the gift—as she who counters the poisoned gift of historical deception with the claim that it could not have been thus—to silence? Rather Derrida recommends that we acquiesce to a transcendental illusion of the gift, not in straightforward imitation of Kant's notion of the transcendental but rather as acceding to the aleatory character of existence. Resorting to the imperative voice, Derrida proclaims:

> *Know* still what giving *wants to say, know how to give,* know what you want and want to say when you give, know what you intend to give, know how the gift annuls itself, commit yourself *[engage toi]* even if commitment is the destruction of the gift by the gift, give economy its chance.[38]

Exteriority is imbricated in economy and cannot be severed from it.

In sum, the heterological historian brings to the fore the historical object as a gift in the sense just described: the gift is both manifest and self-annulling. She commits herself to carrying the past over into the future as that which is held before (in both its temporal and spatial connotations) a community. Although she remains wary of Nietzsche's view of history as "written by the superior man," she might wish to echo his remark that "when the past speaks it always speaks as an oracle; only if you are an architect of the future and know the present will you understand it."[39] What she makes manifest is a tradition always already fissured by the cataclysm so that historical objects cannot be piously reappropriated. Traditions are transmitted as a system of traces, but the historian whose discourse is refracted through the cataclysm may prefer, as does Derrida, to replace this favored term with the more sering locution, cinders: ashes or cinders are traces that are totally consumed. The cinder does not exist, is not. "It testifies to the disappearance of the witness . . . of memory."[40] The blank spaces of historical writing, its silences, point to the effacement of the other, the *tout autre* who solicits the heterological historian. She is commanded to respond to the order of the gift, to give without knowing precisely what is to be given—how can she lay her hands on time—nor who are the recipients, her addressees. Embodied in the imperatives of the great fifth chapter of the *Bṛhadaranyika Upanisad* "What the Thunder Said," verses taken up in the coda of T. S. Eliot's *Wasteland,* is something like the imperative of the gift. Prajapati, the creator god, is depicted as enjoining each of his children, gods, men, and demons respectively, to overcome their particular failings. *Damyata,* be self-controlled, is the charge to the gods who are given over to the exercise of power; *dyadvham,* be compassionate, is the order to the demons whose fault is cruelty; to human beings because they are self-witholding, Prajapati commands *datta,* give. To whom and what? On this point the god is silent.

∞

What role does the heterological historian, the custodian of memory, play in the formation of community? Does the historical artifact she constructs itself fall into "the dustbin of history?" If history hypostatizes the past, does the historian, in Hegel's terms, consign lifeless memories to a crypt? Or can the historical artifact become something else, a gift through which communities may emerge from the plethora of images and information that constitute contemporary culture? To answer these questions she must first engage some dominant and conflicting accounts of social existence.

In classical philosophy, community is embedded in the polis that, like the soul, is required to regulate runaway affects, to bring action into conformity with the unchanging truths delivered by reason. It would seem that proper pedagogy would suffice to assure sound, that is, rational, governance. Yet in order to implement the rule of reason, Plato invokes a myth that can only undo rationality, that of a community of autochthons, of those who see themselves as sprung from the same earth and thus bound by blood. Autochthony assures homogeneity, but reason is unsaid by the consanguity of origin.

Rational community is also undermined by an eros that by its nature is indigent, in want of what it lacks. Plato's *Symposium* can be envisaged as demonstrating the repeated reconquest of love by thought. Yet in the tale told by Diotima the discourse of love is a discourse of alterity, not only because what is said is hearsay but because Poverty loves what she does not have, Plenty, the perpetual other. Love has become desire, the craving for what one lacks. The heterological historian observes that, in Plato's discourse on love, Poverty exhibits the desire for an irredicible alterity that cannot be reined in by reason.

Aristotle's ethics continues the endorsement of reason's rule sanctioning what is good in relation to oneself. In his disquisition on friendship this self-regarding position persists: the friend is another myself. Yet Aristotle concedes that rather than aiming at one's own happiness, one should seek the happiness of another, that of the friend, for his sake and not for any benefit that might accrue to oneself.

When the classical discourses of autochthony and eros reinforce one another, an aporia is generated not unlike that confronted by the heterological historian. The love of one for another that is born of consanguinity may generate political power which, if it is to be effective as power, can lack nothing whereas love is lack. Either the ties that bind the consanguine community cannot be those of love or love must cease to be lack. The dilemma for the historian who chronicles the social bonds of communities is that autochthonous history may become heroic history, a dangerous remythologization of the divine origin. Yet if she turns to the inverse of autochthony, to the burial places hidden in the cataclysm, she realizes that the space of ethics from which her narrative issues is one of silence.

The modern view of community grounded in production receives its most powerful expression and critique in Marx: production depends upon labor, and labor is alienated. Human beings produce their own essence as production, an essence that circulates within a totality without aperture. Sartre both maintains and criticizes production as the foundation of community. To the oppressiveness of the totality, a reified entity that resists the modifications of praxis, Sartre opposes the open-ended process of totalization that allows for conscious participation. What is more, totalization incorporates the perspectives of the critical investigator who along with all the others takes on the persona of anyone at all, *"n'importe qui."*

Because need is intrinsic to human existence, societies cannot escape production. With the persistence of socially generated scarcity, violence and war will continue and may even be seen as necessary. For Sartre, there can be no community unless there is scarcity, unless need is felt as common need and unless there is a passion against the inertness of the totality. Growth in communal consciousness is reflected in the progression from sheer co-existence to the acquisition of a temporally limited common purpose and thence to authentic community, the relation of each to every other member of a group by way of the group's established common purpose. The hetero-logical historian may note that collective purpose is achieved at the price of yielding to the identity of *n'importe qui,* the universal subject in the arena of political action.

How is one to escape from the community of production whose com-plexity is that of interior differentiation but from which there is no egress. In giving thought to this problem, Bataille uncovers a hidden aporia in communities of production, a certain mortuary alterity, the otherness of death. Purporting to serve the principle of utility, production gone wild creates only death in the form of war and extermination and the pseudo-immortality of images. Yet what social bond can there be that would unite the community other than death, the willingness to die for the others? Death as the ultimate negation is a non-product, a workless work whose value cannot be determined by labor.

If there is to be a community in which exteriority figures, in which the I of the subject proclaims its nullity, for Bataille this exteriority must be a source of ecstasy, an ecstasy that precludes fusion into an undifferentiated one but rather is a release of that which is excessive. The heteorlogical historian remains suspicious of an exteriority that is ecstatic, one that is reminiscent of the *il y a* identified with pagan sacrality by Levinas. Has the culture of the spectacle not introduced killing as a form of *jouissance* in a re-figuration of the drunkenness described in Plato's *Symposium,* the inebria-tion of affect without language? For the heterological historian, exteriority ethically re-figured is the cataclysm, a power that overpowers, constrained by language so as to resist mythologization as sheer will to power. Language as Saying, as promising to speak for the dead others, attests the fact of signi-fication and regiments what Nietzsche recognized as power's self-accretion.

The discourse of cataclysm and alterity as the pre-originary conditions of justice remains a foray into the unthinkable and appears cordoned off from the problems of actual justice. In order for there to be justice, the other must become an an-iconic indication of all the others as Sartre realized. It is the gap between its pre-originary conditions and "real life" that opens the possibility of injustice, the inequity of power between oppressed and oppressor. Although the resolution of actual discrepancies is beyond the jurisdiction of the historian, she becomes both the narrator of events and litigant for the powerless. As such, she is always already at risk, in danger of abandoning either the historical object or her stand in the discursive space of ethics.

Does the onus of responsibility for the dead other preclude joy in communal life, the self-mortification of an asceticism redescribed as ethics? Would not the joys that remain under this austere regimen not be the pallid pleasures excoriated by Nietzsche? The claim that joy is absent results from seeing joy as contingent upon the exercise of freedom which, in turn, presupposes an independent subject whereas responsibility de-nucleates the I. Yet the response to another need not be a joyless encounter but rather a movement of welcoming and hospitality. What is more, responsibility is not bound up with measure in the classical sense but is intemperate, often violating rule-bound behavior.

How is time to be understood in the community where intemperate generosity prevails? On the one hand, such a community is the object of hope; on the other, there is, *per impossibile,* a desire for immediacy, for hope's presence here and now. To be what it is, hope must create the future in the mode of the now. It is the nature of hope to be a desire for presence, a presence that must be deferred. Yet hope cannot be conceived as totally vain for hope then becomes despair, nor is hope calculative, a banking on what is likely or probable. To be hope, both its fulfillment and its frustration must be possible. If fulfilled, the future takes on the urgency of presence, a spur to activity, so that hope becomes other than itself in that it must enter into relations of power and risk violence. The heterological historian herself may set this violence into motion.

In speaking for the dead others, the historian enters into a temporal zone that is neither past, present, nor future. The tense in which her promise is inscribed is that of the future-present, an impossible new time in which the future as promise cannot lose its sense of presence. A historical artifact is also a gift of the past to a present affected with futurity. What is inscribed in the gift is not only the *vouloir dire* of a people that has been silenced, of the dead others, but is, in addition, what giving wants to say.

NOTES

PROLOGUE

1. Edward Rothstein, "Technology: On the Web, Tuning in to Timothy Leary's Last Trip, Live from His Deathbed," *New York Times,* April 29, 1996, sec. D.

CHAPTER ONE

1. Hayden White, "The Historical Text as Literary Artifact," in *The Writing of History: Literary Form and Historical Understanding,* ed. Robert H. Canary and Henry Kozicki (Madison: University of Wisconsin Press, 1978), p. 59.

2. Citations from individual works of Aristotle are from the *Basic Works of Aristotle,* trans. Richard McKeon (New York: Random House, 1941).

3. Insofar as these criticisms have been successful, they have undermined a sense of history altogether so that their own oppositional force is diminished. See Fredrick Jameson, *Postmodernism, or the Cultural Logic of Late Capitalism* (Durham, NC: Duke University Press, 1991), p. 268.

4. Tzvetan Todorov, *The Morals of History,* trans. Alyson Waters (Minneapolis: University of Minnesota Press, 1995), p. 54.

5. Hayden White, "The Value of Narrativity in the Representation of Reality," in *The Content of the Form* (Baltimore: Johns Hopkins University Press, 1987), p. 14.

6. Toni Morrison, *Beloved* (New York: Penguin Plume, 1988), p. 116.

7. Fernand Braudel, *On History,* trans. Sarah Matthews (Chicago: University of Chicago Press, 1969), p. 213. It is worth noting that, with the globalization of the arms trade, heretofore isolated killing zones are reconfigured. Serbian trainers have entered the conflict in Zaire. Howard W. French, in "In Zaire's Eccentric War, Serbs Train Refugee Force," *New York Times,* February 12, 1997, sec. A, writes that the Serbians both supply arms and train anti-rebel Zairean forces: "Zairean government forces with little appetite for battle have distributed assault rifles and mortar charges by the planeful to Hutu refugees from neighboring Rwanda. Some of the Hutu are militia members

who organized mass killings of members of their home country's Tutsi minority in 1994 while others are members of the Rwandan army, which was defeated by the Tutsi led forces now in power in Rwanda."

8. This view, described and rejected by Bernard Williams, is cited and the rejection endorsed by Richard Rorty in *Objectivity, Relativism and Truth, Philosophical Papers,* vol. 1 (Cambridge: Cambridge University Press, 1991), p. 8. The resistance to the centrality of epistemology is developed in Rorty's *Philosophy and the Mirror of Nature* (Princeton: Princeton University Press, 1979), p. 134. He reiterates this position in a reply to his critics, in Herman A. Saatkamp, Jr., *Rorty and Pragmatism: The Philosopher Responds to His Critics* (Nashville: Vanderbilt University Press, 1995). See esp. his response to Susan Haack, pp. 148–153.

9. Arthur C. Danto, *Narration and Knowledge,* including the integral text of *Analytical Philosophy of History* (New York: Columbia University Press, 1985), p. xii.

10. Jacques Rancière, *The Names of History: On the Poetics of Knowledge,* trans. Hassan Melehy (Minneapolis: University of Minnesota Press, 1994), p. 97.

11. Emmanuel Levinas, "Language and Proximity," in *Selected Philosophical Papers,* trans. Alphonso Lingis (The Hague: Martinus Nijhoff, 1987), p. 109.

12. Cited and commented upon in Richard Rorty, *Philosophy and the Mirror of Nature,* p. 158. The holistic, antifoundationalist, and pragmatist treatment of Davidson is challenged by Frank B. Farrell, in *Rorty and Pragmatism,* pp. 154–188.

13. Cited in Jean-François Lyotard, *The Differend: Phrases in Dispute,* trans. Georges Van Den Abeele (Minneapolis: University of Minnesota Press, 1988), p. 39.

14. Ibid., p. 40. Cf. Gilles Deleuze and Felix Guattari, *What Is Philosophy?* trans. Hugh Tomlinson and Graham Burchell (New York: Columbia University Press, 1991), p. 64. They write: "Conceptual personae are the philosopher's heteronyms and the philosopher's name is the simple pseudonym of his personae."

15. Jacques Derrida, *Speech and Phenomena and Other Essays on Husserl's Theory of Signs,* trans. David Allison (Evanston: Northwestern University Press, 1973), p. 130. As inscribed in contemporary thought, differance, "neither word nor concept" is manifested as "the difference of forces in Nietzsche, Saussure's principle of semiological difference, difference as the possibility of [neurone] facilitation, impression and delayed effect in Freud, . . . the irreducibility of the trace of the other in Levinas, and the ontic-ontological difference in Heidegger."

16. Ibid., p. 64; cf. p. 152.

17. Ibid., p. 7.

18. Emmanuel Levinas, "Language and Proximity," in *Collected Philosophical Papers,* p. 116.

19. See Gilles Deleuze and Felix Guattari, *What Is Philosophy?* pp. 66–67.

20. See Emmanuel Levinas, "Phenomenon and Enigma," in *Collected Philosophical Papers,* p. 66.

21. "Language and Proximity," in ibid., p. 116.

22. Jean François Lyotard, *The Differend,* p. 115.

23. Emmanuel Levinas, "Language and Proximity," in *Collected Philosophical Papers,* p. 119.

24. Jean François Lyotard, *The Differend,* p. 33

25. Ibid., p. 50.

26. Benveniste is cited in Giorgio Agamben, *Language and Death: The Place of Negativ-*

ity, trans. Michael Hardt (Minneapolis: University of Minnesota Press, 1991), p. 23. See Agamben's summary of the history of ostension, pp. 19–26.

27. Jacques Derrida, *The Ear of the Other: Otobiography, Transference, Translation*, trans. Peggy Kanuf (Lincoln: University of Nebraska Press, 1985), p. 7.

28. Ibid., p. 5.

29. Ibid., p. 52.

30. Gilles Deleuze and Felix Guattari, *What Is Philosophy?* p. 54.

31. See Jean François Lyotard, *The Differend*, p. 35.

32. The expression is that of Roland Barthes. It is consistent with Emmanuel Levinas's development of faciality as a pervasive theme in his work.

33. Homi Bhabha, in *The Location of Culture* (London: Routledge, 1994), p. 25, sees the language of critique as opening up "a space of translation: a place of hybridity" for the creation of a new political object that is "neither the one nor the other." Yet what such an object would be remains unclear.

34. Jacques Derrida, *The Ear of the Other*, p. 89.

35. Anaximander, frag. 1, in Philip Wheelright, *The Pre-Socratics* (New York: Odyssey Press, 1966), p. 34. Although he does not mention Anaximander, Aristotle's remark that it is "impossible to exceed every assigned magnitude" may refer to the *apeiron*. See his *Physics* 207b.

36. The thorny question of how successfully ordinary language can explain natural phenomena without recourse to mathematical language is not the issue here but rather the similarity of the tropes that are invoked when ordinary language is used.

37. Stephen Hawking, *A Brief History of Time: From the Big Bang to Black Holes* (New York: Bantam Books, 1988), p. 152. For Hawking's account of the expansion and contraction of the universe in relation to time, see pp. 123–153.

38. Jacques Derrida, *On the Name*, trans. David Wood (Stanford: Stanford University Press, 1995), p. 95.

39. Emmanuel Levinas, *Existence and Existents*, trans. Alphonso Lingis (The Hague: Martinus Nijhoff, 1978) p. 57. Cf. *Totality and Infinity*, trans. Alphonso Lingis (Pittsburgh: Duquesne University Press, 1969), p. 141.

40. Giorgio Agamben, *Language and Death*, p. 25.

41. Jacques Derrida, *On the Name*, p. xiv.

42. Ibid., p. xvi.

43. Jacques Rancière, *The Names of History*, p. 63.

44. Arthur C. Danto, *Narration and Knowledge*, p. 341.

45. Roland Barthes, "The Discourse of History," in *Comparative Criticism: A Yearbook*, ed. E. S. Shaffer (Cambridge: Cambridge University Press, 1981), pp. 16–18.

46. Ibid., pp. 17–18.

47. Hayden White, *The Content of the Form*, p. 4.

48. Ibid., p. 5. For an excellent overview of varying responses by postmodern theory to the meaning and function of historical narrative, see Rudiger Kunow, "The Return of Historical Narrative," in *Ethics and Aesthetics: The Moral Turn of Postmodernism*, ed. Gerhard Hoffmann and Alfred Hornung (Heidelberg: Universitätsverlag C. Winter, 1996), pp. 265–274.

49. Ibid., p. 25.

50. Richard Rorty, *Philosophy and the Mirror of Nature*, p. 178.

51. Ibid., pp. 182–184.

52. Hayden White, *The Content of the Form,* p. 20.

53. Ibid., p. 77.

54. Michelet's work will be discussed in Chapter 3.

55. Jacques Rancière, *The Names of History,* p. 8.

56. Ibid., p. 28.

57. Hayden White, *Metahistory: The Historical Imagination in Nineteenth Century Europe* (Baltimore: Johns Hopkins University Press, 1973), p. 27.

58. Jacques Rancière, *The Names of History,* p. 29.

59. Jean-François Lyotard, *The Differend,* p. 9.

60. Jacques Rancière, *The Names of History,* p. 98.

61. Hayden White, *Metahistory,* p. 12.

62. Blaise Pascal, *Pensées,* trans. William Finlayson Trotter (London: J. M. Dent and Sons, 1940). Translation is from the edition of the text prepared by Leon Brunschvig.

63. Martin Heidegger, *What Is a Thing?* trans. W. B. Barton Jr. and Vera Deutsch (South Bend, IN: Regnery Gateway, 1967), p. 43.

64. Jacques Rancière, *The Names of History,* p. 82.

65. Fernand Braudel, *On History,* pp. 66–67. It is possible to interpret the long event as the synchronic element in history in accordance with structuralist princples.

66. Gilles Deleuze and Felix Guattari, *What Is Philosophy?* p. 118.

67. Fernand Braudel, *On History,* p. 39.

68. Hayden White in *The Content of the Form,* p. 78.

69. George Steiner, *A Reader* (New York: Oxford University Press, 1984), p. 398.

70. Augustin Duran's account of Moctezuma is cited in Tzvetan Todorov, *The Morals of History,* p. 25. What is taken for granted here is the accuracy of Duran's report of Moctezuma's words, a chain of transmission that itself invites closer inspection.

71. Ibid., p. 41.

72. Jean-Jacques Rousseau, *Reveries of a Solitary Walker,* trans. Peter France (London: Penguin Books, 1979), pp. 64–65. Hereafter cited in text as *RSW.*

73. *The Twilight of the Idols,* in *The Portable Nietzsche,* trans. Walter Kaufmann (New York: Viking Press, 1982), p. 485.

74. Ibid., p. 484.

75. Ibid., p. 486.

76. *The Antichrist,* in *The Portable Nietzsche,* p. 640.

77. Arthur C. Danto, *Narration and Knowledge,* p. 361.

78. "On Truth and the Lie," in *The Portable Nietzsche,* pp. 46–47.

79. Ibid., pp. 46–47. Derrida makes this passage a focus for his "White Mythology: Metaphor in the Text of Philosophy," in *Margins of Philosophy,* trans. Alan Bass (Chicago: University of Chicago Press, 1982), pp. 207–229.

80. Jean François Lyotard, *The Differend,* pp. 151–152.

81. Jacques Rancière, *The Names of History,* pp. 58–59.

82. Jorge Luis Borges, "The God's Script," trans. L. A. Murillo, in *Labyrinths,* ed. Donald A. Yates and James E. Irby (New York: New Directions, 1964), p. 171.

83. Jorge Luis Borges, "Pierre Menard: Author of the Quixote," trans. James E. Irby, ibid., p. 40. Yosef Hayim Yerushalmi, in his study of Jewish memory in its relation to history, *Zakhor: Jewish History and Memory* (Seattle: University of Washington Press, 1982), cites another Borges story, "Funes the Memorious," a tale that points to the danger of infinite recall. Because Funes can forget nothing, a present event triggers an infi-

nite series of past events. Yerushalmi concludes: "[The tale] looms as a possibly demonic parable for a potential denouement to modern historiography as a whole" (p. 102).

84. Michel Foucault, *The Order of Things: The Archeology of the Human Sciences,* (New York: Vintage Books, 1973), pp. xvi–xvii.

85. Ibid., p. xxiii.

86. Michel Foucault, *The Archeology of Knowledge,* trans. A. M. Sheridan Smith (London: Tavistock, 1972), p. 91.

87. Michel Foucault, *The Order of Things,* p. 353.

88. Hayden White "Foucault Decoded: Notes from the Underground," in *Tropics of Discourse* (Baltimore: Johns Hopkins Press, 1978), p. 235. White misses the anti-Hegelianism of Foucault.

89. Cf. Richard Rorty, *Philosophy and the Mirror of Nature,* p. 391n.

90. Michel Foucault, *The Archeology of Knowledge,* p. 38.

91. The role of the historian as internal and external to the historical narrative is brought out by Arthur C. Danto in the context of defending historical reality against historical relativism. He writes, "To hold a historical belief is to hold that there is (was) some bit of history-as-reality it describes, external to the belief in question. And this is so even though the beliefs themselves . . . compose a portion of historical reality. Historical beliefs are thus internal and external to historical reality." See his *Narration and Knowledge,* p. 330.

92. Fernand Braudel, *On History,* p. 31.

93. Friedrich Nietzsche, *The Will to Power,* trans. Walter Kaufmann (New York: Vintage Books, 1968). Cited in the text as *WP.*

94. Jacques Rancière, *The Names of History,* p. 8. There is no reference here to Foucault.

95. Friedrich Nietzsche, *On the Uses and Disadvantages of History for Life,* in *Untimely Meditations,* trans. R. J. Hollingdale (Cambridge: Cambridge University Press, 1983), p. 93.

CHAPTER TWO

1. H. G. Wells, *The Time Machine* (New York: Berkeley Books, 1979), p. 24.

2. For an analysis of the role of immanent critique in contemporary French thought, see Vincent Descombes, *Objects of All Sorts, a Philosophical Grammar,* trans. Lorna Scott-Fox and Jeremy Harding (Baltimore: Johns Hopkins Press, 1986).

3. Kant's well-known arguments against the ontological and cosmological proofs for God's existence demonstrate the inherent conflict between Kantian and scholastic rationality. Kant's refutation of the former rests on his rejection of the argument's supposition that existence is a real predicate; of the latter, that it hangs on a notion of cause that is applicable to the phenomenal world but is applied transcendentally. In the *Critique of Pure Reason,* trans. Norman Kemp Smith (London: Macmillan and Co., 1958), Kant discusses the ontological proof in A592, B620–A602, B630 (pp. 500–507); the cosmological proof in A603, B631–A614, B642 (pp. 507–514).

4. Immanuel Kant, *On History,* trans. Lewis White Beck (New York: Liberal Arts Press, 1963), pp. 41–42. Cited in the text as *OH.*

5. For a persuasive interpretation of Heidegger's view of the way in which quality is transformed into quantity and sheer magnitude rules contemporary existence, see Michel

Haar, *Heidegger and the Essence of Man,* trans. William McNeill (Albany: State University of New York Press, 1993), pp. 165–176. He writes: "At a certain point of objectification, the meaning of what has been objectified undergoes a qualitative change: what has been calculated and manipulated becomes the 'incalculable,' the 'immense,' something beyond our grasp and without measure" (p. 166).

6. Emmanuel Levinas, "Narcissism or the Primacy of the Same," in *Collected Philosophical Papers,* p. 51.

7. Jean-François Lyotard, *The Differend,* p. 64.

8. Immanuel Kant, *Foundations of the Metaphysics of Morals* (Indianapolis: Liberal Arts Press, 1959), p. 39.

9. The notion of obligatoriness in the absence of foundation is given an excellent interpretation in John D. Caputo, *Against Ethics* (Bloomington: Indiana University Press, 1993). Strikingly expounded in Kierkegaardian fashion, Caputo writes: "[O]bligation happens, the obligation of me to you and of both of us to others. It is all around us, on every side, constantly tugging at our sleeves, calling upon us for a response" (p. 6).

10. Emmanuel Levinas, "Meaning and Sense," in *Collected Philosophical Papers,* p. 97.

11. See Jacques Rancière, *The Names of History,* p. 97, for development of this theme.

12. Alan Cowell, "Memories of Wartime Brutalities Revive Czech-German Animosity," *New York Times,* February 9, 1996, sec. A. It was also pointed out that the Christian Democrats risked losing Sudetan German support in the Bavarian elections if they backed down on the demand for Czech restitution.

13. Immanuel Kant, *Critique of Judgment,* trans. J. H. Bernard (New York: Hafner Press, 1951). Cited in the text as *CJ.*

14. Gilles Deleuze and Felix Guattarti, *What is Philosophy?* p. 95.

15. Ibid., p. 94.

16. Ibid., p. 110.

17. Ibid., p. 111.

18. It should be noted that Kant includes women as historical subjects (*OH,* p. 58).

19. G. W. F. Hegel, in *Philosophy of Right,* trans. T. M. Knox (London: Oxford University Press, 1967), 167, p. 106, writes that the laws are not alien to the subject but reflect the Spirit's own essence.

20. Friedrich von Schiller, "On the Sublime," in *Naive and Sentimental Poetry and On the Sublime: Two Essays,* trans. Julius A. Elias (New York: Frederick Ungar, 1966), p. 207.

21. Mark C. Taylor has persuasively demonstrated this point in his *Disfiguring: Art, Architecture, Religion* (Chicago: University of Chicago Press, 1992), esp. chap. 3, pp. 50–95.

22. Original reads "Helmut Kohl (CDU) und Fraktionschef Wolfgang Schauble lehnen die Verhüllung ab. Schauble warnt, mit den Reichstag durfe nicht experimentiert werden" in "Christos and Jean Claude," *Berliner Zeitung,* supplement, distributed on site, July, 18, 1995.

23. *New York Times,* October 29, 1995, sec. A.

24. Hayden White, "The Politics of Historical Interpretation: Discipline and De-Sublimation," in *The Content of the Form,* pp. 74–75.

25. Ibid., p. 75.

26. Ibid., p. 74.

27. The problem of whether a philosophy can stand or fall because of the politics of the philosopher who promulgates it is nowhere exemplified more strikingly than in the

celebrated Heidegger affair and the vast literature it has generated. Philippe Lacoue-Labarthe, in *Heidegger, Art, and Politics,* trans. Chris Turner (Basil Blackwell: Oxford, 1990), frames the question thus: "From where might one 'criticize' Heidegger? From what 'point of view'? This much, however, is true: recognition of the importance of his thought—or indeed unreserved admiration for it—in no way excludes infinite mistrust" (p. 14).

28. Emmanuel Levinas, *Existence and Existents,* trans. by Alphonso Lingis (The Hague: Martinus Nijhoff, 1978), p. 57.

29. See a succinct formulation of this relation in Adriaan Peperzak, *To the Other: An Introduction to the Philosophy of Emmanuel Levinas* (West Lafayette, IN: Purdue University Press, 1981), p. 230.

30. Emmanuel Levinas, *Otherwise than Being or Beyond Essence,* trans. Alphonso Lingis (The Hague: Martinus Nijhoff, 1981), p. 164.

CHAPTER THREE

1. Jacques Derrida, *Of Grammatology,* trans. Gayatri Chakravorty Spivak (Baltimore: John Hopkins University Press, 1974), p. 6.

2. Ibid., p. 9. The term "artifical intelligence" (AI) would likely supplant "cybernetics" used by Derrida in this 1967 work.

3. Nowhere has the question of the relation of representation to figuration been more insightfully argued than in Mark C. Taylor, *Disfiguring: Art, Architecture, Religion.* See esp. chap. 6, pp. 185–228.

4. Guy Debord, *The Society of the Spectacle,* trans. Donald Nicholson-Smith (New York: Zone Books, 1994), esp. pp. 11–24.

5. Jean Baudrillard, *Simulations,* trans. Paul Foss, Paul Patton, and Philip Beitchman (Semiotexte, Columbia University, 1983), p. 142. Hereafter cited in the text as *Sim.*

6. These words appear to be an afterthought and do not appear in the original edition but in the 1992 Introduction (Editions Gallimard). They are cited in the English translation used here, p. 10.

7. This essay was first delivered as a lecture on June 9, 1938, at the University of Freiburg im Breisgau, and later published in *Holzwege* (Frankfurt: Vittorio Klosterman, 1952). It appears in *The Question concerning Technology and Other Essays* (New York: Harper and Row, 1977), pp. 115–154.

8. Guy Debord, *Society of the Spectacle,* p. 130.

9. Ibid., p. 123; cf. p. 93 for a more critical view of cyclical time. Cf. the notion of cyclical time with that of "repeating as handing down explicity," in Martin Heidegger, *Being and Time,* trans. John Macquarrie and Edward Robinson (New York: Harper and Row, 1962), p. 437 (H385). Numbered references cited in my text hereafter are found in the margins of the English translation and refer to *Sein und Zeit* (Tübingen: Niemeyer, 1943).

10. Gilles Deleuze, *Difference and Repetition,* trans. Paul Patton (New York: Columbia University Press, 1994), p. 127.

11. Gilles Deleuze and Felix Guattari, *What Is Philosophy?* p. 8.

12. Walter Benjamin, "The Work of Art in the Mechanical Age of Reproduction," in *Illuminations: Essays and Reflections,* trans. Harry Zohn (New York: Harcourt, Brace, Jovanovich, 1968), p. 221. Hereafter cited in the text as *Il.*

13. Martin Heidegger, in the title essay, in *The Question concerning Technology and Other Essays,* p. 14. See also Jacques Lacan, *Speech, Language and Psychoanalysis,* trans. Anthony Wilden (Baltimore: Johns Hopkins University Press, 1968), pp. 296ff for remarks on the lost object.

14. Susan Sontag, *On Photography* (New York: Farrar, Strauss and Giroux, 1973), pp. 175–176.

15. Roland Barthes, *Camera Lucida: Reflections on Photography,* trans. Richard Howard (New York: Hill and Wang, 1981), p. 87. Hereafter cited in the text as *CL.*

16. See Epicurus's "Letter to Herodotus," In *The Stoic and Epicurean Philosophers,* trans. Cyril Bailey (New York: Modern Library, 1957), p. 5.

17. For an account of Lacan's view of the partial object as anterior to the relation with a person and as that with which he wishes to unite, see Anthony Wilden, "Lacan and the Discourse of the Other," in Jacques Lacan, *Speech and Language in Psychoanalysis,* pp. 162–163.

18. Susan Sontag, *On Photography,* p. 23.

19. Photograph accompanies news article by Nicholas D. Kristof, *New York Times,* July 30, 1995, sec. 2.

20. Douglas Hubbard, in *The Guide to the Museum of the Pacific War* (Fredricksburg, TX: Awani Press, 1989). P. 28n.48 notes that the Japanese foreman, landscapers, carpenters, and interpreter arrived in San Antonio from Tokyo, having left Japan for the first time. They brought their own equipment and uniforms and a month's food supply asking only for more hot water for bathing. Uniforms were soon replaced by jeans and straw cowboy hats. With local crews, the workplace became a multilingual site.

21. Media coverage has been given to comparable issues bound up with the Smithsonian's installation of the Enola Gay at the National Science Museum and the proposed Library of Congress exhibition on Freud. Thus Paul Goldberger, in "Historical Shows on Trial: Who Judges?" *New York Times,* February 11, 1996, sec. 2, writes:

> A spate of cancellations and quickly retailored exhibitions—on subjects as diverse as slave life on Southern plantations, the history of lynching, the dropping of the atomic bomb on Hiroshima and the theories of Freud—has raised tough questions about how . . . cultural institutions now go about their business. (P. 1)

22. See news article: Steven Kinzer, "They're Coming Again! Russians Relish Germany," *New York Times,* November 30, 1995, sec. A.

23. Steve Lowe, "Huge Photo Archive Bought by Software Billionaire Gates," *New York Times,* October 11, 1995, sec. 1.

24. David MacDougall, "Films of Memory," in *Visualizing Theory: Selected Essays from V.A.R. 1990–1994,* ed. Lucien Taylor (New York: Routledge, 1994), p. 261.

25. Letter to Jean Beaufret, November 23, 1945, cited in Giorgio Agamben, *Language and Death: The Place of Negativity,* p. 4 in his analysis of Dasein and negativity.

26. Giorgio Agamben, *The Coming Community,* trans. Michael Hardt (Minneapolis: University of Minnesota Press, 1993), pp. 90–91.

27. Bill Rodriguez, "Reality Bytes: Animating Human Beings," *New York Times,* December 3, 1995, sec. 2.

28. Jean-Paul Sartre, *Being and Nothingness: An Essay on Phenomenological Ontology,* trans. Hazel E. Barnes (New York: Philosophical Library, 1956), p. 255.

29. Michel Foucault, *Discipline and Punish: The Birth of the Prison*, trans. Alan Sheridan (New York: Vintage Books, 1979), p. 173.

30. Ibid., p. 171.

31. In the director's cut (unlike the released version), the replicant status of Deckerd is unambiguous. There is an interesting account of the use of this film as an analogue for the co-optation of consciousness in Slavoj Zizek, *Tarrying with the Negative*, trans. Jon Barnes (Durham: Duke University Press, 1993), pp. 10–12.

32. Andrzej Wajda, *Double Vision: My Life in Film*, trans. into English from French translation of Polish (translators are not named), (New York: Henry Holt and Co., 1989), pp. 79–80. Reprinted as *On Film: A Master's Notes* (Los Angeles: Acrobat Books, 1991). Hereafter cited in the text as *DV*. (Citations are from 1989 edition.)

33. For a nontechnical account of miniaturization as the way to speed computation, see Bill Gates with Nathan Myhrvold and Peter Rinearson, *The Road Ahead* (New York: Viking Press, 1995); "In order to take advantages at the molecular level, computers will have to be very small, even microscopic. We already understand the science that would allow us to build these superfast computers. What we need is an engineering break-through" (p. 33).

34. Edmund Husserl, *Phenomenology of Internal Time Consciousness*, trans. James S. Churchill (Indianapolis: Indiana University Press, 1964), p. 80.

35. Jacques Derrida, *Speech and Phenomena*, p. 64 cites Husserl, *Phenomenology of Internal Time Consciousness*, para. 17, p. 64.

36. See my "The Art in Ethics: Aesthetics, Objectivity, and Alterity in the Philosophy of Emmanuel Levinas," in *Ethics as First Philosophy: The Significance of Emmanuel Levinas for Philosophy, Literature and Religion*, ed. Adriaan T. Peperzak (New York: Routledge, 1995), pp. 137–150.

37. Herbert Muschamp, "Monuments in Peril: A Top 100 Countdown," *New York Times*, March 31, 1996, sec. 2.

38. "A Conversation between Eric Foner and John Sayles," in *Past Imperfect: History according to the Movies*, ed. Mark C. Carnes (New York: Henry Holt and Co., 1995), p. 28.

39. George E. Marcus, "The Modernist Sensibility in Recent Ethnographic Writing and the Cinematic Metaphor of Montage," in George E. Marcus in Lucien Taylor, *Visualizing Theory*, p. 43.

40. Homi Bhabha/Victor Burgin, "Visualizing Theory: 'In Dialogue,'" in *Visualizing Theory*, p. 454.

41. Homi Bhabha, *The Location of Culture* (London: Routledge, 1994), p. 36.

42. Ibid., pp. 36–38.

43. Guests at this meeting included Gudrun Burwitz, the daughter of Heinrich Himmler, chief of the SS and the Gestapo. Stephen Kinzer, *New York Times*, December 18, 1995, sec. 1.

44. Levinas departs from Husserl's segregation of perception from sign and image whose belonging together in Husserl is noted by Derrida in "Signs and the Blink of an Eye," in *Speech and Phenomena*, p. 60n.1.

45. Emmanuel Levinas, "Reality and Its Shadow," *Collected Philosophical Papers*, p. 6.

46. Ibid.

47. Ibid.

48. Emmanuel Levinas, "The Ego and the Totality," in *Collected Philosophical Papers*, p. 41.

49. Levinas would be likely to resist this interpretation of the image both because of his stress on language and his fear of the idolatrous potential of the image.

50. Phillip Gourevitch, "Letter from Rwanda: After the Genocide," *New Yorker*, December 18, 1995, pp. 76–95. Most of the estimated 700,000 who died were Tutsi but, in a retaliatory strike, 4000 Hutu were killed in the village of Kibeho in southern Rwanda in April 1995. An exception to technologically advanced delivery of death, the killings were largely low-tech murders by machete.

51. David MacDougall, in Lucien Taylor, *Visualizing Theory*, pp. 263–264.

52. Ibid., p. 264. While MacDougall's account applies to significant segments of Lanzmann's 9-1/2-hour film, James E. Young in *Writing and Rewriting the Holocaust: Narrative and the Consequences of Interpretation* (Bloomington: Indiana University Press, 1988) pinpoints Lanzman's relentless questioning of a survivor, Abraham Bomba, a Tel Aviv barber who also cut hair in Treblinka, virtually compelling the reluctant witness to exhibit his painful memories.

53. George E. Marcus, "The Modernist Sensibility in Ethnographic Writing," in *Visualizing Theory*, pp. 48–52.

54. Phillip Gourevitch, "Letter from Rwanda," in the *New Yorker*, December 15, 1995, p. 84.

55. Jean Baudrillard, *The Illusion of the End*, trans. Chris Turner (Stanford: Stanford University Press, 1994), p. 22. Hereafter cited in the text as *IE*.

56. Friedrich Nietzsche, "On the Uses and Disadvantages of History for Life," in *Untimely Meditations*, pp. 120–123.

57. Having been present at a post-performance discussion of the play, I observed little interest in this matter. Müller's position is echoed in the claim that German children identify Hitler with Chaplin. "It is hard to believe that Hitler will recover from the ridiculousness that Chaplin revealed," writes Peter Schneider, "The Sins of the Grandfathers," *New York Times Magazine*, December 3, 1995, p. 74.

58. These comments are not meant to undermine the power of either the text, direction, or the performance of the actual play as critique but rather as an interrogation of the overlapping of political and formal elements in artistic works. For a recent English language press appreciation of Heiner Müller, see Stephen Kinzer, "Germany Can't Forget a Legendary Director," *New York Times*, Sunday, March 31, 1996, sec. 2.

59. His comment is cited by Walter Benjamin (*Il*, p. 227).

60. Roland Barthes, *Michelet*, trans. Richard Howard (Berkeley: University of California Press, 1987), p. 77.

61. Simon Schama, *Citizens: A Chronicle of the French Revolution* (New York: Knopf, 1989), p. 5. His own impassioned style brings to life the fervor of Michelet, a passion anticipated in Walter Benjamin's comment in "Theses on the Philosophy of History" (*Il*, p. 261) about the Revolution's explosive power. "Thus to Robespierre ancient Rome was a past charged with the time of the now which he blasted out of the continuum of history," a now that inaugurated a new calendar that served as a "historical time-lapse camera."

62. Cited in Hayden White, *Metahistory*, p. 154.

63. *The New Science of Giambattista Vico*, trans. Thomas Goddar Bergin and Max Harold Fisch (Ithaca: Cornell University Press, 1986), p. 819.

64. Cited in Roland Barthes, *Michelet*, p. 99.

65. *Journal de Michelet*, vol. 1, 1842, p. 382. Cf. vol 2, January 1851, p. 147, where Michelet acknowledges he is no artist but that the vitality of his thought is attributable to the fact that it is his: "my life, my study, my word: three things that are only one" (translation mine).

66. Ibid., vol. 1, p. 384.

67. Ibid.

68. Roland Barthes, *Michelet*, pp. 67–68.

69. Ibid., p. 102.

70. Ibid.

71. In this context Kant (surprisingly) would side with Rorty's endorsement of world disclosure against Habermas's valuing of problem solving within social practices. See Richard Rorty, *Contingency, Irony and Solidarity* (New York: Cambridge University Press, 1989), pp. 61–69.

72. See Simon Schama, *Citizens*, pp. 746–750.

73. Roland Barthes, *Michelet*, p. 76.

74. Ibid., p. 115.

75. Jules Michelet, *Histoire de la Révolution française*, vol. 2 (Paris: Editions Robert Laffont, 1979), p. 745.

76. Cited from Simon Schama, *Citizens*, p. 82.

77. For an account of the film's reception in France, see Robert Darnton, "Danton," in *Past Imperfect*, ed. Mark C. Carnes, p. 104. Darnton presupposes that narrative history is likely to be more truthful than film (p. 108).

78. Richard Reeves in "Nixon Revisited by Way of the Creative Camera," *New York Times*, December 17, 1995, sec. 2.

79. Kip S. Thorne, *Black Holes and Time Warps: Einstein's Outrageous Legacy* (New York: W. W. Norton, 1994), p. 557.

80. Nicholas Negroponte, *Being Digital* (New York: Alfred A. Knopf, New York, 1995), p. 14. This account and that of Bill Gates in *The Road Ahead* are those of enthusiasts. Digitization's advantage is that it achieves high levels of data compression thereby increasing the amount of data that can be transmitted. With the increased bandwidth or "number of bits that can be moved through a given circuit in a second" of fiber optic (glass or plastic) cable, the transmission of information is expected to expand even further (Gates, pp. 30–31).

81. Bill Gates, *The Road Ahead*, pp. 30–31.

82. Ibid., pp. 131–132.

83. Paul Virilio, "The Last Vehicle," in *Looking Back on the End of the World*, ed. Dietmar Kamper and Dieter Lenzen (New York: Semiotext[e], 1989), p. 112.

84. Nicholas Negroponte, *Being Digital*, p. 14.

85. James Sterngold, "Digital Studios: It's the Economy Stupid," *New York Times*, December 25, 1995, sec. D.

86. Cited in Bill Gates, *The Road Ahead*, p. 30.

CHAPTER FOUR

1. Karl Löwith, *Martin Heidegger's European Nihilism*, ed. Richard Wolin (New York: Columbia University Press, 1995), p. 198.

2. The term "One-All" is used by Gilles Deleuze and Felix Guattari in *What Is Philosophy?* p. 35, to designate "an *Omnitudo* that includes all concepts on one and the same plane."

3. Martin Heidegger, *Hegel's Phenomenology of Spirit,* trans. Parvis Emad and Kenneth Maly (Bloomington: Indiana University Press, 1988), p. 7. Hereafter cited in the text as *HPoS*.

4. From a letter, December 22, 1822, to Edouard-Casimir Duboc, a French hat manufacturer turned philosopher who became enamored with Hegel's thought, in *Hegel: The Letters,* trans. Clark Butler and Christiane Seiler, commentary by Clark Butler (Bloomington: Indiana University Press, 1984), p. 494.

5. G. W. F. Hegel, *Lectures on the Philosophy of World History,* with *Introduction: Reason in History,* trans. H. B. Nesbitt (Cambridge: Cambridge University Press, 1975), pp. 25–26. Hereafter cited in the text as *RH*.

6. Fernand Braudel, *Capitalism and Material Life, 1400–1800,* trans. Miriam Kochan (New York: Harper and Row, 1973), pp. 18–20, 32–37, passim.

7. For an account of the construction and uses of this archetype, see Marianna Torgovnik, *Gone Primitive: Savage Intellects, Modern Lives* (Chicago: University of Chicago Press, 1990). For the way in which the image of the primitive has affected analyses of human existence in mid-twentieth-century philosophy, see my "Fear of Primitives, Primitive Fears: Anthropology in Heidegger and Levinas," in *Emotion and Postmodernism,* ed. G. Hoffman and A. Hornung (Heidelberg: Universitätsverlag C. Winter, 1997).

8. Martin Heidegger, *Hegel's Concept of Experience,* trans. Kenley Royce Dove (New York: Harper and Row, 1970), p. 38. Hereafter cited in the text as *HCE*.

9. Heidegger explicitly denies the relation between Husserlian and Hegelian phenomenology: "[Hegel's] *Phenomenology* has nothing whatever to do with a phenomenology of consciousness as currently understood in Husserl's sense—either in its theme or in the manner of its treatment, or above all in terms of its basic questioning and intention." He goes on to assert the truth of this claim even if their foundational objectives, the grounding of the sciences and human culture with reference to consciousness, are the same, thereby conceding a significant affinity (*HPoS*, p. 28).

10. Edmund Husserl, *The Idea of Phenomenology,* trans. William P. Alston and George Nakhnikian (The Hague: Martinus Nijhoff, 1964), p. 59.

11. These lectures were delivered from 1933 to 1939 at the École des Hautes Études. Translator's note in Alexander Kojève, *Introduction to the Reading of Hegel,* trans. James H. Nichols Jr. (New York: Basic Books, 1969), p. xiii.

12. Ibid., p. 173.

13. G. W. F. Hegel, *Phenomenology of Spirit,,* trans. A. V. Miller (Oxford: Oxford Press, 1977), 797, p. 485. Hereafter cited in the text as *Phen*.

14. Jacques Derrida, *Glas,* trans. John P. Leavey Jr. and Richard Rand, *Glas* (Lincoln: University of Nebraska Press, 1986), p. 92; cf. pp. 218–219.

15. Jean-Luc Marion, *God without Being: Hors-texte,* trans. Thomas A. Carlson (Chicago: University of Chicago Press, 1991), pp. 126–130.

16. See Emmanuel Levinas, "Façon de parler," in *Dieu qui vient à l'idée* (Paris: Vrin, 1982), pp. 266–270; for an analysis of Levinas's view of skepticism in comparison with contemporary analytic treatments, see Jan de Greef "Skepticism and Reason," in *Face to Face with Levinas,* ed. Richard A. Cohen (Albany: State Uinversity of New York Press, 1986), pp. 159–180.

17. Jean Baudrillard, "Fatal Strategies," in *Selected Writings,* trans. Mark Poster (Stanford: Stanford University Press, 1988), p. 197. Hereafter cited in the text as *FS.*

18. Arthur Cohen, *The Tremendum: A Theological Interpretation of the Holocaust* (New York: Crossroad Publishing Company, 1981), pp. 108–109.

19. This is a central theme of Lawrence L. Langer, in *Holocaust Testimonies: The Ruins of Memory* (New Haven: Yale University Press, 1991), p. 58, passim.

20. This view is a version of an earlier account of sacrifice in George Bataille's *Theory of Religion,* trans. Robert Hurley (New York: Zone Books, 1989). Bataille writes:

> [T]he destruction that sacrifice is intended to bring about is not annihilation. The thing—only the thing—is what sacrifice means to destroy in the victim. Sacrifice destroys the object's real ties of subordination; it draws the victim out of the world of utility and restores it to that of unintelligible caprice. (P. 43)

For a discussion of a comparable view of sacrifice that echoes that of Bataille, see my "Tainted Greatness: Depravity and Sacrifice in Genet," in *Tainted Greatness,* ed. Nancy Harrowitz (Philadelphia: Temple University Press, 1994), pp. 253–276.

21. Lawrence L. Langer, *Holocaust Testimonies,* p. 158.

22. Ibid., p. 178.

23. Jean Baudrillard, *The Ecstasy of Communication,* trans. Bernard and Caroline Schutz (New York: Semiotexte, Autonomedia, 1988), p. 93. Baudrillard's bypassing of the subject distances the interpretation of the object from a Lacanian psychoanalytic context still retained in Deleuze's independently authored work. He writes: "The child constructs for itself another object, a quite different kind of object which is a virtual object or centre and which then governs and compensates for the progresses and failures of its real activity." See *Difference and Repetition,* trans. Paul Patton (New York: Columbia University Press, 1994), p. 99.

24. Jean Baudrillard, *The Ecstasy of Communication,* p. 66.

25. Ibid., p. 68.

26. G. W. F. Hegel, *Philosophy of Mind,* pt. 3 of the *Encyclopedia of the Philosophical Sciences* (1830), trans. William Wallace together with the *Zusätze* in Boumann's Text (1845), trans. A. V. Miller (Oxford: Oxford Press, 1971), 577, p. 315. Hereafter cited in the text as PhM.

27. *Hegel's Philosophy of Nature,* trans. Michael Petry (London: Allen and Unwin, 1970). Hereafter cited in the text as *PhN.*

28. Werner Heisenberg, *Physics and Beyond: Encounters and Conversations,* trans. Arnold J. Pomeranz (New York: Harper and Row, 1971), p. 21. The philosophical consequences of this shift are explored in Chap. 5.

29. In Jacques Derrida's nuanced analysis of Spirit in Heidegger, Hegel's view of Spirit is seen to appear as a ghost. In *Of Spirit: Heidegger and the Question,* trans. Geoff Bennington and Rachel Bowlby (Chicago: University of Chicago Press, 1989), p. 37, Derrida writes: "[I]n a sense which would like to think itself not Hegelian, historicity is immediately and essentially determined as spiritual."

30. Hegel approves this remark found in Karl Friedrich Göschel (1784–1861): "Aphorismen uber Nichtwissen und absolutes Wissen im Verhältnisse zur christlichen Glaubenserkenntnis," p. 157 as cited by the editor. See his Introduction, *PhN,* 1:99.

31. G. W. F. Hegel, *Lectures in the Philosophy of Religion,* trans. E. B. Speirs and J. Burdon Sanderson (1895; reprint, New York: Humanities Press, 1974), 3:366.

32. Whether Nietzsche is himself a postmodernist in the various non-chronological senses attributed to the term is a hotly debated issue. For an analysis on both sides of this question, see Clayton Koelb, ed., *Nietzsche as Postmodernist: Essays Pro and Contra* (Albany: State University of New York Press, 1990).

33. Friedrich Nietzsche, *Thus Spake Zarathustra*, in *The Portable Nietzsche*, trans. Walter Kaufmann (New York: Viking Press, 1954), p. 245. Hereafter cited in the text as *Z*.

34. Cf. Chap. 11n.35 citing Aristotle's critique of Anaximander.

35. Becoming means there is no final state for Nietzsche. See WP 708, p. 377.

36. Gilles Deleuze, *Difference and Repetition*, p. 50.

37. The works in which this subject figures are legion. For an interesting, if brief, recent exchange, see Stephen Houlgate, "Hegel and Fichte: Recognition, Otherness and Absolute Knowing," in *The Owl of Minerva* 26, no. 1 (biannual journal of the Hegel Society of America) (Fall 1994): 3–19; and Robert R. Williams, "Discernment in the Realm of Shadows: Absolute Knowing and Otherness," in ibid., vol. 26, no. 2, 133–148. Houlgate argues that Heidegger, Levinas, Derrida, et al. fail to see that the Absolute has relinquished its identity as selfhood and so could not absorb an object, whereas to posit the contrary is to think in Fichtean rather than Hegelian terms. Yet, paradoxically, he concedes that being must cease to be other in order for thought to disclose its otherness. Williams argues that the complexity of absolute knowing needs the other and otherness, that Spirit is not an ego but a community characterized by multiple internal modes of being. Robert B. Pippin, in *Hegel's Idealism* (Cambridge: Cambridge University Press, 1989), pp. 3–15, offers a bird's-eye view of attitudes toward Hegel in continental and American philosophy in the context of his own argument that Hegel's idealism is a continuation of Kant's theory of transcendental apperception.

38. Jacques Derrida, *Speech and Phenomena*, p. 102.

39. A careful analysis of the question of closure can be found in Simon Critchley, *Ethics of Deconstruction* (Cambridge, MA: Blackwell, 1992), pp. 76–88.

40. François Laruelle, *Philosophie et non-philosophie* (Liege: Pierre Mardaga, 1989), p. 218. I have followed the original graphematically.

41. Jacques Derrida, *Positions*, trans. Alan Bass (Chicago: University of Chicago Press, 1981), p. 57.

42. Ibid., p. 104.

43. Ibid., p. 105n.31.

44. Jacques Derrida, *Edmund Husserl's Origin of Geometry: An Introduction*, trans. John P. Leavey Jr. (Stony Brook, NY: Nicholas Hays Lts., 1978), p. 153.

45. For a meticulous reading of Derridean infrastructures, see Rodolphe Gasché, *The Tain of the Mirror* (Cambridge, MA: Harvard University Press, 1986), pp. 142–153.

46. Comment cited in *Hegel: The Letters*, p. 667.

47. G. W. F. Hegel, *The Philosophy of History*, trans. J. Sibree (1899; reprint New York: Dover, 1956), p. 444.

48. Ibid., pp. 443–444.

49. Ibid., p. 450.

50. See Martin Heidegger, "The Question concerning Technology," in *The Question concerning Technology*, pp. 3–35.

51. Ibid., p. 24.

52. Heidegger, "The Turning," in *The Question concerning Technology*, p. 48.

53. For opening the way into a particularly nuanced thinking of the not, see Mark

C. Taylor, *nOts* (Chicago: University of Chicago Press, 1993). His analysis of architect Daniel Libeskind's City Edge project for the city of Berlin captures the relation of Libeskind and many others to that city in an unexcelled way. Taylor writes: "Few cities are more of a border—margin, limen, edge—than Berlin. Berlin is the city that simultaneously holds apart and brings together the differences that define our era: East/West, communism/capitalism, statism/consumerism." Neither modern nor postmodern, Berlin is "not here, not there, and yet not nowhere. To build (in) the placeless place of the gap, it is necessary to construct otherwise by building not" (p. 134).

54. Martin Heidegger, "Letter on Humanism," trans. Frank A. Capuzzi in *Basic Writings* (New York: Harper and Row, 1977), p. 238. Jacques Taminaux in "Finitude and the Absolute: Remarks on Hegel and Heidegger," in *Heidegger the Man and the Thinker,* ed. Thomas Sheehan (Chicago: Precedent Publishing, n.d.), p. 204, shows that Hegel and Heidegger are closer than is immediately apparent. Both Hegel and Heidegger resist anthropological interpretations of the nothing and instead refer the going-beyond that characterizes human existence to Being itself or to the Absolute. This affinity is also developed in William H. Werkmeister, "Hegel and Heidegger," in *New Studies in Hegel's Philosophy,* ed. Warren E. Steinkraus (New York: Holt, Rinehart and Winston Inc., 1971), pp. 142–155.

55. Maurice Blanchot, *Writing of the Disaster,* trans. Ann Smock (Lincoln: University of Nebraska Press, 1986), p. 28. Hereafter cited in the text as *WoD.*

56. The photo in *Ende und Anfang: Photographen in Deutschland um 1945,* ed. Klaus Honnef and Ursula Breymayer (Berlin: Deutsches Historisches Museum, 1995), p. 137, is described as that of a "Jewish youth." He is identified as "the Belgian Jew Sieg Mandaag [who] survived the dying after the liberation of the camp by the British army" (p. 202).

CHAPTER FIVE

1. H. G. Wells, *The Time Machine* (New York: Berkeley Books, 1979), p. 10.

2. Nietzsche's perspectivism has received much critical scrutiny. For a subtle analysis of the point at issue see Babette E. Babich, *Nietzsche's Philosophy of Science: Reflecting Science on the Ground of Art and Life* (Albany: SUNY Press, 1994); and Tracy Strong, *French Nietzsche and the Politics of Transfiguration* (Berkeley: University of California Press, 1988), p. 51. Alexander Nehemas in *Nietzsche: Life as Literature* (Cambridge, MA: Harvard University Press, 1985) rejects the view that perspectivism is self-refuting in that it acknowledges itself as a perspective (pp. 66–67). Maudmarie Clark in *Nietzsche on Truth and Philosophy* (Cambridge: Cambridge University Press, 1990) sees Nietzsche's perspectivism as limited to attacking foundationalism and things-in-themselves and suggests that Nietzsche retains "cognitive interests and standards of rational acceptability" (p. 141).

3. William James, *Some Problems of Philosophy,* in *Collected Works of William James,* ed. Frederick Burkhardt and Friedson Bowers (Cambridge, MA: Harvard University Press, 1979), p. 80.

4. *Pluralistic Universe,* in *Collected Works of William James,* (1977), p. 128.

5. Friedrich Nietzsche, *The Gay Science,* trans. Walter Kaufmann (New York: Vintage Books, 1974), 374, p. 336.

6. H. G. Wells, *The Time Machine* pp. 6–7.

7. Ibid., p. 11.

8. Ibid., p. 77.

9. David Deutsch and Michael Lockwood, "The Quantum Physics of Time Travel," in *Scientific American,* 270:3 (March 1994), p. 68.

10. Ibid.

11. Ibid., p. 74.

12. Friedrich Nietzsche, *Thus Spoke Zarathustra,* trans. R. J. Hollingdale (Harmondsworth: Penguin Books, 1961), 3, 2, p. 179. Hereafter cited in the text as *Z.*

13. Kip S. Thorne, *Black Holes and Time Warps: Einstein's Outrageous Legacy,* pp. 484-485.

14. Ibid., pp. 55-56; cf. pp. 502-503.

15. Ibid., p. 521. It is worth noting that although Stephen Hawking has not yielded to Kip Thorne on the matter of wormholes he has conceded to Thorne and Dr. John P. Preskill that naked singularities might exist. Malcolm S. Browne, "Bet on a Cosmic Scale, and a Concession, Sort of," *New York Times,* February 12, 1997, sec. A, writes that, in a famous bet, Hawking denied that "a singularity . . . a mathematical point at which space and time are infinitely distorted, where matter is infinitely dense, and where the rules of relativistic physics and quantum mechanics break down," heretofore thought to exist in black holes, now admits that they might exist "bereft of a black-hole shell" and theoretically become visible to an outside observer.

16. Michael Heim, *The Metaphysics of Virtual Reality* (New York: Oxford University Press, 1993), pp. 180-181.

17. Kip S. Thorne, *Black Holes and Time Warps,* p. 527. Lawrence W. Fagg, in *The Becoming of Time: Integrating Religious and Physical Time* (Atlanta: Scholar's Press, 1995), comments: "The concept of four dimensional spacetime has been very useful in making mathematical calculations in relativity theory . . . but has been in part responsible for the tendency to spatialize time" (p. 33).

18. Kip S. Thorne, *Black Holes and Time Warps,* p. 502.

19. S. Samursky and S. Pines, in *The Concept of Time in Late Neo-Platonism: Texts with Translations, Introduction and Notes* (Jerusalem: The Israel Academy of Sciences, 1971), note that Plotinus's view of time is by no means a replication of Plato's treatment in the *Timaeus.* Plotinus addresses and rejects the accounts of Aristotle and other later philosophers who treat time as the measure of motion and argues that time is produced by a movement of Soul. Iamblichus in the fourth century hypostatizes time as an independent entity, while Damascius in the sixth century sees time as a series of extensionless now points whose movement is explained in terms of sudden leaps or jumps.

20. Augustine, *Confessions,* trans. R. F. Pine Coffin (London: Penguin Books, 1961). Subsequent citations will be from this edition.

21. Maurice Blanchot, *The Step Not Beyond,* trans. Lycette Nelson (New York: State University of New York Press, 1992), p. 22. For an excellent concise interpretation of this passage, see Mark C. Taylor, *Altarity* (Chicago: University of Chicago Press, 1987), p. 239.

22. Gilles Deleuze, "Active and Reactive," trans. Richard Cohen, in *The New Nietzsche,* ed. David Allison (Cambridge, MA: MIT Press, 1985), p. 86.

23. Gilles Deleuze, *Difference and Repetition,* p. 13. For Deleuze the connotations and denotations of the term "concept" are complicated matters (pp. 11-15). In a fuller account, Gilles Deleuze and Felix Guattari, *What is Philosophy?* pp. 15-34, write: "The concept is defined by the inseparability of a finite number of heterogeneous components

traversed by a point of absolute survey at infinite speed" (p. 21). "The concept is knowl-edge—but knowledge of itself, and what it knows is the pure event, which must not be confused with the state of affairs in which it is embodied" (p. 33).

24. Gilles Deleuze, *Difference and Repetition*, p. 241.

25. Gilles Deleuze, "Active and Reactive," in *The New Nietzsche*, pp. 85–86.

26. A caveat expressed by Joan Stambaugh with respect to any discussion of Nietzsche's eternal return is noteworthy. Commenting on "the intricacies, abysses and virtually insoluble problems," that arise in pondering the eternal recurrence, she warns: "Anyone who has tried long enough to grope his way around that philosophical terrain often returns from it as something far worse than the 'burnt child' [of the three meta-morpheses in Zarathustra] and begins to fear that the element of recurrence is taking place precisely in his own desperate attempts to make sense of that doctrine." See her *The Other Nietzsche* (Albany: SUNY Press, 1994), p. 62.

27. Gilles Deleuze, *The New Nietzsche*, p. 86.

28. Michel Haar, "Nietzsche and Metaphysical Language," in *The New Nietzsche*, p. 33.

29. Gilles Deleuze, *The New Nietzsche*, p. 100.

30. Ibid., p. 74.

31. Ibid., p. 86. Kathleen Higgins, "Nietzsche and Postmodern Subjectivity," in *Nietzsche as Postmodernist*, p. 215 replicates a misunderstanding commonly attributed to postmodern interpretations of Nietzsche that "all is empty, all is the same and all has been." It is clear that the allegation of sameness and vacancy does not apply to De-leuze's interpretation.

32. David Farrell Krell, *Of Memory, Reminiscence and Writing: On the Verge* (Blooming-ton: Indiana University Press, 1990), pp. 240–241.

33. German captures this distinction more forcefully than the English distinction between "I was in the past" and "I used to be."

34. Gilles Deleuze, *Proust and Signs*, trans. Richard Howard (New York: George Braziller, 1972), p. 138.

35. See Babette Babich's interpretation of these passages in her *Nietzsche's Philosophy of Science*, pp. 293–294.

36. Friedrich Nietzsche, *The Gay Science*, p. 336.

37. See Mark C. Taylor, *Disfiguring*, for a powerful and original analysis of abstract art that links it to its conceptual matrix. The interpretation of logic as a style rather than as a way of making progress in epistemology is likely to be resisted by most analysts. It would, however, have the advantage of breaking with the bifurcation as usually per-ceived that the method of analytical philosophies may be identified with that of the sciences, and that of continental philosophy with that of the arts. Vincent Descombes, in *Objects of All Sorts*, proposes the antithesis of the "positive" or the "speculative" de-pending upon whether one deals with the phenomena or their possibilities. Positivism, for example, embraces both its naturalistic form in Anglo-American philosophy and a historical cultural form in Continental thought, for example, Foucault, Althusser, and Levi-Strauss (pp. 11–12).

38. S. Sambursky and S. Pines in *The Concept of Time in Late Neo-Platonism* show that the early sixth-century neo-Platonic philosopher Damascius had observed that the rela-tion of earlier and later never changes. The statement that the Trojan War happened before the Peloponesian is true no matter when it is asserted (p. 20).

39. My description attempts to take account of the summaries of the controversies in the essays of L. Nathan Oaklander, Quentin Smith, George Schlessinger, and David Kaplan in *The New Theory of Time,* ed. Oaklander and Quentin Smith (New Haven: Yale University Press, 1994). Individidual essays will be cited when necessary.

40. J. M. E. McTaggart, *The Nature of Existence,* vol. 2, ed. C. D. Broad (New York, 1927), pp. 9–31.

41. See Quentin Smith, "Problems with the New Tenseless Theory," in *New Theory of Time,* p. 41.

42. L. Nathan Oaklander, p. 160. "Introduction: McTaggart's Paradox and the Tensed Theory of Time," in *The New Theory of Time,* p. 160.

43. It would be misleading to suggest that detensers have not tried to overcome this difficulty by developing strategies for appropriating the phenomenological properties of tensed time in their accounts of tenseless time. Among analysts the jury is still out as to whether these moves are successful. See the essays in pt. 2, *The New Theory of Time,* esp. exchanges between D. H. Mellor Oaklander and Quentin Smith, pp. 157–201.

44. In his *Truth and Other Enigmas* (London: Duckworth Press, 1978), pp. 358–374.

45. Ibid., pp. 358–359.

46. Ibid., p. 361.

47. Friedrich Nietzsche, *The Gay Science,* 110, p. 169.

48. Michael Dummett, *Truth and Other Enigmas,* p. 170.

49. Ibid., p. 370.

50. Nolte's comments in essays and letters on various occasions and responses to them can be found in *Forever in the Shadow of Hitler? The Dispute about the German Understanding of History,* ed. James Knowlton and Truett Cates (Atlantic Highlands, NJ: Humanities Press, 1993).

51. Jean Baudrillard, "The Anorexic Ruins," in *Looking Back on the End of the World,* trans. David Antal, ed. Dietmar Kamper and Christoph Wulf (New York: Semiotext(e), 1989), pp. 34–35.

52. Cf. Derrida's messianism as treated in John D. Caputo, *The Prayers and Tears of Jacques Derrida: Religion without Religion* (Bloomington, IN: Indiana University Press, 1997).

53. Arthur C. Danto, *Narration and Knowledge,* p. 11; cf. pp. 349–350.

54. L. Nathan Oaklander, "Introduction," pt. 2, *New Theory of Time,* p. 160.

55. See his *Philosophical Explanations* (Cambridge, MA: Harvard University Press, 1981), p. 548.

CHAPTER SIX

1. Mary Carruthers, *The Book of Memory in Medieval Culture* (Cambridge: Cambridge University Press, 1990), p. 58.

2. For puzzle cases and subtle variations of these modes, see Edward S. Casey, *Remembering* (Bloomington: Indiana University Press, 1987), pp. 122–141.

3. For the subsequent use of the Platonic metaphors of seal imprint and aviary in medieval thought, see Mary Carruthers, *The Book of Memory: A Study in Medieval Culture,* esp. pp. 16–45. Janet Coleman in *Ancient and Medieval Memories: Studies in the Reconstruction of the Past* (Cambridge: Cambridge University Press, 1992), p. 6, touches on but

does not explicate the key problems of the *Theaetetus* as a focus for medieval accounts of memory.

4. David Farrell Krell, in *Of Memory, Reminiscence and Writing*, pp. 13–50, develops a valuable classification of the functions that have been attributed to memory in the history of Western thought. The *typos* or impressing of an imprint seeks to account for the passive and active dimensions of the mechanism of memory. This is so whether impressed by a seal or the work of a faculty. The *icon* enables me to affirm that what I remember is the same as what was originally experienced. *Engrammatology* is the convergence of the preceding two, a process of writing that ranges from wax tablets to computers. Krell's extraordinarily subtle analysis nevertheless misses some novel elements that cannot be envisaged by way of the engrammatological trope.

5. *De Memoria Reminiscentia*, 450b, p. 609, from the *Parva Naturalia* (Short Physical Treatises) in *Collected Works of Aristotle*, p. 609.

6. The phrase is a play on the title of the well-known work in ethics by Alasdair McIntyre, *Whose Justice, Which Rationality?*

7. Jacques Derrida, "Passages—from Traumatism to Promise," trans. Peggy Kamuf, in *Points . . . Interviews, 1974–1994* (Stanford: Stanford University Press, 1995), p. 381.

8. Mary Carruthers, *The Book of Memory*, p. 58.

9. *The Transparency of Evil*, trans. James Benedict (London: Verso, 1993), p. 92.

10. Ibid., p. 90.

11. Jean Baudrillard, "Symbolic Exchange and Death," in *Selected Writings*, ed. Mark Poster, p. 122.

12. See the reprinted articles and letters by Frederick Nolte in *Forever in the Shadow of Hitler? The Dispute about the German Understanding of History*, esp. pp. 18–23.

13. "Symbolic Exchange and Death," in *Selected Writings*, p. 122.

14. Frances A. Yates [London: Routledge and Kegan Paul, 1966), pp. 6–17; cf. Mary Carruthers, *The Art of Memory*, pp. 71–72.

15. Jonathan Spence, *Memory Palace of Matteo Ricci* (New York: Penguin Books, 1984), pp. 1–3. Ricci provides a phonic equivalent of Simonides name.

16. Ibid., p. 3. For reference to textual source, see p. 271n.3.

17. Francis A. Yates, *The Art of Memory*, pp. 129–159.

18. "Memory: Luba Art and the Making of History," exhibit at the Museum of African Art in New York City (February 2–September 8, 1996).

19. I am indebted to the excellent essays of Mary Nooter Roberts and Allen F. Roberts, esp. their "Audacities of Memory" in the exhibit's catalogue that they edit, *Memory: Luba Art and the Making of History* (Munich: Prester Verlag, 1996), pp. 17–48.

20. V. Y. Mudimbe, "The Idea of 'Luba,'" in Mary Nooter Roberts and Allen F. Roberts, *Memory: Luba Art and the Making of History*, p. 246.

21. Francis A. Yates, *The Art of Memory*, p. 45.

22. Ibid., p. 62.

23. Mary Carruthers, *The Book of Memory*, p. 64.

24. Frances A. Yates in *The Art of Memory* identifies Augustine with the mnemotechnic tradition as understood in the ancient art of rhetoric with which, as a teacher of rhetoric, he must have been familiar. What is more, the actual buildings of the ancient world not yet destroyed could have provided the loci for the practice of the art (p. 48). Mary Carruthers in *The Book of Memory* argues that metaphors used by Augustine are archetypal and need not denote familiarity with pnemotechnics. Moreover, the *Ad Her-*

ennium, although known in Augustine's day, was not much commented upon until after the eleventh century (p. 146).

25. David Farrell Krell in *Of Memory, Reminiscence and Writing,* p. 53.

26. Jacques Lacan, *Speech and Language in Psychoanalysis,* trans. Anthony Wilden (Baltimore: Johns Hopkins University Press, 1968), p. 38.

27. Jean Baudrillard, "On Seduction," in *Selected Writings,* p. 162.

28. Ibid.

29. "Ousia and Grammé," in *Margins of Philosophy,* p. 66.

30. Cited in Jacques Derrida, *Of Grammatology,* p. 3.

31. Jacques Derrida, "Plato's Pharmacy," in *Dissemination,* trans. Barbara Johnson (Chicago: University of Chicago Press, 1981), pp. 92–93. References to Plato as cited by Derrida are not altered but follow his usage.

32. Jacques Derrida, *Of Grammatology,* p. 11.

33. Ibid., pp. 36–37.

34. Ibid.

35. Ibid., pp. 70–71.

36. Jacques Derrida, *Dissemination,* p. 77. See David Farrell Krell, *Of Memory, Reminiscence and Writing,* p. 193. I have altered the gender of the pronouns in order to suggest that this transposition entails rethinking the genealogical chain.

37. Jacques Derrida, *Of Grammatology,* p. 71.

38. Marian Hobson in *Post-Structuralism and the Question of History,* ed. Derek Attridge, Geoff Bennington, and Robert Young (Cambridge: Cambridge University Press, 1987), pp. 109–110. The idea of seriality is developed in a Derridean context.

39. Robert A. Rosenstone, *Visions of the Past: The Challenge of Film to Our Ideas of History* (Cambridge, MA: Harvard University Press, 1995), pp. 49–50. James Young in *Writing and Rewriting the Holocaust* maintains in response to the historian's suspicion of video and cinema: "Even style-less narrative is a style in itself a way of making a text . . . seem natural and true" (p. 164). Richard Corliss in a March 4, 1996, *Time* magazine review of *Anne Frank Remembered* contrasts this film with what he calls "holokitsch," which one may infer to mean sanitization through sentimentality.

40. Jacques Derrida in *Edmund Husserl's Origin of Geometry: An Introduction,* trans. John P. Leavey (Stony Brook, NY: Nicholas Hays, 1978) writes in this regard: "The linguistic neutralization of existence is an original idea only in the technical and thematic signification that phenomenology gives it. . . . Hegel above all had amply explored it [in the *Encyclopedia*]" (p. 67n.62).

41. Jacques Derrida, "The Pit and the Pyramid: Introduction to Hegel's Semiology," in *Margins of Philosophy.* Gloss is of *PhM* 453, p. 209.

42. Hegel takes the opportunity to criticize empirical psychology's view of association as one of ideas subject to laws. The sheer number of laws posited, Hegel claims, suggest that chance and contingency belie the idea of law (*PhM* 455, p. 205).

43. Jacques Derrida, "The Pit and the Pyramid," in *Margins,* p. 77.

44. Jacques Derrida, *Glas,* p. 229.

45. Jacques Derrida, *Points . . . ,* pp. 380–381.

46. Ibid., pp. 389–390.

47. Jacques Derrida, *The Ear of the Other: Otobiography, Transference, Translation,* pp. 50–51. In this analysis of the autobiographical with specific reference to Nietzsche, Derrida fans into a wide range of issues bound up with reading as the hearing of alterity.

Speaking of autobiography, Derrida offers this terse formulation: "It is the ear of the other that signs."

48. Nicholas Negroponte, *Being Digital,* p. 20.

49. John Searle, *New York Review of Books,* November 2, 1995, p. 62. This line of thought is further pursued in his criticism of David J. Chalmers's functionalism defined by Searle as the view that "mental states are functional states and functional states are physical states; but they are physical states defined as functional states in virtue of their causal relations." In refuting this view, Searle invokes a number of reductio ad absurdum arguments intended to show the irreducibility of consciousness.

50. Daniel Dennett, *Consciousness Explained* (Boston: Little, Brown and Co., 1991), p. 253.

51. Ibid., p. 254.

52. Ibid.

53. Daniel Dennett, *Consciousness Explained,* p. 279, dismisses both John Searle's and Hubert Dreyfus's well-known phenomenological defenses of consciousness in this brief passage:

> Philosophers influenced by the Husserlian school of phenomenology have stressed the importance of [the] "background" of conscious experience. But they have typically described it as a mysterious or recalcitrant feature, defying mechanical explanation, rather than the key . . . to providing a computational theory of what happens. [For them] consciousness is the source of some special sort of "intrinsic intentionality." (P. 279)

The positions with which Dennett takes issue are first explicated in the earlier work of Hubert Dreyfus, *What Computers Can't Do* (New York: Harper and Row, 1979); and John Searle, *Intentionality: An Essay in the Philosophy of Mind* (Cambridge: Cambridge University Press, 1983).

54. Ibid., p. 166.

55. Ibid., p. 132.

56. Ibid., p. 410.

57. Ibid., p. 411.

58. Taking neither a semiotic nor a hermeneutical tack, Beth Preston in "Heidegger and Artificial Intelligence," *Philosophy and Phenomenological Research* 53, no. 1 (March 1993): 52, argues that the role of the environment has been misunderstood in standard AI models which work with representational accounts of behavior. Such accounts miss the complex environmental structures and processes, the panoply of relations of organism and world that cannot be described in representational terms. This argument is applicable *mutatis mutandis* to Dennett's view of consciousness.

The *Revue de Métaphyisique et de Morale* 38, no. 2 (1992), contains a number of articles that compare or bridge the conceptual frameworks in terms of which the problem of consciousness is articulated. Claude Debru in "La Conscience du temps" considers the problem of how the constitutive phenomena of time differ from constituted objects in time in Husserl and William James. He finds suggestive answers less in Dennett's critical anti-Cartesian polemics than in his concrete account of "the intrinsic mechanisms that analyze information in accordance with parallel processes possessing distinct modes of temporalization" (p. 293; translation mine). Pierre Buser in "Neurobiologie et conscience" argues for what he calls "emergent materialism." Steering a course between dualism and the radical reduction of mental phenomena to the smallest units at the physico-chemical level, Buser contends that the "mental is the product of the neural ensemble and not of the [particular] neurons" (p. 179; translation mine).

59. William James, *Principles of Psychology* (Cambridge, MA: Harvard University Press, 1983), p. 136.

60. Roger Penrose, *Shadows of the Mind: A Search for the Missing Science of Consciousness* (Oxford: Oxford University Press, 1994), p. 348. Hereafter cited in the text as *SM*.

61. William James, *Principles of Psychology*, p. 143.

62. John Searle, *New York Review of Books,* November 2, 1995, p. 65.

63. Jacques Derrida, *Glas*, p. 229.

64. Jorge Luis Borges, *Labyrinths,* p. 41.

65. Lewis Thomas, *The Lives of a Cell: Notes of a Biology Watcher* (New York: Viking Press, 1974), p. 5.

66. Steven Levy, *Artificial Life: A Report from the Frontier Where Computers Meet Biology* (New York: Vintage Books, 1993), p. 7.

67. Ibid., p. 16.

68. Ibid., p. 61.

69. Ibid., pp. 63–65. Ed Fredken at the AI laboratory of MIT used Toffoli's models to support his own neo-Pythagorean view that the universe is made up of information and that living things can be digitally interpreted. Like Penrose, he argues that the information is chemically triggered.

70. Ibid., p. 76.

71. Ibid., pp. 110–111.

72. The logical commands "and" and "or" can be programmed by combining or separating DNA strands. Gina Kolata, "A Vat of DNA May Become Fast Computer of the Future," *New York Times,* April 11, 1995, sec. B.

73. Ibid. That physicists have not given up on constructing still other models that would defy the present limits of computation is evident in the effort to develop information-processing systems based upon quantum mechanics. George Johnson, in "Quantum Theorists Trying to Surpass Digital Computing," *New York Times,* February 18, 1997, sec. B9, writes: "Theorists recently proved that by manipulating subatomic particles as though they were beads in an abacus, a quantum computer could in principle crack problems that now seem impenetrable."

74. Gina Kolata, "A Vat of DNA May Become Fast Computer of the Future."

75. Jean-François Lyotard, *The Inhuman: Reflections on Time,* trans. Geoffrey Bennington and Rachel Bowlby (Stanford: Stanford University Press, 1991), p. 62.

76. Ibid.

77. Ibid., p. 64. It is worth noting that Yosef Hayim Yerushalmi, in *Zakhor: Jewish History and Jewish Memory,* points to this problem in the context of Jewish history:

> Modern Jewish historiography cannot replace an eroded group memory which . . . never depended on historians in the first place. [Collective memories] were a function of the shared faith, cohesiveness, and will of the group itself, transmitting and recreating its past through an entire complex of interlocking social and religious institutions that functioned organically to achieve this. (P. 94)

78. Ibid.

79. Ibid., p. 65.

80. Emmanuel Levinas, *Totality and Infinity,* p. 21.

81. Jean-François Lyotard, *The Inhuman*, p. 70

82. Steven Levy, *Artificial Life*, pp. 110–111.

CHAPTER SEVEN

1. Jacques Derrida, *Given Time: I. Counterfeit Money*, trans. Peggy Kamuf (Chicago: University of Chicago Press, 1992), p. 122.

2. Selection is from Yehuda Amichai as cited in James Young, *Writing and Rewriting the Holocaust: Narrative and the Consequences of Interpretation* (Bloomington: Indiana University Press, 1990), p. 172.

3. Gilles Deleuze and Felix Guattari in *What Is Philosophy?* dream of a deterritorialization that is outside of history, of pure becoming that defies autochthony as it has heretofore been conceived both in the Greek state and later in the form of the democratic state as a confraternity of language and custom. They see this process of alternating nomadism and reterritorialization even in the contemporary hope for a new earth in the future (p. 110). In conformity with contemporary ecological movements, they place their hope upon the earth. "The earth is not one element among others but rather brings together all the elements within a single embrace while using one or another of them to deterritorialize territory" (p. 85).

4. Jean-Luc Nancy, *The Inoperative Community*, trans. Peter Connor and Lisa Garbus (Minneapolis: University of Minnesota Press, 1991), p. 85.

5. Augustine, *The City of God*, in *The Basic Writings of Saint Augustine*, vol. 2, trans. Whitney J. Oates (New York: Random House, 1948), Book XV, chap. 4, p. 278.

6. Ibid.

7. Jean-Luc Nancy, *The Inoperative Community*, p. 3.

8. I shall focus on Sartre's analysis in *Critique of Dialectical Reason: Theory of Practical Ensembles*, pts. 1 and 2, trans. Alan Sheridan-Smith (Atlantic Highlands, NJ; Humanities Press, 1976). Hereafter cited in the text as *CDR*.

9. For an excellent running commentary on this work, see Joseph S. Catalano, *Jean-Paul Sartre's Critique of Dialectical Reason, Vol. 1, Theory of Practical Ensembles* (Chicago: University of Chicago Press), 1986.

10. "The Last Vehicle," in *Looking Back on the End of the World* (New York: Semiotexte, Columbia University, 1989), p. 118.

11. Joseph Catalano, *Jean-Paul Sartre's Critique of Dialectical Reason*, p. 174.

12. Jean-Luc Nancy, *The Inoperative Community*, p. 4

13. *Assassins of Memory: Essays on the Denial of the Holocaust*, trans. Jeffrey Mehlman (New York: Columbia University Press, 1992), p. 24.

14. Ibid., p. 20.

15. George Bataille, *The Accursed Share*, vol. 2 (New York: Zone Books, 1991), pp. 14–15.

16. Ibid.

17. George Bataille, *The Accursed Share*, 2:421.

18. Jean-Luc Nancy, *The Inoperative Community*, p. 19,

19. Giorgio Agamben, in *The Coming Community*, trans. Michael Hardt (Minneapolis: University of Minnesota Press, 1993), p. 97, comments, "Real predicates express relationship within language; exposure is real relationship with language itself."

20. Robert Nozick, *Anarchy, State and Utopia* (New York: Basic Books, 1974), p. 130.

21. Jean-Luc Nancy, *The Inoperable Community*, p. 20.

22. Robert Nozick, *Anarchy, State and Utopia*, p. 264.

23. Emmanuel Levinas, *Totality and Infinity*, p. 303.

24. For an account in support of multiple types of society, see Robert Nozick, *Anarchy, State and Utopia*, pp. 309–317.

25. See Emmanuel Levinas, *Totality and Infinity*, p. 305.

26. Theodore Adorno, *Prisms*, trans. Samuel and Sherry Weber (Cambridge MA: MIT Press, 1986), p. 34. The work of Paul Celan and Nelly Sachs attest the power of poetry focused on the Holocaust to unsay ordinary descriptive language. A literature about Celan too extensive to cite including comments by Hans-Georg Gadamer and Jacques Derrida addresses this issue.

27. Emmanuel Levinas, "The Servant and Her Master," in *The Levinas Reader*, ed. Sean Hand (Oxford: Basil Blackwell, 1989), p. 156.

28. This expression used by Bataille and Blanchot was adopted by Alphonso Lingis as the title of his work *The Community of Those Who Have Nothing in Common* (Bloomington: Indiana University Press, 1994). Lingis finds in the midst of the rational community another, that of those who have "death, their mortality, in common" (p. 13).

29. Maurice Blanchot, *The Infinite Conversation*, trans. Susan Hanson (Minneapolis: University of Minnesota Press, 1993), p. 41.

30. Jacques Derrida, *Points . . .* , p. 83.

31. Maurice Blanchot, *The Infinite Conversation*, p. 41.

32. Ibid., p. 42.

33. Pierre Vidal-Naquet, *The Assassins of Memory*, p. 104. The danger of fabrication is explored by Arthur Schlesinger Jr. in an op-ed, "History as Therapy, a Dangerous Idea," in the *New York Times*, May 3, 1996, in which he cites a text from an address delivered by John Lothrop Motley on December 16, 1868, at the New York Historical Society that is premonitory of Baudrillard's dismissal of history. It reads: "There is no such thing as human history. Nothing can be more profoundly sadly true. The annals of mankind never have been written, never can be written. . . . It is all confused babel of which the key is lost." Schlesinger as a working historian acknowledges that the questioning of historical discourse may be useful but does not attempt to provide responses to the numerous doubts that have been raised.

34. See John D. Caputo, *The Prayers and Tears of Jacques Derrida: Religion without Religion*, chap. 6.

35. For Derrida's account of Nietzsche and the gift, see his *The Gift of Death*, trans. David Wills (Chicago: University of Chicago Press, 1995), pp. 11–115.

36. Jacques Derrida, *Given Time I: Counterfeit Money*, pp. 7–10.

37. Ibid., p. 101n.18.

38. Ibid., p. 30.

39. Friedrich Nietzsche, "On the Uses and Diasadvantages of History for Life," in *Untimely Meditations*, p. 94.

40. Jacques Derrida, *Points . . .* , p. 208.

INDEX